CHRONICLE OF THE RUSSIAN TSARS

ЦРЬ ВЕЛИКІЙ
КНЗЬ АЛЕѮЕЙ
МИХАЙЛОВИЧЪ
ВСЕѦ ВЕЛИКІА
И МАЛЫА
И БѢЛЫА
РОСІИ САМО
ДЕРЖЕ

DAVID WARNES

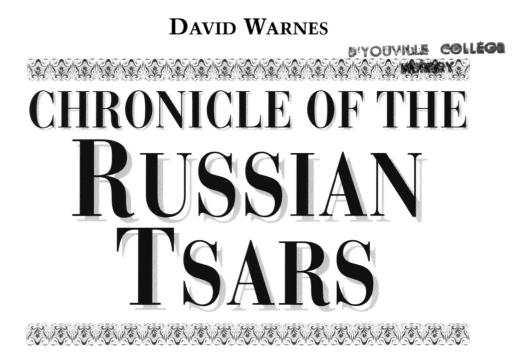

CHRONICLE OF THE
RUSSIAN
TSARS

THE REIGN-BY-REIGN RECORD OF THE
RULERS OF IMPERIAL RUSSIA

WITH **229** ILLUSTRATIONS
100 IN COLOR

THAMES AND HUDSON

Моей любимой матери
и моему покойному отцу,
вечная память ему.

*To my dear mother and my
late father, eternal memory
to him.*

© 1999 Thames and Hudson Ltd,
London

First published in hardcover in the
United States of America in 1999 by
Thames and Hudson Inc., 500 Fifth
Avenue, New York, New York 10110

Library of Congress Catalog Card
Number 98-61289

ISBN 0-500-05093-7

Printed and bound in Slovenia

CONTENTS

pages 6–7
Preface: Lives of the Tsars

pages 8–13
Introduction: The Background to Tsarism

Special Feature

p. 12 Alexander Nevsky

pages 14–59

THE FOUNDING AND TESTING OF TSARISM
1462–1613
*The gathering of the Russian lands; the foundation of the Russian
empire by Ivan the Terrible; the Time of Troubles*

Special Features

p. 22 The Moscow Kremlin
p. 36 Kazan: Art of Empire
p. 39 The English Connection
p. 56 Murder at Uglich?

pages 60–109

THE RISE OF THE ROMANOVS
1613–1725
*A new dynasty; Russia becomes more open to Western influences;
Peter the Great establishes Russia as a European power*

Special Features

p. 82 Palaces and Treasures
p. 94 The Great Embassy
p. 102 St Petersburg

Ivan IV

Mikhail

Peter I

Nicholas II

pages 110–161

THE ZENITH OF TSARISM
1725–1825

The 'Empresses of the Guard'; Catherine the Great's attempts at modernization; the role of Alexander I's Russia in the downfall of Napoleon

Special Features

p. 124 Elizabethan Palaces
p. 142 Catherine II and Classicism
p. 154 Alexander I and the War of 1812

pages 162–209

THE CHALLENGES OF MODERNIZATION
1825–1917

Successive emperors face the issue of whether it is possible to modernize Russia while maintaining the autocracy intact; crises of growth weaken and finally destroy the Romanov dynasty

Special Features

p. 166 Palace Square
p. 173 The Emperor and the Poet
p. 196 Historical Painting and the Slavic Revival
p. 204 The 1905 Revolution

pages 212–217

EPILOGUE
1917–1988

Special Feature

p. 214 Tsars on Film

pages 218–219
Select Bibliography

page 220
Illustration and Text Credits

pages 221–224
Index

PREFACE:
LIVES OF THE
TSARS

Alexander I. This portrait is by the French painter François-Pascal-Simon Gérard (1770–1837).

Which tsar asked for political asylum in England? Which tsar married a girl of peasant origin and made her an empress? Which empress forced a nobleman to spend his wedding night in an ice palace? The exploits and foibles of the Rurikids and the Romanovs still have the power to surprise us. The rulers of imperial Russia sought to exercise an absolute authority over their subjects. 'Everything that is mine belongs to the tsar', ran one Russian proverb. 'Near the tsar, near death', asserted another. Ivan the Terrible's cruelty and Peter the Great's ruthless pursuit of modernization have been used, respectively, as symbols of the perils and the possibilities of autocracy.

The Russian tsars transformed a vulnerable principality into a vast empire, yet their power was limited. The size of their domains and the lack of an adequate number of educated and honest officials meant that their policies were either patchily implemented or not implemented at all. Nor were the policies necessarily theirs. Able and energetic rulers could implement their ideas, but when the ruler was a minor or lacking in ability, initiative passed into the hands of aristocratic factions and favourites. In the 19th century the business of government became too complex to be mastered by one individual, however able. Russia's last few autocrats exercised power by delegating it to ministers and by refereeing disputes between them. They could no longer govern personally, but they still had the power to prevent others from governing effectively. As the thwarted reformer Mikhail Speransky said of Alexander I: 'He is too feeble to reign and too strong to be ruled.'

Surviving letters and writings enable us to catch something of the style and character of many of Russia's rulers: clipped and sarcastic in the case of Ivan the Terrible, warm-hearted, witty and urbane in the case of Catherine the Great. Catherine is Russia's most famous empress, yet she was German and owed her power to a coup d'état. Eighty years earlier the regent Sophia had become the first Romanov woman to play an active role in government. The myths that developed around both of them – of repulsive ugliness in the case of Sophia and of sexual insatiability in the case of Catherine – tell us much about the reactions of their male contemporaries to women in positions of power.

The cathedrals and palaces of the Moscow Kremlin were intended to embody the authority and the values of the princes who built them. Impatient with those values, and seeking an authority of a different kind, Peter the Great began work on a new capital, St Petersburg, in the early 18th century. The city itself, its palaces and public buildings are expressions not only of the personal tastes and aspirations of Peter and his successors, but also of their conception of monarchy. By forcing the Russian nobility to embrace Western European culture they made possible a remarkable outburst of literary and musical creativity. Their attempts to control and to harness that creativity by means of patronage and censorship were only partially successful.

'God makes only the future, while the tsar remakes the past!' Prince Kozlovski's epigram reminds us that Russia's rulers, both tsarist and Communist, have drawn on the past to justify their policies and manipulated the truth to strengthen their rule. Historians, artists and film directors also remake the past. *Chronicle of the Russian Tsars* explores the ways in which they have shaped our view of Russia's imperial era. The new Russia is a country which has lost an empire but has yet to find nation-statehood. No understanding of its turbulent present or its uncertain future is possible without some knowledge of the old Russia. As Pavel Alexandrovich Florensky – scientist, priest and martyr – put it: *'proshloe ne proshlo'*, the past has not passed away.

Catherine II. A coloured engraving.

Sophia Alexeyevna, regent from 1682 to 1689. This painting by Ilya Yefimovich Repin (1844–1930), completed in 1879, depicts the aftermath of the rebellion of the streltsy in 1698 (p. 96). Peter I believed that Sophia had instigated the revolt and ordered some of the rebels to be hanged outside the windows of her rooms in the Novodevichy Convent. Repin has included this grim detail.

INTRODUCTION: THE BACKGROUND TO TSARISM

A painted banner showing Vladimir I, grand prince of Kiev, and his followers from Novgorod. Vladimir, who died in 1015, was the first grand prince to adopt the Orthodox faith, and was later canonized.

The first Russian state, a federation of Slavs centred on Kiev, emerged in the late 9th century AD. Kiev lay on the Viking or Varangian trade route from the Baltic to the Black Sea, and most Western historians accept that its rulers were of Scandinavian origin. Rurik, the legendary Viking ancestor of the grand princes of Kiev, Vladimir-Suzdal and Moscow, remains a shadowy figure.

In 988, during the reign of Grand Prince Vladimir I, the Kievan Rus became Christian, adopting the Eastern Orthodox faith. By the first half of the 11th century Kiev was an important, if loosely organized, federation with significant international links, but in the ensuing decades it was weakened by internal conflicts, encouraged by the practice of dividing lands among the ruler's sons. By the time that the Tatar (Mongol) invasions began in 1223, power had shifted to the area of Vladimir-Suzdal, hitherto sparsely populated by Finnish tribes. There a succession of vigorous Rurikid princes encouraged colonization by Slav immigrants from the south. Their belief that the principality was the private property or patrimony of the ruler was to be an important element in the development of the concept of tsarism.

In 1237 Tatar forces commanded by Batu, a grandson of Genghis Khan, invaded Russia, sacking Vladimir in 1238 and Kiev in 1240. The Tatars settled in the lower Volga area, establishing the khanate of the Golden Horde, which exercised suzerainty over the Russian lands. Alexander Nevsky, prince of Novgorod from 1236, saw that resistance was futile and, in return for offering his allegiance to the khan, was rewarded with the title of 'grand prince' in 1252.

Some historians have suggested that the medieval rulers of Russia derived their institutions and their autocratic aspirations from the Tatar khans, who forced the Russian princes to levy troops and taxes for them, and took savage reprisals against any principality which reneged on these

The Cathedral of St Sophia in the Detinets (kremlin) at Novgorod was constructed in the mid-11th century, and was the first stone building in the city. The distinctive onion-shaped domes date from a later period. Scholars used to attribute the use of the onion dome in Russia to Tatar influence, but there are examples which predate the Tatar invasion. The shape may have been devised as a means of preventing a heavy weight of snow from accumulating on the dome in winter.

A late 16th-century representation of Moscow, taken from Braun and Hogenberg's *Civitates Orbis Terrarum* (1570). This early picture of the Kremlin is not topographically accurate.

obligations. Others point out that the khanate was loosely organized and argue that it was from Kievan tradition and from the example of Byzantium that the Russian princes acquired concepts of monarchy which developed, in the late 15th and 16th centuries, into the Muscovite autocracy.

The 13th and 14th centuries were a time of cultural and linguistic differentiation, with the Belorussians and Ukrainians emerging as populations distinct from the Great Russians. In the north-west Novgorod grew into a prosperous city-state controlling a vast area of northern Russia and styling itself 'Lord Novgorod the Great'. The western parts of the Kievan Rus came under the control of the grand princes of Lithuania. This period of Russian history is often referred to as the appanage era, after the practice by which princes divided their estates among their sons. One of the smaller appanages was centred on Moscow, which Alexander Nevsky settled on his youngest son, Daniel. Daniel's son Yury secured the grand princedom by marrying the sister of the khan of the Golden Horde.

The Muscovite appanage was further enlarged in the 14th century, and Daniel's great-grandson Dmitry Donskoi (1359–1389) defeated the Tatars in the battle of Kulikovo Field in 1380. This victory marked the beginning of the end of Tatar domination of Russia. The power of the Golden Horde never fully recovered after Tamerlane's attack on the khanate in the 1390s, and in the 15th century the Tatar state fell apart. The successor khanates of Kazan, the Great Horde and the Crimea remained a threat to the Russian lands. The Crimean khanate came under Ottoman Turkish suzerainty in 1475, giving the Turks strategic bases on the northern coast of the Black Sea.

Moscow's geographical location made it less vulnerable to foreign attack than some principalities and gave it commercial advantages. It is

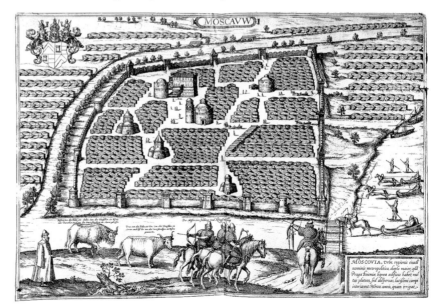

A grand prince of Moscow receiving petitions in the Kremlin. From a manuscript in the National Historical Museum in Moscow.

located close to the headwaters of the Don and the Dnieper, and on a tributary of the Oka, which flows into the Volga. Its rulers consolidated the principality by bequeathing the title of grand prince and the largest share of their lands to their eldest sons. Moscow's emergence as an important religious centre and the seat of the metropolitan, the head of the Orthodox church in Russia, further enhanced the authority of the grand princes. The nature of the authority to which the grand princes aspired was expressed in their adoption of the title 'gosudar'. This word was used to describe the absolute power of a landowner over the slaves on his estate.

The second quarter of the 15th century was a period of civil strife in Muscovy. Vasily II, Grand Prince of Moscow (1425–1462), blinded by a rival during these struggles, successfully asserted his authority in the closing years of his reign, confiscating the lands of his opponents, and in 1456 depriving the Novgorodians of the right to conduct a separate foreign policy. During Vasily's reign the Orthodox church in Russia became autocephalous, that is to say independent of the authority of the emperor and patriarch in Constantinople. When Constantinople fell to the Turks in 1453, Muscovy became the largest remaining Orthodox state. The creation in 1458 of a separate metropolitanate for Lithuania, based in Kiev, meant that Muscovy and Lithuania developed distinct national churches. This helped to foster a growing identity of interests between church and state in Muscovy, where the clergy sought to enhance the authority of the grand prince.

Primary sources

Narrative sources for early Russian history are mainly ecclesiastical in their authorship, and reflect the values and policies of the church and the political perspectives of the principality in which they were written. They concentrate on rituals and on the deeds of rulers rather than on their character and personal appearance. The testimony of foreign visitors to Muscovy is colourful, but cannot be accepted at face value. Those who published their impressions had reason to sensationalize their accounts, while others were influenced in their writings by diplomatic and commercial considerations. The most candid Russian accounts of personalities and events before 1905 were written by defectors and exiles, since the tsarist government operated a system of censorship, and important information was suppressed.

Russian historians

Chronicle of the Russian Tsars contains one extract from the writings of a historical practitioner of the Soviet era, others by a distinguished contemporary Russian historian, and a number of extracts from the work

Grand Prince Dmitry Donskoi (1359–89), who defeated the Tatars at Kulikovo Field in 1380, considerably enlarged the Muscovite state, as did his son Vasily I (1389–1425). By the end of Vasily's reign the principalities of Yaroslavl, Rostov and Tver were almost completely surrounded by Muscovite territory. The reign of Vasily II (1425–62) was marked by civil strife and Tatar invasions, yet Vasily added further lands to the grand princedom and, in 1456, signed a treaty with Novgorod. In 1462 Muscovy was still vulnerable to Lithuanian and Tatar attacks, but the waning of Tatar power was to make further territorial expansion possible in the reigns of Ivan III (1462–1505) and Vasily III (1505–1533).

of two great Russian historians, Karamzin and Kliuchevsky. Nikolai Mikhailovich Karamzin (1766–1826) wrote a massive and unfinished *History of the Russian State*, a project which Alexander I supported by awarding him a life pension. The extracts reproduced in *Chronicle of the Russian Tsars* are from a much briefer work, the *Memoir on Ancient and Modern Russia* which Karamzin wrote in the years 1810–11, almost certainly at the suggestion of the Grand Duchess Catherine, a sister of Alexander I. The purpose of Karamzin's lively and polemical essay was to persuade the emperor that autocracy was the only viable form of government for Russia. Catherine gave the *Memoir* to her brother, though it is not known whether Alexander read it.

Vasily Osipovich Kliuchevsky (1841–1911) was the son of a village priest in Penza Province. He was educated at Moscow University, and taught there and in other institutions, becoming one of the most

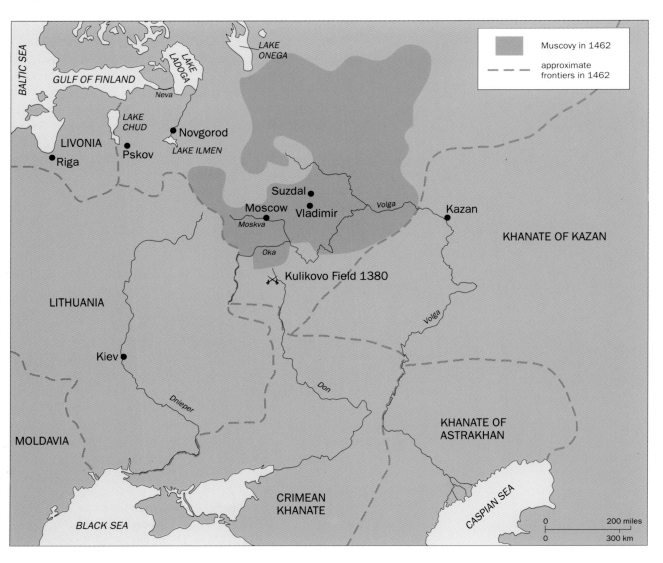

ALEXANDER NEVSKY

Alexander Nevsky was born in 1219, the second son of Grand Prince Yaroslav of Vladimir. He became Prince of Novgorod in 1236. The title Nevsky, which was not applied to him in his lifetime, commemorated his defeat of a Swedish army in a battle on the banks of the River Neva in 1240. Just under two years later, on 5 April 1242, he overcame an invading army of Teutonic knights in a battle fought on the frozen surface of Lake Chud (or Peipus).

It is important to try to disentangle fact from legend when studying Alexander Nevsky's career. Eisenstein's powerful film, at the climax of which the ice on Lake Chud breaks under the weight of the mail-clad German knights, and the musical score by Prokofiev have reinforced the heroic image. The problem is that the sources for these events are of questionable reliability, with the fatality figures for the German side in the battle of Lake Chud ranging from an improbably high 400 to an unimpressive 20. In recent years some historians, particularly Professor John Fennell, have questioned whether the threat from the west was as great as has been believed, and have suggested that the battle was not an important historical turning point. Alexander's decision to cooperate with the Tatars resulted in him being given the title of grand prince of Vladimir, which had previously been held by his younger brother Andrei, who had rebelled against Tatar rule. Was Alexander's policy one of appeasement or commendable pragmatism? The debate continues.

The defeat of the Teutonic knights soon came to be seen as a triumph of Orthodoxy over papally-inspired Catholic aggression, and Alexander Nevsky was canonized early in the reign of Ivan the Terrible. Peter the Great paid tribute to the warrior-saint by ordering the construction of the Alexander Nevsky Lavra on the supposed site of the prince's victory over the Swedes in 1240. The Empress Elizabeth encouraged the cult by commissioning a massive silver shrine for the relics of the saint, which was made in the St Petersburg Mint between 1750 and 1753. His place in the pantheon of Russian heroes was so secure that Stalin, who had to contend with a German invasion on a much larger scale, inaugurated a military decoration named after him.

(Above) A wall-painting of St Alexander Nevsky in the Archangel Michael Cathedral in the Moscow Kremlin. The painting dates from the mid-17th century, though it may have been modelled on a 16th-century original.

(Above right) The Alexander Nevsky medal, a military decoration inaugurated by Stalin in July 1942.

(Right) The battle on the ice between the Russians and the Teutonic knights in Sergei Eisenstein's Alexander Nevsky. The film was first screened in 1938, when anti-German feeling was strong in Russia, but withdrawn from circulation in August 1939, when a non-aggression pact was signed between the Nazi and Soviet regimes.

influential scholars of his era. Kliuchevsky was suspicious of theoretical approaches to history, preferring a critical examination of original sources based on a broad range of disciplines. A superb stylist, his writing combined scholarly precision with poetic grace and economy of expression. He believed that economic and social forces were more important than ideologies or the deeds of individuals.

Dating systems

In 1582 the Roman Catholic church implemented a reform under which the Julian Calendar was replaced by the Gregorian Calendar, named after Pope Gregory XIII. The discrepancy between the two calendars was 10 days. Further adjustments were made in 1700, 1800 and 1900, so that the gap became 11 days in the 18th century, 12 days in the 19th century and 13 days in the 20th century. In Russia calendar reform was not implemented until 1 February 1918.

There is the further complication that until 1700 Russians counted their years from the supposed date of the creation of the world (1 September 5509 BC, according to Orthodox theologians), with the year beginning on 1 September. Peter I decreed the adoption of the Western system of year numbering and of starting the year on 1 January. When exact dates are given in this book they are in Old Style (Julian), using the Western system of year numbering, with years beginning on 1 January. The exceptions to this rule are the dates of battles and treaties or other international incidents, where both dates are given, and dates occurring after the calendar reform of February 1918, which are given only in the New Style (NS). In the few cases where the regnal dates of a ruler are affected by the calendar discrepancy, this fact is clearly signalled, but the Old Style year is used.

Transliteration and names

I believe that the main aims of the transliterator should be to make the text accessible to readers and to give them some clue as to how the words should be pronounced. These aims are not always compatible. Choosing the familiar inevitably leads to inconsistencies, for example 'Ekaterinburg' and 'Yeltsin', both of which begin with E, the sixth letter of the Russian alphabet, which is pronounced 'ye' as in the English word 'yet'. I have used 'Alexeyev' rather than 'Alekseev', and 'Feodor' rather than 'Fedor' or 'Fyodor'. I have stuck to well-known versions of surnames such as 'Tchaikovsky', to the familiar 'x' as opposed to the more accurate 'ks', and to 'y' rather than 'ii' in name endings. I have used the equivalent English personal names for rulers, except in the case of Mikhail, where the English and the Russian names are very similar. Place names are given in the familiar versions, for example 'Moscow' rather than 'Moskva'. I have used the Russian word 'tsaritsa' rather than the English 'tsarina'. Anachronistic use is made of names such as the Ukraine and of terms such as 'intelligentsia' for the sake of intelligibility.

THE RURIKIDS

Ivan III
('The Great')
1462–1505

Vasily III
1505–1533

Ivan IV
('The Terrible')
1533–1584

Feodor I
1584–1598

THE TIME OF TROUBLES

Boris Godunov
1598–1605

Feodor II
1605

False Dmitry I
1605–1606

Vasily Shuisky
1606–1610

Interregnum – several claimants
1610–1613

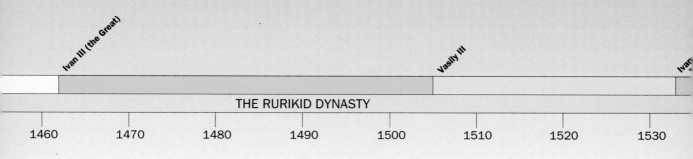

THE RURIKID DYNASTY

1460   1470   1480   1490   1500   1510   1520   1530

Ivan III

Ivan IV

Feodor I

Boris Godunov

THE FOUNDING AND TESTING OF TSARISM
The Rurikids 1462–1598
The Time of Troubles 1598–1613

IVAN THE TERRIBLE and Boris Godunov are the best known of the early tsars, the former for his legendary cruelty and the latter as the tragically flawed hero of Mussorgsky's opera. Ivan was the first ruler of Muscovy to be crowned as tsar (derived from the Latin Caesar), a title which had occasionally been used by his father and grandfather. Though the early tsars also used the title 'autocrat', the word had no precise constitutional meaning. They could only rule in cooperation with the boyars, an aristocratic elite, and when the tsar was a minor or incapable of ruling, boyar factions vied for power.

During his young manhood, Ivan the Terrible laid the foundations of the Russian empire. His attempts to curb the influence of the boyars and to centralize and strengthen the government were undermined by lengthy and costly wars and a succession crisis of his own making. On the death of the last Rurikid ruler, the ineffectual Feodor I, the era known as the Time of Troubles began. Many boyars were unwilling to accept the authority of Boris Godunov, who was elected tsar in 1598. The institution of tsarism survived the civil strife and foreign invasions which followed Boris' death, and in 1613 Muscovites rallied round Mikhail Romanov, the founder of the dynasty which was to rule until 1917.

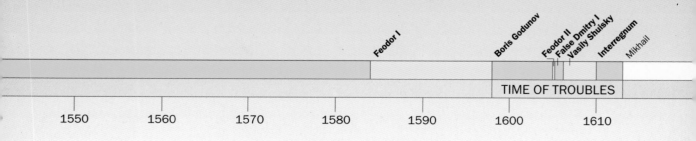

Feodor I

Boris Godunov

Feodor II
False Dmitry I
Vasily Shuisky

Interregnum

Mikhail

TIME OF TROUBLES

1550   1560   1570   1580   1590   1600   1610

Иван III Великий **Ivan III**
('The Great')
1462–1505

Василий III **Vasily III**
1505–1533

A portrait of Ivan III. This stylized image, dating from the 16th century, provides no reliable evidence of the grand prince's physical appearance.

IVAN III	
Full name Ivan Vasilievich also known as Ivan the Great *Father* Vasily II ('the Dark' or 'the Blind') *Mother* Maria Yaroslavna *Born* Moscow 22 January 1440 *Accession* 27 March 1462 *Died* Moscow 27 October 1505 Natural causes *Wives* (1) 1452 Maria, daughter of Prince Boris of Tver Died 1467	(2) 1472 Sophia (Zoe) Palaeologue, niece of Constantine XI, the last Byzantine emperor Died 1503 *Child by (1)* Ivan (1458) *Children by (2)* Yelena (1474) Yelena (1476) **Vasily** (1479) Yury (1480) Dmitry (1481) Feodosia (1485) Simeon (1487) Andrei (1490) Evdokia (1492)

IVAN III

The Duke may be thirty-five years of age; he is tall and thin, and handsome.... When the Duke spoke to me I retired from him, but he approached me with great kindness. I answered all his questions, and thanked him appropriately, and we conversed for more than an hour. He showed me, with great good nature, some of his dresses of cloth of gold, lined with ermine, which were most beautiful.

Ambrogio Contarini,
an Italian traveller who visited Moscow in the reign of Ivan III

Moreover he was so hostile to women that if any woman met him by chance, they almost fainted with terror at the sight of him. No access was allowed to him for poor men, who were oppressed by the more powerful or unjustly treated; he generally drank so excessively at dinner as to fall asleep, and while his guests were all struck with terror and sitting in silence, he would awake, rub his eyes, and then first begin to joke and make merry with them.

Sigismund von Herberstein,
envoy of the Holy Roman Emperor to Muscovy

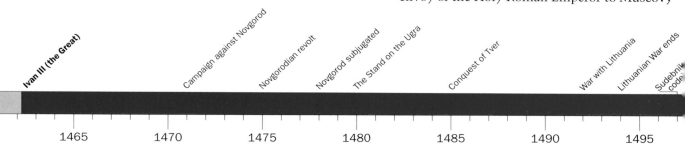

Ivan III (the Great) | Campaign against Novgorod | Novgorodian revolt | Novgorod subjugated | The Stand on the Ugra | Conquest of Tver | War with Lithuania | Lithuanian War ends | Sudebnik code

1465   1470   1475   1480   1485   1490   1495

Vasily II, grand prince of Moscow, died in March 1462. He had been suffering from a wasting disease, and his suggestion that lighted wooden spills be applied to his skin resulted not in the cure for which he had hoped, but in multiple burns which turned gangrenous. The 22-year-old Ivan III, who succeeded him, was by no means inexperienced. He had been a political prisoner at the age of six, and joint ruler with his father from the age of eight. He had married Princess Maria of Tver at the age of 12, a few months after leading, at least in name, his first military expedition. His actions suggest a cautious man determined to increase the size and power of the Muscovite state, by diplomacy and assertiveness if possible and by war if necessary. It remains a matter of debate whether he followed a predetermined plan, or seized opportunities as they arose. The demands of warfare, poor communications and the primitive nature of the royal administration meant that Ivan was dependent on the help of the boyars. He showed considerable skill in securing their cooperation.

The gathering of the lands

Vasily II had settled appanages on his four surviving younger sons. Ivan III managed to gain control of almost all these territories. When two of his brothers died without heirs, Ivan appropriated their lands, though custom said that they should be divided among the family. These seizures, and other assertions of power, provoked two of his brothers, Boris and Andrei the Elder, into rebellion in 1480. Ivan, facing a Tatar attack, was forced to compromise with them, but by the time of his death he had acquired all of Andrei's lands and half of Boris' appanage, by confiscation or by inheritance. By means of aggression, dynastic marriage and inheritance Ivan was able to acquire the principalities of Vereia, Beloozero, Yaroslavl, Rostov, Tver and the city-state of Viatka as well as part of Riazan.

By far the largest of Ivan's acquisitions was the vast territory owned by the city-state of Novgorod. When the Novgorodians broke the treaty of 1456 by making an alliance with Casimir IV of Lithuania, Ivan went to war. He defeated the Novgorodian army in 1471 and granted a magnanimous treaty which left the city's institutions intact. This attempt indirectly to rule Novgorod was unsuccessful. In 1478 Ivan imposed direct rule, confiscating the estates of members of the anti-Muscovite faction, as well as a substantial amount of ecclesiastical land and the district of Torzhok. Subsequently Ivan had to deal with several incipient revolts, after which there were further forfeitures. These confiscations put three million acres of Novgorodian land at his disposal. Much of it

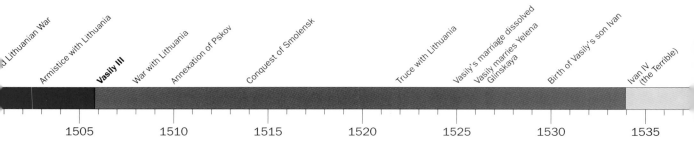

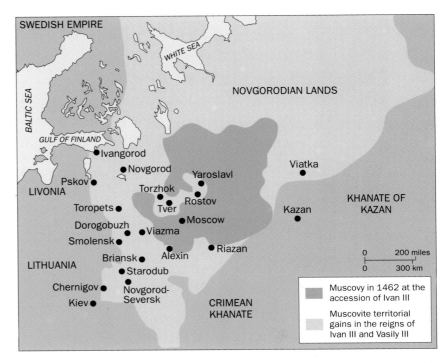

In the reigns of Ivan III (1462–1505) and his son Vasily III (1505–33) the grand princedom of Muscovy was dramatically enlarged and the Tatar yoke formally repudiated. The decline of Tatar power created an opportunity for eastwards expansion which Vasily III's son Ivan IV (1533–1584) successfully exploited.

was granted to Muscovites in order to strengthen Ivan's grip on the region. The grants were conditional on military service. This system of so-called *pomestie* land tenure was not new, but it had never before been used on such a scale. It enabled the grand prince to create a much larger gentry class who owed their land and status to him and who knew that they would lose both if they failed to render military service. These

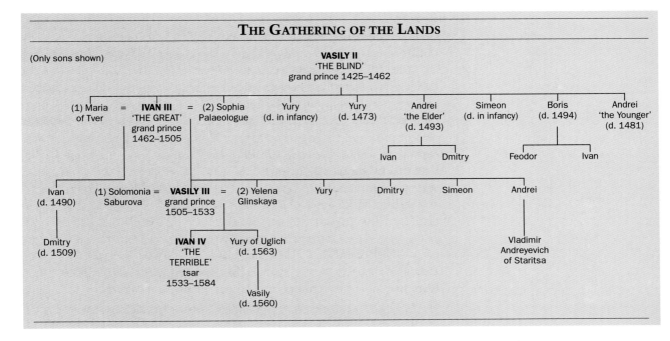

THE GATHERING OF THE LANDS

ВЕЛИКЇЙ НОВЪ ГРАДЪ   РЕВНЯЯ

Novgorod. A 17th-century wood engraving. In the foreground is the commercial district on the east bank of the River Volkhov. The bridge leads directly to the east gate of the Detinets (kremlin). The river formed part of the important medieval trade route from the Baltic to the Black Sea. In the 14th and 15th centuries Novgorod was a powerful city-state ruling a vast area of northern and western Russia, and governed by an elected city council, the *veche*. In 1478 Ivan III removed to Moscow the bell that summoned members of the *veche* to meetings, so symbolizing the end of the city-state's independence.

service gentry were to become the backbone of Muscovy's cavalry forces.

In 1497 Ivan issued a new law code for his realm, the Sudebnik, which made armed rebellion and conspiracy against the sovereign capital offences. The Sudebnik was a response to the enlargement of Muscovy, and an attempt to ensure a degree of uniformity in the administration of justice.

Relations with the Tatars

By the time Ivan came to the throne the Tatars were past the zenith of their power, and no tribute had been paid to them for some years. The khanates nevertheless represented a threat to the grand princedom and it was in Ivan's interest to foster rivalries between them. In 1472 the armies of Ahmed, khan of the Great Horde, attacked Alexin on the River Oka before retreating in the face of superior Muscovite forces. Ivan sought to neutralize the threat from Ahmed, who had allied himself with Lithuania, by befriending Ahmed's enemy, Mengli-Girey, khan of the Crimea. In 1480 they agreed a defensive pact against Ahmed and an offensive pact against Lithuania. The treaty was timely. Ivan was facing a rebellion by his brothers, as well as attacks in the north-west by the armies of the Livonian Order, the Germanic knights who had been the ruling class in Livonia since the 12th century, and in the south by the forces of Ahmed. Expecting that Casimir IV of Lithuania would also attack Muscovy, Ahmed gave as his reason for invading the fact that Ivan had not paid tribute to him. It is unclear whether this was a deliberate act of defiance by Ivan, since the tribute payments had lapsed in an earlier reign.

A Tatar soldier. Woodcut from Hans Weigel's *Trachtenbuch* of 1566.

Ivan III receiving the news of the victory over Lithuania in the Battle of the Vedrosha River, 1500. A 19th-century lithograph by P. Ivanov. In the background a boyar raises his tall hat and gives thanks to God.

The Muscovite and Tatar armies confronted each other across the River Ugra. There was little fighting. The assistance promised by Casimir IV did not materialize and when news came of a Muscovite advance towards the Tatar heartland in the Lower Volga region Ahmed's forces withdrew. Contemporaries criticized Ivan III for not being sufficiently aggressive during the 1480 campaign, yet the 'stand on the Ugra' produced the desired result. The failure of the last great Tatar attack came to symbolize the achievement of independence by Muscovy and the Great Horde soon ceased to be a significant threat.

Ivan maintained good relations with the Crimean khanate, and sought to ensure that the khanate of Kazan was ruled by men favourably disposed to Muscovy. Twice, in 1468 and in 1469, he had attempted unsuccessfully to establish a puppet khan of Kazan in power. In 1480 Ivan forced Khan Ibrahim to swear allegiance to him. Ibrahim's death in 1482 resulted in a succession dispute between two of his sons, Ali-Khan and Mohammed-Emin. In 1487 Ivan came down decisively on the side of Mohammed-Emin, who was installed as khan by Muscovite forces and who proved a reliable ally for most of the rest of Ivan's reign.

Lithuania, Livonia and Sweden

For Ivan III Lithuania represented both a threat and an opportunity. The threat was that the Lithuanians and the Tatars might mount a joint invasion of his principality. The opportunity arose from the possibility that landowners in eastern Lithuania, Russian by race and Orthodox by religion, might be persuaded to throw in their lot with Muscovy. To encourage this Ivan permitted raids on the Lithuanian borderlands. In the 1480s a number of landowners, finding that Casimir IV of Lithuania could not defend his eastern frontier, transferred their allegiance to Muscovy, and then joined in the process by attacking their western neighbours. While Ivan encouraged non-Muscovites to offer their allegiance to him, he broke with custom by treating as a traitor any Muscovite who sought to transfer his allegiance to another ruler.

Casimir's death in 1492 enabled Ivan to take advantage of his inexperienced successor, Alexander, by launching an invasion of Viazma, an area that had come under Lithuanian control at the end of the 14th century. The Lithuanians were already seeking a treaty with Muscovy, including a marriage alliance between Alexander and Ivan's daughter, Yelena. Ivan preferred to negotiate from a position of strength once the conquest of Viazma was complete. Serious talks began in January 1494. The resulting treaty affirmed Ivan's right to the lands that he had already acquired, including Viazma, and acknowledged his new title, Sovereign of all Russia, which announced his claim to all the Russian lands under Lithuanian rule. Yelena and Alexander were married in 1495.

Ivan did not intend that the peace should be permanent, but a further war against Lithuania could not be attempted until he felt more secure. The acquisition of the Novgorodian lands meant that Muscovy now had common frontiers with Livonia and Sweden, and an outlet to the

The coronation of Alexander the Jagiellonian, king of Lithuania and son-in-law of Ivan III, as king of Poland in 1501. A miniature from the *Pontifical* of Erazm Ciołek, Bishop of Płock, dating from 1515. The original is in the Czartoryski Collection in the National Museum in Kraków. Alexander was the younger son of Casimir IV, who had ruled both Poland and Lithuania. On Casimir's death in 1492 Poland went to his elder son, Jan Olbracht, and Lithuania to Alexander. The kingdoms were reunited under Alexander's rule when Jan Olbracht died in 1501.

Gulf of Finland. Ivan constructed a fortress, Ivangorod, to defend his north-western frontier. He hoped to gain control of the northern shoreline of the Gulf of Finland from Sweden. An alliance was negotiated with Denmark in 1493, and the two states went to war with Sweden in 1495. The Danes were the main beneficiaries of the conflict, with King Johannes gaining control of Sweden in 1497. Ivan acquired no new territory as a result of the war.

In 1500 a number of princes who were subjects of the grand duke of Lithuania transferred their allegiance to Muscovy, protesting that they had been persecuted for their Orthodox faith. The alleged persecutions provided Ivan with an excuse to attack Lithuania, justifying his aggression as a crusade. Muscovite forces quickly captured Briansk, Dorogobuzh and Toropets, and defeated the Lithuanians on the River Vedrosha in July 1500. After these initial setbacks, the Lithuanians rallied. In 1501, on the death of the Polish king Jan Olbracht, Alexander became joint ruler of Poland and Lithuania, and secured an alliance with the Livonian Order. Ivan was thus forced to divert substantial forces to deal with the Livonian threat, and was unable to mount the all-out attack on Smolensk that he had planned. By the end of 1502 he had gained no further territory. Alexander, however, was ready to discuss peace. A six-year truce was negotiated in 1503. The truce left Ivan in control of a sizeable area of Lithuania. By the time of his death in 1505 there was localized fighting along the truce boundary, and a further war seemed inevitable.

A dynastic marriage

Ivan III's first wife, Maria of Tver, died in 1467, having produced a male heir, Ivan the Younger, in 1458. The grand prince seems to have been genuinely fond of his wife, and did not remarry for five years. He chose as his second bride Sophia (Zoe) Palaeologue, niece of the last Byzantine emperor, Constantine XI. One source describes Sophia as ugly, intelligent, scheming and obese. The great bed of the grand princesses is said to have broken under her weight during her first night in Moscow. The prestige to be gained from such a union outweighed any distaste that Ivan may have felt, and the couple were married in 1472. He resisted suggestions from the Vatican, which had encouraged the match, that Muscovy should cooperate in a Western alliance against the Turks. Ivan added the Byzantine double-headed eagle to his regalia, and encouraged the use of the titles 'tsar' and 'autocrat' with reference to himself. Chroniclers began to disseminate legends intended to glorify the dynasty, including an imaginative genealogy tracing Ivan's descent from Prus, a supposed kinsman of the Roman emperor Augustus. Ivan's extensive building programme in the Moscow Kremlin was also intended to enhance his prestige.

THE MOSCOW KREMLIN

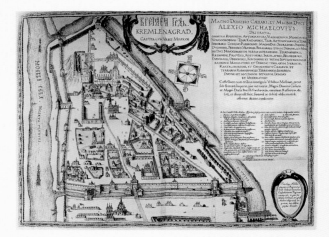

Kreml is a Russian word for citadel or fortress, and many of the historic towns of Russia have their kremlin. The Moscow Kremlin occupies a roughly triangular site on a low hill rising above the River Moskva. Moscow first enters the historical record in 1147, though there is archaeological evidence of much earlier settlement on the Kremlin site. The first fortifications, built by Yury Dolgoruky in the mid-12th century, were captured and destroyed by the Tatar forces of Batu Khan 90 years later, and rebuilt on a grander scale in the 13th, and again in the 14th centuries.

Ivan III's first great building project in the Kremlin was the construction of a new Dormition Cathedral, the foundations for which were laid in 1471. The uncompleted structure was damaged in an earthquake in 1474, and Ivan decided that foreign expertise was needed. He hired an Italian architect and engineer, Aristotele Fioravanti (*c.* 1415–*c.* 1485/86), who had been official engineer to the city of Bologna. His brief was that the new church was to be modelled on the 12th-century Cathedral of the Dormition in Vladimir, but was to surpass it in splendour. The new building was completed in 1479. Fioravanti used iron tie-rods to strengthen the arches and walls, a technique which was new to the Russian masons who worked under him. The result was a lofty and spacious structure which, while making use of traditional Russian features, has a light and airy interior that is untypical of medieval Russian church architecture.

Ivan's second major work of reconstruction in the Kremlin was the Annunciation Cathedral (1484–89), built by craftsmen from Pskov and used for private worship by the tsars.

Damaged in the great fire of 1547, the cathedral was restored by Ivan IV in 1564.

Just before his death in 1505 Ivan III commissioned another Italian architect, Alevisio Novi, to rebuild the cathedral of St Michael the Archangel. The project was completed in 1509. The exterior of the cathedral is elaborately decorated in the Renaissance style. The cathedral was the burial place of the tsars until the time of Peter the Great.

Ivan III ordered the building of more than 1¼ miles of brick wall round the Kremlin's 60-acre site, with 20 towers. The work began in 1485 under the direction of an Italian architect, Pietro Antonio Solari, and was completed during the reign of Vasily III. The original appearance of these fortifications can only be conjectured, for the upper parts of the walls and

(Left) The Moscow Kremlin. A miniature from the Book of the Election of Tsar Mikhail to the Throne, 1672–73. The painting shows, on the left, the Cathedral of St Michael the Archangel, with its Italianate pilasters and the carved scallop shell recesses under each gable. The procession is passing the rusticated façade of the Faceted Palace, and the Dormition Cathedral can be seen on the right.

(Right above) The Spasskaya (Redeemer) Tower of the Kremlin seen from Red Square in a watercolour sketch of 1912.

(Below) The Ivan the Great Belltower. The additions made on the orders of Tsar Boris Godunov brought the height of the structure to 266 ft (81 m). In 1812 the tower withstood an attempt by the retreating French forces to blow it up.

towers underwent considerable alterations in the 17th century. The most impressive of Solari's structures was the Spasskaya (Redeemer) Tower, built in 1491. The tower got its name in the 17th century, when Tsar Alexei Mikhailovich installed an icon of the Saviour on it, and issued an edict that everyone, including himself, must dismount from their horses and remove their hats when they passed under the arch. The octagonal clock turret was added in the reign of Tsar Mikhail, on whose orders an English craftsman, Christopher Galloway, installed a clock, which had to be replaced after a fire in 1654.

The main secular building in the Kremlin dating from the reign of Ivan III is the Faceted Palace, built by Solari and Marco Ruffo. The palace, which was completed in the reign of Vasily III, takes its name from the rusticated masonry façade. The upper floor consists of a hall whose vault was supported by a single, central square pier. Here successive tsars received foreign ambassadors. The walls of the hall were first decorated in the reign of Tsar Feodor I. The present decorations date from the late 19th century, though the artists stuck to the late 16th-century iconography. The Faceted Palace was damaged by fires in the 16th century, badly damaged by the occupying Polish forces during the Time of Troubles, and heavily restored in the 19th century.

The building in the Kremlin that is most popularly associated with Ivan III, the 'Ivan the Great Belltower', was begun in the period 1505–08 by an Italian master, Marco Bono. An additional campanile, designed by Petrok Maly, was added in 1532–43. The upper tiers of the main tower were completed in the reign of Boris Godunov.

(Opposite above) Plan of the Kremlin in the time of Alexei Mikhailovich, from Jan Blaeu's Cosmographie Blaviane of 1663.

(Opposite) The Dormition Cathedral, consecrated in 1479 in the presence of Grand Prince Ivan III. It is likely that its architect, Fioravanti, a famous military engineer, accompanied Ivan III on his campaigns against Novgorod. The final appearance of the cathedral may have been influenced by the style of church architecture he saw there. The Faceted Palace can be seen on the left.

An Argument and a Betrothal

The wedding of Ivan III and Sophia (Zoe) Palaeologue in Moscow in 1472. An illustration from the late 16th-century Litsevoy Chronicle.

This account of the arrival of the Princess Sophia Paleologue in Moscow is taken from the *Nikonian Chronicle*, and was written some decades after the events described took place. The *Nikonian Chronicle* was compiled by Orthodox churchmen, and their beliefs about the duty of the grand prince to obey the church authorities show clearly in this account. This source also offers some evidence of how decisions were arrived at during the reign of Ivan III, and indicates that the grand prince's mother, Grand Princess Maria, was an influential figure.

When they were in the vicinity of Moscow the Grand Prince was told that the Pope's envoy, legate Antonio, who accompanied the Princess, had a Latin [crucifix] carried before him…. Hearing this, the Grand Prince deliberated with his mother, with his brothers and with the boyars and some said, 'Let us not prohibit him this.' And others said, 'Such a thing has never been in our lands, that the Latin [Roman Catholic] faith should be honoured…' The Grand Prince, however, sent to his father [i.e. his spiritual father, Metropolitan Filipp], announcing it to him. The

Metropolitan replied, 'It is not possible that such should enter this city or approach it. If you permit, he would even enter the gate of the city. I, your father, would leave through the other gate. We should neither hear nor see this, because if one loves and praises a foreign faith then it means he offends his own.' Hearing this from His Holiness, the Grand Prince sent to the legate [saying] that he should not have a cross borne openly before him and should order that it be hidden. The other resisted for a time concerning this but did according to the will of the Grand Prince…. Thereafter, on the twelfth day of November, they entered the city. The Metropolitan himself entered the church, put the vestments on her, blessed the Princess with the sign of the cross, as well as the other Christians accompanying her, and let her go from the church. And with her [everyone] went to Grand Princess Maria. Soon thereafter Grand Prince Ivan also came to his mother, and he became betrothed to the Princess according to the custom, as is due Their Majesties' honour; and they went to church to the liturgy.

The succession crisis

In 1490 Ivan the Younger, the son of Ivan III and his first wife, died, leaving a son named Dmitry. His death raised the question of whether Dmitry, or Vasily, Ivan III's eldest son by his marriage to Sophia, had the better claim to the succession. Both candidates were backed by ambitious mothers. The rivalry between Sophia Palaeologue and Yelena Stepanovna, the mother of Dmitry, may have had its origins in the lavish gifts with which Ivan III rewarded Yelena for giving birth to his first grandchild. Ivan is not recorded as having shown similar generosity to Sophia when their sons were born. It was rumoured that Sophia had poisoned Ivan the Younger in order to improve her son's prospects of inheriting the throne. There was also a religious dimension to the crisis. Yelena belonged to a heretical sect, the 'Judaizers'. Ivan III had tolerated this heresy for some years because its followers condemned the wealth of the monasteries, and he wished to confiscate the monastic estates. Given Yelena's heretical beliefs, it was natural for the Orthodox clergy to oppose the claims of her son.

In 1497, the crisis came to a head. Vasily and his mother believed that Ivan was about to name Dmitry as his heir, and involved themselves in a plan to poison Dmitry. The conspirators were disgruntled courtiers who resented the power of the principal boyar families, in particular Prince Patrikeyev, governor of Moscow and president of the Boyar Duma. Ivan III uncovered the plot and executed the conspirators, who were the first victims of the new legal code. Vasily and his mother were placed under close surveillance and in 1498 Dmitry was crowned as co-ruler. But Vasily's disgrace did not last for long. Sophia schemed successfully to undermine her husband's confidence in Patrikeyev. In January 1499 Ivan III arrested Patrikeyev and his family. Vasily was rehabilitated and granted the titles Prince of Novgorod and Pskov. A year later he was designated as co-ruler and heir. In 1502 Dmitry and his mother were arrested. Both died in captivity, almost certainly by violence; Yelena in 1504 and Dmitry in 1509.

Ivan abandoned his hopes of expropriating the monastic estates, and bowed to the wishes of the Orthodox party. A church council in 1504 condemned the leaders of the 'Judaizers' to the stake. At the same time an important dispute within the Orthodox church was settled, the struggle between the 'Possessors' and the 'Non-Possessors'. The former faction, led by Abbot Joseph of Volokolamsk, argued that the church should keep its lands and privileges, and that in return for guaranteeing these privileges, the grand prince should enjoy authority over the church. The Non-Possessors, whose principal spokesman was Nil Sorsky, argued for the separation of church and state, and were critical of the ritualism and the wealth of the church. Ivan III may have sympathized with the Non-Possessors' enthusiasm for ecclesiastical poverty, since he wished to confiscate church lands, but in 1503 a church council found in favour of the Possessors, a decision which cemented the relationship between the Orthodox church and the Muscovite state.

Ivan III died in the early hours of 27 October 1505 at the age of 65. Though the final years of his reign were clouded by failure, he and his successor Vasily III trebled the size of the grand princedom in the period 1462–1533. His contribution to this achievement earned him the title 'Ivan the Great'.

VASILY III	
Full name	*Wives*
Vasily Ivanovich	(1) 1505 Solomonia
Father	Saburova
Ivan III	Marriage annulled
Mother	1525
Sophia (Zoe)	(2) 1526 Yelena
Palaeologue	Glinskaya
Born	Died 1538
Moscow	*Children by (2)*
25 March 1479	**Ivan** (1530)
Accession	Yury (1532)
27 October 1505	
Died	
Moscow	
3 December 1533	
Septicaemia	

VASILY III

He surpasses all other kings and princes in the power he has and uses over his own people; what his father began he completed. That is, he turned out the princes and others from all the fortresses, neither leaving nor entrusting any fortress to his brothers. He holds one and all in the same subjection.

Sigismund von Herberstein, envoy of the Holy Roman Emperor to Muscovy

Vasily III (1505–1533) was an active, energetic man who enjoyed hunting and religious pilgrimages. During his reign the gathering of the lands continued. Ivan had bequeathed appanages to his four younger sons, but

(Right) The Battle of Orsha, 1514, by a contemporary Polish painter.

BOYARS

The term 'boyar' can be traced back to the late 10th century, when it was used to describe the principal advisers of the ruling princes, a courtly elite of counsellors and warriors. The most important boyars could trace their ancestry back to the princely descendants of Rurik, but grand princes and tsars conferred the status of boyar on men of lesser lineage. By the 17th century the Boyar Duma (Council) included non-titled royal servitors, members of the landed gentry who provided cavalry contingents for the tsar's armies, and senior civil servants. Under the system of precedence (*mestnichestvo*) the most important and lucrative positions and military commands were reserved for boyars. The term boyar has been used by historians to describe both the princely class and the entire membership of the Boyar Duma.

Grigory Kotoshikhin, a junior clerk in the Department of Foreign Affairs in the reign of Tsar Alexei (1645–76), commented: '...the tsar confers the boyar rank on many not according to their intelligence but according to their ancient lineage, and many of them are illiterate and have had no schooling.'

Traditional boyar dress. An illustration from Adam Olearius' Vermehrte Neue Beschreibung der Moskowitischen und Persianischen Reise *(1656)*

Vasily forbade his brothers to marry until he himself had produced an heir, and when two of them died unmarried he took control of their lands. He gained control of Pskov in 1510 and the remainder of Riazan in the early 1520s. Vasily struggled to maintain Muscovy's influence over the khanate of Kazan, and by 1532 had managed once more to install a khan who acknowledged his overlordship. In 1512 Khan Mengli-Girey of the Crimea broke off his alliance with Muscovy and sided with Lithuania. Fighting between Muscovy and Lithuania had resumed in 1508, even before the six years of the truce had elapsed. In 1514 Muscovite forces captured Smolensk, and though the Lithuanians won a major victory at Orsha in the same year they were unable to retake the city. Several years of skirmishing and negotiation followed, and then in 1522 a five-year truce was agreed, under which the Lithuanians conceded Muscovy's territorial gains. Vasily broadened the grand princedom's diplomatic horizons, cultivating relations with the Holy Roman Empire, the papacy, the Turkish sultanate and the Mughal empire. He extended his authority over the boyars and, like his father, treated as treasonable any attempt by a Muscovite noble to transfer his services to another ruler.

The sinews of power

During Vasily's reign the administration continued to develop. Ivan III had begun to appoint a new type of official, the *diaki* or state secretaries,

ORTHODOXY

The Orthodox church played an important part in the creation and the sustaining of tsarism and of the Russian national identity. Its beliefs and rituals both enriched Russia and separated her from the West.

The schism of 1054 that divided eastern from western Christendom was the climax of a long process of separation. The fall of the Western Roman empire and the rise of Islam destroyed the religious order established by the Emperor Constantine. Language became a barrier, with the knowledge of Greek almost dying out in Western Europe, and Latin falling into disuse in Byzantium, the capital of the Eastern Roman empire. Theological disagreements completed the rupture, and the Eastern church opposed the supremacist claims of the popes. The pillaging of Constantinople by the Crusaders in 1204 added bitterness to these doctrinal divisions.

Orthodoxy places great emphasis on tradition, and much of this tradition is handed down in the words and actions of the liturgy and in the style and content of the icons, whose purpose is to reveal the divine to human beings. Russian Orthodoxy emphasizes mystical experience and the undefined power of God, and places less

emphasis on rational, abstract thought than Roman Catholicism. These differences are arguably the most important explanation of the divergent cultural, social and intellectual development of Russia and Western Europe in the period covered by this book.

The conversion of Russia began with the work of missionaries from Constantinople. The brothers Cyril and Methodius preached the Orthodox faith in Moravia in the 9th century, translating the Bible and the liturgy into Slavonic and devising an alphabet, which became known as Cyrillic, for the purpose. Orthodoxy spread to Bulgaria, Serbia and Russia through the efforts of later generations of missionaries. A church had been established at Kiev, the principal city of Russia, by 945, and in 988 Grand Prince Vladimir of Kiev (980–1015) was baptised. The Russian *Primary Chronicle*, the principal source for the period, contains the legend that Vladimir investigated a number of religions, rejecting Judaism and Islam because he found the prospects of circumcision and abstention from alcohol repellent, and embracing Orthodox Christianity because the envoys he had sent to Byzantium were deeply impressed by the worship that they attended. 'We do not know whether we were in heaven or upon earth,' they told the grand prince, 'for there is not upon earth such sight or beauty.'

Monasticism was from the start a vital element in Russian Orthodoxy. The monks were colonizers and cultivators of remote and inhospitable areas. Fortified monasteries and convents were important military outposts in the Tatar era. One example is the Holy Trinity and St Sergius Monastery near Moscow. This was founded in the 14th century by Sergius of Radonezh, whose piety and humility made him the trusted spiritual adviser of the grand princes of Moscow. Under the influence of St Sergius, who died in 1392, Russian ecclesiastical art reached its zenith. The great icon-painter Andrei Rublev (*c.* 1370–1430), who was himself to be canonized by the Orthodox church, was born in the closing years of Sergius' life.

(Above) icon of the Old Testament Trinity by Andrei Rublev. Rublev was a monk at the Holy Trinity and St Sergius Monastery, and this icon is believed to be a work of his later years. The three angels who visited Abraham and Sarah at the Oaks of Mamre (Genesis 18) are interpreted in the Orthodox Church as a manifestation of the Holy Trinity.

(Left) The Holy Trinity and St Sergius Monastery at Sergiev Posad (known as Zagorsk in the Soviet era). The monastery was established in 1340 by St Sergius of Radonezh, and became an important religious and cultural centre of the grand princedom of Moscow, and one of only four monasteries in Russia to have the status of Lavra, or major monastery.

Vasily III. A mid-16th-century woodcut from von Herberstein's *Actiones*. This stylized portrait offers no reliable evidence as to the grand prince's appearance.

men from non-aristocratic backgrounds who had the expertise needed to manage the treasury and to deal with foreign affairs. Vasily increased their numbers, and began to reform the way in which the provinces were administered. A new class of official, the town overseers, was appointed, through whom the grand prince could exercise a more direct control over local affairs.

The alliance between the Orthodox church and the Muscovite state was further strengthened. Filofei, a monk from Pskov, wrote an epistle propounding the doctrine that Moscow was the 'Third Rome', the successor to Constantinople as the centre of the Orthodox world. 'Observe then, and take heed, o pious tsar, for all Christian realms are reduced to your realm alone, and two Romes have fallen, the third stands, and a fourth there will not be.' Filofei was stressing the tsar's duty to defend the Orthodox faith. In return, the clergy would uphold the power of the grand prince. The position of the Possessors was consolidated in 1522 by the appointment of Daniel, a disciple of Abbot Joseph of Volokolamsk, as metropolitan of Moscow, head of the Orthodox church in Muscovy. Vasily had to abandon any hope of expropriating church lands, but he benefited from the fact that Daniel was a strong supporter of the autocracy and cemented his alliance with the Orthodox hierarchy by building churches and founding new monasteries.

A dynastic crisis

Vasily's first wife, Solomonia Saburova, was selected in 1505 from a bride show of 1,500 noble virgins. She was a beautiful girl and a descendant of Rurik, but from a dynastic point of view Vasily chose badly. Twenty years of fruitless wedlock ensued. The Orthodox church did not recognize childlessness as grounds for divorce, but Metropolitan Daniel granted Vasily an annulment, against the advice of the Orthodox patriarchs. In

A RELUCTANT NUN

Sigismund von Herberstein, the envoy of the Holy Roman Emperor, visited Russia in 1526–27, shortly after Vasily III repudiated his first wife, Solomonia, and forced her to take the veil. He later wrote down this version of events, which he heard from an unknown source.

When the metropolitan, upon her arrival at the convent weeping and sobbing, cut off her hair and offered to put on the hood, she was so indignant at its being placed upon her that she took it and, hurling it to the ground, stamped upon it with her feet. One of *the chief councillors, irritated at the sight of this indignity, not only reviled her bitterly, but beat her with a scourge, and asked her, 'darest thou resist the will of my lord? And delayest thou to obey his commands?' When Salomea [Solomonia] in return asked him by what authority he beat her, he replied, 'by the will of his lord;' upon which she, broken-hearted, protested in the presence of all, that she took the hood unwillingly and under compulsion, and invoked the vengeance of God on her behalf for so great an injury.*

THE PAIN OF CHILDLESSNESS

The *Pskov Chronicle* gives a moving, though not necessarily reliable account of how Vasily III decided to divorce his first wife. The grand prince was travelling through the countryside of northern Russia. He noticed a bird's nest in a tree, and commented:

I feel sadness. To whom could I liken myself? Not to the birds – they bear offspring; not to the animals – they are prolific; not to the streams – they play with waves and abound in fish. Oh Lord! And not to the earth can I liken myself, since it produces fruit and thus glorifies Thee!

1525 the outraged Solomonia was banished to a convent. The following January the grand prince married Yelena Glinskaya, a 23-year-old princess of Tatar descent. Vasily, who was 46 when he remarried, was besotted with his new wife and defied Orthodox custom by trimming his beard to please her, but it was not until 1530 that Yelena provided him with an heir. Their first child, Ivan, was born during a thunderstorm on 25 August. A second son, Yury, was born in 1532. Since he was a deaf-mute, the future hopes of the dynasty rested on the first-born.

Vasily was interested in Western ideas and practices, and employed a physician from Lübeck named Nicholas, a learned man who also studied astrology and astronomy. Yet even Nicholas was unable to save the grand prince when an ulcer on his left thigh led to blood poisoning. Knowing that he was dying, Vasily gathered together Metropolitan Daniel and a number of leading boyars and asked them to recognize his three-year-old son Ivan as his heir. His request to be made a monk was granted, and on 3 December 1533 he died.

The Church of the Ascension at Kolomenskoe on the outskirts of Moscow. The church was constructed in the years 1530–32 and is believed to have been commissioned by Vasily III as a thank-offering for the birth of his son and heir, the future Ivan IV. The church is built in the 'tent style', and may be a reinterpretation in brick and stone of the traditional wooden churches of Russia. Berlioz, who visited Russia in the 1840s, was much moved by it. 'Nothing impressed me more than the monument to ancient Russian architecture which stands in the village of Kolomenskoe … here I was confronted by a unity. My entire being trembled. There was a mysterious stillness in the harmony of the exquisite shapes.'

Иван IV Грозный Ivan IV
('The Terrible')
1533–1584

Portrait of Ivan IV, painted on wood in the late 16th century by an unknown Russian artist, and now in the National Museum, Copenhagen.

IVAN IV	
Full name Ivan Vasilievich also known as Ivan the Terrible	(4) 1572 Anna Koltovskaya Banished to a convent 1575
Father Vasily III	(5) 1575 Anna Vassilchikova Died 1577
Mother Yelena Glinskaya	(6) 1576 Vassilissa Melentievna Banished to a convent 1577
Born Kolomenskoe 25 August 1530	(7) 1580 Maria Nagaya Died 1608
Accession 3 December 1533	*Children by (1)* Anna (1548)
Died Moscow 18 March 1584 Seizure	Maria (1551) Dmitry (1552) Ivan (1554) Evdokia (1556)
Wives (1) 1547 Anastasia Romanovna Zakharina Died 1560	**Feodor** (1557) *Child by (2)* Vasily (1563; died in infancy)
(2) 1561 Kucheney (aka Maria Temriukovna or Cherkasskaya) Died 1569	*Child by (7)* Dmitry (1582)
(3) 1571 Marfa Sobakina Died 1571	

IVAN IV

…and there hence being conducted into the chamber of presence, our men began to wonder at the majesty of the emperor. His seat was aloft in a very royal throne, having on his head a diadem or crown of gold, apparelled with a robe all of goldsmith's work, and in his hands he held a sceptre garnished and beset with precious stones; and besides all other notes and appearances of honour, there was a majesty in his countenance proportionable with the excellency of his estate.

Richard Chancellor, an English visitor to Russia in 1553

When Vasily III set aside his first wife in order to marry Yelena Glinskaya, the patriarch of Jerusalem is reported to have laid a curse on the grand prince. 'If you do this evil thing, you shall have an evil son. Your nation shall become prey to terror and tears.' The first offspring of the marriage was the man known to history as Ivan the Terrible. The English translation 'the Terrible' is misleading. The Russian word *grozny* means 'dread' or 'awesome', and the appellation was used in Ivan's lifetime.

Ivan IV (1533–1584) succeeded to the throne at the age of three. From 1533 to 1538 the dominant figures in the government were his mother

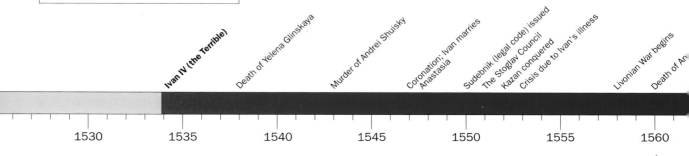

Ivan IV (the Terrible)

Death of Yelena Glinskaya

Murder of Andrei Shuisky

Coronation; Ivan marries Anastasia

Sudebnik (legal code) issued
The Stoglav Council
Kazan conquered
Crisis due to Ivan's illness

Livonian War begins

Death of An

1530   1535   1540   1545   1550   1555   1560

The arrival of Ivan IV at the Holy Trinity and St Sergius Monastery, to which he made a number of pilgrimages. A 16th-century engraving.

The *Shapka Monomakh* (Cap of Monomakh) was made by an unknown craftsman in the late 13th or early 14th century and used in the coronation rituals of Muscovite grand princes and tsars until the late 17th century.

Yelena and her lover, Prince Ivan Obolensky. Yelena and her advisers governed effectively. The surviving brothers of Vasily III were imprisoned when they attempted to seize the throne, and their appanages were reclaimed. A single currency was established for the whole of Muscovy, the frontier defences were strengthened and a border war with Lithuania ended in victory. Yelena's rule provoked resentment among the boyars. She died in 1538, possibly as a result of poisoning. Obolensky was imprisoned by his rivals and later starved to death. Over the following nine years the government was dominated in turn by the Shuisky, Belsky, Vorontsov and Glinsky families. The fact that the boyars vied for control of the government, but none attempted to seize the throne for himself, is significant. There seems to have been a tacit understanding that the office of grand prince was a means of preventing Muscovy from descending into chaos. Ivan was at first a victim of this power game. One source, whose reliability has been questioned, records that he grew into a violent teenager who enjoyed dropping dogs to their deaths from the top of the Kremlin's towers, and who exhibited an unusual mixture of loutish brutality and scholarly piety. Evenings were spent rampaging through the streets of Moscow with a gang of friends and beating people up; days were devoted to reading the scriptures, the Fathers and the lives of the saints, with the encouragement of Metropolitan Makary. The young prince was physically impressive, almost 6 ft (1.8 m) tall, well built, with grey eyes, auburn hair and an aquiline nose.

Ivan's first political initiative came in December 1543 when he had Prince Andrei Shuisky arrested and murdered. Thirty boyars associated with the Shuisky faction were hanged. It would be wrong to suppose that this act gave the young grand prince complete independence. From 1546 the dominant figures in the government were Ivan's maternal uncles Yury and Mikhail Glinsky.

Coronation and marriage

In January 1547 Ivan IV was anointed and crowned in the Cathedral of the Assumption in the Moscow Kremlin by Metropolitan Makary, who proclaimed him 'Tsar of all Russia'. This title had been used occasionally in documents issued by Ivan III's government, but Ivan IV was the first grand prince to be so designated in his coronation ceremony. In earlier centuries Russians had applied the title to the Tatar khans and to the Byzantine emperors. The coronation rituals were designed to demonstrate the imperial continuity between Constantinople and Moscow. The regalia included the 'Shapka Monomakh', the cap traditionally believed

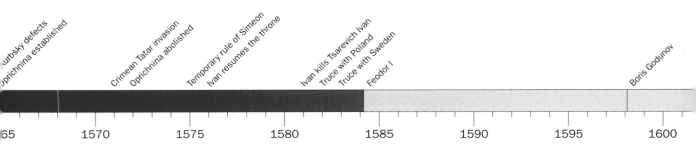

Ivan IV being showered with gold
coins during his coronation ritual.
A miniature from the 16th-century
Book of the Tsar. The scattering of coins,
a regular part of the coronation ritual of
the tsars, symbolized that all the wealth
of Russia was at their disposal.

to have been presented to Vladimir Monomakh, grand prince of Kiev
(1113–1125), by the Byzantine emperor Constantine Monomachus, but
which was in fact of a later date. In the address that he delivered to the
tsar in the course of the ceremony, Makary emphasized not only the
divine origin of imperial power but also the duty of the tsar faithfully to
defend the Orthodox church. A few weeks after the coronation, Ivan
married Anastasia, the daughter of the boyar Roman Yurievich Zakharin,
an influential member of the Boyar Duma or Council. The family, which
came to be known as the Romanovs, were descended from a nobleman
named Andrei Ivanovich Kobyla, who had moved to Moscow in the early
14th century. The marriage appears to have been a happy one, with Anastasia acting as a moderating influence on her husband.

In June 1547 Moscow was devastated by fire. The populace rose up in
revolt, angered by the corruption and cruelty of the Glinsky regime and
convinced that Anna Glinskaya, the tsar's grandmother, had started the
fire by witchcraft. Yury Glinsky was dragged from the Dormition Cathedral in the Kremlin and strangled. Many Glinsky retainers were
murdered, and the mob marched out to Vorobevo, the tsar's summer residence on the Sparrow Hills near the city, to demand that the other
members of the Glinsky family be handed over to them. Ivan's troops dispersed the crowd, but the power of the Glinskys was broken.

THE HISTORIAN KLIUCHEVSKY ON IVAN THE TERRIBLE

Whenever he could not understand a given matter or subject he would fall to stimulating and goading his brain with the spur of emotion, until, with the aid of such forced self-inspiration, he not infrequently succeeded in firing his mind to bold and lofty schemes, and inflating his diction to the point of burning eloquence. At such moments the keenest witticisms, the most caustic sarcasms, the most apposite similes, the most unexpected turns of thought would fly from his tongue or pen like sparks from a blacksmith's hammer. The mere fact that he had the most ungovernable temper in Moscow made him one of the finest writers and orators of his day.

Reforms

The outburst of violence ushered in the most constructive phase of Ivan IV's reign. At the time of his coronation a courtier named Ivan Peresvetov had presented Ivan with a petition in which he recommended that the tsar should appoint officials on merit, regardless of their social class, and should ensure that the law was applied consistently throughout his realm. These ideas appear to have influenced the group of advisers who gathered round Ivan, which included Alexei Adashev, one of the tsar's childhood friends and the son of a government official; Ivan Viskovaty, a civil servant; and Sylvester, the archpriest of the Annunciation Cathedral. Some historians refer to this circle of advisers as the Chosen Council. The extent to which Ivan himself devised policies is not clear. One source states that the reform programme was launched at a joint assembly of boyars and senior clergy in February 1549. Ivan castigated the boyars for their greed and corruption, and announced the creation of a Petitions Chancery, headed by Adashev, to deal with pleas and complaints from the lower classes. At the same time the judicial powers which provincial governors (*namestniki*) had exercised over the minor nobility and the gentry were limited. The 1549 assembly was the first of a series of meetings, and the practice of consulting the minor nobility as well as the boyars and the ecclesiastical hierarchy led to the emergence of the Assembly of the Land (*zemsky sobor*). The Assembly served as a useful counterweight to the power of the boyars, but was not a decision-making body and met only occasionally. Its function was to support and to endorse the policies of the tsar and his advisers. Further reforms followed. Chanceries were established to deal with the issues of Brigandage, the Postal System and Military Affairs, and departments which had begun to evolve in the previous reigns, such as the Foreign Office and the Treasury, were given an independent and distinct existence. A new department was created to keep track of those nobles who held their land under the *pomestie* system of tenure (p. 18). In 1550 a new law code or Sudebnik was published. The Sudebnik condemned corruption in judges and tax-collectors and limited the powers of provincial governors.

The Small State Seal of Ivan IV, 1569. On one side is the double-headed eagle and the inscription 'By the grace of God Tsar and Grand Prince Ivan Vasilievich'; on the other side, a unicorn, symbol of kingly authority and strength (Psalm 92:10), and an abbreviated version of the tsar's titles emphasizing his sovereignty over all Russia, Vladimir, Moscow and Novgorod.

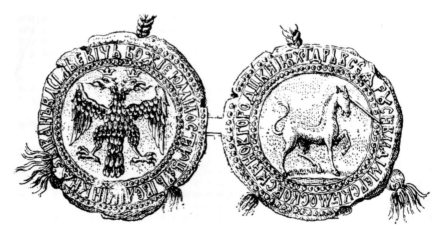

Ivan's government also reformed the army. The complex system of precedence (*mestnichestvo*) among field commanders, which had led to costly disputes on the battlefield about who should obey whom, was modified, though the changes did not amount to a complete solution to the problem. Six companies of full-time, salaried musketeers or *streltsy* – 3,000 men in all – were established, forming Muscovy's first standing army. The Book of the Thousand was drawn up, listing 1,000 men on whom lands near to Moscow would be settled. The intention was to secure their services for the army and the administration, but lack of available land may have prevented the plan from being fully realized.

Ivan IV, like his grandfather Ivan III, showed signs of a desire to limit the property owned by the church and to remove its tax immunities. Metropolitan Makary objected to this. As he had made clear in his coronation precept, he expected the tsar to protect the privileges of the church. In return the church would support the crown. In 1551 the tsar summoned a church council which became known as the Stoglav (Hundred Chapter) Council. Whether Ivan made the speeches that are attributed to him in the record of the proceedings is open to question. If he did so, his remarks were a cunning mixture of threats and flattery. On the one hand he reminded the churchmen of the fate of Sodom and Gomorrah, cities which had failed to reform themselves. On the other hand he proclaimed himself a repentant sinner. The decisions of the Council were a blend of the conservative and the reformist. Traditional styles of icon painting and church music were affirmed, and secular music and drama were condemned. One chapter reasserted the duty of Orthodox men to grow beards, after the manner of their Saviour, and another banned the eating of black pudding. Clerical corruption and licentiousness were condemned. Church lands and tax exemptions were declared inviolable, but it was agreed that future acquisitions of land would require the tsar's permission. The Stoglav Council also approved the new law code.

The founding of the Russian empire

One issue on which church and state were in complete accord was the conquest of Kazan, which Metropolitan Makary proclaimed as a crusade against the Muslims. The death of Khan Safa-Girey in 1551 provided Ivan with the opportunity to install a puppet khan, Shah-Ali, but this experiment in indirect rule broke down and in 1552 Ivan decided to conquer the khanate. It was a prize worth having. The city of Kazan lay at the junction of a number of important trade routes, and the khanate included fertile land with which the tsar could secure and reward the services of the gentry.

Ivan himself led the campaign, and laid siege to Kazan. Success at first eluded him. The defenders of the city displayed their contempt for the Russians by baring their hindquarters and breaking wind at them. The Russian soldiery believed this was witchcraft and that it accounted for

The Kazan Banner, carried before Ivan IV in the Kazan campaign. It bears a representation of the face of Christ in a traditional design known as 'the image of Christ not made with human hands'.

Russian artillery in action at the siege of Kazan, from a 16th-century miniature.

the storms which were impeding the siege. The relic of the True Cross which formed part of the coronation regalia was brought from Moscow, and the weather improved. On the morning of the final assault Ivan is said to have lingered long at his devotions and appeared reluctant to join in the fighting. Despite this, the Russians took the city on 2 October 1552, and the tsar made a triumphant entry into Kazan two days later.

Though the subjugation of the khanate took five more years, the capture of Kazan made Muscovy an imperial power and released powerful patriotic emotions. The victory was commemorated by an unusually large icon in which the Archangel Michael and the tsar were portrayed at the head of the Muscovite armies. The other great monument to the victory was the cathedral in Red Square now known as St Basil's. In 1556 Ivan's forces added the khanate of Astrakhan to his empire.

Lacking defensible natural frontiers and an ice-free coastline, Ivan and his successors, tsarist and Communist, could only seek security and trading outlets by continuing to expand their territory. Westwards expansion was to bring them up against technologically more developed nation states, and to confront them with the need to modernize. This imperative was to cost the Russian people dear in terms of taxation, military obligations and the regimentation of society.

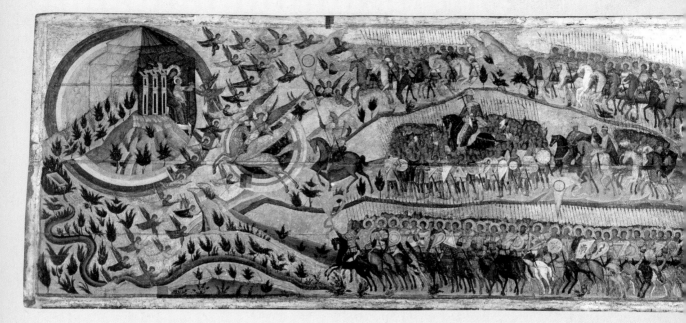

(Above) The Icon The Blessed Army, *now in the Tretyakov Gallery, Moscow.*

(Opposite) The Cathedral of the Intercession, Moscow, better known in the West as St Basil the Blessed.

(Below) The Shapka Kazansky (Kazan Cap), *a piece of ceremonial headgear made in the 16th century to commemorate the conquest of Kazan.*

KAZAN: ART OF EMPIRE

The city of Kazan was captured on the Feast of the Intercession of the Virgin in the year 1552. Tradition has it that when Ivan IV decided to build a cathedral adjacent to the Moscow Kremlin to commemorate his victory, he ordered that it should be dedicated to the Intercession, and that the central church, built in the 'tent' style, should be surrounded by chapels dedicated to the saints and holy days on which other victories in the war had taken place. The cathedral was built between 1555 and 1560. The architects were Postnik and Barma, though some Russian scholars have suggested that there was only one of them, named Postnik Barma. There is no evidence to support the story that Ivan had them blinded once the work had been completed, to prevent them from building anything as splendid for another ruler. The building strikes the casual observer as oriental in its outline and its richness of colour and ornament, but the motifs and decorations used all derive from Russian tradition.

The cathedral soon became known as St Basil the Blessed. Basil was a religious visionary of the type known as a 'holy fool', reputedly gifted with powers of healing and prophecy. He is said to have foretold the Moscow fire of 1547. Since most of the buildings in the city were made of wood and conflagrations were commonplace this was not a particularly impressive feat. 'Holy fools' used their position to criticize those in authority, usually with impunity. Basil was revered by Ivan and the Tsaritsa Anastasia, who both visited him on his deathbed in 1552. He was buried in the graveyard of a church dedicated to the Holy Trinity which was demolished to make way for the Cathedral of the Intercession, and subsequently reburied in a shrine attached to the new cathedral, which became a focus of his cult.

The capture of Kazan was commemorated by an unusually large icon in which the Archangel Michael and Ivan IV were portrayed at the head of the Russian armies, marching back from Sodom (Kazan), which is depicted in flames, towards the Celestial City (Moscow), where the Virgin and the infant Jesus wait to welcome them. Above Ivan's head, a trio of angels hold the Shapka Monomakh, the cap used at his coronation. The cap was believed to have been presented to Vladimir Monomakh by the Byzantine Emperor Constantine Monomachus (pp. 31–32). Its inclusion in the icon is an indirect reminder of the concept that Muscovy was spiritually the successor state of the Byzantine Empire. Vladimir Monomakh himself appears among the procession of victorious Muscovite warriors, mounted on horseback and carrying a cross. He was grand prince of Kiev from 1113 to 1125, and a direct ancestor of Ivan IV. His presence in the icon suggests a parallel between his victories over the Polovtsians and Ivan's conquest of the khanate of Kazan.

A crisis and further reforms

Ivan IV fell ill in March 1553. Fearing for his life, he tried to secure the succession for his infant son Dmitry. This proposal caused serious disagreement, with one faction arguing that the crown should pass to an adult and advancing the claims of Ivan's cousin, Vladimir Andreyevich of Staritsa. Ivan's recovery brought the dispute to an end, but the experience made him hostile towards his cousin and the boyar group who had supported his claim.

During the 1550s there were further reforms of the administration. The office of provincial governor soon disappeared from most areas of Muscovy. The system known as *kormlenie* (feeding), under which local people contributed to the upkeep of governors, who retained a proportion of the revenues that they raised in lieu of a salary, was abolished. The new arrangements, under which the administration of justice and the collection of taxes were supervised by local boards consisting of elected representatives of the gentry, the townspeople and the peasants, were in theory less open to corruption. Officials were directly answerable to the tsar, but in practice it proved difficult to keep track of their behaviour. The new system was not applied to frontier provinces. There local administration was in the hands of the *voevoda*, a military official appointed by the tsar.

In 1556 a Decree on Service defined the military obligations of all landowners. As well as serving in person, they had to provide one fully equipped cavalryman for every 410 acres of land. This reform sought to ensure that the burden of military service was more fairly shared, and increased the service obligations of many boyars.

War and trade

In the second half of the 1550s Ivan's advisers were divided as to how to use Muscovy's military power. Adashev favoured an attempt to defeat the Crimean khanate, but a series of military ventures across the southern frontier failed. Ivan Viskovaty argued for a policy of westwards expansion, with Livonia as the first objective. The conquest of Livonia would give Muscovy better access to the Baltic than was provided by the small coastal strip at the mouth of the River Neva. Though Ivan's government had made a trading agreement with the English in 1555, the trade route was via the port of Archangel and the White Sea, and Archangel was icebound for many months each year.

In the first phase of the Livonian War, from 1558 to 1564, the Muscovites made rapid gains, and the capture of Narva in 1558 gave them a Baltic port. The partial collapse of Livonia encouraged the Danes, the Poles and the Swedes to join in what had become a partition process.

THE ENGLISH CONNECTION

Queen Elizabeth I of England. The 'Pelican' portrait of 1572–76 by Nicholas Hilliard.

In 1553 an English expedition attempting to find a north-east passage to Asia came to grief in the Russian Arctic. The surviving vessel, commanded by Richard Chancellor, landed on the White Sea coast. Chancellor was royally welcomed by Ivan IV and returned home with a charter granting English merchants privileged access to Muscovy. In 1555 the Muscovy or Russia Company was established by a royal charter of Queen Mary. Thereafter the aim of English diplomacy was to maintain and extend the trading and taxational privileges enjoyed by the Company.

Ivan's view of the relationship was broader. He saw England not only as a valuable trading partner but also as a place of refuge for himself if he lost control of his kingdom. He twice tried, unsuccessfully, to persuade Elizabeth I into an offensive and defensive military alliance with Muscovy. Towards the end of his life another theme entered into the diplomacy – his hope of an English marriage. In 1582 he sent Feodor Andreyevich Pissemsky to negotiate a marriage alliance with Lady Mary Hastings, cousin to Queen Elizabeth and a daughter of the Earl of Huntingdon. Elizabeth had no intention either of agreeing to the offensive-defensive alliance which Pissemsky proposed, or of sacrificing her cousin to her country's commercial interests. Pissemsky was told that Lady Mary had been seriously disfigured by smallpox and was suffering from a disease. He was not permitted to meet her until 1583. He later informed Ivan that she was 'tall and slender, with a pale

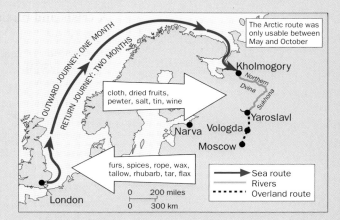

The Arctic route was only usable between May and October

OUTWARD JOURNEY: ONE MONTH

RETURN JOURNEY: TWO MONTHS

cloth, dried fruits, pewter, salt, tin, wine

Kholmogory

Northern Dvina

Sukhona

Yaroslavl

Narva Vologda

Moscow

furs, spices, rope, wax, tallow, rhubarb, tar, flax

London

| 0 | 200 miles |
| 0 | 300 km |

➤ Sea route
— Rivers
┄┄┄ Overland route

face, grey eyes, a straight nose, and long tapering fingers.' Elizabeth sent Sir Jerome Bowes to Moscow with a letter explaining that her cousin did not wish to marry the tsar, and could not be forced to do so.

…as over the rest of our subjects, so especially over the noble houses, and families, we have no further authority than by waye of persuasion to induce them to like of such matches as are tendered them.

The English Merchants' House in Moscow after restoration in 1962. This 16th-century house was given to the Muscovy Company by Ivan IV to use as their headquarters. It is located close to Red Square and the Kremlin.

Though unwilling to bind her country to the kind of alliance that Ivan sought, Elizabeth understood the importance of maintaining good relations with the tsars. Diplomacy was sweetened by presents. When Jerome Horsey travelled to Moscow in 1586 he took with him dogs, lions, bulls, pistols, armour, wines, drugs, organs and other costly gifts for Tsar Feodor and his chief adviser, Boris Godunov. Elizabeth later sent a carriage as a gift to Boris Godunov, but Boris' hopes of securing English aristocratic marriages for his son and daughter were not realized.

A model of the carriage sent by Elizabeth I to Boris Godunov. The model is in the Science Museum, London, and the carriage itself in the Kremlin Armoury Museum.

In 1561 the Livonian Order was disbanded. Its last Master made himself a vassal of the king of Poland, and was granted the title Duke of Courland. Ivan's government thus found itself at war with Poland. The Russians' capture of Polotsk in 1563, which was the high point of the first phase of the Livonian War, was followed by a defeat on the Ulla River in 1564.

In 1560 Ivan's wife Anastasia died. It was rumoured that she had been poisoned, and a modern autopsy whose results were published in 1996 lent credence to that view, for the tsaritsa's hair was found to contain large quantities of mercury salts. In the 16th century, however, this poisonous substance was believed to be a cure for leprosy and syphilis, so the case remains open. In his grief, Ivan was further alienated from two of his principal advisers, Adashev and Sylvester. The former died of a fever in a prison cell, and the latter was exiled to a remote monastery. The death of Metropolitan Makary in 1563 removed another restraining influence. Ivan's behaviour became increasingly violent and irrational. Senior boyars were arraigned on charges of treason and executed. In April 1564 Prince Andrei Kurbsky, one of Ivan's generals, defected to the Poles. He had lost an important battle and feared Ivan's retribution.

Ivan IV's extensive conquests in the east were not matched by equal success in the south or the west. In the south the Crimean Tatars, who had come under the overlordship of the Ottoman empire, remained a serious threat to Muscovy. In the west, the main beneficiaries of the partition of Livonia were Sweden and Lithuania-Poland, the dual state formed by the Union of Lublin in 1569. In 1598 Russia had a limited coastline on the Gulf of Finland, but this territory was lost to the Swedes by the terms of the Peace of Stolbovo in 1617. It was not until the reign of Peter the Great (1682–1725) that Russia secured a permanent outlet to the Baltic.

Russia and her Neighbours 1533–98

Russia in 1533

Russia in 1598

THE IVAN–KURBSKY CORRESPONDENCE

If they are genuine, the letters exchanged between Prince Andrei Mikhailovich Kurbsky and Tsar Ivan IV are one of the most important sources for the study of 16th-century Russian history. In 1971 the historian Edward Keenan put forward the view that the letters dated from the 17th rather than the 16th century, and a complex and detailed scholarly argument ensued. Was Ivan the educated, theologically literate ruler suggested by the letters, or an irascible and possibly illiterate invalid? The question has not been, and may never be, conclusively answered. Kurbsky was a senior Muscovite boyar who defected to the Lithuanians in 1564. The first of his five letters to Ivan purports to have been written shortly afterwards.

Kurbsky: *Wherefore, O tsar, have you destroyed the strong in Israel and subjected to various forms of death the voevodas [generals] given to you by God? And wherefore have you spilt their victorious, holy blood in the churches of God during sacerdotal ceremonies, and stained the thresholds of the churches with their blood of martyrs? And why have you conceived against your well-wishers and against those who lay down their lives for you unheard-of-torments and persecutions and death, falsely accusing the Orthodox of treachery and magic and other abuses, and endeavouring with zeal to turn light into darkness and to call sweet bitter?*

Ivan: *How is it that you feel no shame when you call the evil-doers martyrs without considering the reason for the suffering of any of them? Yet the apostle cries out: 'If a man be tormented for his transgressions, that is to say not for his faith, he is not crowned.' And the divine Chrysostom and the great Athanasius say in all their teaching: 'Thieves and brigands and evil-doers and adulterers shall be tormented; for such are not blessed, since they shall be tormented for their sins and not for the sake of God.'*

Ivan then offers a lengthy justification of his policies, including some autobiographical elements to explain his hatred and distrust of the boyars.
Ivan: *When I had entered upon my eighth year of life and when thus our subjects had achieved their desire, namely to have the kingdom without a ruler, they did not deem us, their sovereigns, worthy of any loving care, but themselves ran after wealth and glory, and so leapt on one another. And what did they do then! How many boyars and well-wishers of our father and voevodas did they massacre! And the courts and the villages and the possessions of our uncles did they seize and they set themselves up in them!*

Ivan protests about the treatment that he and his brother received at the hands of the boyars when they were children:
Ivan: *...they began to feed us as though we were foreigners or the most wretched menials ... everything was contrary to my will and unbefitting my tender years. I recall one thing: whilst we were playing childish games in our infancy Prince Ivan Vasil'evich Shuisky is sitting on a bench, leaning with his elbows on our father's bed and with his leg up on a chair; and he did not even incline his head towards us, either in parental manner, or even as master – nor was there any servility to be found. Who can endure such arrogance?*

Kurbsky: *I have received your grandiloquent and big-sounding screed, and I have understood it and realized that it was belched forth in untameable wrath with poisonous words, such as is unbecoming not only to a tsar, so great and glorified throughout the universe, but even to a simple lowly soldier....*

Ivan: *And why did you separate me from my wife? If only you had not taken from me my young [wife], then there would have been no 'sacrifices to Cronus'. You will say: 'that I was unable to endure this and that I did not preserve my purity' – well, we are all human.*

Kurbsky: *Recall your first days in which you ruled blessedly! Destroy not further yourself and your house! As David said: 'he that loveth injustice, his soul hateth' – how much more swiftly will those that swim in Christian blood disappear with all their house!*

The Oprichnina

In December 1564 Ivan abruptly left Moscow with his second wife Maria and his sons Ivan and Feodor. Ivan knew that many boyars disapproved of the Livonian War and felt that he should instead be concentrating on defeating the Crimean Tatars. He was also alarmed by Kurbsky's defection. Ivan sought refuge at Alexandrovskaya Sloboda, some 70 miles from the city, and from there announced that he had laid down the office of tsar. A delegation of churchmen and boyars travelled to Alexandrovskaya Sloboda to persuade him to resume the throne, as Ivan had probably calculated that they would. He agreed to do so, stipulating that he must have a free hand to deal with traitors. When he returned to Moscow a few

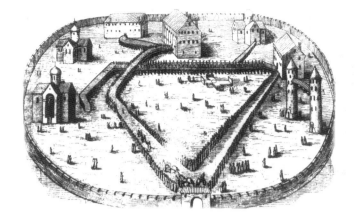

'SHORTY' AND 'DIRTY' – TWO PROMINENT OPRICHNIKI

Two of the most feared members of the Oprichnina went by the misleadingly homely nicknames of 'Shorty' and 'Dirty'. Grigory Liukanovich Skuratov-Belsky, captain of Ivan IV's personal bodyguard and effectively his chief of police, was known as Maliuta ('Shorty'). Skuratov was responsible for a large number of killings. His most distinguished victim was Metropolitan Filipp, smothered in December 1569 in the monastery cell in which he had been imprisoned. In the bizarre imitation of monastic life that Ivan commanded to be played out at Alexandrovskaya Sloboda, the Oprichnina base north of Moscow, Skuratov played the role of sacristan. Prince Andrei Kurbsky described him as 'a ferocious and inhuman child of darkness'. Skuratov died in battle in 1573, hit by a cannon ball during the assault on the fortress of Weissenstein in Swedish Estonia. Ivan IV's revenge for the loss of his retainer was to have the fortress' commander roasted alive. Boris Godunov was one of Skuratov's protégés, and he married Skuratov's daughter, Maria.

Skuratov's chief assistant was Vasily Griaznoi (the surname is derived from the Russian word meaning 'dirty'), who was unfortunate enough to be captured by the khan of the Crimea during a reconnaissance expedition on the southern borders of Muscovy in 1573. He wrote to Ivan IV begging to be released in exchange for a prominent Tatar captive. Ivan was unsympathetic. 'The Crimeans,' he wrote back, 'do not fall asleep as you do and can easily capture milksops like you.' Despite the fact that Vasily had played a key part in the purging of Novgorod and the Livonian War, and had been a favourite drinking companion of the tsar's, Ivan refused to arrange his release.

weeks later, he announced his intention of dividing the territory of the state. He would rule parts of it, assisted by hand-picked landowners. This royal domain, a collection of scattered lands rather than a consolidated holding, would be known as the Oprichnina – derived from the Russian word for dowry. The rest of Muscovy, known as the Zemshchina, would be ruled separately by traditional institutions. Even the capital was divided into two zones, and the tsar moved from the Kremlin to a new fortified mansion.

The oprichniki who ruled Ivan's domain terrorized the rest of the population with impunity, since their privileges included complete legal immunity. Mounted on black horses, and dressed in black uniforms and hoods, they carried on their saddles the twin emblems of a broom and a dog's head, symbolizing their mission to rid the land of traitors. They had a strong incentive to persecute the wealthy since they received a quarter of the property of anyone whom they arrested. A second quarter went to whoever had denounced the victim, and the remainder to the tsar. Some historians have seen the Oprichnina experiment as a device for destroying the boyars and replacing them with men who would be loyal to the crown because they owed their wealth and position to Ivan, but the selection of both victims and oprichniki cut across class barriers, and appears to have been based on the tsar's personal feelings. Those whom he trusted were invited to join the Oprichnina, and those whom he distrusted were liable to become its victims. Whole families were slaughtered. Prominent victims included Metropolitan Filipp, imprisoned because he denounced the crimes of the oprichniki, and then strangled on Ivan's orders, and Vladimir Andreyevich of Staritsa, accused of plotting to poison the tsar.

During the Oprichnina experiment, Ivan became more fearful for his own safety. Alexandrovskaya Sloboda was turned into a heavily fortified residence where the tsar and 300 trusted oprichniki lived a lifestyle blended of monastic piety, drunken debauchery and bizarre cruelty. Ivan even wrote to Queen Elizabeth I of England in 1567 asking her to grant him political asylum should the need arise. The climax of the terror came in 1570. Ivan, convinced that the Novgorodians were conspiring to hand

(*Above*) The black uniform of an oprichnik.

(*Opposite*) Alexandrovskaya Sloboda. A 16th-century engraving of Ivan IV's fortified compound near Moscow. In the *Life of Ivan IV* attributed to Prince Andrei Kurbsky it is described as 'that bloody fortress ... filled with the blood of Christians.'

Stefan Báthory (1533–86), a contemporary engraving. Báthory, who became prince of Transylvania in 1571, was king of Poland from 1576 to 1586, and is remembered for his administrative reforms and soldierly abilities.

over their city to the Poles, conducted a brutal purge of leading citizens and their families. In July 116 prisoners were executed in Red Square by a variety of cruel means. Ivan Viskovaty, once one of the tsar's closest advisers, was hacked to pieces by the oprichniki, and Nikita Funikov, the royal treasurer, was tortured to death by being alternately doused in boiling and cold water. Later that year the Oprichnina system began to devour its own enforcers, and in 1572 Ivan abruptly halted the experiment, issuing a decree forbidding his subjects even to mention it.

The Livonian War continues

Victory in Livonia proved elusive. In 1564 Ivan's government signed a seven-year truce with Sweden and opened negotiations with Poland. The results did not satisfy Ivan, who wished to continue the war, and in 1566 summoned a meeting of the Assembly of the Land to discuss the terms that the Poles had offered. The delegates endorsed his decision to reject the peace terms, and the conflict was resumed. In 1569 Poland and Lithuania became a single kingdom as a result of the Union of Lublin. Ivan now faced a strengthened enemy. His pact with Prince Magnus of Denmark, whom he made puppet king of Livonia in 1570 in return for his help against the Swedes, backfired, since Magnus was militarily unsuccessful and unpopular with the Livonian population.

In 1571 Devlet-Girey, khan of the Crimea, invaded Muscovy and reached the outskirts of Moscow. The fires started by his troops in the suburbs spread to the city itself, with catastrophic results. Ivan blamed the disaster on the oprichniki, and the system of divided command that he himself had created. In 1572 a united force drawn from both the Oprichnina and the Zemshchina successfully saw off a second Tatar invasion.

The death of Sigismund II of Poland in 1572 created a vacancy there and diplomatic and military opportunities for Ivan's government. Ivan put forward both himself and his second son Feodor as candidates. The choice fell first on Henry of Valois, but in 1574 he left to succeed his dead brother on the throne of France. In 1575 a second election gave the crown to Stefan Báthory, a Hungarian-born nobleman who had been ruler of Transylvania since 1571. Ivan's government took advantage of Stefan's inexperience to seize much of Livonia, taking territory both from the Swedes and the Poles, and thus driving these two powers into an anti-Russian alliance. Polish and Swedish counterattacks began in 1578 and wiped out the Muscovite gains. Narva fell to the Swedes in 1581. The truce agreements that Ivan's government signed with Poland in 1582 and with Sweden in 1583 restored the frontiers to where they had been at the beginning of the Livonian War. The drive to the Baltic had failed, though a small area on the Gulf of Finland including the mouth of the River Neva was retained. The war left Muscovy in a ruinous condition. Taxation impoverished the population and peasants reacted by deserting their lands in large numbers and fleeing south. Land fell out of cultivation and famines ensued.

Tsar Simeon

In 1575 there was a further outbreak of brutal executions, and it seemed as though Ivan was contemplating a return to the Oprichnina terror. Then, in the autumn of that year, Ivan announced that he was abdicating. Henceforward he would be an appanage prince with the title Ivan of Moscow. Simeon Bekbulatovich, a descendant of Genghis Khan, was enthroned as tsar. Simeon was one of Ivan's military commanders. His elevation to the tsardom baffled contemporaries and still puzzles historians. Superstition may have been a factor. Soothsayers had warned Ivan that in the year 7084 (which began on 1 September 1575) the tsar of Muscovy would die. Ivan resumed the tsardom once the year was over, and pensioned off Simeon by making him grand prince of Tver.

Dynastic difficulties

Ivan married seven times in all, a conjugal persistence which was not rewarded with many surviving offspring. Dmitry, his first-born son, was drowned as an infant when his nurse dropped him in a river. His other two sons by Anastasia, the intelligent and capable Ivan, and the gentle and half-witted Feodor, survived into adulthood. His second marriage, to the Circassian princess Kucheney, also known as Maria Temriukovna or Maria Cherkasskaya, gave Ivan a son who died in infancy. Maria died in 1569. Ivan's third wife, a Novgorodian girl named Marfa Sobakina, died in 1571 after only 16 days of marriage. The Orthodox church did not permit a fourth marriage, but Ivan claimed that his marriage to Marfa had never been consummated and was allowed to marry Anna Koltovskaya, who was banished to a convent after three years, having failed to produce any children. She was rapidly succeeded by Anna Vassilchikova, who died after only two years, and Vassilissa Melentievna, whose alleged adultery resulted in her banishment to a convent and her lover's execution. Ivan's final and seventh marriage was to Maria Nagaya, the daughter of a court official of Tatar descent. Since the Orthodox church did not sanction his last three marriages, Ivan's son by Maria, Dmitry, was canonically illegitimate. The prospects for a stable succession therefore depended on Ivan's eldest surviving son, the Tsarevich Ivan.

Relations between the two men were strained. The tsar had taken against his son's first two wives, banishing both of them to nunneries, and he was no fonder of the third wife, Yelena Sheremetieva. There may also have been political disagreements between father and son, with the tsarevich favouring the continuation of the war against Poland at a time when Ivan IV had decided to negotiate peace. By 1581 Yelena was pregnant. One day the tsar entered her apartments and found that she was not wearing the clothing prescribed by the church for women in her condition. In a fit of rage he knocked her to the ground and began kicking her. The tsarevich, hearing her cries, rushed to her aid, and his father lashed out at him with the iron-shod staff that he always carried, fracturing his skull. The tsarevich died of his injuries some days later. Yelena

The face of Ivan IV. The distinguished Russian anthropologist M. Gerasimov made this sculptural reconstruction of the tsar's features in the 1960s after examining his skull.

miscarried and soon afterwards died. These events left Ivan racked with guilt, as well they might.

The death of Ivan

By the early months of 1584 the tsar was seriously ill. He summoned a group of 60 astrologers to predict the exact day of his death, and was told that he would die on 18 March. On 17 March he warned them that if they were wrong they would be executed by burning. On the morning of the predicted day he felt well enough to take a bath. Long soakings in hot water relieved the chronic back pain from which he suffered. He was even heard to sing. Then he lay on his bed and ordered that a chessboard be made ready for a game. Suddenly he gave out a loud cry and fell backwards onto the bed. He was found to be dead. He was buried in the Archangel Michael Cathedral in the Kremlin next to the son whom he had killed.

Ivan's reign was a transitional period. In Muscovy, as in many European states in the late 15th and 16th centuries, a medieval system of monarchy was developing into a more centralized and autocratic institution. Yet though Ivan's reforms, and his creation of a court elite of service gentry and officials, were an attempt to strengthen the monarchy at the expense of boyar influence, the boyars remained a powerful and privileged force because of the system of precedence (*mestnichestvo*) which Ivan's reforms had modified rather than abolished. The 30 years after Ivan IV's death were to demonstrate that the boyars were still in a position to exploit the weaknesses of the tsar.

AN ACCOUNT OF IVAN IV FROM THE STALIN ERA

Soviet historians of the Stalin era saw Ivan IV as a dynamic nation-builder engaged in a class war against the boyars. Andrei Kurbsky, the Russian commander who defected to Poland during the reign of Ivan, was reviled as a traitor who fled abroad and, from a place of safety, engaged in a propaganda war with the leader. The parallel with Trotsky would have been obvious to politically educated readers. The study of Ivan IV from which this extract is taken was originally published in 1922, but was revised for second and third editions published in 1942 and 1947 respectively. Its author, the historian Wipper, had originally been a monarchist, but, as this extract makes clear, modified his views after the Bolshevik Revolution. Stalin read and was fascinated by the book.

It has long been the custom in Russian historiography to depict the institution of the Oprichnina primarily as a gesture of horror and despair, which conformed to the high-strung character of Ivan IV, before whom yawned a chasm of disloyalty and treachery among what had seemed his best servants and counsellors. This naive and romantic presentation of the subject must be abandoned once and for all. It is time to understand that the institution of the Oprichnina was primarily a great military administrative reform, called forth by the growing difficulties of the great war for access to the Black Sea and for the opening of intercourse with Western Europe.... The reform was designed to remove those who were dangerous to the country and to utilize the idle elements in the interests of the state; the resistance it encountered transformed it into a weapon for their extermination. As a consequence, the reform developed into an internal war. Ivan Grozny's policy, both foreign and domestic, clearly expressed the class character of the rising monarchy. Moreover, the definite social change that was exceptionally marked by the institution of the Oprichnina in 1564 should be noted. The tsar acted mainly in the interests of the middle landed gentry, from whose representatives he formed what was, to use J.V. Stalin's classically precise term, an 'aristocratic military bureaucracy'.

Фёдор I	Feodor I
	1584–1598
Борис Годунов	Boris Godunov
	1598–1605
Фёдор II	Feodor II
	1605
Лжедмитрий I	False Dmitry I
	1605–1606
Василий Шуйский	Vasily Shuisky
	1606–1610
Междуцарствие	Interregnum
	1610–1613
	Several claimants

Feodor I. A late 16th-century portrait.

FEODOR I	
Full name	*Accession*
Feodor Ivanovich	18 March 1584
also known as	*Died*
Feodor the Angelic	Moscow
Father	7 January 1598
Ivan IV	Natural causes
Mother	*Wife*
Anastasia	1580 Irina
Romanovna	Feodorovna
Zakharina	Godunova
Born	Died 1603
Moscow	*Child*
31 May 1557	Feodosia (1592)

FEODOR I

The emperor … is for his person of a mean stature, somewhat low and gross, of a sallow complexion, and inclining to the dropsy, hawk-nosed, unsteady in his pace by reason of some weakness of his limbs, heavy and inactive, yet commonly smiling almost to a laughter. For quality otherwise simple and slow-witted but very gentle and of an easy nature, quiet, merciful, of no martial disposition nor greatly apt for matters of policy, very superstitious and infinite that way.

Giles Fletcher, envoy of Queen Elizabeth I of England

Feodor I, although pious and fond of bell-ringing and religious pilgrimages, was ill-equipped to rule, being physically and mentally feeble. Ivan IV had, in his will, designated a group of five courtiers to act as a regency council. Boris Godunov, the new tsar's brother-in-law, immediately showed himself the most able of them. By 1588 he had

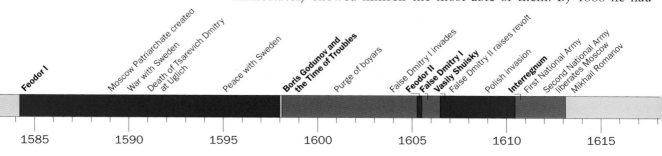

outmanoeuvred his rivals and he was unchallenged for the rest of Feodor's reign.

It is often said that Boris was of Tatar princely descent, but there is no reliable evidence of this. The Godunov family traced their ancestry back to the Kostroma district. In 1571 Boris joined the Oprichnina. Elevated to the rank of boyar in 1580, he became a trusted adviser of Ivan IV, a relationship cemented by the marriage between his sister Irina and Ivan's son Feodor. One account of Ivan IV's fatal wounding of his son says that Boris was present on that occasion, and tried to protect the tsarevich.

Muscovite foreign policy in the reign of Feodor was largely successful. Boris maintained good relations with Elizabeth I of England. The death of Stefan Báthory, king of Poland, in 1586 presented an opportunity to exploit the weakness of an enemy. Feodor's government proposed that he should be king of Poland as well as Muscovy, though it is unlikely that they expected this candidacy to succeed. The choice of Sigismund Vasa, heir to the throne of Sweden, seemed to threaten a Polish-Swedish coalition against Muscovy, but the Poles gave no active support to the Swedes in the Russo-Swedish War of 1590–95, during which Moscow retook much of the coast of the Gulf of Finland and parts of Karelia. Boris Godunov also consolidated Muscovy's grip on western Siberia. The first Russian penetration of the area had been by the Stroganovs, a merchant dynasty who hired the Cossack hetman (chieftain) Yermak to defeat the Siberian Tatars. Yermak was killed in battle, but Muscovite troops soon established a permanent presence in the region.

In domestic policy the most important development of Feodor's reign was the establishment of the patriarchate. In 1589 Metropolitan Job, a

LIFE AT THE COURT OF FEODOR I

The Englishman Giles Fletcher visited Russia in 1588–89, and wrote *Of the Russe Commonwealth* on the basis of his experiences. The book, which contained some unflattering descriptions of Russian customs and manners, was suppressed by Queen Elizabeth I at the request of the Muscovy Company, who feared that it might prejudice the Russians against trading with England. Of Feodor I Fletcher wrote:

After dinner he layeth him down to rest where commonly he taketh three hours sleep except he employ one of the hours to bathing or boxing. And this custom for sleeping is an ordinary matter with him as with all the Russes. After his sleep he goeth to evensong … and, thence returning, for the most part recreateth himself with the empress till suppertime with jesters and dwarfs, men and women that tumble before him and sing many songs after the Russe manner.

The Zaporozhian Cossack hetman Petro Konashevich Sahaidachny. A 17th-century woodcut. Sahaidachny is a Ukrainian national hero.

COSSACKS

The original meaning of the term 'cossack', which is of Turkish origin, was a migrant worker, a man who was not tied to the land. In southern Muscovy many of them were hunters and fishermen living adjacent to the Tatars, and often in conflict with them. With the break-up of the khanate of the Golden Horde, communities of cossacks began to settle in areas of the steppes previously dominated by the Tatars, particularly in the valleys of the Don and the Dnieper. Some of them tilled the land, others were mercenaries and freebooters. The Don Cossacks were the first to come under the influence of Muscovy. The Zaporozhian Cossacks of the Dnieper region remained a law unto themselves for much longer, sometimes fighting alongside the Poles against the Muscovites, and sometimes alongside the Muscovites against the Poles. A warrior brotherhood governed by an elected *hetman* (chieftain), the Zaporozhians practised a rough and ready democracy, in which unpopular leaders were disposed of by drowning. Any man who appeared sufficiently comradely and bellicose was welcomed into the community, and the Zaporozhians developed into a kind of foreign legion, many of whose members were fugitives from Muscovy, from the Tatar khanates or from Poland. In the early 17th century their only firm tie to Russia was their Orthodoxy.

Feodor I. A late 16th-century portrait.

close ally of Boris Godunov, was elevated to the rank of patriarch with the consent of the patriarch of Constantinople. The head of the Russian church now ranked fifth in seniority in the Orthodox world, behind the patriarchs of Constantinople, Alexandria, Antioch and Jerusalem. This enhancement of the church's status proved to be opportune, for at the worst moment of the Time of Troubles – the period of calamities and civil strife that began during Boris Godunov's reign as tsar – it was Patriarch Hermogen who rallied a divided Muscovy against the Poles.

A time of crisis

Feodor's government had to contend with an acute economic and social crisis. Famines and taxation had reduced some peasants to slavery and forced many others to migrate. This led to labour shortages and a decline in tax revenues. Noblemen were unable to cultivate their estates, and therefore unable to render military service to the tsar. Boris Godunov tried to solve these problems by reducing taxation, by limiting the freedom of peasants to migrate, and by giving nobles the right to haul recent migrants back to their estates, but these measures did not match the scale of the problems. The movement of people to the southern and eastern frontier regions also represented a challenge to the authority of the government, since the runaway peasants and Cossack warrior bands were not amenable to authority. The establishment of new fortified settlements in these areas helped to give Moscow a greater degree of control over the Cossacks.

In 1591 Prince Dmitry, the nine-year-old half-brother of Tsar Feodor, was found dead with a wound in his throat in the courtyard of his residence in Uglich. The boyar Vasily Shuisky, appointed by Boris Godunov to investigate the boy's death, concluded that Dmitry had suffered an epileptic fit while playing with a knife, accidentally sustaining a fatal injury. But after Boris became tsar it was rumoured that he had ordered the boy's murder to secure the throne for himself. Tsar Feodor died on 7 January 1598, leaving no male heir and having designated no successor. The Muscovite dynasty thus came to an end and Boris was well placed to make a bid for the throne.

BORIS GODUNOV	
Full name	*Died*
Boris Feodorovich Godunov	Moscow 13 April 1605 Haemorrhage
Father	*Wife*
Feodor Ivanovich Godunov	c. 1570 Maria Grigorievna Skuratova
Mother	
Stepanida Ivanovna	Murdered 1605
Born	*Children*
c. 1552	**Feodor** (1589)
Accession	Xenia
21 February 1598	

BORIS GODUNOV

He is a comely person, well favoured, affable, easy and apt to ill counsel, but dangerous in the end to the giver, of good capacity, about forty-five years of age, affected much to necromancy, not learned but of sudden apprehension, and a natural good orator to deliver his mind with an audible voice, subtle, very precipitate, revengeful, not much given to luxury, temperate of diet, heroical in outward show; gave great entertainment to foreign ambassadors, sent rich presents to foreign princes.

Sir Jerome Horsey, envoy of Queen Elizabeth I of England

Tsar Boris Godunov. This portrait shows the tsar with his coronation regalia.

Boris Godunov's throne, now in the Moscow Kremlin Armoury Museum, was made in Persia and presented to the tsar by Shah Abbas in 1604. The throne is covered with plates of gold embossed with floral designs and studded with precious stones.

The death of Feodor I was followed by several months of manoeuvring and intrigue, as a result of which Boris Godunov (1598–1605), with the help of Patriarch Job, was chosen as tsar by the Assembly of the Land and crowned. Boris refused to acknowledge any limitations on his authority, and many boyars who had cooperated with him during the reign of Feodor were unwilling to accept that authority because Boris had no hereditary claim to the tsardom. In the early years of the reign he

THE CHARITABLE WORKS OF BORIS GODUNOV

Captain Jacques Margeret was a French officer who served in Russia during the Time of Troubles. He arrived in Moscow in 1600. After the death of Feodor II he transferred his allegiance to False Dmitry I, leaving Russia at the beginning of the reign of Vasily Shuisky. He returned in 1609 and served False Dmitry II and later the Polish king.

His book *The State of the Empire of Russia and the Grand Duchy of Muscovy*, which is an important source for this period, was published in 1607.

The sum that the Emperor Boris spent on the poor is incredible. Beside the disbursement which was made in Moscow, there was not a town in all of Russia to which Boris did not contribute something for the care of these poor. I know that he sent to Smolensk by a man known to me 20,000 roubles. He had the good quality of ordinarily giving great alms and much property to the clergy, who were all devoted to him.

The title page of an 18th-century edition of Jacques Margeret's book The State of the Empire of Russia and the Grand Duchy of Muscovy, *first published in 1607.*

ESTAT
DE L'EMPIRE
DE RVSSIE,
ET GRANDE DVCHE'
DE MOSCOVIE

Avec ce qui s'y est passé de plus memorable et tragique, pendant le regne de quatre Empereurs : à sçavoir depuis l'an 1590. iusques en l'an 1606. en Septembre.

Par le Capitaine MARGERET.

NOVVELLE EDITION,
Precedée d'une Notice biographique et bibliographique

Par HENRI CHEVREVL.

A PARIS
Chez L. POTIER, Libraire,
quai Malaquais, n° 9.
cIɔ Iɔ ccc LV.

BORIS GODUNOV AND THE RECTOR OF WOOLLEY

Boris Godunov was a convinced Westernizer. In the early years of his reign he actively negotiated with Elizabeth I in the hope of marrying his son and daughter to members of the English aristocracy. He encouraged foreigners to settle in Muscovy, and employed Western physicians. In 1602–03 he sent four young Russians to England to study, and in the following years 14 other scholars were sent to Western Europe. The hope was that they would bring back Western learning and skills, but none of them returned. One of them, Nikifor Olferiev Grigoriev, graduated from the University of Cambridge, took holy orders, married an English woman and settled down as rector of Woolley in Huntingdonshire.

Tsar Mikhail tried to persuade Mikifer Alphery, as he became known in England, to return to Russia. In 1621 a Russian envoy delivered a personal letter from Tsar Mikhail to James I, in which the tsar protested that Alphery '...by reason of his younger years hath forsaken our true and undoubted religion and is become a priest, whether urged thereto against his will or willingly is to us unknown.' Alphery explained that he had no wish to return home and James I refused the ambassador's request that the rector should be forced to do so. Alphery was ejected from his living during the Civil War, but returned to it on the Restoration in 1660. Shortly after that he retired and died at his son's house in Hammersmith in 1668.

KARAMZIN ON BORIS GODUNOV

The theme of Karamzin's *Memoir on Ancient and Modern Russia*, which was written in the early 19th century, was that tsarist autocracy was the only workable form of government for Russia. Karamzin shared the general belief that Boris Godunov was guilty of the murder of Dmitry of Uglich. In this extract he argues that Boris' guilt caused him to weaken the autocracy.

A crime, plotted secretly but uncovered by history, cut off the dynasty of Ivan. Godunov, a Tatar by origin, a Cromwell by disposition, assumed the throne with all the prerogatives of a legitimate monarch, and under the same regime of integral monarchy. This unfortunate man, overthrown by the shadow of the tsarevich he had slain, perished amid deeds of great wisdom and apparent virtue, the victim of an immoderate, illicit thirst for power, as an example for ages and peoples. Troubled by his conscience, Godunov sought to stifle its sacred reproaches by means of gentle deeds, and as a consequence began to loosen the reins of autocratic power. Blood ceased to flow at the place of execution.... The moral strength of tsardom was weakened in the hands of this elected ruler.

neutralized his main rivals. These included Feodor Nikitich Romanov, a first cousin of Feodor I, who was arrested in 1600 on charges of necromancy and attempting to assassinate the tsar, and was forced to enter a monastery, taking the name Filaret. A number of other boyars were purged in 1601, and Boris developed an elaborate system of informers to enable him to curb opposition.

Boris' reign was marked by a succession of disasters, and ushered in a period known as the Time of Troubles. Drought and famine in 1601 were followed by further crop failures in 1602 and 1603, resulting in mass starvation, epidemics and a breakdown of law and order, with hungry peasants and runaway slaves in open revolt. The government's programme of relief, though extensive and innovative, was insufficient to solve these problems.

In the summer of 1604 Muscovy was invaded by a force of Poles, Cossacks and Russian dissidents commanded by a young man who claimed to be Prince Dmitry, who had in reality died at Uglich in 1591. Boris Godunov's government insisted that the False Dmitry, as he became known, was a runaway monk, Grigory Otrepiev, who had spent several years in the Chudov Monastery in the Moscow Kremlin and was therefore familiar with court life. He was believed to have been a retainer of the Romanovs, who had every reason to promote an alternative claimant to the throne. He had secured support for his claim in Poland by secretly embracing Roman Catholicism and by betrothing himself to Marina Mniszek, the daughter of a Polish nobleman. Many contemporaries accepted his claim and disaffected elements in Muscovite society rallied to the pretender's cause. Though Boris' troops easily defeated the False Dmitry's army, they were unable to capture the pretender, whose support continued to grow during the early months of 1605. Then, in April 1605, Boris Godunov died. He had been in poor health since 1602, and had probably suffered a stroke in 1604.

FEODOR II	
Full name	*Accession*
Feodor Borisovich	13 April 1605
Godunov	*Died*
Father	Moscow
Boris Godunov	10 June 1605
Mother	Murdered
Maria Grigorievna	*Unmarried*
Skuratova	No issue
Born	
Moscow 1589	

FEODOR II

Boris Godunov's successor was his 16-year-old son Feodor (r. 1605), but though he was a physically robust and well-educated youth the boyars who had accepted Boris' authority were unwilling to swear allegiance to him, and some of them transferred their support to the False Dmitry. In June 1605, as the pretender's armies approached Moscow, a group of boyars seized control of the city and arrested the tsar. Feodor and his mother Maria were murdered shortly afterwards, on the orders of the pretender. Patriarch Job was ejected from office, and the gates were opened to receive the False Dmitry.

FALSE DMITRY I

He was beardless, had a moderate stature and strong, sinewy limbs. He had a dark complexion and a wart very near his nose, under his right eye. He was agile, generous, had a magnanimous disposition, and a forgiving nature.

Jacques Margeret, a French soldier in the Russian service

The late sovereign had a heroic and manly spirit, and displayed many splendid virtues, but he also had his failings, namely over-confidence and vanity, because of which, without a doubt, God visited such punishments upon him…. His vainglory increased daily, and also that of his tsaritsa, and it showed not only in that he exceeded all former tsars in his luxury and ostentation, but he also commanded that he be styled 'tsar of tsars'.

Conrad Bussow, a German in the Russian service

(*Below*) False Dmitry I. This woodcut portrait was included in his wedding brochure.

(*Below right*) Marina Mniszek (?1588–1614). An illustration from a pamphlet published in 1605. Marina was the daughter of an impoverished Polish noble, who hoped to restore his fortunes by promoting the cause of False Dmitry I.

The claim of the False Dmitry (1605–1606) was soon endorsed by the real Dmitry's mother Maria, and her family. Vasily Shuisky, who had previously declared that Dmitry was the victim of an accident, now claimed that assassins sent by Boris Godunov had murdered one of Dmitry's playmates by mistake. The boyars exiled by Boris Godunov acknowledged the pretender's legitimacy and were restored to favour. Feodor Nikitich Romanov, now the monk Filaret, was promoted to be

The coronation of False Dmitry I and Marina Mniszek. A contemporary Polish painting.

THE DOWNFALL OF FALSE DMITRY I

This account of the reasons why Muscovites turned against False Dmitry I is taken from Conrad Bussow's *The Disturbed State of the Russian Realm*, a contemporary account of the Time of Troubles by a foreigner who visited Russia.

Bussow was a German and a Lutheran, who was employed as a secret agent by Boris Godunov. He was an eyewitness to some important events during the Time of Troubles, and his account of them was written only a few years after they happened.

On the third day of the marriage, the tsar ordered everything in the kitchen to be prepared in the Polish fashion, and among other dishes he ordered baked and roasted veal. When the Russian cooks saw this and related it to all, the Russians grew very suspicious of the tsar, and said that truly he was a Pole and not a Muscovite, since the Muscovites consider veal to be unclean and not to be eaten. They suffered this in silence, awaiting the opportune moment. On the same day, 10 May, with Dmitry's permission an Evangelical Lutheran sermon was heard in the Moscow Kremlin for the first time, preached by Martin Beer of Neustadt....

On 12 May it was rumoured openly among the people that the tsar was a pagan. He no longer went to church diligently as before, he lived by adhering in all things to foreign ceremonies and customs, ate unclean food, went to church without cleansing himself, did not revere the icon of St Nicholas, and although from the first day of his marriage a bath had been prepared for him every morning, neither he nor his pagan consort had taken a bath. It therefore followed that he was not a Muscovite, and consequently could not be the true Dmitry.

metropolitan of Rostov. While it suited these nobles to accept the False Dmitry's claim, since it enabled them to regain their influence, popular feeling soon turned against the pretender. His Polish retainers provoked resentment as they swaggered round Moscow. The presence of Jesuits in his retinue gave rise to a well-founded suspicion that he had secretly become a Catholic. His marriage, in May 1606, to a Polish Catholic, Marina Mniszek, made matters worse. Moreover he was clean-shaven, in public defiance of Orthodox teaching, and did not consume alcohol.

Vasily Shuisky soon turned against the pretender. By late 1605 he had changed his story for the second time, and was asserting that Dmitry had indeed been murdered in 1591. The False Dmitry spared his life and soon allowed him to return to Moscow. This magnanimity proved to be his undoing, for in May 1606 Shuisky and other boyars deposed the False Dmitry and killed him, after which the populace of Moscow murdered hundreds of his Russian and Polish supporters.

VASILY SHUISKY

The aforementioned Vasily, without the consent of the people of the entire land, by chance and hurriedly, to the extent that haste was possible in such a matter, was first acclaimed in his own courtyard and was then installed as tsar of all great Russia, solely by the people who were here present in the ruling city, and without any resistance on his part.

From the *Chronicle* of Ivan Timofeyev

His wolf-like advance to power was distasteful and unpleasant to many people. When fortune suddenly raises an equal above those who have seen him their equal, it does not happen without envy.

Hetman Stanislaus Żółkiewski, commander of the Polish forces that invaded Russia in 1610

VASILY SHUISKY	
Full name	*Accession*
Vasily Ivanovich Shuisky	1 June 1606
Parentage	*Deposition*
Scholars have debated whether he was the son of Ivan Petrovich Shuisky or of Ivan Andreyevich Shuisky. The two men were distant cousins.	17 July 1610
	Died
	Warsaw September 1612
	Natural causes
	Wives
	(1) Maria Repnina
	(2) Catherine Rostovskaya
	Children by (2)
Born	Anna (1609)
c. 1552–53	Anastasia (1610)

Vasily Ivanovich Shuisky

Vasily Shuisky's supporters then proclaimed him as tsar (1606–1610). The body of the False Dmitry was displayed in Red Square, to demonstrate that he was dead. It was then cremated, and the ashes were fired from a cannon in the direction of Poland. To establish that the real Dmitry had indeed died in 1591, the new tsar ordered that his body be reburied in Moscow. It was given out that Dmitry's corpse had suffered no decay, and on the basis of this evidence the dead prince was canonized.

Vasily Shuisky was of short stature, almost blind, and superstitious and conspiratorial by temperament. His claim to the office of tsar rested in part on a family tree which included the elder brother of Alexander Nevsky. Vasily had been a member of Ivan IV's bodyguard in his youth. He had supporters among Moscow's merchant community, but was viewed with suspicion by many of the boyars and deemed it advisable to make certain promises to them. In future no boyar would be

The house of the Boyar Romanov in Moscow. This 16th-century stone building was built for Nikita Romanov, brother-in-law of Ivan IV, and is believed to have been the birthplace of the first Romanov tsar, Mikhail. The building was drastically restored in 1858 on the orders of Tsar Alexander II. Its condition prior to restoration was so ruinous that its present appearance offers little evidence of its original design.

Mikhail Skopin-Shuisky (1586–1610). An early 17th-century painting of the Moscow school. Skopin-Shuisky's military successes made him popular, and his sudden death on 23 April 1610 gave rise to rumours that he had been poisoned because Tsar Vasily Shuisky feared he might try to seize the throne.

executed without the agreement of the Boyar Duma, and the practice of punishing a guilty man's innocent relatives would be abandoned. Vasily's attempts to restore order by preventing peasants from leaving their landlords' estates, and by creating a register of slaves, were abortive because his authority did not extend to much of the country. He soon alienated leading boyar families, including the Romanovs. Rumours began to circulate that the False Dmitry had miraculously escaped. A False Peter emerged briefly as a figurehead of revolt, his supporters claiming that he was a son of Tsar Feodor I. Vasily Shuisky's government survived a large-scale rebellion in 1606–07 led by Prince Shakhovskoi and a Cossack hetman and former galley-slave named Ivan Bolotnikov. Vasily's victory over the rebels owed much to the talented generalship of his nephew, Prince Mikhail Skopin-Shuisky. The rebels were weakened by the fact that their leaders, one a disgruntled aristocrat and the other a social revolutionary, could not agree on the purpose of the revolt. By the time the rebellion had been crushed in October 1607, and the False Peter had been hanged, another pretender to the throne had emerged. False Dmitry II, like his predecessor, was easily able to gather an army of Poles, Cossacks and disaffected Russians. Neither he nor his supporters really believed that he was the son of Ivan IV. Though he bore no resemblance to False Dmitry I, both Maria, the mother of the real Dmitry, and Marina, the wife of False Dmitry I, supported his claims. Indeed Marina lived with him and provided him with a male heir. In 1608 False Dmitry II set up his headquarters at Tushino near Moscow, from where he exercised authority over a large area of southern Muscovy, earning himself the nickname 'the Brigand of Tushino'. Filaret Romanov and other leading boyars supported his claim.

Unable to dislodge False Dmitry II, Vasily Shuisky called in Swedish help in 1609. The price of this support was high. Vasily had to renounce Russia's claims to Livonia, give up some territory and promise to side with the Swedes against Poland. False Dmitry II was driven from Tushino, but his supporters, led by Filaret Romanov, turned to the Poles for help. King Sigismund III played along with their suggestion that his son Wladyslaw should become tsar. The death of the able and successful Mikhail Skopin-Shuisky in April 1610 further weakened Vasily Shuisky's position.

Moscow was now threatened not only by an invading Polish army, determined to place Wladyslaw on the throne, but also by a counter-attack by False Dmitry II. In July 1610 Vasily Shuisky was deposed in a coup d'état engineered by the Romanovs and their allies, who forced him to become a monk. He was sent as a member of the grand embassy to the king of Poland, and he died as a prisoner in Warsaw in 1612.

Vasily Shuisky appearing before Sigismund III of Poland and the Warsaw *Sejm* (Diet) in 1611. A contemporary engraving. After being deposed from the throne he was sent to Warsaw as a member of a Muscovite delegation. He died there in 1612.

MURDER AT UGLICH?

A 17th-century icon showing the murder of Dmitry at Uglich. The perpetrators can be seen making off to the left. Their victim is portrayed with a halo. His mother, Maria Nagaya, the seventh wife of Ivan the Terrible, emerges from the palace on the right.

The victim
Dmitry Ivanovich, the son of Ivan the Terrible by his marriage to Maria Nagaya, was born in 1582.

The location
Uglich is 125 miles north of Moscow. It was an appanage that had been granted to younger sons of the grand princes of Muscovy in the past, and the child Dmitry lived there, cared for by guardians appointed by Boris Godunov, who was the dominant figure in the government of Tsar Feodor I.

The facts
There is general agreement that Dmitry died of a knife wound to the throat which he sustained while playing in the courtyard of the palace at Uglich on 6 May 1591. Later, during the Time of Troubles, three pretenders to the throne claimed that they were Dmitry. Though the claims of two of them were endorsed by Dmitry's mother, it is clear that none of them was the prince, whose death was a publicly established fact, and had provoked a riot in Uglich.

The prime suspect and the possible motives
Those who believed that Dmitry had been murdered immediately pinned the blame on Boris Godunov, the powerful brother-in-law of Tsar Feodor. The motive, they suggested, was that Boris wished to succeed Feodor on the throne, and that Dmitry, as the tsar's half-brother, had a better claim.

The investigator
Vasily Shuisky, who investigated Dmitry's death, muddied the waters by changing his publicly stated opinion on several occasions. His initial conclusion was that Dmitry had suffered an epileptic fit while playing with a knife, and had sustained the fatal injury when he fell. In 1605 it suited the interests of Shuisky to accept the claims of the first False Dmitry, and he came up with a version of events in which Boris Godunov's assassins had stabbed the wrong boy. Once Shuisky himself became tsar, in 1606, it was important for him to establish that False Dmitry I, whom he had overthrown, was bogus. He had the body of Dmitry exhumed and reburied in the Moscow Kremlin, and the boy was canonized as a martyr.

The legend
For nearly 300 years, Boris Godunov was widely believed to be responsible for the death of Dmitry, and the plot of Mussorgsky's opera is based on the assumption of his guilt.

The truth?
Most historians now believe that Boris Godunov was innocent. Boris' motive for having Dmitry killed was not strong. As the son of a seventh and therefore uncanonical marriage, Dmitry's claim to the throne was questionable. In 1591 there was still every chance that Tsar Feodor, a man in his early 30s, would produce a male heir. If Boris had wanted to get rid of Dmitry, would he not have done it in a more subtle way in order to avoid being a suspect?

Icon cloth of 1656 showing Dmitry with selected saints. The tsarevich is depicted holding a martyr's cross in his right hand.

False Dmitry II (?–1610), known as the Brigand of Tushino. A contemporary engraving.

The uprising of the Muscovites against the invaders, 1611. A 19th-century watercolour by Lissner.

Interregnum

After the deposition of Vasily Shuisky the government fell into the hands of seven senior boyars. Faced with a choice between a Polish prince and False Dmitry II at the head of a disorderly rabble, they decided to offer the throne to Wladyslaw, admitted Polish troops to Moscow and sent a grand embassy, headed by Filaret Romanov, to Sigismund III's headquarters near Smolensk. False Dmitry II retreated and was murdered by one of his own men later in 1610.

The Polish solution proved to be elusive. Sigismund III, believing that he could conquer Muscovy for himself, arrested the delegation when they refused to agree to this, and dispatched them to imprisonment in Poland. In the autumn of 1610 the Swedes invaded north-western Russia and advanced towards Novgorod. With a Polish army in Moscow, Swedish and Polish forces occupying an extensive part of its territory, and brigands and runaway slaves devastating the countryside, the Muscovite state appeared to be on the brink of disintegration. In this moment of extreme crisis it was Patriarch Hermogen of Moscow who rallied the Russians against the threat of Polish rule and the imposition of Roman Catholicism.

In the early months of 1611 a diverse army of provincial troops and Cossacks marched on Moscow in response to the patriarch's call, with the aim of driving out the Poles. As this National Army advanced, the Polish garrison burned down much of the city and retreated into the Kremlin. Their commander ordered the arrest of the patriarch. By the summer of 1611 the Russian forces seemed poised to capture the Kremlin. They were prevented from doing so by tensions within their own ranks. The provincial nobles whose contingents formed part of the

POZHARSKY'S APPEAL TO THE PEOPLE

Prince Dmitry Pozharsky, one of the leaders of the Second National Army, issued this appeal for support in April 1612. The document gives an insight into the motives of those who invited Mikhail Romanov to ascend the throne in 1613.

And now, sirs, we Orthodox Christians, having exchanged messages with the entire land, have vowed to God by common agreement and have pledged our souls not to serve their [the Poles'] knavish tsar … or Marina and her son, but to stand firmly against the enemies and depredators of the Christian faith, the Poles and Lithuanians. And you, sirs, should take counsel together with all the people, mindful of God and of our faith, lest we remain without a sovereign in these times of utter ruin, so that by counsel of the entire state we may choose a sovereign by common agreement, whomever God may grant us in his righteous love of mankind, lest the Muscovite state be utterly destroyed by such calamities. You know yourselves, sirs: how can we defend ourselves now, without a sovereign, against our common enemies, the Poles and Lithuanians and Germans [Swedes], and the Russian rogues who are renewing bloody strife in the state? How can we, without a sovereign, negotiate with neighbouring sovereigns about great matters of the state and of the land? And how can our realm stand firm and unshakeable henceforth?

The monument to Minin and Pozharsky, the heroes of the Time of Troubles, is the work of Ivan Petrovich Martos (1754–1835), who studied in Rome, where he acquired the neoclassical style.

National Army had a conservative social and political agenda, while the Cossacks, peasants and fugitive slaves who were fighting alongside them had no wish to see a return to the old order. In July 1611 the Cossacks murdered Prokopy Liapunov, the leader of the aristocratic faction, and the National Army fell apart. Shortly before that, Polish troops had captured Smolensk, and in mid-July Novgorod fell to the Swedes. To add to the confusion a third False Dmitry emerged in the city of Pskov, while the Cossacks rallied round the claims of the infant son of False Dmitry II and Marina Mniszek, known as the 'Baby Brigand'.

In response to a message smuggled out of his prison by Patriarch Hermogen, a second national rallying began in the autumn of 1611. The leaders of this Second National Army were Kuzma Minin, a merchant from Nizhny-Novgorod, and Prince Dmitry Pozharsky. Their programme was the defeat of the Poles and the Swedes, the restoration of tsarism and a return to social order. They established a provisional government in Yaroslavl, and in September of 1612 laid siege to Moscow. The Kremlin fell to them in October.

Having liberated the capital, the leaders of the national movement summoned a meeting of the Assembly of the Land. Representatives from all parts of Muscovy gathered in Moscow in January 1613 to select a tsar. In February 1613 they elected Mikhail Romanov, the 16-year-old son of Filaret, who was still a prisoner of the Poles. Mikhail had been the choice of Patriarch Hermogen, who had died in prison shortly before the liberation of Moscow. The boyars may have felt that they could easily dominate an inexperienced teenager. His dynastic claim was a reasonable one, since his great aunt Anastasia had been married to Ivan IV. Mikhail's mother was understandably reluctant to allow her son to leave the relative security of the Ipatiev Monastery in Kostroma, where he had taken refuge, and embark on the hazardous undertaking of tsardom.

Tsarism survived the Time of Troubles because it had not been seriously challenged as an institution. In so far as the strife and bloodshed were motivated by political considerations, they were about who should be tsar, not about whether tsarism was the proper form of government. Even the social rebel Ivan Bolotnikov claimed to be acting on behalf of pretenders to the throne. The chaos of the interregnum after the deposition of Vasily Shuisky strengthened the case for believing that an effective autocracy was the only guarantee of peace and stability. The events of 1611–12 have been seen by some Russian historians as the time when a Russian national consciousness emerged, with the Orthodox church functioning as a unifying factor in the absence of a tsar.

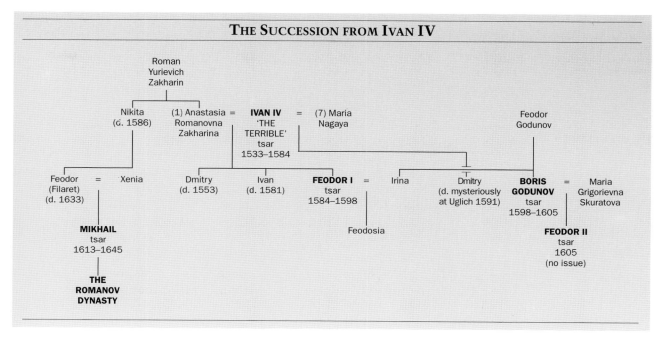

THE SUCCESSION FROM IVAN IV

Mikhail
1613–1645

Alexei Mikhailovich
1645–1676

Feodor III
1676–1682

Regency of Sophia
1682–1689

Ivan V
1682–1696

Peter I
('The Great')
1682–1725

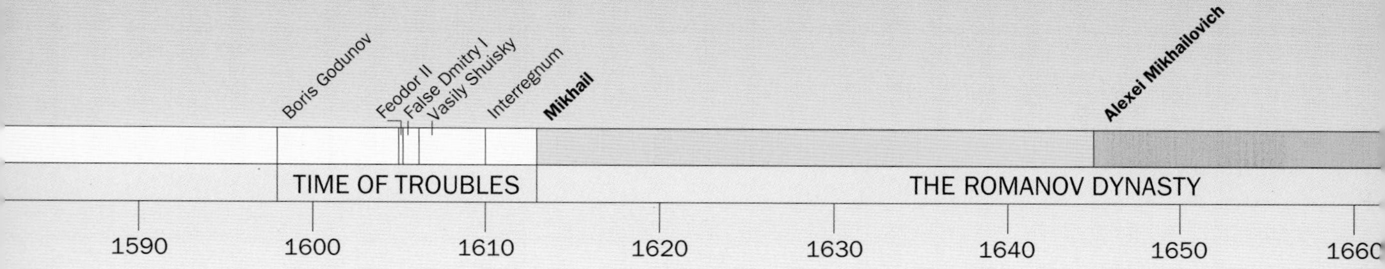

Boris Godunov
Feodor II
False Dmitny I
Vasily Shuisky
Interregnum
Mikhail
Alexei Mikhailovich

TIME OF TROUBLES

THE ROMANOV DYNASTY

1590 · 1600 · 1610 · 1620 · 1630 · 1640 · 1650 · 1660

Mikhail

Alexei Mikhailovich

Feodor III

Peter I

THE RISE OF THE ROMANOVS

THE 17TH CENTURY saw the completion of the process by which the bulk of the Russian population was enserfed. The Russian empire continued to expand. The Orthodox church, which had played an important part in the establishment of the Romanov dynasty, was riven by theological and liturgical disputes. It was permanently weakened by the Great Schism that resulted. The reign of Peter the Great, a dynamically brutal modernizer, used to be seen as marking a decisive break between the old Muscovy and the new Russia. In reality Peter inherited most of his aims from his Romanov predecessors. His father, the warm-hearted and hot-tempered Alexei Mikhailovich, sought to modernize the army using Western expertise and was the first tsar directly to involve himself in agricultural and industrial development. Peter's half-sister Sophia, who was the first Russian woman to style herself autocrat, attempted to pursue an expansionist foreign policy.

Peter differed from his predecessors in his methods and the extent of his success. He understood that the survival of the Russian empire depended on its becoming, both territorially and culturally, a European power. In forcing the nobility to adopt Western European manners, Peter further separated them from the mass of the population. His attempts to modernize Russia's administrative systems were hampered by a lack of educated officials, and by the vast size and the economic backwardness of his realm. His successes were in the main the product of his forceful personality, and his reach considerably exceeded his grasp.

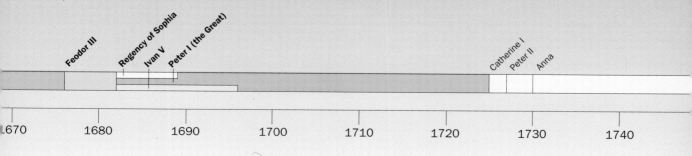

Михаил Mikhail
1613–1645

Алексей Михайлович Alexei Mikhailovich
1645–1676

Tsar Mikhail, the first of the Romanov tsars. A 17th-century engraved portrait.

MIKHAIL	
Full name	*Wives*
Mikhail Feodorovich	(1) 1624 Maria
Romanov	Dolgorukaya
Father	Died 1625
Feodor Nikitich	(2) 1626 Evdokia
Romanov (Filaret)	Streshnieva
Mother	Died 1645
Maria Ivanovna	*Children by (2)*
Chestova	Irina (1627)
Born	Pelagia (1628)
Moscow	**Alexei** (1629)
12 July 1596	Marfa (1631)
Accession	Anna (1632)
11 February 1613	Ivan (1633)
Died	Sophia (1634)
Moscow	Tatiana (1636)
13 July 1645	Evdokia (1637)
Natural causes	Vasily (1639)

MIKHAIL

He is like unto a sun partially obscured by stormy clouds, so that the soil of Muscovy has not yet received the heat of his rays. The princes of the blood have no authority, he himself cannot write, and I am not sure whether he can read.

Isaac Massa, a Dutch envoy who visited Moscow in 1614

His Tsarist Majesty was seated on the throne attired in a robe set with all sorts of precious stones and embroidered with large pearls. His crown, which he wore over a black sable hat, was encrusted with large diamonds, as was the golden sceptre, which, probably because of its weight, he transferred now and then from one hand to the other.

Adam Olearius, envoy of the Duke of Holstein to the Russian Court in the 1630s

Mikhail Feodorovich Romanov was, at the time of his accession, a pale, pious youth, afflicted by a nervous tic in the left eye and a weakness in the legs which caused him to topple over in public under the weight of the royal regalia on the day of his coronation.

Interregnum | Mikhail | Peace of Stolbovo with Sweden | Deulino Truce with Poland | Filaret returns to Russia | War with Poland | Filaret dies | Peace with Poland | Alexei Mik

1610　1615　1620　1625　1630　1635　1640　1645

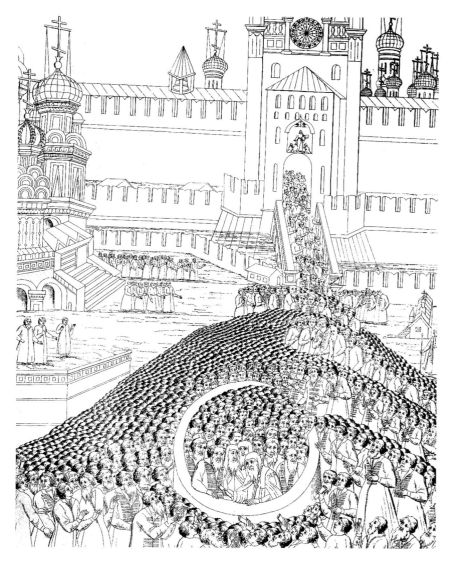

The announcement of Mikhail Romanov's nomination as tsar. Miniature from *The Book of the Election of Tsar Mikhail to the Throne*, 1672–73. The ceremony is shown taking place in Red Square. St Basil's Cathedral can be seen on the left, and the Spasskaya Tower of the Kremlin in the background.

The new tsar's youth and inexperience were political assets. He had not collaborated with the Poles during the Time of Troubles. His father, Filaret, had offered the crown to Prince Wladyslaw of Poland, but this was outweighed in people's minds by the fact that Filaret had been, since 1610, a prisoner of the Poles. Filaret's involvement with the second False Dmitry had made the Romanovs popular with the Cossacks, who supported the decision to offer Mikhail the throne. The Romanovs could not

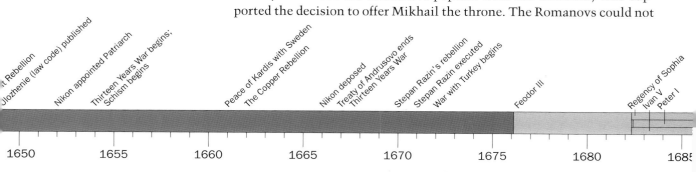

t Rebellion
Ulozhenie (law code) published
Nikon appointed Patriarch
Thirteen Years War begins; Schism begins
Peace of Kardis with Sweden
The Copper Rebellion
Nikon deposed
Treaty of Andrusovo ends Thirteen Years War
Stepan Razin's rebellion
Stepan Razin executed
War with Turkey begins
Feodor III
Regency of Sophia
Ivan V
Peter I

1650   1655   1660   1665   1670   1675   1680   1685

Tsar Mikhail Feodorovich Romanov.
A 17th-century portrait.

claim Rurikid ancestry, but Filaret was a first cousin of Feodor I, the last legitimate monarch. Mikhail had been the chosen candidate of the late Patriarch Hermogen, and had the blessing of the church hierarchy. For the first six years of his reign he ruled in close consultation with the Boyar Duma and the Assembly of the Land (*zemsky sobor*). Some historians have suggested that this cooperation was the result of a constitutional agreement, but it is more likely that it arose from the tsar's inexperience and from the difficulties that confronted him.

Those difficulties included the presence of Polish and Swedish armies on Russian soil, and the continuing rebellion by the Cossack leader Zarutsky, accompanied by Marina Mniszek and the 'Baby Brigand', her son by False Dmitry II. Zarutsky was captured at Astrakhan in 1614 and publicly impaled in Moscow later that year. The 'Baby Brigand' was executed, and Marina Mniszek died in prison. It took longer to deal with the Swedish threat. King Gustavus Adolphus – the most renowned warrior of all Sweden's rulers – laid siege to Pskov in 1615, but failed to capture the city. Mediation by John Merrick, the envoy of King James I of England, helped to secure the Treaty of Stolbovo in 1617. The Swedes agreed to hand Novgorod back to the Russians and to recognize Mikhail as tsar. In return, they regained control of the coastal towns on the Gulf of Finland and their hinterland, Ingria. The war with Poland went badly in the early years of the reign, but was suspended by the Treaty of Deulino in 1618, a 14-year armistice under which the Poles kept Smolensk and other territories in western Russia that they had conquered, though Wladyslaw refused to relinquish his claim to the Muscovite throne.

A monastery besieged by the Swedes in 1613. One of the scenes from the border of the icon of the Virgin of Tikhvin, painted *c.* 1680.

The consecration of Filaret Romanov as patriarch. Miniature from *The Book of the Election of Tsar Mikhail to the Throne*, 1672–73.

The rule of Filaret

Under the terms of the Deulino agreement, the tsar's 66-year-old father Filaret, who had been a prisoner in Poland, returned to Moscow in June 1619. He was confirmed in office as patriarch, granted the title 'Great Sovereign' and accorded formal equality with Mikhail. In ceremonies they shared the royal regalia, but Filaret was the real ruler of Russia until his death in 1633, and his grip on the reins of power was firm. The Assembly of the Land was consulted less frequently after 1622 than it had been in the early years of the reign. The Boyar Duma was deprived of some of the functions that it had previously enjoyed, and a privy council of four leading boyars advised Filaret and the tsar on important matters.

Filaret was described by a contemporary, Bishop Pachomius of Astrakhan, as 'of medium height and bulk, had some knowledge of theology, was irritable and mistrustful, and so overbearing that even the tsar himself was afraid of him. He kept the boyars and the tsar's other councillors in check by sending them to exile or imposing other punishments on them. To the clerics he was kind and not avaricious.' He had been something of a dandy in his youth and even as patriarch he employed a monk to trim his hair and beard every two months. He was, perhaps because of his long imprisonment in Poland, a strong nationalist. He was also determined to maintain the traditions of the Orthodox church.

TSAR MIKHAIL AND HIS SUBJECTS CELEBRATE EASTER

Adam Olearius, the Duke of Holstein's envoy, wrote an account of his visits to Russia during the reign of Mikhail.

On April 17, Holy Easter Day, there was great rejoicing among the Russians, partly because of the Resurrection of Christ, partly because it was the end of their long fast. That day, and for 14 days thereafter, practically everyone – notables and commoners, young and old – carries coloured eggs. In every street a multitude of egg vendors sit, hawking boiled eggs decorated in various colours. When they meet on the street, they greet each other with kisses on the mouth. One says 'Khristos voskrese', that is 'Christ has risen'; and the other answers, 'Voistinu voskrese', which means 'Indeed he is risen'. And no one, neither man nor woman, neither magnate nor commoner, refuses to another a kiss and greeting and an egg. The Grand Prince himself distributes Easter eggs to his courtiers

The tsar leading the Easter celebrations in 17th-century Moscow. An engraving from a 1718 edition of Adam Olearius' Vermehrte Neue Beschreibung der Moskowitischen und Persianischen Reise. St Basil's Cathedral can be seen on the left, and the walls of the Kremlin and the Spasskaya Tower in the background.

and servants. It was also his custom, the night before Easter, before he went to morning prayer, to visit the prison, open the cells, and give each prisoner (there were always many) an egg and a sheepskin coat, saying: 'Let them be happy. For Christ, who died for their sins, has indeed risen.' Then he ordered the prison shut again and went off to church.

The patriarch's hopes of founding a dynasty depended on his son producing an heir. In 1624 Mikhail married Maria Dolgorukaya, a princess who could trace her ancestry back to Rurik. She died the following January, and in 1626 Mikhail took a second wife, Evdokia Streshnieva, who bore him three sons and seven daughters.

Government and revenue

Eleven new departments of state (*prikazy*) were created in the first six years of Mikhail's reign to carry out specific tasks or to address particular problems, including a Masonry Department to rebuild Moscow and other towns damaged in the Time of Troubles, a Brigand Department to restore order, and an Apothecary Department to look after the tsar's health. Later in the reign a Siberian Department was created. The intention was to centralize the government, but the size of Russia made this difficult to realize. Most of the departments had more than one function, and some of them operated only for a few years. The tsar's government came to rely more and more on the military governors as the principal local officials, and their responsibilities were broadened to include many administrative, judicial and financial affairs. There was no shortage of aspirants for these posts, which were lucrative and influential.

In 1613 the treasury was empty. One of the first acts of Mikhail's government was to write to the wealthy Stroganov family requesting a loan so that the army could be paid and fed. Work began in 1619 on a census of lands and population, partly to determine what direct taxes the population should pay. The survey was also intended to record which peasants were serving on which estates. Progress was slow, and was hindered by a fire in 1626 that destroyed some of the accumulated records. The drift of population southwards from the central region continued, and in 1642 the government extended to ten years the period of time during which a runaway peasant could be forced to return home. This step in the direction of serfdom was unpopular with those landowners who were benefiting from the influx of labour. Impoverished peasants

THE HISTORIAN KLIUCHEVSKY ON THE 17TH CENTURY

Kliuchevsky's prose is clear and stylish. His fondness for metaphor and his grasp of the broad sweep of history are evident in this passage.

Such are the main innovations that come to light in the 17th century: a new dynasty, new territorial boundaries, a new social structure with a new ruling class, and new developments in the national economy. The inter-relationships among these things seem perplexing. At first glance it is easy to detect in them two parallel currents:
(1) In this period the territorial expansion of the state was inversely proportional to the people's freedom within it.
(2) The political rights of the working classes were inversely proportional to the economic productivity of their labour; that is, the more productive labour was, the less free it became.... The sweep of state authority grew mightier and mightier in its expanding territory, but the people's spirit of initiative and enterprise weakened. In its external successes and inner weaknesses the new Russia resembled a bird caught in a whirlwind and hurled aloft, regardless of the strength of its wings.

were only too willing to serve landlords who offered them cash advances to buy tools and food, and found themselves tied to those landlords by their inability to repay the loans.

Mikhail's reign was a period of economic recovery. Manufacturing and foreign trade revived, and the government encouraged this by granting tax immunities and other privileges to corporations of merchants, and permitting them to travel abroad for purposes of trade. New enterprises were founded, the most important of which was located in the Tula district, where a Dutchman, Andrei Vinius, was granted a monopoly to exploit metal ores. Stronger economic links with the West did not lead to the adoption of Western manners and customs. Filaret was thoroughly reactionary in his defence of Orthodox beliefs and practices, and his attitudes lived on after him. The sale of tobacco ('the herb that is an abomination unto the Lord') was forbidden by a decree of 1634.

Foreign policy

Aware that the Deulino truce with Poland was of limited duration, Filaret and Mikhail sought to strengthen the army. The streltsy and the contingents provided by the nobility were barely adequate for the defence of the realm. For the coming war with Poland the government raised new paid regiments, trained and officered by foreigners such as Alexander Leslie, who was sent abroad to raise recruits. These new infantry, light cavalry and heavy cavalry units were very expensive to run, since the soldiers received pay and an allowance for food. They were demobilized in 1634 at the end of the Polish War.

The foreign policy of Mikhail's government was influenced by the events which came to be known as the Thirty Years War (1618–48). The preoccupation of the Austrian Habsburgs with this complex series of conflicts prevented them from offering continuous support to Poland, and brought Austria into confrontation with Sweden. Filaret saw these tensions as providing an opportunity for Russia to regain Smolensk from the Poles. During the 1620s Russia supported Denmark and Sweden by selling grain to both countries at low prices. Filaret encouraged Gustavus Adolphus of Sweden to consider a joint attack on Poland, with the Polish crown as the reward for the Swedish king.

The death of King Sigismund III in 1632, and the succession dispute that broke out in Poland as a result, created a good opportunity for a Russian offensive. The campaign began in the late summer of that year, and the Russian armies under the command of the boyar general, Mikhail Borisovich Shein, were at first successful. Then Gustavus Adolphus was killed, and the negotiations for a firm military alliance between Sweden and Russia were stalled. Shein laid siege to Smolensk through the winter of 1632–33 but failed to capture the city. An invasion of Russia by the Crimean Tatars and a vigorous counterattack by Poland's new king, Wladyslaw IV, undermined the Russian war effort. At this stage in the

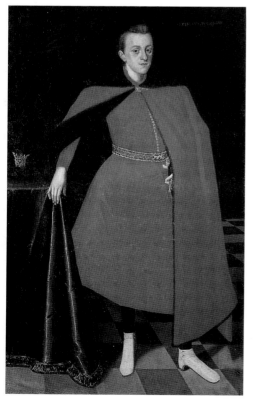

Wladyslaw IV, king of Poland (1632–1648), in coronation robes. An anonymous miniature in the Palazzo Pitti, Florence. Wladyslaw was born in 1595, and became king in 1632 on the death of his father Sigismund Vasa. Sigismund had been king of Sweden until 1599, when he was deposed. His son's attempts to regain the Swedish throne were unsuccessful.

campaign Filaret Romanov died. In early 1634 Shein concluded an armistice with the Poles, a surrender for which he was later to pay with his life. It was a humiliating end to the war, and the Peace of Polianovka confirmed the Poles in their possession of Smolensk and the other Russian territories that they had gained during the Time of Troubles. Moscow had to pay an indemnity of 20,000 roubles, and the only benefit that the Russians gained from the treaty was that Wladyslaw renounced his claim to the Muscovite throne and recognized Mikhail as tsar. The Smolensk War placed a great strain on the national finances.

The Tatar invasion of 1633 had been an alarming reminder of the vulnerability of Russia's southern frontier. In 1635 Mikhail's government began to construct the chain of fortified settlements which became known as the Belgorod Line. Twenty-nine new towns were built in the next 15 years, and by 1650 the line stretched from the Vorskla River to Tambov and beyond, passing through Belgorod and Voronezh.

While the tsar's government pursued a defensive policy along the southern frontier, the Cossacks who lived beyond that frontier took advantage of a war between Turkey and Persia to seize the Turkish fortress of Azov in 1637. Azov, where the River Don flows into the sea, was of great strategic importance. The Turks attempted unsuccessfully in 1641 to retake the fortress. Though the Don Cossacks withstood a siege of four months, they realized that they could not hold Azov against repeated Turkish assaults, and they therefore offered it to the tsar. Mikhail's advisers knew that the cost of garrisoning and defending the fortress would be great. An Assembly of the Land was convened in 1642 to discuss what should be done. Financial caution prevailed, and the Cossacks followed the tsar's instruction to abandon Azov to the Turks.

Family matters

Mikhail's later years were clouded by tragedy and depression. Two of his sons, Ivan and Vasily, died young. In 1642 Mikhail proposed a marriage alliance between his eldest daughter Irina and Prince Waldemar Christian, the son of Christian IV of Denmark. Waldemar, as the product of a morganatic marriage, was excluded from the Danish succession. Mikhail may have wanted Waldemar as a son-in-law in order to secure the dynasty against the danger of his surviving son, Alexei, dying before he had produced an heir. The Danish prince was induced to travel to Moscow by an understanding that he would not be expected to give up his Lutheran faith if he married Irina. On his arrival in 1644 he became the object of a heavy-handed attempt by Mikhail to force him to convert to Orthodoxy, and found himself under house arrest. An escape attempt failed, and only after Mikhail's death was Waldemar allowed to return home, unmarried. When the tsar was taken ill in the summer of 1645 he designated his 16-year-old son Alexei as his heir. Mikhail died in the small hours of 13 July 1645.

ALEXEI MIKHAILOVICH	
Full name Alexei Mikhailovich Romanov also known as 'the quietest' or 'the gentlest' tsar	(2) 1671 Natalya Kirillovna Naryshkina Died 1694
Father Mikhail Romanov	*Children by (1)* Dmitry (1648) Evdokia (1650)
Mother Evdokia Streshnieva	Marfa (1652) Alexei (1654) Anna (1655)
Born Moscow 9 March 1629	Sophia (1657) Catherine (1658) Maria (1660)
Accession 13 July 1645	**Feodor** (1661) Feodosia (1662) Simeon (1665)
Died Moscow 29 January 1676 Natural causes	**Ivan** (1666) Evdokia (1669) *Children by (2)*
Wives (1) 1648 Maria Miloslavskaya Died 1669	**Peter** (1672) Natalia (1673) Feodora (1674)

Tsar Alexei Mikhailovich in coronation regalia. A portrait from the *Titulyarnik* of 1672.

ALEXEI MIKHAILOVICH

His Imperial Majesty is a goodly person ... of a sanguine complexion, light brown hair, his beard uncut, he is tall and fat, of a majestical Deportment, severe in his anger, bountiful, charitable, chastly uxorious, very kind to his Sisters and Children, of a strong memory, strict in his Devotions, and a favourer of his Religion....

Samuel Collins, Tsar Alexei Mikhailovich's English doctor

Alexei Mikhailovich (1645–1676) was born in 1629. His education was supervised by the boyar Boris Ivanovich Morozov, an enthusiast for Western culture who encouraged the boy to wear German clothing and provided him with German toys. Alexei mastered the complexities of church music and liturgy, and as an adult would roundly curse any priest who made a mistake in church. He was genuinely devout, with a strong belief in the divine origins of his office. Though quick to anger and harsh in his punishing of wrongdoers, he was also cheerful and courteous, and became known as 'the quietest' tsar. Nineteenth-century Slavophiles saw his reign as a final flowering of Muscovite tradition, while other historians have portrayed him as a figurehead, dominated by powerful advisers. There is a strong case for seeing Alexei as an able ruler with a modernizing agenda.

Government and taxation

The new tsar was at first dependent on advisers such as Morozov and Prince Ilya Miloslavsky, whose daughter Maria he married in January 1648. At the beginning of his reign the Assembly of the Land was still a powerful institution, but once he had secured its approval for the war with Poland in 1653, Alexei never summoned it again. Although he transformed the Boyar Duma by including in it a large number of men drawn from the service gentry rather than the aristocracy, by the end of the reign it rarely met in full session. Alexei continued to employ

ALEXEI'S LETTER OF CONDOLENCE TO ODOEVSKY

Prince Nikita Odoevsky was an army commander, diplomat and friend of the tsar. His son Mikhail died in 1652. This is an extract from the letter of condolence that Alexei wrote to Odoevsky.

Do not grieve too much. Of course you must grieve and shed tears to some extent, but not immoderately lest Almighty God be angered. You must imitate the righteous Job.

He was tempted by our common enemy Satan; he suffered so many calamities. Yet did he not bear them and did not God give him sons and daughters again? And why? – because he did not sin in his mouth; the deaths of his children did not make him resentful.... You know that everything that God does is for our good. Besides he was in a state of grace when he was taken.... How would you feel if your son had died by falling from his horse without an opportunity to repent?

The seal of Tsar Alexei Mikhailovich.

Bogdan Khmelnitsky, hetman of the Zaporozhian Cossacks. A contemporary engraved portrait of 1651 by William Hondius. In October 1943 a military decoration named after Khmelnitsky was inaugurated. The inscription on the medal was in Ukrainian rather than in Russian, in recognition of the heroism of Ukrainian soldiers in the Red Army and Ukrainian partisans.

aristocrats, including the soldier, diplomat and administrator Prince Nikita Odoevsky, but he also promoted talented men from less exalted backgrounds, such as Afanasy Lavrentievich Ordin-Nashchokin and Artamon Sergeyevich Matveyev.

Alexei and his advisers were forced to resort to unpopular taxational measures in the early years of the reign. They quadrupled the tax on salt and permitted the sale of tobacco, while imposing a heavy duty on it. These new taxes, together with the reputation for corruption that the Miloslavsky faction acquired, provoked the Salt Rebellion of 1648. Though the new salt tax had by then been abolished, Muscovites had other grievances. Government employees had been dismissed or forced to accept reductions in pay, and the streltsy had not been paid on time. In June 1648 an angry crowd gathered outside the Kremlin to demand that Morozov and other unpopular advisers be handed over to them. The mob burned down the houses of those they wished to lynch, and the fires spread through Moscow, causing extensive damage. By handing over two officials for summary execution, distributing bribes and promising that Morozov would be exiled, Alexei pacified the situation in Moscow, but there were rebellions in Novgorod and Pskov in 1650. The tobacco duty was abolished, and Morozov was allowed to return to Moscow when the unrest had subsided.

The Ulozhenie and serfdom

In the aftermath of the Salt Rebellion, Alexei summoned a meeting of the Assembly of the Land. The Assembly elected a commission which drew up a new legal code, the Ulozhenie of 1649. The Ulozhenie prescribed severe penalties for those who challenged the political or religious order. It also completed the process by which serfdom was legally established. The period in which fugitive peasants could be returned to their masters became indefinite and in future all peasants and their offspring were to be legally bound to the land. The new code bound merchants and artisans to their towns and cities as closely as it bound peasants to the land. No subject of the tsar might travel abroad without the permission of the sovereign. The code also limited the rights of the church to acquire additional lands, and Alexei created the Monastery Department in 1649 to oversee the church estates and enforce this law.

The Thirteen Years War

In 1654 Alexei's government embarked on a war with Poland which was to last until 1667. The war, which also brought Muscovy into conflict with Sweden, placed great strains on the economy. The territorial gains that resulted did not match the hopes of Alexei and his advisers, but they paved the way for the successes of Peter the Great. The war also brought the Muscovites into closer contact with Western culture and ideas, particularly through their acquisition of Kiev, an important centre of learning.

The opportunity for expansion was created by a Ukrainian revolt against Polish rule led by Bogdan Khmelnitsky, the hetman of the Zaporozhian Cossacks. Khmelnitsky had been urging the Russians to intervene almost since the beginning of the rebellion in 1648, but it was not until 1653 that the Assembly of the Land endorsed the decision to go to war. The price that Khmelnitsky had to pay for Muscovite support was a high one. In the Treaty of Pereiaslavl (1654) he and other Cossack leaders swore allegiance to Tsar Alexei, and their lands, in the area that later became known as the Ukraine, were incorporated into Russia. Despite the treaty, the Cossacks proved unreliable as allies, since they were not willing to give up their independence in the long term.

The Russian campaign began in the spring of 1654. The objectives were the expulsion of Polish forces from the Ukraine, the conquest of Belorussia and the capture of Smolensk, and considerable progress was made in the first year of fighting. Alexei himself took part in the siege of Smolensk, which surrendered in September 1654. That summer the plague struck Moscow and other cities. It has been estimated that almost 80 per cent of Moscow's taxpayers died. Patriarch Nikon, who had prudently removed the tsar's family from the city, was given the job of ruling in the tsar's absence, and in the autumn of 1654 Alexei conferred on him the title 'Great Sovereign'.

The year 1655 was disastrous for the Poles. While Russian forces took Minsk, Vilno, Lvov, Kovno, and Mogilev, a Swedish army commanded by King Charles X invaded Poland and captured Warsaw. Alexei returned to Moscow in triumph in December. The Swedish intervention raised the dangerous possibility of a permanent Swedish presence in Poland. Alexei's advisers urged him to ally himself with the Poles against the Swedes. The chief architect of this new policy was Ordin-Nashchokin, who saw not only the chance of gaining a Baltic coastline for Russia by seizing the port of Riga, but also the possibility that when the childless

REFUSING A RESIGNATION

In 1660 the son of Afanasy Lavrentievich Ordin-Nashchokin, Tsar Alexei's chief minister, fled to Poland. Ordin-Nashchokin was deeply embarrassed, since previous tsars had regarded such flight as treasonable, and tendered his resignation. Alexei refused to accept it, and replied in these terms:

You ask to be dismissed; but what could have made you ask that? Excessive sorrow, I think. Your son has done a silly thing, but there's nothing extraordinary about it, it was just foolishness on his part. He is young, he wanted to have a look at God's world and at what is happening there. Just as a bird flies hither and thither and having had enough of it flies back to its nest, so your son will recall his nest and his spiritual attachment, and soon return to you.

Afanasy Lavrentievich Ordin-Nashchokin (?1605–80). An anonymous 17th-century portrait, now in the State Historical Museum in Moscow. Ordin-Nashchokin was a member of a noble family from Pskov. He served Tsar Mikhail and Tsar Alexei as soldier, courtier and diplomat.

King Jan Casimir of Poland died, the Polish nobility might elect a Romanov in his place.

A ceasefire was agreed with the Poles in April 1656, but Alexei rashly declared war on Sweden the following month, before his negotiators had achieved a peace treaty with Poland. Alexei was unable to capture Riga from the Swedes, though his armies occupied large areas of Latvia, Estonia and Finland. By the end of the year the Muscovite negotiators seemed to be close to securing a treaty with Poland by which Alexei would be nominated as Jan Casimir's successor. The Cossacks feared that such a union between Muscovy and Poland would mean the end of their independence. When their leader Khmelnitsky died in July 1657, fighting broke out in the Ukraine between those who favoured continued cooperation with Moscow and those who believed that their best interests would be served by helping the Poles to remain independent. These developments strengthened the hand of the party in Poland who opposed the idea of a Romanov king, and the ceasefire between Poland and Muscovy broke down in November 1658. Alexei, knowing that he could not defeat both Poland and Sweden, signed a truce with the Swedes in December 1658.

The Muscovite armies fared badly in 1659 and the Poles, who made peace with Sweden by the Treaty of Oliva in May 1660, found themselves in a strong position. Alexei's advisers knew that they must secure a lasting peace with the Swedes. The price proved to be high. Under the Treaty of Kardis (June 1661) the Muscovites had to give up all the Swedish territory that they had conquered. The war with Poland continued until 1667, with the Muscovites losing ground in Belorussia and Lithuania, but retaining control of the eastern part of the Ukraine. War weariness, the threat of a Tatar invasion, and an internal

Russia's Western Frontier in the Seventeenth Century

- Swedish territory after 1629
- Russia's gains by the Treaty of Andrusovo 1667

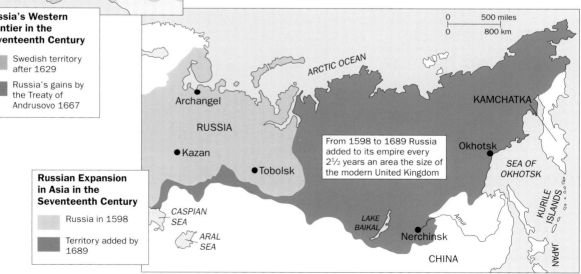

From 1598 to 1689 Russia added to its empire every 2½ years an area the size of the modern United Kingdom

Russian Expansion in Asia in the Seventeenth Century

- Russia in 1598
- Territory added by 1689

The German Quarter (*Nemetskaya Sloboda*) on the outskirts of Moscow, c. 1700, in an engraving by Hendrik de Witt (1671–1716). *Nemets*, plural *nemtsy*, means both foreigner and German, and derives from the Russian word for 'dumb' in the sense of unable to speak. By the time this engraving was made, the Quarter had developed into a European town approximately one-fifth the size of Moscow. In the foreground are the residences of the wealthier members of the foreign community, including the palace that Peter I built for his favourite, François Lefort (p. 92). In the distance, beyond the River Yauza, is the more crowded quarter where the poorer merchants lived.

rebellion made the Poles willing to negotiate. Under the Treaty of Andrusovo, signed in 1667 and valid for 13 years and 6 months, Russia gained Smolensk and other territories, including the parts of the Ukraine east of the Dnieper, while the Poles retained the rest of the Ukraine and Belorussia. Kiev was to be held by Russia until 1669, but when the time came Alexei refused to hand it back. The Poles ultimately ceded Kiev to Muscovy in 1686 (p. 89).

The Schism

At the beginning of the reign of Alexei two reform movements were active within the Russian Orthodox church. One of them – the more controversial – sought to bring the rituals and religious texts used in Russia, which had been corrupted by mistranslations and by local variations, back into line with Greek Orthodox practices. The other group, known as the Zealots of Piety, wished to raise the moral and educational level of the parish clergy and the laity. The tsar was receptive to both groups' reformist ideas. He issued laws to punish profanity, ban public entertainments and limit the sale of alcoholic drinks. In 1652 he decreed

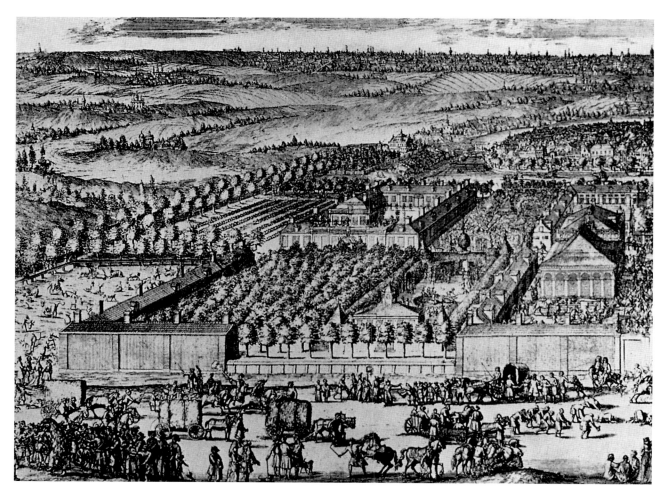

that all non-Orthodox foreigners in Moscow must reside outside the walls in an area which became known as the German Quarter. The intention was to limit contacts between Russians and the non-Orthodox.

In 1652 the patriarchate fell vacant, and Alexei secured the appointment of Metropolitan Nikon of Novgorod, a known supporter of reform. Nikon, a strikingly tall man from a peasant background, was determined to prevent the state from encroaching on the liberties of the church. He disapproved of the way in which the Ulozhenie of 1649 had established state supervision of church lands, and as patriarch he managed significantly to limit the operation of the Monastery Department.

Nikon, however, was also insistent that the Russian church should conform to Greek Orthodox rituals and practices. This, combined with his arrogance, soon alienated other reformers, such as the Archpriest Avvakum. Avvakum and his followers thought that the Greek Orthodox church was discredited because its leaders had, in the 15th century, been willing to contemplate reunion with Rome. The issues on which they

Patriarch Nikon accompanied by clergy and nuns. A contemporary painting dating from *c.* 1660. The picture conveys Nikon's impressive stature, which gave rise to scurrilous and improbable rumours that he was the father of Peter I, who was also very tall.

The Patriarch's Palace and the Church of the Twelve Apostles in the Moscow Kremlin. The palace and church were built by Patriarch Nikon in the 1650s. The rooms in the patriarch's residence outdid those of the adjacent Terem Palace in size. The church, completed in 1656, represents a return to the traditional Russian style and a reaction against the elaborate detail fashionable in the first half of the 17th century.

challenged Nikon, including the correct spelling of the name of Jesus and the question of whether the sign of the cross should be made with three fingers or with two, may appear trivial to secular minds, but liturgy and ritual were and are of central importance to Orthodoxy. The dispute led to a schism in which those who clung to traditional Russian practices (the Old Believers or Schismatics) formed a separate church in defiance of the patriarch and the tsar. Alexei continued to support Nikon's reforms, and the powers of the state were used against the Schismatics.

By 1657 relations between Alexei and Nikon were deteriorating. Alexei may have been uneasy about the ways in which Nikon was trying to assert the authority of the church over the state. When Alexei appointed a new metropolitan to the see of Kiev in 1657, Nikon refused to consecrate him, arguing that Kiev came under the authority of the patriarch of Constantinople. In 1658 Alexei forbade Nikon to use the title 'Great Sovereign' which he himself had conferred on him in 1654. Nikon denounced the tsar from the pulpit, and withdrew to a monastery.

Nikon had not resigned as patriarch, and Alexei found it difficult to depose him. The assembly of Russian bishops which he convened in Moscow in 1660 for that purpose advised the tsar that they did not have the right to dismiss the patriarch. In 1664 Nikon attempted to stage a dramatic come-back. He arrived unexpectedly at the Assumption Cathedral in the Kremlin, seized the patriarch's crozier, and took control

KLIUCHEVSKY ON LITURGICAL REFORM AND THE GREAT SCHISM

As the son of a country priest, the historian Kliuchevsky had an excellent grasp of matters theological and liturgical. In his multi-volume *Course in Russian History*, published between 1904 and 1922, he demonstrated a deep understanding of what moved the Schismatics to object to the reforms proposed by Patriarch Nikon.

Dogmas and commandments are expressed in sacred texts and embodied in church ritual. All this is only an outer covering of the doctrine and not its essence. But religious as well as aesthetic comprehension differs from the logical and mathematical in that the idea, or the musical phrase, is inseparable from the form in which it is expressed. We can understand a logically deduced conception or a mathematically demonstrated theorem in whatever style, symbols, or language known to us they may be formulated. The case is different with religious and aesthetic perception. Here, by the law of psychological association, the idea and the motif are organically interconnected with the text, the rite, the image, the rhythm, the sound. If you forget the picture or the musical combination of sounds that has invoked a certain mood in you, you will not be able to reproduce that mood.

The most magnificent poem rewritten in prose will lose all its charm.

Sacred texts and liturgical rites were created in the course of history, and are not unchangeable or inviolable. One might invent better, more perfect texts and images than those that have developed our religious feeling, but they will not replace for us the old, inferior ones. When an Orthodox Russian priest intones at the altar, 'Lift up your hearts,' Orthodox believers experience a familiar feeling of exaltation that helps them 'to lay aside all earthly care'. But let the same priest say in Latin, 'Sursum corda', which stylistically is even more impressive, and the believers, however well they may understand the words, will have no sense of exaltation simply because they are not used to them. The religious beliefs and feelings of every community are inextricably interwoven with the rituals and formulas that have helped to form them.

A Russian Orthodox archbishop giving a blessing. An engraving by J.-B. Le Prince dating from 1769. The two-branched candlestick symbolizes the two natures of Christ and the three-branched candlestick the Holy Trinity.

of the service that was in progress. But when Alexei ordered him to leave Moscow, he obeyed.

Alexei arranged for a church council to meet in Moscow in 1666, and persuaded the patriarchs of Antioch and Alexandria to attend. The council deposed Nikon, who was exiled to a remote northern monastery. Thereafter, Alexei treated him kindly, sending him money and gifts. The deposition of Nikon did not bring the debate about the relationship between church and state to an end. A church council of 1666–67 ruled that the tsar's authority was only supreme in secular affairs. The Monastery Department declined in influence and in 1675 Patriarch Joachim persuaded Alexei to abolish it. Nikon's successors continued his liturgical reforms. The Old Believers were vigorously persecuted by the

TSAR ALEXEI'S SHOPPING LIST

In 1659 Tsar Alexei drew up a list of items which he required John Hebdon, his English purchasing agent, to obtain for him. The list included:

- The very best sort of doctor who can find cures using herbs available in Muscovy

- An alchemist of the very best kind and an amiable fellow, who understands these herbs and can concoct them

- A reliable herbal book that deals with Russian and Polish as well as foreign herbs

- Mineralogists expert in all kinds of silver, copper, lead and iron ores

- A goldsmith who can gild

- An illustrated book in four volumes on trajectories and someone who can make them all work

- A pamphlet about the tsar's campaigns

- Monthly news sheets from all states

- Good birds – singing parrots, finches and canaries

- A master glass-maker who knows how to make clear glass and all kinds of embossed and cut-glass vessels, and who knows the sort of earth from which such glass is made

- 2½ cwt of camphor

state. Many endured exile, imprisonment or execution. Some immolated themselves on bonfires, while others engaged in armed rebellion.

Western influences

Alexei was keenly interested in Western learning and culture. Among his chief advisers was Feodor Mikhailovich Rtishchev (1625–73), a pious and scholarly boyar whose charitable works included the building of almshouses and a scheme for rescuing Moscow's drunks from the gutter, a not inconsiderable undertaking. Rtishchev established a monastery with a free school, inviting monks from Kiev, a city where Western learning flourished, to teach Latin, Greek, rhetoric and philosophy. Alexei himself employed a distinguished Latinist, Simeon Polotsky, as court poet and tutor to his children and became a patron of the theatre, though the Orthodox church condemned drama as a dangerous illusion. The birth of Alexei's son Peter in 1672 was celebrated by a performance of *Esther*, a biblical play written and staged by Johann Gregory, the pastor of the Lutheran church in Moscow's German Quarter. The tsar was fascinated by astronomy, and frescoes depicting the stars and planets were painted on ceilings both in the Kremlin and at Kolomenskoe. Alexei employed foreign physicians, including the Englishman Samuel Collins.

The Copper Rebellion

In 1656 Alexei began to debase the currency in order to meet the costs of the war. Copper coins were minted to the same nominal value as silver coins. Officials, including the tsar's father-in-law Ilya Miloslavsky, enriched themselves by having coins struck from their own stocks of copper. When the fraud was uncovered Miloslavsky and the other guilty men were let off lightly. The inflation caused by this increase in the money supply led to an uprising in Moscow in July 1662. Five thousand aggrieved citizens marched out to the tsar's summer residence at Kolomenskoe to demand that Alexei punish those responsible for the inflation. Alexei, who was in church when the mob arrived, ordered Ilya Miloslavsky and his associates to hide, sent messengers to Moscow to fetch troops, and then addressed the crowd, reproaching them for interrupting the liturgy and promising to deal with their grievances. Satisfied, the mob set off back towards Moscow. On the way they met a second and more volatile crowd, who persuaded them to return to Kolomenskoe, where they demanded that the 'traitors' be handed over to them, and jostled the tsar. Fortunately for Alexei, the reinforcements he had summoned from Moscow arrived, and he ordered them to attack. Some of the demonstrators were cut down where they stood. Others, who fled down the hill towards the Moskva, found themselves trapped and were drowned when they attempted to escape across the river. In the weeks that followed hundreds were executed, mutilated or exiled for their part in the riots. A decree of 1663 re-established the silver currency and ordered the melting down of the copper coins.

Reforms and the economy

Alexei created new regiments of Russian soldiers who were officered and trained by foreign experts. Engineers and firearms makers were recruited from abroad, and the government arranged for the publication in 1649 of a translation of *The Art of Infantry Warfare* by the Dutchman van Wallhausen. There were no radical alterations to the central administration during the reign, though the tsar created a number of new government departments to carry out specific functions. The most important of these was the Secret Department, set up in 1654 to run Alexei's falconry establishment – no mean task, given that the tsar owned 3,000 falcons which were cared for by 200 falconers. It developed into a private office, supervising his personal finances and correspondence, and serving as a training ground for promising officials.

TSAR ALEXEI ON FALCONRY

Scholars are not certain that Alexei wrote the *Statute and Regulations for the Falconry Service* himself, though it is clear that the work reflects his outlook and values. The passage highlighted at the end of this extract, which is from the introduction to the work, was certainly written by the tsar, since it is in his own hand. Though the *Statute* is concerned with falconry, it may give some insight into the tsar's thinking on government.

...let there be nothing done without stateliness, or without well-regulated and admirable order; and let all things have their honour and their place and their model regulated by writ, because, though a thing be small, but if it be in due form honoured, well-proportioned, harmonious, stately, no one will shame it, nor blame it; everyone will praise, everyone will honour and admire, that even so small a business is honoured and regulated and ordered in due measure.... What is necessary to everything? Measure, proportion, consistency, strength; then in it and around it, stateliness, harmony, good order. Nothing unless it be well proportioned, and have all the afore described qualities, can become consistent and strong....

Be sportsmanlike, amuse yourself with this good sport and enjoy it joyously and heartily and cheerfully, for it is good to keep away all sorrow and spleen. Choose your days, ride out often, let the birds fly on a catch, without sloth and spleen, that the birds might not forget their cunning and beautiful art. O my glorious counsellors, my true and able sportsmen, be joyous and mirthful, let your hearts enjoy and appreciate this goodly and cheery sport in all years to come. These maxims for your souls and bodies; but never forget about truth and justice, and charitable love and military exercise; there is one time for work, and another for enjoyment.

The Secret Department was given charge of the crown estates, which developed into the largest agricultural and industrial enterprise in Muscovy. At Ismailovo, a royal hunting lodge near Moscow, orchards, market gardens and experimental farms were created, together with factories where foreign craftsmen trained Russian workers in glass-blowing and brick-making. The park was laid out in the French style, and Alexei set up Russia's first zoo, the most exotic inmates being some moose imported from North America. Other royal estates became centres of rope-making and the manufacture of potash. The tsar encouraged Dutch entrepreneurs to settle in Russia and set up ironworks. Alexei himself owned three such enterprises, though their output was not large.

Russian merchants petitioned the tsar to abolish the privileges which foreign traders enjoyed. After the execution of Charles I in 1649 Alexei deprived the English merchants of their special privileges and during the 1650s he sent envoys and money to encourage the exiled Charles II. The Commercial Charter of 1654 raised the taxes on goods bought and sold in Russia by foreign merchants. In 1667 the New Trade Code, drafted by Ordin-Nashchokin, laid down uniform trading terms for all foreigners and afforded some protection to Russian merchants. The Code also reduced taxes on all items except luxury goods. The other main taxational reform was the abandonment of the tax on plough lands, which was easy to evade, in favour of a tax on households.

Family life

In 1669 Alexei's wife Maria died shortly after giving birth to their 13th child and in 1670 Alexei's heir, the Tsarevich Alexei, died just short of his 16th birthday. Neither of Alexei's surviving sons, Feodor and Ivan, was physically robust, so there were dynastic reasons for Alexei to remarry. The tsar chose Natalya Naryshkina, the ward of his close friend and adviser Matveyev. Samuel Collins grudgingly describes Natalya as 'a tolerable beauty', but other sources are more flattering. The marriage, which took place in January 1671, was resented by the Miloslavskys, the family of the dead tsaritsa Maria. On 30 May 1672, Natalya was delivered

A medal struck in 1672 to commemorate the birth of Peter Alexeyevich, later Peter I. The medal bears portraits of the infant's parents, Tsar Alexei and his second wife Natalya Naryshkina.

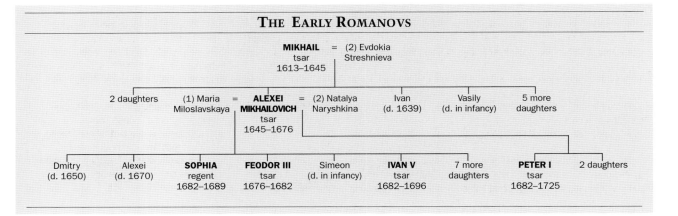

THE EARLY ROMANOVS

MIKHAIL tsar 1613–1645 = (2) Evdokia Streshnieva

2 daughters — (1) Maria Miloslavskaya = **ALEXEI MIKHAILOVICH** tsar 1645–1676 = (2) Natalya Naryshkina — Ivan (d. 1639) — Vasily (d. in infancy) — 5 more daughters

Dmitry (d. 1650) — Alexei (d. 1670) — **SOPHIA** regent 1682–1689 — **FEODOR III** tsar 1676–1682 — Simeon (d. in infancy) — **IVAN V** tsar 1682–1696 — 7 more daughters — **PETER I** tsar 1682–1725 — 2 daughters

Stepan (Stenka) Razin. A German engraving of the Cossack rebel leader executed in 1671.

of a son, Peter, who grew into a strong, healthy child quite unlike his ailing half-brothers Feodor and Ivan. This intensified the rivalries between the Miloslavskys and the Naryshkins. The Naryshkin faction hoped that one day Peter would succeed to the throne.

Stepan Razin's rebellion

The most serious rebellion of Alexei's reign was led by Stepan Timofeyevich (Stenka) Razin. At first Razin seems to have been motivated mainly by a desire for plunder, though the band of Don Cossacks and fugitive serfs that he led from 1667 onwards also murdered government officials. After a period of piracy on the Caspian Sea in 1668, Razin's forces turned back towards central Muscovy. His promise that he would liberate people from the burdens imposed on them by the government attracted considerable peasant support. The Zaporozhian Cossacks also rose in revolt. By late 1670 the government had lost control of much of eastern Russia, and Razin had 20,000 men under his command. He claimed to be acting on behalf of the Tsarevich Alexei, the eldest son of the tsar, though Alexei had died in 1670. Razin's entourage included not only a False Alexei but also someone who claimed to be the deposed Patriarch Nikon.

Razin's failure to capture Simbirsk was the first major setback of the rebellion. A relief force of government troops defeated and scattered his army. In April 1671 he was arrested by Cossacks loyal to the government and handed over to the authorities. Razin was questioned by Tsar Alexei himself, who ordered him to be tortured and executed. Government forces killed tens of thousands of rebels in the Don region, and the Don Cossacks were brought under more direct Muscovite jurisdiction.

War with Turkey

Alexei's acquisition of Ukrainian territory brought him into conflict with the Turks. The sultan's forces invaded the Polish Ukraine in 1672, and Alexei, who was once again interested in the vacant Polish throne, attacked the Turkish forces and their Cossack allies as a way of showing his commitment to the defence of Poland. The campaign was a failure. The Poles elected Jan Sobieski as their king and the Turks drove the Russians out of the Polish Ukraine. The war was still in progress when Alexei died on 29 January 1676 at the age of 46. The agenda of modernization and conquest which Alexei's government had set was taken up by his energetic youngest son, Peter the Great.

(*Opposite*) Stepan Razin carrying off a Russian princess by boat on the lower reaches of the Volga. An engraving from Jan Struys' *Reysen*, published in Amsterdam in 1676.

(*Right*) Jan Sobieski, king of Poland. An anonymous portrait dated 1674 in the Palazzo Pitti, Florence. Jan Sobieski (1624–96) was appointed commander-in-chief of the Polish army in 1668. His early military success against the Turks at Khotin in 1673 helped to gain him election to the throne the following year. In 1683 he raised the Turkish siege of Vienna.

PALACES AND TREASURES

The Terem Palace

The construction of the Terem Palace in the Moscow Kremlin began in the period 1635–36. The uppermost floor of the palace contained the private chambers, where, during the 17th century, the female members of the Romanov family lived in seclusion, surrounded by elaborate protocol. Even physicians were only admitted in extreme cases, and they were obliged to examine their patients in semi-darkness, and to take their pulse through a veil. When the royal ladies ventured out of the Terem they had to cover their faces, and travel in closed carriages. Since rank prevented them from marrying outside the royal family, and religion ruled out foreign husbands, the Terem was, for the majority of Romanov women, a gilded cage. The Regent Sophia was the first to defy many of these conventions, and Peter the Great abolished them altogether.

(Above) The golden domes of the Terem churches. Eleven small churches were constructed next to the Terem Palace between the 14th and the 17th centuries, though subsequent alterations reduced their number to six.

(Opposite above) The Council Chamber of the Terem Palace is painted with mid-19th-century murals, though their vivid colours and floral motifs reflect the original decorative scheme. Tsar Alexei Mikhailovich imported Flemish and Persian tapestries and oriental carpets to add magnificence to the rooms, and the ceiling of the dining room was decorated with an astronomical mural showing planets and stars.

(Left) One of the windows in the Terem Palace is decorated with an elaborate stone surround. This was the Petition Window of the tsar's study, from which a box was lowered in which people could place petitions. The box became known as the 'Long Box' because responses to petitions were tardy. 'Leaving your business in the Long Box' became a proverbial expression for indefinite delay.

The Kremlin workshops

Russia's rulers in the 17th century were important patrons of the goldsmith's and silversmith's art, and the Kremlin workshops produced many important items.

A cover for a copy of the Gospels made in the Kremlin workshops in 1678, and decorated with enamels and precious stones. The central panel shows Christ flanked by the Blessed Virgin Mary and St John the Baptist. The four evangelists are depicted in the four corners: St John and St Matthew at the top, and St Mark and St Luke at the bottom.

A goblet made for Tsar Mikhail in the Kremlin workshops in 1628 by a foreign craftsman, Jakob Frick.

The palace at Kolomenskoe. An 18th-century engraving.

Kolomenskoe

Kolomenskoe, just over six miles from the Kremlin, had long been one of the summer residences of the grand princes. It was rebuilt in timber in the period 1667–81 by Tsar Alexei and his son Feodor Alexeyevich. The chief designers were Muscovites – Ivan Mikhailov and Simon Petrov – and the range of buildings that they produced drew on traditional Russian styles and contemporary Western European influences. From a distance the palace, which had well over 200 rooms, must have had the appearance of a fantasy village rather than a single structure. The exterior was elaborately carved and gilded, and decorated with motifs made from copper and tin. The interior was decorated with murals, including portraits of Julius Caesar and Alexander the Great, and one of the rooms had an astronomical ceiling.

Kolomenskoe was demolished in the 18th century on the orders of Catherine II. She was prejudiced against wooden houses, in part because in the spring of 1748 she was nearly killed when a wooden building in which she had been sleeping broke loose from its foundations and slid down a hill, causing 19 fatalities. A detailed model of the palace was commissioned, and this survives, giving a clear idea of the building's appearance.

Федор III **Feodor III**
1676–1682

Софья **The Regency of Sophia**
1682–1689

Иван V **Ivan V and Peter I**
Петр I Великий **(joint reign)**
1682–1696

Feodor III. Detail of a portrait of the young tsar now in the State Historical Museum, Moscow.

FEODOR III	
Full name	*Died*
Feodor Alexeyevich	Moscow
Romanov	27 April 1682
Father	Natural causes
Alexei	*Wives*
Mikhailovich	(1) 1680 Agafia
Mother	Grushevskaya
Maria	Died 1681
Miloslavskaya	(2) 1682 Marfa
Born	Apraxina
Moscow	Died 1716
30 May 1661	*Child by (1)*
Accession	Ilya (1681; died
29 January 1676	1681)

FEODOR III

The tsar was consecrated last Sunday according to the manners and customs of this country. The people and the courtiers were all superbly turned out, dressed in cloth of gold and silver; a number of them had their coats and tall hats very richly embroidered, decked with a quantity of pearls. Prince Mikhail Dolgoruky threw liberal handfuls of gold and silver pieces to the people. There was present a teeming mass of people of all sorts, shouting at the tops of their voices, wishing the prince all kinds of prosperity. However certain of them, over eager to gather up the money, were trampled under foot.

Van Zeller, a Dutch statesman present at the coronation of Feodor III

Feodor was 14 at the time of his accession. Most contemporary accounts of his reign stress his ill health, though his participation in religious pilgrimages and lengthy rituals suggests that he was not a permanent invalid. He was well educated and devout, had literary aspirations, and contributed verse translations of two psalms to a psalter published in 1679. At first he was dominated by the faction led by the Miloslavskys, the family of his mother. They persuaded him to

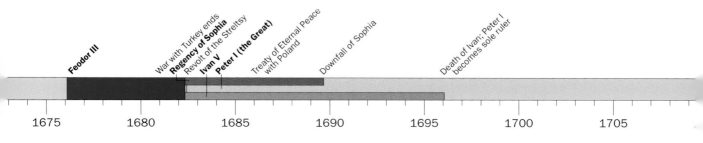

Feodor III · War with Turkey ends · **Regency of Sophia** · Revolt of the Streltsy · Ivan V · **Peter I (the Great)** · Treaty of Eternal Peace with Poland · Downfall of Sophia · Death of Ivan; Peter I becomes sole ruler

1675　1680　1685　1690　1695　1700　1705

FEODOR III ABOLISHES THE PRECEDENCE SYSTEM

Feodor's reasons for acting on the issue of precedence (*mestnichestvo*) were practical and forward-looking.

It has come to the great sovereign's attention that in the recent hostilities the enemy displayed new military skills in their engagements with his majesty's troops, thereby hoping to inflict defeats upon the sovereign's men. The enemy's newfangled device obliges us to review and reorganize our armies in order to provide them with more trustworthy methods of defence and protection against the enemy in time of war.

Yet the case for its abolition that he made to a gathering of boyars and senior clergy in January 1682 was theological rather than pragmatic. This approach reflected Feodor's character but also made political sense, since it helped to secure the support of the clergy for his proposals.

That crafty disseminator of evil and common foe, the Devil, seeing how Christian people enjoyed peace and tranquillity as a result of their glorious victories in battle, and how the foes of Christianity were embittered and annihilated, implanted in the mild hearts of the glorious warriors the idea of precedence. In times gone by this system brought about great misfortune in war, diplomacy and other affairs of state, and led to the disparagement of our troops by the enemy.... Therefore we, the sovereign, desire, and Divine Providence, the author of peace and earthly well-being by his Almighty will, commands that this Code of Precedence, the destroyer of love, be abolished, and the hearts torn apart by this perfidy unite in peaceful and blessed love.

exile Matveyev, the ablest member of the Naryshkin faction, to Russia's arctic north. Later in the reign the boyar Vasily Golitsyn became one of the dominant figures in the government.

There were no radical departures from the policies of the previous reign. In 1680 Feodor agreed that Nikon could return to Moscow, but he died during the homeward journey in 1681. The rank of patriarch was posthumously restored to him. The persecution of the Old Believers continued. A church council in 1681 condemned Avvakum to death, and in April 1682 he was burned alive in a wooden cage.

The Treaty of Bakhchisarai, agreed in 1681 and confirmed by the sultan in 1682, brought the Turkish War to an end. The Turks retained Podolia in return for their recognition of Muscovy's right to Kiev. Feodor appointed Vasily Golitsyn to head a commission to reform the army. The commission recommended not only structural changes, but the abolition of the precedence (*mestnichestvo*) system, under which the hierarchy of command was determined by ancestry rather than by ability. The recommendation was accepted and the registers of precedence were burned.

Feodor's government abolished the practice of cutting off the hands and feet of thieves, substituting for it the penalty of deportation to Siberia. The most ambitious policy initiative of the reign was the land survey, begun in 1680. Work on the survey continued after Feodor's death until 1686. By then most of the land in central Russia had been registered, but in many areas the surveyors merely negotiated an agreed statement with the landowner. An accurate survey of who owned what was beyond the capacity of the government.

In 1680 Feodor married Agafia Grushevskaya, the daughter of an Orthodox Polish nobleman. Polish manners and dress became prevalent at the court. Agafia gave birth to a son, Ilya, in July 1681, but both she and the child died within a few days. The grieving tsar was urged by his advisers to remarry as soon as possible for dynastic reasons. He married his second wife, Marfa Apraxina, in February 1682. By Easter 1682 Feodor was seriously ill, and he died on 27 April without designating an heir.

IVAN V	
Full name	*Died*
Ivan Alexeyevich Romanov	Moscow 29 January 1696
Father	Natural causes
Alexei Mikhailovich	*Wife*
Mother	1684 Praskovia
Maria Miloslavskaya	Feodorovna Saltykova
Born	Died 1723
Moscow 27 August 1666	*Children*
Accession	Maria (1689) Feodosia (1690)
May 1682 (as a result of the Streltsy revolt)	Catherine (1692) **Anna** (1693) Praskovia (1694)
Coronation (with Peter I) 6 July 1682	

JOINT REIGN OF IVAN V AND PETER I AND REGENCY OF SOPHIA

Tsar Ivan is very infirm and congenitally blind, with a growth of skin right over his eyes. So one can well imagine that the dual monarchy will not last long. It's true that Peter has the greater support from the boyars and magnates, but sister Sophia, who is about 26 and said to possess great wit and judgment, has promoted the elder brother. But it should be evident to anyone that such a feeble-minded and sickly man is by nature unfit to rule.

Johann Eberhardt Hövel, Austrian envoy to the Russian court

I believe that Sophia has not been rendered the justice due to her. She conducted the affairs of the Empire for many years with all the sagacity that anyone would have desired.

Catherine the Great *Memoirs*

The death of Feodor led to uncertainty about who should be tsar and a renewal of the power struggle between the Miloslavsky and Naryshkin factions. Patriarch Joachim hastily convoked an assembly which decided that the crown should pass to Peter, then just short of his tenth birthday,

(*Below*) Peter Alexeyevich, later Peter I, as a child. A contemporary oil painting by an unknown artist.

(*Below right*) An 18th-century portrait of Sophia Alexeyevna as regent. The sceptre, orb and crown all symbolize Sophia's authority.

Natalya Kirillovna Naryshkina (1651–94), the mother of Peter the Great. An anonymous 17th-century portrait.

The revolt of the streltsy and the murder of Artamon Matveyev. A miniature from the *History of Peter the Great* by Peter Krekshin (1684–1763). The artist has also shown the streltsy searching the Kremlin for the members of the Naryshkin family. The court dwarves were forced, at knife point, to assist in the search, and one of them can be seen in the picture.

with his mother Natalya Naryshkina acting as regent. Ivan, though older than Peter, was passed over because he suffered from a number of handicaps, including poor vision and a speech defect. This arrangement was soon challenged by the streltsy, the infantry regiments set up in the reign of Ivan IV (p. 34).

The Revolt of the Streltsy

Most accounts of the crisis of April–May 1682 claim that the revolt of the streltsy was encouraged by Tsar Alexei's daughter Sophia and the Miloslavsky faction in the hope of placing Ivan on the throne and exercising power on his behalf. The evidence is far from conclusive, and the streltsy, who were owed massive arrears of pay and resented the way their commanders were exploiting them as unskilled labour, needed little encouragement to revolt. The Naryshkin faction and Artamon Matveyev, whom they had recalled from exile, took no steps to placate the streltsy.

When, on 15 May, a rumour spread that Ivan had been murdered, a mob of angry soldiers broke into the Kremlin demanding to know the truth. Natalya brought Peter and Ivan out onto the Red Staircase to show the streltsy that Ivan was in good health. This strategy might have worked had not Prince Mikhail Dolgoruky, chief of the Streltsy Department, intervened and roundly condemned the mutineers. He was dragged from the staircase, thrown on to the pikes of the streltsy and hacked to pieces before the eyes of Natalya, Peter and Ivan. The streltsy then rampaged through the palace, murdering Matveyev and several members of the Naryshkin family and faction. They returned the next day to demand that Ivan Naryshkin, who had hidden in a cupboard in the Terem Palace, be handed over to them. Ivan gave himself up to prevent a general massacre, and was tortured and killed. Further violence followed, and on 23 May Prince Ivan Khovansky, the self-appointed leader of the streltsy, demanded that Ivan be appointed joint ruler with Peter. This arrangement was agreed. Ivan was capable of fulfilling ceremonial and dynastic functions, though in the former he frequently needed physical support from courtiers. It is not clear whether Sophia was formally

The *Shapka Monomakh* of the Second Order, now in the Kremlin Armoury Museum, was made for the coronation of the ten-year-old Peter I in 1682. Extra regalia was needed because Peter was jointly crowned with his older half-brother Ivan V.

LETTERS FROM THE REGENT SOPHIA TO VASILY GOLITSYN

The letters from which these extracts were taken were written in 1689. The biblical allusions refer, allegorically, to Vasily Golitsyn's second campaign in the Crimea.

By the grace of God and the Holy Mother of God and your own good sense and good fortune you have defeated the Hagarene; may God grant you future victories over your enemies. I, my light, shall be unable to believe that you will return to us until I actually see you in my embrace. You write that I should pray, being a sinner and unworthy in the eyes of God; still, I dare to trust in his goodness, sinner though I be. Be healthy and prosper, my light, in Christ for countless ages. Amen.

My lord and light and hope, may you have long life and prosperity. Joyful to me indeed is this day on which the Lord God has glorified his holy Name and the name of his mother the blessed Mother of God through you, my light, the like of which has not been heard throughout the ages, nor have our fathers recounted such divine mercy, for God has delivered you, as once he delivered the Israelites out of the land of Egypt by his prophet Moses; now praise be to God for the mercy he has shown us through you, my dear. My lord, how can you be repaid for your innumerable labours? My joy, my light, I can hardly believe that I shall ever see you again. Great indeed will be the day when I have you with me again, my dear. If it were possible, I would have you before me in a single day.

The language used in the letters is likely to give the modern reader the impression that Sophia and Golitsyn were, as contemporary gossip asserted, lovers. The problem that historians face in using these letters as evidence of the nature of their relationship is that we have no other letters from powerful Russian women of the late 17th century to their political collaborators. It is therefore impossible to be sure how much we should read into the terms of endearment used. It may be significant that both letters were written in code.

A contemporary allegorical engraving by I. Shchirsky showing Christ blessing Ivan V and Peter I. It contains flattering references to the Regent Sophia. The winged female figure above Christ represents Holy Wisdom (Sophia is the Greek word for wisdom) and the double-headed eagle at the bottom is lodged in a temple with seven pillars on whose arch is inscribed the biblical text referring to the seven pillars of wisdom (Proverbs 9:1).

appointed regent at that stage, but there is no doubt that she emerged from the crisis as the dominant figure in the government. Her reputation of being ugly, obese, Machiavellian and immoral rests on unreliable evidence. She was an educated, able and determined woman and her emergence from the seclusion of the Terem to play the leading role in government was without precedent.

Sophia and her advisers moved rapidly to pacify the streltsy by paying them the 240,000 roubles of back pay that they were demanding. Within a few months she had disposed of the troublesome Prince Khovansky and transferred 12 of the streltsy regiments to frontier duties. Her government was constructive, though not particularly innovative. Dutch and German merchants were given permission to establish a textile industry in Russia. The harsh treatment of the Old Believers continued, and Sophia was scrupulous in her religious observances. This behaviour may have been as much the product of political consideration as of piety. Vasily Golitsyn, her principal adviser and, gossip alleged, her lover, attempted to tackle the squalor of Moscow, organizing the construction of many stone buildings and a stone bridge over the River Moskva. A decree of 1686 ordered the removal of refuse from the streets. The penalty of burial alive customarily applied to women who murdered their husbands was abolished.

Foreign policy

In 1689 Russia became the first European state to sign an equal trade treaty with China, the Treaty of Nerchinsk. The price of peace and trading access to China was a Russian withdrawal from territory in the Amur valley, a remote area that the Russians were unable to defend. When Sophia came to power Russia was at peace with her traditional

Vasily Vasilievich Golitsyn (1643–1714), the principal adviser to the Regent Sophia, holding the 1686 Treaty of Eternal Peace with Poland.

A medal struck to commemorate the 1686 Treaty of Eternal Peace between Russia and Poland. The medal shows personifications of the two countries hand in hand. Russo-Polish relations in the ensuing hundred years proved to be less amicable.

enemies, Poland, Turkey and Sweden, though none of the peace treaties that her predecessors had signed with those states had removed the causes of conflict.

The Turkish and Polish questions were closely linked, since the Poles hoped to persuade Muscovy to join the Holy League against the Turks which they, the Austrians and the Venetians had formed in 1684. Sophia's government was not averse to this idea, provided that the Poles were willing to make territorial concessions. In April 1686 the Treaty of Eternal Peace with Poland was agreed. The price of Russia's support in the war against Turkey was high. The Poles had to recognize as permanent Russia's possession of Kiev and the other territories that Russia had conquered in recent decades. In return Russia would pay the Poles an indemnity of 146,000 roubles, and seek for further allies in Western Europe. The resulting diplomatic offensive achieved no tangible results, but the visits by Russian missions to 11 capitals were a significant step towards Russia's acceptance as a European power.

The Russian contribution to the anti-Turkish crusade was an invasion of the Crimea, which Golitsyn launched in the spring of 1687. The march across the steppes turned into a disaster as grass fires deprived the horses of fodder and the army ran short of water. In June Golitsyn gave the order to turn back. The celebrations on his return to Moscow could not disguise his failure.

Sophia's ambitions

As Peter grew to manhood, Sophia's position became increasingly precarious. She probably hoped to exercise power in the long term. From 1684 coins and medals were being issued with her likeness on them, and in 1686 she assumed the title of Autocrat. Her best prospect was that Ivan might, by producing a male heir, provide an excuse for a prolongation of the regency. Ivan married Praskovia Saltykova in 1684, but their first child, born in 1689, was a daughter. Early in 1689 the 16-year-old Peter married Evdokia Lopukhina. This was the political context in which Golitsyn set out on his second Crimean campaign in 1689. His forces reached Perekop, but once again lack of water and fodder created problems, and Golitsyn chose to negotiate rather than to fight. The retreating Russian army was harried by Tatars and Turkish irregulars. Again Sophia attempted to pass off failure as victory, but Peter pointedly refused to attend the solemn Te Deum that marked Golitsyn's return.

By the summer of 1689 both Sophia and Peter believed that the other was about to use violence to resolve the conflict between them. There is no firm evidence that Sophia planned a coup d'état against Peter, though Peter believed that his life was in danger. In August he panicked and fled to the fortified Troitsky-Sergius Monastery near Moscow. Over the following weeks an increasing number of officials and officers defected to his camp. By early September Sophia no longer had sufficient support to refuse Peter's demands that she hand her advisers over into his custody and retire to the Novodevichy Convent. Vasily Golitsyn was exiled.

Петр I Великий

Peter I

('The Great')

1682–1725

Miniature portrait of Peter I, painted
c. 1720, now in the Hermitage,
St Petersburg.

PETER I	
Full name	Repudiated by Peter
Peter Alexeyevich	in 1698
Romanov	Died 1731
also known as Peter	(2) 1712* Marfa
the Great	Skavronskaya
Father	(**Catherine I**)
Alexei Mikhailovich	Died 1727
Mother	*They were
Natalya Kirillovna	secretly married
Naryshkina	in 1707
Born	*Children by (1)*
Moscow	Alexei (1690)
30 May 1672	Alexander (1691)
Accession	Paul (1693)
27 April 1682	*Children by (2)*
Sole ruler from	Paul (1704)
29 January 1696	Peter (1705)
Died	Catherine (1707)
St Petersburg	Anna (1708)
28 January 1725	**Elizabeth** (1709)
Gangrenous	Natalya (1713)
complications from	Margarita (1714)
a urinary tract	Peter (1715)
infection	Paul (1717)
Wives	Natalya (1718)
(1) 1689 Evdokia	Peter (1723)
Feodorovna	Paul (1724)
Lopukhina	

PETER I

The tsar was a very tall man, exceedingly well made; rather thin, his face somewhat round, a high forehead, good eyebrows, a rather short nose, but not too short, and large at the end, rather thick lips, complexion reddish brown, good black eyes, large, bright, piercing, and well open; his look majestic and gracious when he liked, but when otherwise, severe and stern, with a twitching of the face, not often occurring, but which appeared to contract his eyes and all his physiognomy, and was frightful to see; it lasted for a moment, gave him a wild and terrible air, and passed away.

The Duc de Saint-Simon *Memoirs*

Peter the Great (1682–1725) was in every sense larger than life. He was 6 ft 7 in (2 m) tall, with enormous appetites. Energetic and inquisitive, he loved to learn new skills, including dentistry, which he practised on any courtier foolish enough to admit to toothache. He was fascinated by dwarfs and physical freaks and was capable of great generosity and great cruelty. His achievements have kept him at the forefront of debate about Russian history. In the 19th century he was a hero to progressives and

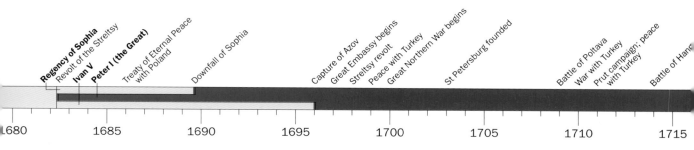

Regency of Sophia
Revolt of the Streltsy
Ivan V
Peter I (the Great)
Treaty of Eternal Peace with Poland
Downfall of Sophia
Capture of Azov
Great Embassy begins
Streltsy revolt
Peace with Turkey
Great Northern War begins
St Petersburg founded
Battle of Poltava
War with Turkey
Prut campaign; peace with Turkey
Battle of Hang

1680   1685   1690   1695   1700   1705   1710   1715

Westernizers and a villain to the Slavophiles, who believed that his reforms had damaged Russian society by cutting it adrift from its traditions. Soviet historians found much to admire in Peter's ruthless pursuit of progress. Stalin described Peter's reign as 'a singular attempt to jump out of our country's frame of backwardness'. Alexander Solzhenitsyn characterized Peter as 'a man of mediocre, if not savage, mind', and emphasized the spiritual, cultural and human costs of his policies.

Early life

After his coronation in 1682, Peter and his mother, Natalya Naryshkina, resided at Preobrazhenskoe near Moscow. There is no reliable evidence that Sophia banished them there, and Peter made regular ceremonial appearances at court with his half-brother and co-tsar Ivan. Peter's tutor Nikita Zotov inspired him with stories of the military exploits of earlier tsars. A Dutchman, Karsten Brand, repaired an old boat for him,

Peter I's dentistry tools are preserved in the Hermitage in St Petersburg, as is the bag of teeth which he extracted from courtiers and commoners in his long career as an amateur dentist. He became interested in tooth-drawing during his visit to Holland, and received some instruction from a travelling practitioner whom he encountered in the market at Amsterdam. Peter's size and physical strength were a considerable asset when it came to controlling his patients, not all of whom were willing victims. His enthusiasm was such that in some cases he reportedly removed not only the diseased tooth but also a section of the gum.

A drawing showing the play regiments formed by the young Peter I attacking some fortifications. Though the cannon fired non-explosive leather balls, these mock battles were not without serious injuries and fatalities.

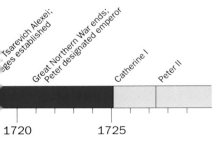

Tsarevich Alexei;
ges established

Great Northern War ends;
Peter designated emperor

Catherine I

Peter II

1720   1725

(*Right*) François (Franz Jakob) Lefort (1656–99). An engraving by P. Schenk made in 1698. Lefort was born in Geneva and travelled to Russia in 1675. He joined the Russian army three years later, serving under Vasily Vasilievich Golitsyn. He became an officer in one of Peter's play regiments, and was rapidly promoted when Peter took power. Peter lavished money and gifts on him, but Lefort was extravagantly hospitable and died in near poverty.

(*Opposite*) This portrait of Prince Alexander Danilovich Menshikov (1673–1729) dressed in armour and decorations and carrying a field marshal's baton was painted by Gottfried Danhauer in 1727, only months before Menshikov was ousted from power and exiled to Siberia. By then the former stable boy had, thanks to Peter's patronage and his own talents, amassed the following titles: Most Serene Prince, Prince of the Holy Roman Empire, Duke of Izhora, Count of Dubrovna, Gorki and Potchep, hereditary sovereign of Oranienbaum and Baturin, and Governor-General of St Petersburg. Menshikov was also lieutenant colonel of three regiments, a Senator, and a knight of various orders of chivalry.

launching a lifelong enthusiasm for things nautical. Peter formed squads of servants and young noblemen, and with the help of foreign experts recruited from Moscow's German Quarter, these play regiments developed into the Preobrazhensky and Semeonovsky Guards, the elite of the modern army that Peter was to create.

After the downfall of Sophia, Peter left the government in the hands of his mother and her boyar advisers, who had no difficulty in controlling his co-ruler, Tsar Ivan V. Peter was thus able to pursue his enthusiasms for shipbuilding and debauchery in the German Quarter. He valued his friendships with foreigners such as Patrick Gordon and François Lefort,

Peter the Great's first boat has been an important historical symbol in Russia since his own lifetime, and is known as 'the grandfather of the Russian Navy'. In 1722, after the end of the Great Northern War, Peter had the boat placed in the Alexander Nevsky Monastery in St Petersburg. In the 1760s it was moved to a specially built pavilion in the St Peter and Paul Fortress. Stalin gave it pride of place in the main hall of the St Petersburg Naval Museum in 1939, where it remains to this day.

A medal struck to commemorate the capture of Azov by the Russians in 1696.

both of whom had rallied to him in the crisis of 1689. Gordon and Lefort encouraged Peter's love of drinking and firework displays, pastimes which led to accidental deaths among his friends, as did his practice of training his regiments with live ammunition. From Lefort he inherited a mistress, Anna Mons, the daughter of a German innkeeper. Peter visited Archangel in 1693, and, delighted by his first sea trip, ordered the construction in Holland of a 44-gun frigate.

Peter's circle included men of humble origins, such as Peter Shafirov, a Polish-Jewish merchant, and Alexander Danilovich Menshikov, who was rumoured to have been a Moscow pie-seller, but was in reality a stable lad at Preobrazhenskoe. The boyars resented the power that such men came to enjoy. Peter organized his cronies into a 'Most Drunken Synod of Fools and Jesters', whose conclaves took the form of drinking bouts and parodies of Orthodox ritual, which scandalized the faithful, including Peter's wife Evdokia. They had married in 1689, and the birth of their son Alexei in 1690 strengthened Peter's dynastic position, since Ivan's children were all daughters. Evdokia bore Peter two other sons, who both died in infancy.

Peter's aims

After the death of his mother in 1694, Peter began to take a more active role in government. His principal goals were the enhancement of Russia's international standing, the establishment of a Russian presence on the Black Sea, and gaining access to the Baltic at the expense of Sweden. His actions do not suggest a preconceived strategy. He seized opportunities when they presented themselves, and suffered serious reverses. His internal reforms were largely dictated by the needs of war. Most of his goals were inherited from his forebears. Only in the creation of a navy, in the subordination of the church to the state and in the enforcement of Western customs did he attempt a complete break with the past. In other areas what differentiated Peter's reign from those of his predecessors was the greatly accelerated rate of change.

In 1695 Peter went to war against Turkey, with the intention of capturing Azov. After an unsuccessful siege, the Russians retreated. Peter's response to this setback was that Azov could be taken if Russia had a fleet with which to conduct a blockade. Shipyards were created at Voronezh, and Peter himself laboured alongside the foreign experts and conscript workers. By the time the fleet was ready, Peter was sole ruler of Russia, Ivan having died on 29 January 1696. Three of Ivan's five daughters survived beyond infancy. One of them, Anna, was to be empress of Russia, and Ivan's great-grandson and namesake was briefly to occupy the throne in succession to her. The combination of a naval blockade and a land assault secured the capture of Azov in July 1696.

The Great Embassy, revolt and reaction

Having achieved a military success, Peter felt able to set out for Western Europe. The Great Embassy of 1697–98, though it is remembered chiefly

THE GREAT EMBASSY

Peter I was the first reigning Russian sovereign to travel abroad, other than at the head of an army, since the 11th century. Peter travelled incognito under the name Peter Mikhailov, and his friend François Lefort was in nominal charge of the Embassy, but the tall tsar attracted attention wherever he went, enjoying the hospitality of the rulers of the territories that he passed through or visited.

Acquiring technical expertise and technology was one of the main purposes of the Great Embassy. In Holland Peter made for Zaandam, a shipbuilding centre of whose reputation he knew. Approaching the town he happened upon Gerrit Kist, a Dutch blacksmith who had worked for him at Voronezh. Kist arranged for Peter to stay in the house of a neighbour, and he spent a week labouring in the shipyards. Moving on to Amsterdam he enjoyed more shipbuilding experience in the yards of the Dutch East India Company and visited numerous other workshops and factories, gaining a knowledge of clock-making, copper engraving and dentistry, and watching anatomical dissections.

Peter had also travelled abroad in search of ideas. In London he had talks with senior churchmen, and attended a communion service at Lambeth Palace. Gilbert Burnet, bishop of Salisbury, found the tsar to be '...a man of very hot temper, soon inflamed, and very brutal in his passion; he raises his natural heat by drinking much brandy.' Burnet also noted that Peter 'has read the scriptures carefully. He hearkened to no part of what I told him more attentively than when I explained the authority that the Christian Emperors assumed in matters of religion and the supremacy of our kings.' Peter's

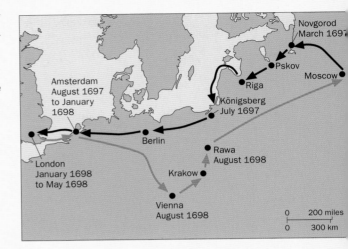

subsequent subordination of the Orthodox church to the state in Russia may have been inspired by these conversations. The tsar also visited the Woolwich Arsenal and the Royal Observatory at Greenwich.

During part of his stay in England Peter studied shipbuilding at Deptford, and lived at Sayes Court, a house owned by the diarist John Evelyn. Evelyn's butler, horrified at the vandalism committed by the tsar and his friends, wrote to his master: 'There is a house full of people, and right nasty'. After their departure, the architect Christopher Wren calculated that they had done more than £350 worth of damage, which included breaking 300 panes of glass, destroying 21 pictures, causing an explosion on the kitchen floor and wrecking a holly hedge

(Opposite above) Peter the Great at Deptford Dockyard. *A painting by the Irish artist Daniel Maclise (1806–70), whose anecdotal and 'subject' paintings were widely admired. The picture was completed in 1857 and is owned by Royal Holloway College, London.*

(Opposite below) This portrait of Peter I was painted by Sir Godfrey Kneller (?1649–1723), the German-born artist who was Principal Painter to King William III at the time of Peter I's visit to England. Kneller was known to work very rapidly, using sketches. He is said to have accommodated 14 sitters in a single day.

The exterior of the house at Zaandam in Holland where Peter I stayed while he worked in the shipyards there.

and three wheelbarrows as a result of horseplay in the garden. Peter also enjoyed a liaison with an actress, Laetitia Cross. King William III arranged for the tsar to watch the House of Lords in session, commissioned Sir Godfrey Kneller to paint his portrait, and gave him a yacht, *The Royal Transport*. It is said that in return Peter handed the king an object wrapped in a grubby piece of paper which turned out, when unpacked, to be a huge uncut diamond.

Diplomatically the Great Embassy was not a success. Peter was unable to persuade the Holy Roman Emperor Leopold I to rejoin the fight against Turkey. Indeed he found that Leopold was inclined to accept a Turkish peace offer. His meeting with the new king of Poland, Augustus II, was more successful. The 354 illegitimate children that Augustus is reputed to have fathered suggest that he was, like Peter, a man of strong appetites. The two sovereigns got on famously, enjoying drinking bouts, military reviews and a cannon firing competition, and laying the foundations of an anti-Swedish alliance.

Peter brought back from the Great Embassy 260 chests filled with weapons, scientific and mathematical instruments, tools and a stuffed crocodile. He had also recruited a large number of military and technical experts, whose function would be to teach their skills to Russians. The vigorous programme of Westernization upon which he embarked soon after his return clearly owed much to his experiences during the 18-month journey.

for Peter's quest for technological expertise, had serious diplomatic purposes. Peter hoped to strengthen the treaty with Austria and the Venetian Republic which committed those states to an offensive alliance against Turkey. Jan Sobieski, king of Poland, died in June 1696. Peter supported the successful candidate for the Polish throne, Augustus, Elector of Saxony, in the hope that Augustus would keep the Poles in the anti-Turkish alliance. The Great Embassy was not a diplomatic success. The Treaty of Friendship with Prussia which Peter signed in July 1697 did not commit the Prussians to give military help to Russia, and the Austrians, preoccupied with the succession to the Spanish crown, no longer wished to continue the war against Turkey. Peter chose to make peace with Turkey in 1699 – retaining Azov but agreeing to destroy the Russian-held fortresses in the lower Dniester region.

A revolt by the streltsy forced Peter to return to Moscow. The revolt was motivated partly by the fear that Peter, who favoured further Westernization of the armed forces, would abolish the corps. By the time Peter reached Cracow, the streltsy had been crushed. He was thus able to break his journey to meet Augustus II, the new king of Poland, with whom he established a rapport that was to bear fruit in the form of an alliance between Saxony-Poland, Denmark and Russia in 1699, aimed against Sweden.

Peter reached Moscow in August 1698 and established a commission to investigate the streltsy revolt. Extensive use was made of torture. More than 1,000 streltsy were executed, some of them hanged outside the windows of the rooms at the Novodevichy Convent in which the former Regent Sophia lived. Peter believed that she had encouraged the

The execution of the streltsy in 1698–99. An engraving from Johan Georg Korb's *Diarium Itineris in Moscoviam*. Peter ordered the destruction of any copies of the book that were found in Russia.

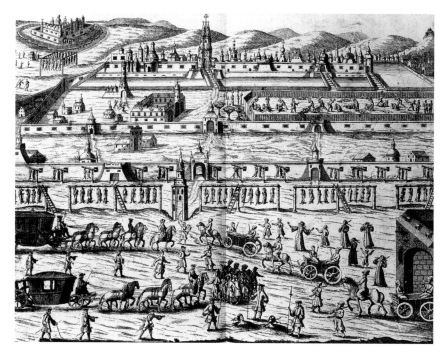

uprising, in the hope of regaining power. The Moscow streltsy regiments were dissolved, and their members exiled to the provinces. The savagery of Peter's reaction may in part be explained by his terrifying memories of the 1682 revolt, but the streltsy were also a symbol of the backward-looking forces in Russian society which he was determined to overcome. Though there was no proof of her involvement in the revolt, Sophia was forced to take the veil. She died in 1704. Peter also consigned his wife Evdokia to a convent. He may have contemplated marrying his mistress Anna Mons, but in 1703 he discovered that she had been unfaithful, and abandoned her.

Peter's celebrated trimming of the boyars' beards in August 1698 was more than a crude practical joke. He was determined to introduce Western customs into Russia. He imposed a tax on beards and decreed that courtiers and officials must wear Western clothes. In December 1699 he ordered the adoption of the Western New Year and the Julian version of the Western calendar. The Gregorian calendar was viewed in

The Church of the Transfiguration in the Novodevichy Convent, completed in 1689, was one of the buildings commissioned by the Regent Sophia, a generous patron of the community. After her downfall Sophia was sent to live in the convent and later forced to become a nun.

(*Right*) A Schismatic or Old Believer having his beard trimmed as a result of Peter I's edict. Anonymous 18th-century woodcut.

(*Below*) Bronze medallions such as this were issued as receipts to those who had paid the beard tax imposed by Peter I. Noblemen and important officials had to pay 100 roubles a year to avoid shaving, and peasants half a kopeck every time they entered or left a city. The Russian words on the token mean: 'Money paid'.

ANISIMOV ON PETER THE GREAT

A modern Russian historian, Evgeny Anisimov, weighs up the impact of Peter I's reforms.

The Petrine era brought not only impressive achievements and brilliant military victories that facilitated the strengthening of national consciousness, the victory of secular over confessional principles in culture, and the inclusion of Russia in the general European family of nations.... The era of the Petrine reforms was the time of the foundation of the totalitarian state, the graphic preaching and inculcation into mass consciousness of the cult of the strong personality – the boss, 'the father of the nation', 'the teacher of the people'.... Peter's era witnessed, too, vices typical of society in the USSR: apathy, social dependency, lack of external and internal freedom for the individual. Finally, triumphs on the battlefield coexisted with a real cult of military force, militarism, and the militarization of civilian life and of consciousness, with the imposition of one's own will on other people's through naked force....

This engraving, published in 1742, shows the forcible replacement of traditional Russian dress with the shorter Hungarian coats and tricorne hats favoured by Peter I.

Russia as Catholic and therefore heretical. The practice of confining royal women to the Terem Palace was abolished in 1702, and court ladies were compelled to attend social functions.

The first phase of the Great Northern War

Sweden appeared to Peter to be an easier target than Turkey. Its ruler, the 18-year-old Charles XII, was inexperienced and the economy was not

Charles XII of Sweden. This equestrian portrait by J.H. Wedekind, now in the Royal Army Museum in Stockholm, was executed in 1701 and shows the king at the crossing of the River Dvina. It was commissioned to celebrate the Swedish victory over the Russians. Born in 1682, Charles ascended the Swedish throne in 1697. Tall, thin and piercing of eye, he was inclined to assault his ministers and smash furniture. His pastimes included heavy drinking, decapitating farm animals with his sabre, and womanizing. A tough and determined soldier, he shared the privations of his troops and was killed in 1718 during a campaign in Norway.

strong enough to support Sweden's Baltic empire. Yet the war against Sweden which began in 1700 went badly. The militarily gifted Charles XII was able to pick his enemies off one by one, forcing the Danes to capitulate on the very day that the Russians entered the conflict. The Russian siege of Narva ended in November 1700 in a disastrous defeat at the hands of a much smaller Swedish force.

The lessons that Peter learned from Narva were that the victory would take time, and would only be achieved by modernization. The Swedish invasion which he feared did not materialize. Charles XII chose to attack Poland, where he became bogged down in a complex situation, and this gave Peter a valuable breathing space.

Narva had revealed that the Russian forces were poorly equipped and trained. An artillery school was established in 1701. New uniforms were introduced, and the English flintlock musket was copied. Within

A Lubok folk print dating from the 1760s and showing the Western styles of uniform which Peter I preferred both for infantry and cavalry.

Catherine, the second wife of Peter 1.
A miniature portrait by G.S. Musikiysky
dating from 1717.

a year of Narva, Russia was producing more cannon than Sweden. Conscription was made more systematic from 1705 onwards, with a levy of one recruit per 20 households which produced almost 45,000 men, who were formed into new regiments, trained and organized along Western European lines. Service was for life, and conscripts were therefore lost to their families. The Admiralty Department, whose task was the construction and equipping of warships, was set up in 1701. The Admiralty dockyards developed into a huge economic enterprise employing a workforce of 10,000. By the end of the reign Russia had a fleet of 800 galleys and 48 ships of the line.

In 1702 Russian forces began to win victories over the Swedes, and in May 1703 they captured the Neva delta, gaining access to the Gulf of Finland. The campaign was pressed forward into Estonia, Livonia and Courland in 1704–06. By then, Charles XII was winning the war in Poland, and in 1706 he forced Augustus II to renounce the Polish crown and make peace. Once again Peter faced the danger of a Swedish invasion, but Russia's position was stronger than it had been after Narva, whereas Sweden was war-weary and economically weakened.

In 1703 Peter met the woman who was to become his second wife and the first empress of Russia. Marfa Skavronskaya, a girl of Lithuanian peasant origin, had fallen into the hands of the Russians when they captured Marienburg. She converted to Orthodoxy, taking the name Catherine. Menshikov made her a member of his household, and it was there that she met the tsar, whose mistress she immediately became. Stocky and buxom, Catherine did Peter's laundry, calmed his rages, shared the discomforts and dangers of his campaigns and gave him 12 children. Peter married her privately in November 1707, and in

The wedding feast to mark the official marriage of Peter I and Catherine on 19 February 1712. An 18th-century engraving by A.F. Zubov. Peter's wedding gift to Catherine was a six-branched candelabra which he himself had made from ivory and ebony.

February 1712 the couple went through a public and official wedding, after which Catherine was acknowledged as tsaritsa.

St Petersburg

The capture of the Neva delta enabled Peter to embark on the development of a new seaport city in May 1703. The chosen site of St Petersburg was impractical, being marshy and prone to flooding. Timber was available in the vicinity, but stone – Peter's preferred building material – and labour were not. The peasants, prisoners of war and criminals who were brought in to construct the city died in their tens of thousands of disease and malnutrition. Peter moved his family to the new city in 1710 and designated it as the capital of Russia in 1712. By the time of his death, St Petersburg had a population of 40,000.

ST PETERSBURG

Peter originally envisaged that his new city would develop on the islands to the north of the main channel of the Neva, with the residential area on the Isle of Birches, where his timber cottage was located. Domenico Trezzini (*c.* 1670–1734), the Swiss-Italian architect, designed three types of timber house to suit the pockets and the needs of the different social classes. More detailed planning of the city was not undertaken until 1716, when the French architect Jean-Baptiste Leblond arrived. Menshikov, who had chosen Vasilievsky Island as the site of his new palace, vetoed the suggestion that the island should become the main area of development, but could not prevent Peter from siting the Twelve Colleges, the administrative centre of the new capital, there. Leblond planned a city on the Admiralty side of the Neva.

The pattern of streets that he proposed, including the Nevsky Prospect, cannot be seen on the map shown here,

which dates from 1720. Peter went to great lengths to obtain building stone for the new city. From 1714 the construction of masonry buildings elsewhere in Russia was forbidden. All coachmen entering the city were obliged to deliver three paving stones, and ships' captains had to bring 30 quarry stones. People were reluctant to move to St Petersburg, which was unhealthy and prone to flooding. Food prices were three times as high as in Moscow. Peter ordered all landlords who owned 30 or more families of serfs to construct a residence in the new city. The coercion involved in its construction, and the huge death toll among the conscript workers and prisoners-of-war who built it, made St Petersburg a powerful symbol of Peter's ruthless pursuit of progress.

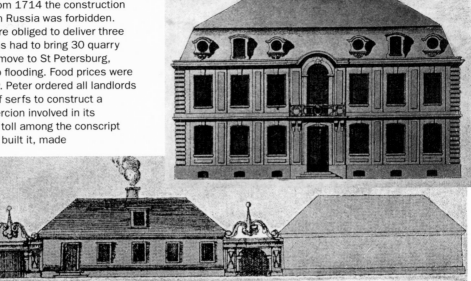

(Opposite above) Miniature portrait of Peter I with St Petersburg in the background. Painted in enamel on gold in the year 1723 by Grigory Semyonovich Musikiysky (1670/71–1739). The Peter and Paul Cathedral can been seen on the left.

(Opposite, main photo) The Peter and Paul Fortress on the Isle of Hares. Construction work began on 16 May 1703, but the fortress, and the Peter and Paul Cathedral inside its walls, were not completed until after Peter's death. The cathedral was designed by Trezzini. The spire, based on German and Scandinavian models, was a revolutionary departure for Russian architecture.

(Opposite inset, left) A medal struck to commemorate the founding of St Petersburg in 1703. The Latin inscriptions and the classical style are evidence of Peter's enthusiasm for Western culture.

(Opposite inset, right) Map of St Petersburg in the time of Peter I by Jean-Baptiste Homann of Nuremberg, c. 1720.

(Above) A nobleman's house and a single-storey artisan's house. Engravings showing Trezzini's designs for housing for the different classes of inhabitants of the new city.

(Below) Trezzini's Summer Palace (1710–14). Peter's residences in the new city were modest. The first Winter Palace was a small building in the Dutch style, and the Summer Palace is almost austere in its simplicity. Like most of the early buildings in the city it was constructed of timber and then decorated with stucco. Peter lived in simply furnished ground-floor rooms. His wife Catherine had more sumptuous apartments on the first floor.

Banner of the Preobrazhensky Guard, dating from 1700.

Peter the Great at the Battle of Poltava, 27 June 1709, painted by Louis Caravaque (1684–1754) in 1718. Charles XII conducted the battle from a litter because he was suffering from a wounded foot and was recovering from a high fever. All but three of the 24 soldiers who were carrying the litter were killed or wounded, and the king was lucky to escape. After the battle Peter I wrote: 'Now, with God's help, the final stone in the foundation of St Petersburg has been laid.'

The economy and society

The desire to build up the armed forces drove the government's economic policies. By 1725 Russia had 86 metal and gun factories and 15 textile factories, and much of this was achieved by state investment. Private manufacturers were exempted from taxation, and Peter protected Russian industry by raising tariffs on imported goods. Conscription and forced labour imposed heavy burdens on the population. The high costs of war were met by debasing the currency, by increasing existing taxes, and by introducing taxes and monopolies on such diverse items as horse-collars, playing cards, mirrors, coffins, cucumbers, baths and weddings. Peter's greatest taxational innovation was the soul tax of 1718, a poll tax which eventually brought in more than four times the revenue raised by all other direct taxes. To keep track of expenditure Peter insisted that government departments maintain proper accounts, and in 1710–11 the first attempt was made to calculate a budget.

These changes were not popular. In the period 1700–10 Peter faced a number of provincial revolts, including a rebellion in Astrakhan in 1705–06, a rebellion among the Don Cossacks in 1707–08 and extensive peasant violence in central and western Russia in 1708–10. The unrest was brutally suppressed. Peter was equally intolerant of political dissent. The Preobrazhensky Prikaz, a department originally established to administer the affairs of the Guards regiment of that name, developed into a ruthless political police force. A decree of 1714 defined the nature of political crimes for the first time, and the government encouraged informers by offering them money.

The Poltava campaign

In 1708 the Swedes invaded Russia. Peter's strategy was to retreat, laying waste to the country, and drawing his enemy into the heart of Russia. Charles XII diverted his forces away from Moscow towards the Ukraine, where he hoped to recruit the support of Mazepa, a Cossack hetman. Less than 2,000 Cossacks followed Mazepa into the Swedish camp, and Charles' hopes of Turkish assistance were disappointed. The Swedish army endured a winter of unusual severity, their privations worsened by Peter's victory over the Swedish supply column at Lesnaya in October 1708. Charles pressed on towards Poltava in the hope of finding provisions for his exhausted and depleted army, and laid siege to the town in April 1709. Peter, who had a preponderance of troops and artillery, mounted a direct attack on 27 June 1709. The battle of Poltava was a decisive victory for the Russians. Peter toasted the captive Swedish commanders with the words 'I drink to the health of those who taught me the art of winning victory'. Charles XII escaped to Turkey, where he remained until 1714.

Administrative reforms

Peter's need for reliable supplies of conscripts and revenue led him to modernize the administration, but his early reforms were improvised and poorly planned. In 1708 he created eight enormous territorial divi-

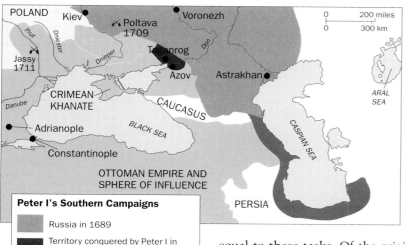

POLAND
Kiev
Poltava 1709
Voronezh
Taganrog
Jassy 1711
Azov
Astrakhan
Prut
Dniester
Dnieper
Don
CRIMEAN KHANATE
CAUCASUS
Danube
Adrianople
BLACK SEA
CASPIAN SEA
Constantinople
ARAL SEA
OTTOMAN EMPIRE AND SPHERE OF INFLUENCE
PERSIA

0   200 miles
0   300 km

Peter I's Southern Campaigns

Russia in 1689

Territory conquered by Peter I in 1696 and lost in 1711

Territory conquered by Peter I in 1723 and retained until 1732

Russian territory which came into Turkey's sphere of influence

sions (*guberny*), each with a governor responsible for policing, roads, the administration of justice, and taxation. Peter soon realized that this system was not satisfactory. The need for a body to administer Russia while he was on campaign led him to create the Senate in 1711. This committee of nine officials became a permanent replacement for the Boyar Duma. It was supposed to supervise the governors, act as the highest court in Russia and translate the tsar's ideas into detailed decrees. The Senate was not equal to these tasks. Of the original members, one was illiterate and two were later punished for corruption. A huge backlog of work accumulated. Peter understood the need to root out corruption and tax evasion, and in 1711 created a body of investigators, known as fiscals, under the control of an Oberfiscal, Alexei Nesterov, who was himself later executed for corruption.

The second Turkish War

In the aftermath of Poltava, Peter helped Augustus II to regain the Polish throne, under Russian suzerainty, and completed the conquest of Karelia and Livonia. His forces captured Riga, Vyborg and Reval in 1710. Charles XII persuaded the Turkish sultan Ahmed III to declare war on Russia in November of that year. On 7 July 1711 a Russian army commanded by the tsar found itself on the banks of the River Prut, surrounded by a much larger Turkish force. After two days of fighting the Russians were facing disaster, and Peter chose to negotiate. The Turkish terms, though harsh, were lighter than he had feared. He had to surrender Azov, Taganrog and the forts on the Dnieper, refrain from further interference in Poland, and allow Charles XII free passage back to Sweden.

The Great Northern War continued

Peter's next campaign, in Finland in 1713–14, was more successful and on 27 July 1714 the Russian fleet won an important naval victory over the Swedes off Cape Hangö. These successes aroused in the minds of other rulers fears that Russia might replace Sweden as the dominant power in the Baltic. Pressure from other powers forced Peter to withdraw his troops from Poland and, in 1717, to abandon his plan to use Mecklenburg as a base from which to attack the Swedes.

Peter's second European journey

Peter's second foreign journey took him to Copenhagen, Amsterdam, Paris and Berlin in 1717. The French court was astonished at the informality of the tsar's behaviour. When he met the seven-year-old King Louis XV, he picked the boy up and embraced him. The only diplomatic result of

The meeting between Peter I and the young Louis XV at the Hotel des Lesdiguières, Paris, on Monday 10 May 1717. Detail of an engraving by Mme L.M.J. Hersent (1784–1862). Though his courtiers were shocked when Peter picked up and embraced the young king, the seven-year-old Louis took it well.

PETER THE GREAT AT TABLE

The Duc de Saint-Simon had the opportunity to observe Peter I during the tsar's visit to France in 1717.

What he ate and drank at his two regular meals is inconceivable, without reckoning the beer, lemonade, and other drinks he swallowed between

these repasts, his suite following his example; a bottle or two of beer, as many more of wine, and occasionally, liqueurs afterwards; at the end of the meal strong drinks, such as brandy, as much sometimes as a quart. This was about the usual quantity at each meal.

The following account was written by a priest, Canon de la Naye, who dined with the tsar during his visit to Spa in 1717.

The tsar presided [at table] in a nightcap and without a cravat.... The second course consisted of a dish containing two loins of veal and four chickens. His Majesty, having noticed a chicken larger than the others, picked it up with his hand, rubbed it under his nose and, having signed to me that it was good, did me the courtesy of throwing it onto my plate.'

Peter I at a German court. An engraving by D. Chodowiecki which indicates the impression Peter's informal manners made during his visits to the West.

the journey was the Treaty of Amsterdam – a triangular friendship agreement between Peter, Louis XV and Friedrich Wilhelm I of Prussia which involved no military obligations. Peter's hope of detaching France from Sweden was not realized. He returned to St Petersburg in October 1717.

Peter and Alexei

Peter's son Alexei showed no taste for military life. Made governor of Moscow in 1708, Alexei found administration boring, preferring to read devotional literature. Peter was angered and disappointed by a son who was a pious, moody drunkard who did not share his enthusiasm for Western ideas. Alexei married Charlotte Christina of Brunswick-Wolfenbüttel in 1711. Charlotte was unhappy, and viewed with alarm the 'prince's party' of boyars and clergy who disapproved of Peter's reforms that gathered round her husband. She presented Alexei with a daughter, Natalya, in 1714, and died in October 1715 shortly after giving birth to a son, Peter Alexeyevich.

Once Peter's wife Catherine gave birth to a son, Peter Petrovich, in 1715, the succession no longer depended solely on Alexei, and relations between the two men deteriorated further, with the tsar threatening to disinherit Alexei and consign him to a monastery. Fear of the latter fate caused Alexei to flee from Russia with his mistress Afrosinia in the autumn of 1716, first to Vienna and then to Naples. In October 1717 Peter's envoys caught up with Alexei and browbeat him into returning home, where he was forced publicly to renounce the crown. Peter believed that Alexei's flight was part of a conspiracy. A new government department, the Secret Chancellery, was established to investigate the case and to root out opposition. Under pressure, Alexei named 50 people as his 'accomplices', including his mother Evdokia. Though many of those he had named were tortured, no evidence of a conspiracy emerged. Alexei was compelled to witness the execution of some of his closest friends. Evdokia was spared but sent to a remote convent.

Afrosinia, who had been imprisoned on her return to Russia, alleged that Alexei had told her that when he was tsar he intended to reverse Peter's policies. Confronted with his mistress' treachery, Alexei admitted that if

Miniature portrait of Peter I and his family by G.S. Musikiysky, painted 1716–17. Now in the Hermitage, St Petersburg. Left to right: Peter, his second wife Catherine, the Tsarevich Alexei Petrovich, the Tsarevna Anna Petrovna, the Tsarevich Peter Petrovich and the Tsarevna Elizabeth Petrovna.

there had been a rebellion against Peter, he would have joined it. After two sessions of torture, he made a fuller confession and was sentenced to death. It was then announced that he had died of a seizure on 15 June 1718. There is no evidence to support the rumour that he died at his father's hand.

Further administrative reforms

In his second period of administrative reforms, Peter adopted a more systematic approach. In 1719 the vast guberny (territorial divisions) were divided into 45 (later 50) provinces, each under the authority of a military governor. The provinces were subdivided into districts, with a land commissar in charge of each. A system of urban local government was created in 1721, with the intention of giving the more prosperous citizens control of policing and internal security. These arrangements, which were based on the Swedish model, did not work well. There were not enough educated and reliable people to operate them, and Peter had increasingly to rely on his soldiers to get things done. By 1722 it was clear that the landowners were not willing or able to collect the soul tax efficiently, and the task was handed over to the army.

In 1718 Peter transformed central government by replacing the system of overlapping departments (*prikazy*) with committees of ministers and senior officials called Colleges. Each of the nine Colleges had a specific area of responsibility and a staff of officials. These arrangements, which were modelled closely on the Swedish system, allowed the development of departmental expertise. The Preobrazhensky Prikaz, Peter's political police department, survived this reorganization. As in provincial administration, Peter's reforms were hindered by a lack of able and educated administrators. In 1721 he created a new post, Procurator General of the Senate, to take over the duties of the Oberfiscal and supervise the Colleges.

Service, education and the church

Peter believed it to be the duty of members of the nobility to serve the state. In 1714 he forced them to entail their estates to a single heir, so that other sons would have to serve in the armed forces or the administration. Traditional titles such as boyar were abandoned in favour of 'count' and 'baron'. In 1722 he issued a Table of Ranks, based on Swedish, Danish and Prussian models, which recognized three categories of service: the armed forces, the court, and the administration. Each category had 14 ranks. Those who reached the eighth rank were accorded a status equivalent to the ancient nobility.

Social status was now dependent on service, and the ladder of rank could not be climbed without education. Peter encouraged the translation into Russian of textbooks on practical subjects such as arithmetic and astronomy, and established schools of mathematics and navigation, civil engineering, surgery and mining. At the end of his reign he was planning the establishment of an Academy of Science. Education was made compulsory for members of the nobility, who from 1714 were forbidden to marry until they had acquired a certificate of elementary education.

(*Above*) A page from Istomin's *Primer*, first published in Moscow in 1694. Charion or Karion Istomin (late 1640s–1717) was a poet, educator, encyclopaedist and monk who worked at the Printing Office in Moscow from 1672. His innovative *Primer* was presented to the Tsaritsa Natalya Kirillovna, mother of Peter I. Each page features a different letter of the alphabet. Istomin included Greek letters as well as Russian, as in this page, devoted to the Greek letter *psi*.

Within a few decades they had embraced Western culture to the extent that French became the spoken and written language of Russia's elite.

The tsar believed that the church should be controlled by and serve the needs of the state. When Patriarch Adrian died in 1700, Peter did not appoint a replacement. The patriarch's lands were placed under the control of the Monastery Department, and their revenues were appropriated by the state. Over the next 20 years the church, whose taxational privileges had been abolished in 1699–1700, was subjected to increasing state control. In 1716 bishops were required to take an oath of obedience to the tsar. Peter promoted churchmen, such as Feofan Prokopovich, archbishop of Novgorod, who preached the absolute authority of the tsar. In 1721 Peter abolished the patriarchate and placed the church under the control of the Holy Synod, a body subject to the right of veto of the Chief Procurator, a lay official appointed by the tsar. Peter's attitude to the Old Believers was relatively tolerant. They were forced to pay double taxes, but were not persecuted. This treatment failed to win them over. Together with many of the Orthodox faithful, the Old Believers were convinced that Peter was the antichrist, partly because he tolerated Lutheran and Catholic worship.

Peter's reforms introduced dangerous contradictions into the Russian polity and society. The church, as the partner of the monarchy, had enthusiastically disseminated the belief that the tsar was God's chosen ruler and that obedience to him was a religious obligation. Peter turned the church into a department of state which his successors exploited, under-funded and neglected, thus undermining the church's ability to legitimate their rule. The educated elite which emerged in Russia as a result of Peter's reforms came to regard the state-controlled church and its teachings with scepticism or contempt. Scepticism about religion led naturally to scepticism about the theological underpinnings of tsarist rule.

The Great Northern War concluded

Peace negotiations between Russia and Sweden began in 1718, but were cut short when Charles XII was killed in action in Norway later that year. Sweden's new ruler Ulrika Eleonora decided to continue the war, hoping for the emergence of an anti-Russian coalition among the European powers. This did not occur and the British, whose navy was unable to prevent Russian galleys from raiding the Swedish coast, persuaded the Swedes to resume negotiations with the Russians. Agreement was reached at Nystad on 30 August (10 September NS) 1721. The treaty allowed Russia to keep most of her territorial gains, though Peter agreed to return the Aaland Islands and most of Finland. Russia now had a Baltic coastline stretching from Riga to Vyborg. Peter celebrated this triumph by assuming the titles 'Peter the Great, father of his country, Emperor of all Russia' in October 1721. The presence, by 1725, of more than 20 permanent diplomatic missions in European capitals demonstrated Peter's determination that Russia should be a respected member of the international community.

IMPERIAL TITLES

In October 1721 the Senate conferred on Peter I the titles 'Emperor and Autocrat of All Russia'. The latter part of the phrase was subtly different from that used by Peter's predecessors, 'of All the Russias', a description which had embodied the tsars' claim to rule all the territories of the former Kievan Rus. The old phrase continued to be used after Peter's time, particularly by foreign writers.

Peter's full titles were, from 1721 onwards: 'Peter I, by the Grace of God Emperor and Autocrat of All Russia, of Moscow, Kiev, Vladimir, and Novgorod; Tsar of Kazan, Tsar of Astrakhan, Tsar of Siberia, Sovereign of Pskov, and Grand Prince of Smolensk; Prince of Estonia, Livonia, Karelia, Tver, Ugra, Perm, Viatka, Bulgaria, and of other principalities; Sovereign and Grand Duke of Nizhny Novgorod, Chernigov, Riazan, Rostov, Yaroslavl, Beloozero, Udoria, Obdoria, Kondia, and Overlord of all the Northern Land; Sovereign of Iveria, and of the Kartalinian and Georgian Tsars; and hereditary Sovereign and Suzerain of Kabardinia and of the Circassian and Mountain Princes.'

Peter's successors altered the titles to include Grand Duke of Finland (1809) and Tsar of Poland (1815).

Peter I on his deathbed. Some authorities have attributed this drawing, now in the Hermitage in St Petersburg, to Gottfried Danhauer, though it is generally believed to be the work of Ivan Nikitin (c. 1690–1740).

Peter's Asian policies

Peter annexed Kamchatka and the Kurile Islands, and at the end of his reign commissioned the Danish explorer Vitus Bering to discover whether there was a land bridge between Siberia and North America. His hopes of increasing Russia's trade with China were disappointed. The embassies that he sent to Peking in 1692 and 1719 secured no concessions from the Chinese. His attempt to establish a protectorate over the khanates of Khiva and Bokhara also failed. His campaigns against Persia in 1722 and 1723 gained Russia a precarious foothold along the western shores of the Caspian Sea.

Personal relationships

The death in 1719 of Peter Petrovich, the only surviving legitimate son of the tsar, created a dynastic problem. Peter was reluctant to leave the crown to Peter Alexeyevich, the son of Alexei. He may have considered repudiating Catherine, whose looks had been ruined by heavy drinking, and marrying his latest mistress, Maria Cantemir, in order to beget a male heir. Yet he remained loyal to Catherine and, in May 1724, crowned her as empress.

In the 1720s Peter began to turn on his closest associates. Menshikov, whose corruption had frequently been forgiven, was arraigned before an investigatory commission in 1723, and was still under suspicion at the time of Peter's death. Vice Chancellor Shafirov was found guilty of embezzlement in the same year and exiled. Even Catherine, who had been having an affair with William Mons, the brother of Peter's former mistress, was in danger. In November 1724 Mons was executed, and it is likely that Peter's death spared her further punishment.

The death of Peter

Peter was now suffering from back pains, abscesses and a urinary tract infection, problems which did not prevent him from wading into the sea to rescue some fishermen whose boat was in danger of capsizing. The fever which he subsequently contracted weakened him further, and in January 1725 he underwent an operation to remove kidney stones. Gangrene set in and he died early on 28 January 1725. Although he had decreed in 1722 that henceforward Russia's emperors would designate their successors, he died without having named an heir.

Unable to defeat both Turkey and Sweden, Peter had wisely chosen to concentrate on the weaker opponent, and his breakthrough to the Baltic established Russia as a European power. His territorial acquisitions and military reforms laid the foundations for future imperial expansion. Many of his administrative reforms proved durable, though some of the institutions that he created were modified or abolished by his successors. His heavy reliance on the army as an organ of government did not survive the reign of Catherine II. In essence the state remained a mechanism for raising, financing and controlling the armed forces. Peter had made that mechanism more elaborate, more specialized and more efficient.

Catherine I
1725–1727

Peter II
1727–1730

Anna
1730–1740

Ivan VI
1740–1741

Elizabeth
1741–1761
(died 25 Dec 1761 Old Style,
5 Jan 1762 New Style)

Peter III
1761–1762

Catherine II
('The Great')
1762–1796

Paul
1796–1801

Alexander I
1801–1825

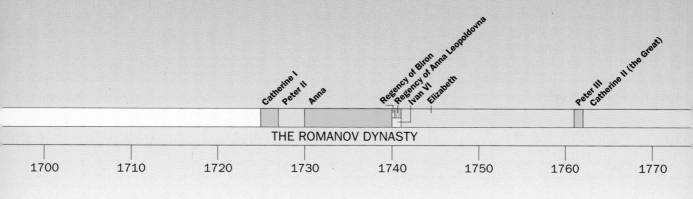

THE ROMANOV DYNASTY

1700   1710   1720   1730   1740   1750   1760   1770

Elizabeth

Catherine II

Paul

Alexander I

THE ZENITH OF TSARISM

In the period from 1725 to 1762 the succession to the Russian throne was determined by the Guards and power rested in the hands of aristocratic factions and court favourites. Yet the reigns of Catherine I, Anna and Elizabeth were not merely an era of frivolity and stagnation. The development of court culture strengthened the prestige of the monarchy and Russia experienced economic progress and an enhancement of her influence in Europe. Catherine the Great, who also owed her power to the Guards and who was notorious for her favourites, was the first ruler since Peter I to strengthen the institutions of government. This success, together with her enlargement of the empire, left Russia capable of withstanding the French invasion in the reign of her grandson, Alexander I.

The leading role that Russia played in the defeat of Napoleon demonstrated her pre-eminence as a European power. Alexander was unable and unwilling to exclude Western European ideas which encouraged Russia's elite to question the status quo. Catherine the Great and Alexander both recognized that serfdom was impeding economic development, but neither was willing to risk its abolition. They dared not alienate the serf-owning nobility, whose privileges Catherine had strengthened, and they lacked the administrative structures that would be needed to control an emancipated peasant population.

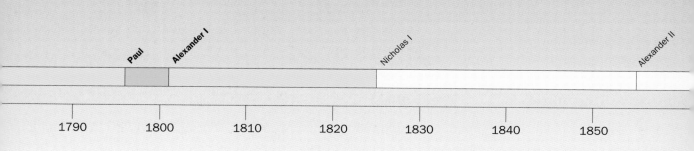

Paul · Alexander I · Nicholas I · Alexander II

1790 1800 1810 1820 1830 1840 1850

Екатерина I **Catherine I**
1725–1727

Петр II **Peter II**
1727–1730

Анна **Anna**
1730–1740

Catherine I by Jean-Marc Nattier (1685–1766), a noted French portraitist. This was a flattering likeness, painted in 1717. Hard drinking and a stressful private life had taken further toll of Catherine's looks by the time of her accession in 1725.

CATHERINE I	
Full name	*Husband*
Marfa	1712* **Peter I**
Skavronskaya	Died 1725
Father	*They were secretly
Samuel	married in 1707
Skavronsky	*Children*
Mother	Paul (1704)
Dorothea Hahn	Peter (1705)
Born	Catherine (1707)
Ringen, near	Anna (1708)
Dorpat	**Elizabeth** (1709)
5 April 1684	Natalya (1713)
Accession	Margarita (1714)
28 January 1725	Peter (1715)
Died	Paul (1717)
St Petersburg	Natalya (1718)
6 May 1727	Peter (1723)
A fever	Paul (1724)

CATHERINE I

The Tsaritsa was short and stocky with a very swarthy complexion, having no distinction or grace. One had only to look at her to tell that she was low born.... She had a dozen orders and relics sewn all along the facings of her dress, so that when she walked you would have thought you heard a mule jingling.

The Margravine of Bayreuth *Memoirs*

During Peter I's final illness, the court was divided on the succession issue. Some, mainly members of leading boyar families, backed the claims of the emperor's grandson, Peter Alexeyevich. Others, whose careers had been advanced by Peter, saw the succession of the Empress Catherine as a means of preserving their own power. The support of Menshikov, colonel of the Preobrazhensky Guards, and of other senior officers strengthened Catherine's cause. On the night of 27–28 January, members of her faction toured the barracks making sure of the officers' loyalty. Immediately after Peter's death, Catherine placed the question of the succession in the hands of the Senate. Her opponents, including the Dolgorukys, were silenced when the building was invaded by Guards

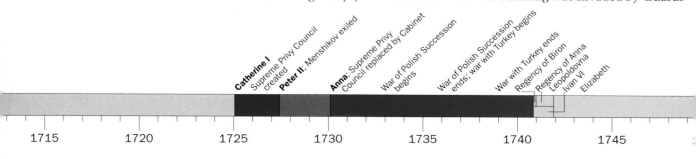

Catherine I; Supreme Privy Council created

Peter II; Menshikov exiled

Anna; Supreme Privy Council replaced by Cabinet

War of Polish Succession begins

War of Polish Succession ends; war with Turkey begins

War with Turkey ends

Regency of Biron

Regency of Anna Leopoldovna

Ivan VI

Elizabeth

1715   1720   1725   1730   1735   1740   1745

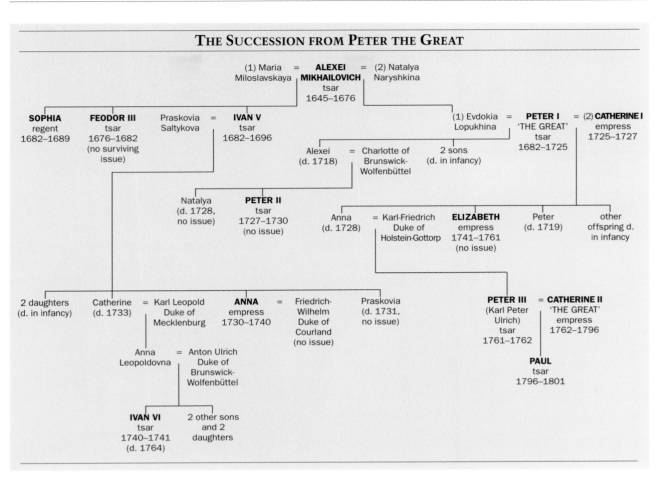

THE SUCCESSION FROM PETER THE GREAT

(1) Maria Miloslavskaya = **ALEXEI MIKHAILOVICH** tsar 1645–1676 = (2) Natalya Naryshkina

SOPHIA regent 1682–1689

FEODOR III tsar 1676–1682 (no surviving issue)

Praskovia Saltykova = **IVAN V** tsar 1682–1696

Alexei (d. 1718) = Charlotte of Brunswick-Wolfenbüttel

2 sons (d. in infancy)

(1) Evdokia Lopukhina = **PETER I** 'THE GREAT' tsar 1682–1725 = (2) **CATHERINE I** empress 1725–1727

Natalya (d. 1728, no issue)

PETER II tsar 1727–1730 (no issue)

Anna (d. 1728) = Karl-Friedrich Duke of Holstein-Gottorp

ELIZABETH empress 1741–1761 (no issue)

Peter (d. 1719)

other offspring d. in infancy

2 daughters (d. in infancy)

Catherine (d. 1733) = Karl Leopold Duke of Mecklenburg

ANNA empress 1730–1740 = Friedrich-Wilhelm Duke of Courland (no issue)

Praskovia (d. 1731, no issue)

PETER III (Karl Peter Ulrich) tsar 1761–1762 = **CATHERINE II** 'THE GREAT' empress 1762–1796

Anna Leopoldovna = Anton Ulrich Duke of Brunswick-Wolfenbüttel

PAUL tsar 1796–1801

IVAN VI tsar 1740–1741 (d. 1764)

2 other sons and 2 daughters

Elizabeth and Anna, daughters of Peter I, in a portrait by Louis Caravaque (1684–1754).

officers. The stout, semi-literate former maidservant was acclaimed as ruler of Russia.

Catherine devoted herself mainly to the pleasures of the table and the bedroom and to indulging her desire for revenge. Evdokia, Peter's first wife, was transferred from her convent to a verminous cell in the Schlüsselburg fortress. Though the Senate had endorsed Catherine's claim to the throne, real power soon lay with the Supreme Privy Council, created in February 1726, and dominated by Menshikov. The office of Procurator General was abolished, as were a number of departments set up by Peter. In the main the Supreme Privy Council continued Peter's policies, though the soul tax was reduced in response to the continuing exodus of peasants from central Russia. Anna, the daughter of Peter the Great, was married to Karl-Friedrich, Duke of Holstein-Gottorp in 1725, and the Russians signed an alliance with Austria in 1726.

The empress wished to designate her daughter Elizabeth as her heir, though public opinion favoured Peter Alexeyevich. The possibility that Peter might eventually marry Elizabeth was discussed, but Menshikov persuaded the ailing Catherine to choose his daughter Maria as Peter's bride. Catherine died on 6 May 1727 of a fever.

PETER II	
Full name	*Accession*
Peter Alexeyevich	6 May 1727
Romanov	*Died*
Father	Moscow
Alexei Petrovich	18 January 1730
Romanov	Smallpox
Mother	*Unmarried*
Charlotte of	Betrothed to
Brunswick-	Catherine
Wolfenbüttel	Alexeyevna
Born	Dolgorukaya
St Petersburg	No issue
12 October 1715	

PETER II

The Emperor is rarely seen, has no drawing room, and seems fond of nothing but hunting. His great favourite, Prince Dolghorucki, keeps him employed in this sport, for fear of being supplanted.... He is very tall, and large-made, for his age, being just turned fifteen; he is fair, but much tanned with hunting, has good features, but a down look, and though he is young and handsome, has nothing attractive nor agreeable.

Mrs Vigor, an English woman resident in St Petersburg

Peter II (1727–1730) ascended the throne at the age of 11. One of his first acts was to release his grandmother, Evdokia, from prison. Menshikov's announcement of the betrothal of his daughter Maria to the emperor deepened the opposition to his rule. An aristocratic faction headed by the Dolgorukys persuaded Peter, who did not relish the prospect of marrying Maria, to exile Menshikov and his family to Siberia in 1727. He died there in 1729.

The fall of Menshikov has been depicted by some historians as the triumph of a conservative, anti-Petrine faction. Although the court was transferred back to Moscow, which once more became the capital, and spending on the navy was reduced, the Supreme Privy Council still included important members of the Petrine administration such as Prince Dmitry Golitsyn and Andrei Osterman. The Dolgoruky faction persuaded Peter II to betroth himself to Catherine, daughter of Alexei Dolgoruky, but in January 1730 Peter died of smallpox on the day appointed for his wedding.

(*Below*) Berezovo in western Siberia, the place of exile of Prince Menshikov, who died there in October 1729. An 18th-century engraving.

(*Above*) Peter II. An engraving by Wortmann. Peter was born in 1715 to the ill-fated Tsarevich Alexei Petrovich and Charlotte of Brunswick-Wolfenbüttel. His mother died shortly after his birth, and his father in 1718. The boy's education was supervised by Menshikov, whom he disliked. He developed a taste for hunting, billiards and dancing.

ANNA	
Full name	*Died*
Anna Ivanovna	St Petersburg
Romanova	17 October 1740
Father	Kidney failure
Ivan V	*Husband*
Mother	1710 Friedrich-
Praskovia Saltykova	Wilhelm, Duke of
Born	Courland
Moscow	Died 1711
28 January 1693	*Children*
Accession	None
25 February 1730	

The Empress Anna. An engraving by Wagner from the portrait by G. Amiconi. Mrs Vigor, who spent a good deal of time in the empress' company, wrote: 'Were I speaking of a private person I should say she has rather strong good sense than wit, though she has a way of saying a short satirical sentence some times that is truly witty, but always tempered with such good nature that it never shocks. She has a fine voice and speaks very distinctly.'

ANNA

...a very large made woman, very well shaped for her size and easy and graceful in her person. She has a brown complexion, black hair, dark and blue eyes; she has an awfulness in her countenance that strikes you at first sight, but when she speaks, she has a smile about her mouth that is inexpressibly sweet.

Mrs Vigor, an English woman resident in St Petersburg

Peter II died without designating an heir. The Supreme Privy Council, dominated by the Golitsyns and Dolgorukys, passed over Peter I's surviving daughter Elizabeth and his grandson Karl Peter Ulrich on the grounds that both Elizabeth and Anna, the mother of Karl Peter Ulrich, had been born out of wedlock. The Council then turned to the descendants of Ivan V. Catherine, his elder surviving daughter, was unacceptable because of her unreliable husband, the Duke of Mecklenburg. Her sister Anna, the widow of Friedrich-Wilhelm Duke of Courland, was believed to be politically pliable. After the briefest of marriages (the Duke had succumbed to a stroke during their wedding journey) she had taken up residence in Courland, consoling herself first with Count Bestuzhev, her High Chamberlain, and later with Ernst Johann Biron or Bühren, a member of a German gentry family in Courland whose wife, Benigna, was one of her ladies in waiting.

The Supreme Privy Council offered Anna the throne on certain conditions. She might neither remarry nor nominate a successor and the Council must continue to run the affairs of the government. Other nobles did not see why the clique which had dominated the previous reign should retain power, and submitted alternative proposals. After her arrival in Moscow Anna was kept informed of these tensions by Andrei Osterman, who had served Peter I as Vice President of the College of Foreign Affairs, and who was determined to thwart the Golitsyns and the Dolgorukys. On 25 February 1730 she signed the conditions and then, responding to a petition from 150 noblemen, tore up the document and announced her intention of ruling autocratically. Several of the Dolgorukys were exiled or executed. Dmitry Golitsyn was eventually sentenced to life imprisonment.

Many historians have characterized Anna's reign (1730–1740) as the Bironovshchina (Biron era), a period of repressive and rapacious government, dominated by Germans. The 19th-century historian Kliuchevsky wrote that '...the Germans littered Russia like dust from a sack with holes in it, infested the court, clustered around the throne, and grabbed all the lucrative jobs in the administration.' Recent Russian scholarship has shown that the percentage of foreign generals in the Russian army actually fell during the reign. There was no 'German Party'; indeed there were bitter rivalries between the Germans who were prominent at court. Although Biron was Anna's lover and High Chamberlain, he made little effort to learn Russian or to grapple with government business. The repressive policies of the regime were supervised by Russians, and the objectives of foreign policy were much the same as in the reign of Peter I. The notion of the Bironovshchina originated in the early years of the reign of Elizabeth (1741–1761), who sought to justify her coup d'état by blackening the memory of her predecessors.

Anna herself took little interest in matters of state. Though the Supreme Privy Council was abolished, the government remained oligarchic, with the Cabinet, informally established at the beginning of the reign, being officially recognized as the main state institution in 1735. From 1732 St Petersburg was once again the capital.

Terror and reforms

The terror which has made the reign notorious had several causes. The childless Anna came to fear that she might be ousted by Elizabeth, the sole surviving offspring of Peter I. Peter's hopes of a dynastic marriage for Elizabeth had been thwarted by the fact that she had been born out of wedlock in 1709. Elizabeth remained unmarried, though by 1732 she was passionately attached to Alexei Razumovsky, a handsome chorister of the Imperial Chapel. She developed a circle of friends which included the Shuvalovs and the Vorontsovs, and became a natural rallying point for those who were discontented with Anna's regime. She also cultivated the support of influential army officers, and earned the nickname 'the Godmother of the Guards'.

Conspirators, real or alleged, were harshly treated by Anna and her advisers. The early years of the reign were marked by crop failures and epidemics which led to a decline in tax revenues. Local officials, threatened with confiscation of property if they did not collect the arrears of tax, adopted brutal methods to extract payment. It has been estimated that between 20,000 and 30,000 people were exiled to Siberia in the period 1730–40.

The reign was not without constructive reforms. The navy, neglected since the death of Peter I, was rehabilitated. Fire brigades were established in Moscow and St Petersburg in 1736, and a postal service was created in 1740. From 1731 noblemen were once again allowed to divide their estates among their offspring, and in 1736 it was decreed that one son from each noble family would be exempted from state service to manage the estates. Nobles who gave good service were permitted to retire after 25 years. The Imperial Corps of Cadets, founded in 1732, provided a broad education for young noblemen. The regime took steps to encourage economic growth. Some state peasants were assigned to work in factories, and a trade treaty was signed with Great Britain in 1734.

Foreign policy

Foreign policy was dominated by Osterman, who maintained good relations with Austria. In the War of the Polish Succession (1733–36), which began with the death of Augustus II of Poland, the Russians drove out Stanislaus Leszczyński, the choice of the majority of the electors,

Anna's garden carriage. There is a portrait of the empress painted on its panelling.

and installed Augustus III of Saxony as king. France was drawn into the war, since Stanislaus Leszczyński was the father-in-law of Louis XV, and Russian forces campaigned with the Austrians against the French in the Rhineland. A costly war with Turkey which began in 1736 saw some victories, including the recapture of Azov, but the Peace of Belgrade (1739) resulted in only limited territorial gains. In order to secure Persian support in this war, Russia agreed to withdraw from the Caspian territories conquered by Peter I. By 1740 the Russians had established a nominal suzerainty over the Kazakh tribes in Central Asia.

Cultural patronage

Anna's patronage of the arts was somewhat selective. She recruited the first permanent imperial theatre troupe, a distinguished group of Italian performers which included the mother of Casanova, and gave Jean-Baptise Landé permission to found the first ballet school in Russia. The architectural splendours of the reign proved to be ephemeral. Rastrelli's timber Annenhof Palace in Moscow was demolished by Catherine II, and Yeropkin's Ice Palace melted. Anna's personal tastes were a mixture of the simple and the extravagant. She disliked drunkenness and elaborate cuisine, yet encouraged gambling at court. She loved hunting, and elaborate ice slides were constructed for her amusement. Like Peter I, she kept an entourage of dwarfs, treating them with alternate brutality and kindness. The talented Neapolitan violinist Pietro Mira, known as Pedrillo, became the empress' favourite jester. He was once blown backwards into a fountain when Anna fired a charge of birdshot at him, but then consoled by a gift of 500 roubles.

The succession

Biron, who was made Duke of Courland in 1737, hoped to consolidate his position by marrying his son to Anna's niece, Anna Leopoldovna. In 1731 the empress had ruled that the succession would pass to any children that Anna Leopoldovna might have. She chose Anton Ulrich, Duke of Brunswick-Wolfenbüttel, as a consort for her niece and they were married in 1739. The empress, whose health was now failing, hoped to be able to pass the crown to a descendant of Ivan V and was delighted when Anna Leopoldovna gave birth to a son, Ivan, in August 1740. She immediately designated the infant as her heir and Biron as regent. Elizabeth was compelled to swear an oath of allegiance to Ivan. Anna Leopoldovna, who had herself hoped to succeed her aunt, was bitterly disappointed. The empress, who had been diagnosed as suffering from an ulcer of the kidneys, died on 17 October 1740 at the age of 47.

THE ICE PALACE

The principal butt of the Empress Anna's cruel sense of humour, Prince Mikhail Alexeyevich Golitsyn, was made to do public imitations of a hen laying eggs as a punishment for marrying an Italian woman and converting to Roman Catholicism. When his wife died Anna forced Golitsyn to marry one of her Kalmyk serving women. They were ordered to pass their wedding night in an elaborate Ice Palace constructed on the frozen River Neva in the harsh winter of 1739–40, and Anna arranged for them to be conveyed there in a cage mounted on the back of an elephant.

The palace, built in the Palladian style, cost 30,000 roubles. It had a façade decorated with ice statues, a garden of trees and shrubs carved from ice, and an ice bath house. Inside, the furniture and fittings were all made of ice. The architect, Peter Yeropkin, was the head of the Commission for the Orderly Development of St Petersburg which Anna established when the city was seriously damaged by fire in 1737. Yeropkin was beheaded in 1740 for his alleged involvement in a conspiracy against the empress.

Иван VI **Ivan VI**
1740–1741

Елизавета **Elizabeth**
1741–1761*

The Empress Elizabeth. An English
engraving of 1761 from the portrait
painted by Count Pietro Rotari
(1707–62).

*Elizabeth died 25 December 1761 Old Style, 5 January 1762 New Style

IVAN VI	
Full name	*Accession*
Ivan Antonovich of	17 October 1740
Brunswick-	*Deposition*
Wolfenbüttel	25 November 1741
Father	*Died*
Anton Ulrich,	Schlüsselburg
Duke of Brunswick-	Fortress
Wolfenbüttel	5 July 1764
Mother	Stabbed to death by
Anna Leopoldovna	his gaolers
of Mecklenburg-	*Unmarried*
Schwerin	No issue
Born	
St Petersburg	
12 August 1740	

IVAN VI

Ivan VI inherited the throne in October 1740 at just under two months
old. Biron, who had been designated as regent by the Empress Anna, was
overthrown in November 1740 in a coup led by his rival Münnich and
exiled to Siberia. Ivan's mother, Anna Leopoldovna, became regent. She
had little interest in affairs of state, and her strong attachment to her
maid of honour Julia Mengden gave rise to scandal.

At first the government was dominated by Münnich, but he resigned
in March 1741 because he felt that the division of responsibilities within
the Cabinet had reduced his power. The Cabinet attempted to speed up
the handling of petitions and to construct an overall budget. Complaints
about the poor quality of army uniforms led to the imposition of controls
on the textile industry, including a maximum working day of 15 hours
and a minimum wage of 15 roubles a year.

Osterman repeatedly warned Anna Leopoldovna that the Swedish and
French ambassadors were encouraging Elizabeth to plot against her. In
November 1741, when Anna confronted her about this, Elizabeth pleaded
her innocence. Though the two women were reconciled, Elizabeth knew

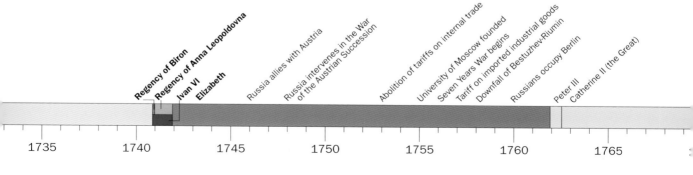

Ivan VI as a baby. The fate of the infant proved very different from that prefigured in this allegorical engraving by I. Leopold, published in Germany in 1741. The deposed emperor spent most of his short life in solitary confinement. It is believed that Catherine II visited 'Nameless Prisoner Number 1', as Ivan was officially known, shortly after she seized power in 1762. In the small hours of 5 July 1764 a disaffected Ukrainian army officer named Mirovich attempted to liberate Ivan, who was immediately stabbed to death in his cell in the Schlüsselburg fortress by his gaolers Vlasov and Chekin. Both Elizabeth and Catherine had ordered that Ivan must murdered in the event of any attempt to release him.

that the Guards units which included her principal supporters had been ordered to leave the capital. Fear that she might be forced to become a nun, a way of life for which she was singularly ill-suited, spurred her into action. In the small hours of 25 November 1741, she led units of the Preobrazhensky Guards to arrest the regent.

Elizabeth promised to allow Anna Leopoldovna, her husband Anton Ulrich and their children to travel to Germany, but detained them in custody until 1744, when she ordered that they be moved to Russia's remote north. Anna Leopoldovna died in childbirth at Kholmogori in 1746. The former Ivan VI was separated from his family and grew up in solitary confinement. Elizabeth gave orders that he was to be killed if any attempt was made to rescue him, and in 1756 had him transferred to the Schlüsselburg fortress. Catherine II subsequently confirmed these orders, and Ivan was stabbed to death by his gaolers in 1764, when a disgruntled army officer attempted to release him. His family remained under house arrest at Kholmogori. Anton Ulrich died there in 1774. In 1780 Catherine II allowed the surviving children to travel to Denmark, where they lived as her pensioners.

ELIZABETH

The Princess Elizabeth is very handsome. She is very fair with light brown hair, large sprightly blue eyes, fine teeth and a pretty mouth. She is inclinable to fat but is very genteel and dances better than anyone I ever saw…. In public she has an unaffected gaiety, and a certain air of giddiness, that seem entirely to possess her whole mind; but in private I have heard her talk in such a strain of good sense and steady reasoning, that I am persuaded the other behaviour is a feint.

Mrs Vigor, an English woman resident in St Petersburg

The Empress Elizabeth had keen natural intelligence, was of a gay disposition, and indulged in excessive pleasures. I think she was kind at heart; she had great high-mindedness and much vanity; she wanted to shine and was fond of admiration. I believe that the beauty of her body and her natural laziness did much damage to her character.

Catherine the Great *Memoirs*

ELIZABETH	
Full name	25 December 1761
Elizabeth Petrovna	(5 January 1762 NS)
Romanova	Stroke
Father	*Marriage*
Peter I	She is said to have
Mother	married Alexei
Catherine I	Razumovsky in
Born	1742. There is no
Kolomenskoe	reliable evidence of
18 December 1709	this, or of any
Accession	children.
25 November 1741	
Died	
St Petersburg	

For many historians Elizabeth's reign has epitomized the corruption of an imperial court whose luxuries depended on the exploitation of millions of serfs. It was also a period of economic growth and cultural progress. The empress understood the extent to which her interests coincided with those of the nobility, whose privileges were strengthened, though not at the expense of the autocracy. Her chief pleasures were dancing, music, the fine arts, and feasting. A confirmed insomniac, she employed ladies-in-waiting to tickle her feet while she lay in bed waiting for her current lover. This frivolous hedonism was coupled with regular attendance at divine worship and frequent pilgrimages.

THE HISTORIAN KARAMZIN ON ELIZABETH

...she re-established the authority of the Senate, she abolished the death penalty, had good-natured lovers, a passion for merrymaking and tender poems. Though she was of a humane disposition, Elizabeth intervened in a war which was as bloody as it was useless for Russia. The foremost statesman of her time was Chancellor Bestuzhev, a man endowed with wisdom and energy, but avaricious and partial. Soothed by indolence, the Queen gave him freedom to traffic in the politics and forces of the realm. At last she had him removed, and then she committed a new blunder by solemnly announcing to the people that this minister, who had personified her whole reign, was the most infamous of mortals!

Portrait of Ivan Ivanovich Shuvalov (1727–97) painted during the 1760s by de Veilly. Shuvalov held no formal state offices, yet exercised a degree of influence over Elizabeth which caused Voltaire to describe him as 'the Pompadour of Russia'.

Kliuchevsky characterized her as 'a clever and kind but disordered and wilful madam'.

The new regime

The view that Elizabeth's coup of 25 November 1741 was solely the work of an aristocratic faction has recently been challenged. Most of the Guardsmen involved were non-noble. They resented the excessive influence of foreigners at court, and revered the memory of Peter I. Elizabeth sought to legitimate her rule by emphasizing that she was Peter's daughter and intended to govern in accordance with his principles. Propaganda glorified Peter's memory and denigrated the reign of Anna and the regency. The Cabinet of ministers was abolished, and the powers of the Senate were restored.

Although Osterman and Münnich were exiled, there was no general purge of foreigners. The empress was careful to remain on good terms with the Orthodox church, which had endorsed her coup, and pursued a punitive policy against the Schismatics. Yet at her coronation in Moscow in 1742 she took the crown from the archbishop of Novgorod and placed it on her own head, a ritual assertion of the subordination of the church to the autocracy. The administration of church lands was handed back to the Holy Synod, but Elizabeth came to regret this decision and in 1756 the lands were returned to lay control.

Succession and government

Elizabeth moved swiftly to settle the succession question. Ivan VI and his family were kept in custody and eventually sent to the arctic north of Russia. Evidence of their existence, including coinage, portraits and legal documents, was destroyed. Another potential rival, her nephew Karl Peter Ulrich of Holstein-Gottorp, was neutralized by summoning him to Russia and designating him as her heir in 1742. Elizabeth arranged a marriage in 1745 between Peter and Sophia Augusta Fredericka of Anhalt-Zerbst, who was received into the Orthodox faith under the name Catherine. The couple's failure to produce offspring caused the empress considerable anxiety. It was not until 1754 that Catherine gave birth to a son, Paul.

Although the empress took some interest in government, routine decision-making remained in the hands of senior officials. She preserved her authority by never committing herself fully to any faction. Razumovsky, whom she may have secretly married in 1742, had no political ambitions. In the 1740s Alexei Petrovich Bestuzhev-Riumin, a man whom she disliked but whose abilities she valued, was the most important of her officials. The dominant figures of the second half of the reign were members of the Vorontsov and Shuvalov families. Ivan Ivanovich Shuvalov, was, as Elizabeth's principal favourite after 1749, a man of considerable influence, but his cousins Alexander and Peter exercised more power. There is no evidence to support the rumours that Elizabeth had children by any of her lovers.

Frederick the Great of Prussia. A Wedgwood cameo portrait dating from the late 18th century.

Equestrian portrait of Elizabeth by Georg Christoph Grooth (1716–49). This painting of 1743 shows Elizabeth as a fit young woman, riding astride.

The War of the Austrian Succession

The empress took an active interest in foreign policy. Bestuzhev-Riumin opposed the francophile faction, led by her physician Armand Lestocq, which surrounded Elizabeth. He favoured maintaining good relations and trading links with Great Britain and believed in an alliance with Austria, since both powers had reason to fear the Turks. A strong Saxony was important to Russia since the Elector of Saxony was also King of Poland.

Elizabeth prosecuted the war against Sweden, which had broken out in the summer of 1741, to a successful conclusion, obtaining part of south-eastern Finland under the terms of the Treaty of Åbo of 1743. The War of the Austrian Succession had begun in 1740 when Frederick II of Prussia invaded Silesia. His expansionist ambitions posed a new threat to Russia's interests in central Europe. France, Spain and Bavaria sought to take advantage of the situation by attacking the Habsburg empire in 1741, and Britain sided with the Austrians. The main parties to the conflict sought by means of bribery and intrigue to secure Russian support. Bestuzhev-Riumin persuaded Elizabeth to renew the Russian Treaty of Friendship with Britain in December 1742. He then outmanoeuvred the French faction and was appointed Chancellor of the College of Foreign Affairs in 1744. Elizabeth, who was reluctant to involve Russia in the war, fearing the human and financial costs, maintained a balance by conferring the Vice-Chancellorship on a francophile, Mikhail Vorontsov.

In 1746 Russia negotiated an alliance with Austria, which secretly committed both countries to common action against Turkey and Prussia. Bestuzhev-Riumin's triumph seemed complete when, in 1747, he secured the downfall of Lestocq, who had been conspiring with the Prussians to place Catherine on the throne. No evidence implicating Catherine in the plot was discovered. Russia finally entered the war when Britain promised to pay her a subsidy. In 1748 a Russian army marched westwards to the Rhine, an unprecedented projection of Russian power which prompted the French to make peace in October of that year. Russia was excluded from the peace talks because her troops had played no part in the fighting, and the British refused to pay the subsidy. This outcome weakened Bestuzhev-Riumin's position.

Court life and culture

Elizabeth was determined that her court should rival Versailles as a centre of culture and fashion.

Mikhail Vasilievich Lomonosov
(1711–65). An engraved portrait.
Lomonosov was a chemist and an
astronomer, and made a significant
contribution to Russian literature.

(*Right*) The Smolny Convent,
St Petersburg, founded by the Empress
Elizabeth in 1748. The name Smolny,
derived from the Russian word for tar,
reflects the fact that the site on which
the convent was built had been used for
tar processing in the reign of Peter I. The
cathedral at its heart was designed by
Bartolommeo Francesco Rastrelli
(1700–71), though his plans were
modified by later architects.

(*Below*) The Boat House in the Peter and
Paul Fortress in St Petersburg, built in
1761 to house the wooden boat in which
Peter the Great learned to sail (p. 92).

She herself decided what was fashionable, punishing any woman who
outdid her in dress or appearance. After her death, Peter III discovered a
closet in the Summer Palace containing 15,000 dresses. Her 'Metamor-
phoses', or transvestite masquerades, were loathed by courtiers and
diplomats, who had to turn out in ball gowns and pay their respects to an
empress dressed as a Dutch sailor. Elizabeth was an influential patron of
the arts, and supported her ministers in their attempts to improve
Russian education. During her reign the scientist and talented polymath
Mikhail Vasilievich Lomonosov (1711–65) reorganized the Academy of
Sciences and founded the University of Moscow in 1755, a project in
which he was supported by Ivan Shuvalov, who also played an important
part in the establishment of the Academy of Fine Arts in 1757. Opera,
ballet and the theatre flourished. The empress, an important patron of
jewellers, painters and craftsmen, was eager to encourage Russian artists.
The baroque style of architecture which she favoured became a means of
demonstrating the power of the autocracy.

Domestic policies

The finances of the state were in a parlous condition in 1741, with 5 million roubles of tax arrears. The salaries of civil servants and officers were reduced as an economy measure, and a census, instituted in 1744, added an extra 1.3 million people to the roll of taxpayers. In the 1750s Peter Shuvalov sought to shift the burden of taxation from the inefficient soul tax to indirect taxes. Increased tariffs on exports and imports, and a new duty on imported industrial goods imposed in 1757, helped to enhance the revenue and to stimulate domestic manufacturing, and the abolition of internal tariffs in 1753 promoted trade. Banks were established to provide loans to nobles to develop their estates. The textile and metallurgical industries boomed, and by the end of the reign Russia's output of pig iron exceeded that of Great Britain.

The wealth generated by these economic developments was concentrated in the hands of the serf-owning nobility, who enjoyed important industrial and trading monopolies. The institution of serfdom was

SERFDOM IN THE REIGN OF ELIZABETH

The draft Legal Code prepared in the reign of Elizabeth but never promulgated, included the following definition of serfdom:

The nobility possesses full authority without exception over the people and peasants of the male and female sex and over their property, except for the taking of life and punishing with the knout* and application of torture to them. And so each nobleman is free to sell and to mortgage those of his people and peasants, to give them as dowries and as conscripts and to indenture them, to set them free and for work and subsistence for a time, and to give widows and maidens for marriage to outsiders, to transfer them from some villages to his other villages and to teach them various arts and crafts, to allow the male sex to marry and the female sex to be married and, at his wish, to use them in service, work and missions, and to apply all punishments, except those above described, and to present them to the courts for punishment and, at his discretion, to institute pardon and thus free them from such punishment.

A grinder sharpens an axe, while peasants work on the construction of an izba, *a traditional wooden house, on the outskirts of St Petersburg. An engraving by J.-B. Le Prince (1734–81), who spent the years 1758 to 1762 travelling in Russia.*

*The knout was a tapering leather whip of considerable length which, in the hands of an expert, could break a spine at a single stroke.

The Russian expression for the policy of 'carrot and stick' is literally translated as the policy of 'knout and ginger biscuit'.

ELIZABETHAN PALACES

Elizabeth's first major architectural commission was the Summer Palace, designed by Bartolommeo Francesco Rastrelli (1700–71), the son of a Florentine sculptor employed by Peter the Great. Rastrelli had been appointed Chief Architect to the Imperial Court in 1736 during the reign of Anna. The Summer Palace, completed in 1744, was, like many of the early buildings in St Petersburg, constructed of wood, with a stucco finish. The building was demolished by the Emperor Paul in the late 1790s.

The original royal residence at Tsarskoe Selo was built for Peter I by his wife Catherine, and was bequeathed to Elizabeth in Catherine's will. Elizabeth asked Rastrelli to rebuild and extend the palace, and work on the Catherine Palace was completed in 1752. Elizabeth wanted something monumental, and Rastrelli produced a building with a very long frontage decorated with massive male caryatids by the sculptor Dunker.

The interior included the famous Amber Room, whose amber panels disappeared during the Second World War, when the Wehrmacht occupied and severely damaged the palace. The room had a painted ceiling whose theme, *The Triumph of Wisdom over Voluptuousness*, was appropriate neither to

(Above right) A corner of the Amber Room in the Catherine Palace at Tsarskoe Selo, showing the results of restoration work.

(Right) The Great Hall of the Catherine Palace.

(Below) Part of the façade of the Catherine Palace, with the gilded domes of the chapel at the far end.

Rastrelli's architecture nor his patroness' private life. The Great Hall of the palace is brilliantly lit by 13 pairs of windows and by mirrors.

In 1754 Elizabeth commissioned Rastrelli to rebuild the Winter Palace on a much vaster scale. Rastrelli's building (heavily restored after a fire in 1837) still stands. It is 978 ft (298 m) long, with a highly ornamented exterior whose original colour scheme consisted of turquoise walls with silvered details. The magnificent Jordan Staircase of the Winter Palace was restored after the 1837 fire in a way which preserved the rococo exuberance of Rastrelli's original.

Elizabeth's palaces were designed to demonstrate that the Russian monarchy was equal to its Western European counterparts in wealth, power and sense of style. The Great Hall of the Catherine Palace was inspired by the Hall of Mirrors at Versailles, and the gardens and parks at Tsarskoe Selo were also remodelled by Rastrelli in the French manner. The monumentality and ornateness of Elizabeth's palaces were

intended to impress. The Russian playwright Denis Fonvizin (1745–92) described a visit to the Catherine Palace:

I confess sincerely that I was amazed by the splendour of the court of our Empress. Everywhere gold shimmered, assemblies of people in light blue and red ribbons, a multitude of beautiful ladies, lastly wonderful music – all this struck my sight and hearing, and the palace seemed to me to be the habitation of a being higher than mortal.

(Above right) The exterior of the Winter Palace.

(Right) The Jordan Staircase in the Winter Palace.

COURT INTRIGUE IN THE REIGN OF ELIZABETH

Countess Natalya Lopukhina was a court beauty of whom the Empress Elizabeth was jealous. When Natalya's lover, Count Löwenwolde, was banished to Siberia, Lopukhina became indiscreet in her criticisms of the empress. Hearing that a young officer called Berger had been posted to Siberia to keep guard on Löwenwolde, Lopukhina gave him a letter to take to her lover. Berger opened it and read it, and discovered that it contained the phrase 'Your trials are perhaps drawing to an end.' This could be interpreted to mean that Lopukhina knew of a conspiracy against Elizabeth. Sensing a way of gaining favour, Berger consulted Lestocq, Elizabeth's French doctor, who advised him to try to obtain more concrete evidence. Berger set out to cultivate Countess Lopukhina's son Ivan, who was known to make critical remarks about the empress when in his cups. Berger invited him to dinner, and Ivan obliged by drinking a toast to Tsar Ivan, hinting that Frederick II of Prussia intended to restore the former Ivan VI to the throne, and also mentioning the Marquis de Botta d'Adorno, until recently the Austrian ambassador in St Petersburg. Berger reported all this to Lestocq, who saw a means of discrediting the pro-Austrian Bestuzhev-Riumin, and furthering the interests of the pro-French party. Questioned further, Ivan Lopukhin claimed that Botta had spoken openly at the Lopukhin's house of the wish of the Austrian government to see Anna Leopoldovna and her son released and restored to power. Elizabeth demanded that Maria Theresa, the Austrian empress, investigate Botta's conduct. The investigations revealed nothing significant, but in order to placate Elizabeth, Maria Theresa sent Botta into a comfortable and temporary banishment. In Russia a detailed investigation was conducted, in which Countess Lopukhina admitted that Botta had made critical remarks about Elizabeth in her house. No written evidence of a plot was discovered, but Elizabeth took a harsh vengeance. The prisoners were sentenced to death, but the sentence was commuted to knouting, the cutting out of their tongues and exile to Siberia. Mikhail Bestuzhev's wife bribed the executioner not to mutilate her tongue too badly. Lopukhina had to be dragged to the block. She was eventually allowed to return to St Petersburg by Peter III.

Count Alexei Petrovich Bestuzhev-Riumin (1692–1766). An engraving by N. Maslov.

strengthened during Elizabeth's reign. Peter I's decree enabling peasants who volunteered for military service to acquire the status of free men had lapsed under his successors and was now officially rescinded. The legal and judicial powers of landlords over their serfs were increased. A decree of 1760 enabled landlords to punish serfs under the age of 40 by sending them to Siberia.

Elizabeth wished to abolish the death penalty, and insisted on sparing the lives of political offenders. The torture of prisoners below the age of 17 was banned in 1742, and facial mutilation was abolished as a punishment for women in 1757. In 1754 the empress created a Commission to draft a new law code. The code, which was never promulgated, would have further strengthened the privileges of the nobility and abolished their obligation to serve the state. Ivan Shuvalov proposed the issuing of fundamental laws defining the powers of the crown and the rights of the nobility, but nothing came of this project, which would have limited the autocratic prerogative.

The Seven Years War and the succession

In 1756 the British negotiated an alliance with Prussia, a development which transformed the diplomatic situation in Europe. France reacted by allying herself with Austria. Bestuzhev-Riumin's policy was discredited and he found himself outnumbered by francophiles on the Conference of the Imperial Court, an advisory cabinet which met for the first time in March 1756.

In June 1756 Elizabeth suffered a stroke, and the succession became the dominant subject of court intrigue. The empress had come to dislike and distrust her nephew Peter, and it was rumoured that she intended to designate her infant great-nephew Paul as her heir. Paul's mother Catherine began secretly to discuss with Bestuzhev-Riumin and the British ambassador how she might secure power for her son and for herself when Elizabeth died.

The conflict which became known as the Seven Years War began with a Prussian invasion of Saxony in August 1756. Elizabeth declared war on Prussia and entered into an alliance with France and Austria. Field Marshal Apraxin, the commander-in-chief of the Russian forces which invaded Prussia in the summer of 1757, was anxious to avoid a major clash with the Prussians. His troops were ill-prepared for war, and he knew that Elizabeth was seriously ill and that her heir Peter, who might succeed to the throne at any moment, was strongly pro-Prussian. Though the Russians defeated the Prussians at Gross-Jägerndorf in August 1757, Apraxin was subsequently dismissed for failing to follow up this advantage.

A further stroke in 1757 made the empress quick-tempered and suspicious. She became convinced that Bestuzhev-Riumin was in the pay of the British and the Prussians, and was responsible for Apraxin's failure vigorously to prosecute the war against Prussia. Fortunately for Catherine, Bestuzhev-Riumin was able to destroy his papers before his arrest in February 1758. He was condemned to exile, and Mikhail Vorontsov became chancellor in his stead. Catherine's avowals of innocence allayed the empress' suspicions, but her position remained precarious and she continued to build up her support among the Guards. Her chief fear was that her husband might denounce her to the empress in order to be free to marry his mistress, Elizabeth Vorontsova.

Apraxin's successors, Generals Fermor and Saltykov, failed to achieve a decisive victory, though Saltykov, with Austrian help, inflicted a massive defeat on the Prussians at Kunersdorf in August 1759. Saltykov was replaced by Elizabeth's former lover, Alexander Buturlin. In September 1760 Russian and Austrian forces briefly occupied Berlin and by December 1761 Prussia was at the point of defeat.

The empress was now very stout, her beauty had faded and she found it difficult to walk. Her health remained a cause of grave concern until the winter of 1761, when she seemed to recover. On 20 December she attended a performance at her private theatre and made a public display of her affection for her great-nephew Paul. Three days later she suffered another stroke, and she died on Christmas afternoon 1761.

Петр III   Peter III
1761–1762

Екатерина II Великая   Catherine II ('The Great')
1762–1796

Catherine II. A portrait by Feodor Stepanovich Rokotov (c. 1735–c. 1808).

PETER III	
Full name	*Died*
Karl Peter Ulrich of Holstein-Gottorp	Ropsha 6 July 1762
Father	Murdered
Karl-Friedrich, Duke of Holstein-Gottorp	*Wife* 1745 Sophia Augusta Fredericka
Mother	of Anhalt-Zerbst
Anna Petrovna Romanova	(**Catherine II**) Died 1796
Born	*Child*
Kiel 21 February 1728	**Paul** (1754; officially the son
Accession	of Peter III, but
25 December 1761 (5 January 1762 NS)	possibly the son of Sergei Saltykov)
Deposition	
28 June 1762	

PETER III

If I can form any judgement of the Emperor's Temper, it is not proper to cross or thwart him first … but rather to appear to enter into his Views. His Imperial Majesty is really open to Reason, especially if it comes from his friends.

Robert Keith, British envoy to Russia

The fault of Peter III consists in having given his spouse too much independence and in having been insufficiently watchful of the party of ambitious men around her.

Louis XV of France

Posterity's verdict on the brief reign of Peter III (1761–1762) illustrates the truth of the saying that history is the propaganda of the victors. Catherine II and her supporters justified the deposition and murder of Peter by portraying him as boorish, immature, uncommitted to the Orthodox faith, and partial to foreigners. Recently a more favourable view, based on the reports of foreign diplomats and on an examination of Peter's policies, has been convincingly put forward.

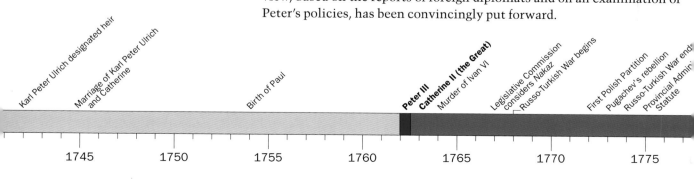

Karl Peter Ulrich designated heir

Marriage of Karl Peter Ulrich and Catherine

Birth of Paul

Peter III

Catherine II (the Great)

Murder of Ivan VI

Legislative Commission considers Nakaz

Russo-Turkish War begins

First Polish Partition

Pugachev's rebellion

Russo-Turkish War ends

Provincial Administ Statute

1745   1750   1755   1760   1765   1770   1775

Family portrait of Peter III, Catherine II and the Tsarevich Paul by R.M. Lisiewska, now in the National Museum, Stockholm. The portrait conveys an illusion of domesticity. In reality Catherine spent little time with either her husband or her son. She was later to cast doubt on the boy's paternity by alleging that the marriage had not been consummated. Peter preferred the company of his mistress, Elizabeth Vorontsova.

Karl Peter Ulrich of Holstein-Gottorp was born at Kiel in 1728, the son of Duke Karl-Friedrich and his wife Anna, the daughter of Peter I. His aunt Elizabeth, empress of Russia, proclaimed him as heir in 1742. As a bride for her nephew, Elizabeth selected Sophia Augusta Fredericka of Anhalt-Zerbst, the daughter of a minor German prince. Sophia, who was born in 1729, arrived in Russia in 1744 and was received into the Orthodox faith under the name of Catherine. By the time of their marriage in 1745 Peter, disfigured by an attack of smallpox, had become physically repellent to her. An intelligent girl with precocious intellectual tastes, Catherine could not share his military enthusiasms. By the early 1750s she had taken a lover, a courtier named Sergei Saltykov. Her first two pregnancies ended in miscarriages, but in 1754 she gave birth to a son, Paul. In her memoirs Catherine hinted that her marriage was never consummated, and Paul's paternity remains a subject of speculation. The infant was immediately removed from his mother's care by the Empress Elizabeth, and brought up under her supervision. Catherine had a daughter by her second lover, the Polish diplomat Stanislaus Poniatowski, but the child died in 1759. By then the ambitious Catherine, who was determined to secure the throne, was deeply involved in political intrigue. Her affair with Grigory Orlov, by whom she had a son in 1762, ensured her support in the officer corps, of which Orlov was an influential member.

Peter as emperor

Peter succeeded to the throne on the death of Elizabeth in December 1761. His manifesto of 18 February 1762, freeing the nobility from compulsory state service, was well received, as was his abolition of the Secret Chancellery. He also abolished the Conference of the Imperial Court, Elizabeth's advisory cabinet, wishing to simplify the structure of government. His proposal for the secularization of church lands was the revival of a project which had been discussed in Elizabeth's reign, and was to be completed in the reign of Catherine.

Peter was strongly pro-Prussian. His accession to the throne saved Frederick the Great, who had been contemplating suicide, from certain defeat. The peace treaty which he signed with Prussia in April 1762 involved the abandonment of all the territories that the Russian armies had occupied. He then negotiated an alliance with Prussia, ratified by Frederick II in June 1762. Neither the peace, nor the Prussian alliance

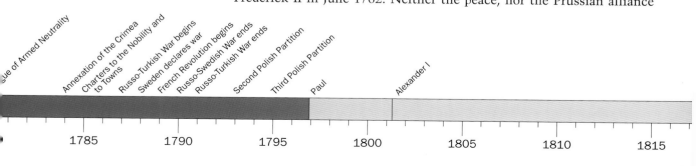

...ue of Armed Neutrality

Annexation of the Crimea

Charters to the Nobility and to Towns

Russo-Turkish War begins

Sweden declares war

French Revolution begins

Russo-Swedish War ends

Russo-Turkish War ends

Second Polish Partition

Third Polish Partition

Paul

Alexander I

1785   1790   1795   1800   1805   1810   1815

The murder of Peter III at Ropsha, as depicted in a contemporary French engraving. The official explanation, that Peter's death had been caused by a fatal attack of piles, was regarded with proper cynicism in France. When Jean le Rond d'Alembert (1717–83), the French mathematician and philosopher, was invited to become tutor to Catherine's son, the Grand Duke Paul, he declined the honour, commenting to Voltaire: 'I am too prone to piles and they are too serious in that country'. The fact that Catherine allowed her husband to take his violin, his negro servant Narcissus, and his favourite dog Mopsy to Ropsha may indicate that she had not decided to have him murdered.

was unacceptable to the Russian elite; indeed Catherine II was to confirm the alliance in the early years of her reign. The aspect of his foreign policy that proved fatal to Peter was his insistence on using Russian money and troops to pursue the interests of the Duchy of Holstein-Gottorp. His plan to wage war against Denmark in order to reconquer Schleswig alienated the Guards. Catherine and her supporters seized the opportunity to revolt.

The coup which overthrew Peter on 28 June 1762 was organized by the Orlov brothers and other Guards officers, with Catherine's knowledge and approval. Peter was placed under house arrest at his country estate at Ropsha, where he was murdered on 6 July by Alexei Orlov and others. The evidence suggests that Catherine had not been informed of the plotters' intention to dispose of her husband. The official explanation, not widely believed, was that he had succumbed to a fatal attack of haemorrhoidal colic.

CATHERINE II

Her figure is noble and agreeably impressive; her gait majestic; her person and deportment graceful in the highest degree.... Her forehead is large and open; the nose borders on the aquiline; her mouth is sweetly fresh, and embellished by a singularly regular and beautiful set of teeth, the chin somewhat plump, and rather inclining to double, but without the smallest tendency to fatness. Her hair is chestnut-coloured, and uncommonly fine; the eyebrows are dark brown; the eyes hazel, and extremely fascinating.

Claude Carloman de Rulhière, an employee of the French embassy in St Petersburg

As a woman and a foreigner, Catherine's position was precarious. Both the imprisoned Ivan VI and her own son Paul had better claims to the throne. The killing of Ivan VI by his gaolers in 1764 removed one potential rival, though during the reign at least 24 pretenders claimed the throne. Paul remained both a threat and an asset, since by siring an heir he could continue the dynasty. Mother and son had scarcely seen each other during the first six years of Paul's life, and had little in common. Apart from a few years of amity in the 1770s, their relations were mutually suspicious. The grandeur of Catherine's court, the elaborate public ceremonial, the projection abroad of the image of Russia as an enlightened and progressive power all served the purpose of glossing over the circumstances of her accession and the flimsiness of her claim to the throne. Her creation in 1763 of the Secret Expedition, a department whose function was to root out political opponents, is further evidence of her sense of insecurity. The Secret Expedition was headed by Stepan Ivanovich Sheshkovsky, a masochist and religious fanatic who personally supervised the interrogation of suspects in a room decorated with icons.

CATHERINE II	

Full name
  Sophia Augusta
  Fredericka of
  Anhalt-Zerbst
  also known as
  Catherine the Great
	6 November 1796
	Stroke
	Husband
	  1745 Karl Peter
	  Ulrich of Holstein-
	  Gottorp (**Peter III**)

Father
  Christian Augustus,
  Prince of Anhalt-
  Zerbst
	Murdered 1762
	Children
	  Paul (1754;
	  officially fathered by
	  Peter III, but

Mother
  Johanna Elizabeth
  of Holstein-Gottorp
	possibly by Sergei
	  Saltykov)
	  Anna (1757;

Born
  Stettin
  2 May 1729
	fathered by
	  Stanislaus
	  Poniatowski)

Accession
  28 June 1762
	Alexei Bobrinskoy
	  (1762; fathered by

Died St Petersburg	Grigory Orlov)

An equestrian portrait of Catherine II. The picture, completed by Vigilius Ericksen in 1765, is a representation of the coup d'état. Having secured control of St Petersburg, Catherine put on the green uniform of a colonel in the Preobrazhensky Guard and, mounted on her horse Brilliant, led a column of troops out of the city towards Oranienbaum, with the intention of arresting her husband.

An illustration from a handbill issued in the reign of Catherine II to persuade people of the dangers of smallpox and the benefits of being inoculated against it. The man on the right is a victim of the disease.

KLIUCHEVSKY ON CATHERINE II

V.O. Kliuchevsky, the brilliant 19th-century Russian historian, was noted for the depth of his psychological insight into the personalities he wrote about. This is his assessment of Catherine II:

She was capable of effort, of intense and even excessive labour; therefore, to herself and others she seemed stronger than she was. But she worked more on her manners, on the way she handled people, than on herself, on her ideas and feelings; therefore, her manners and her handling of people were better than her feelings and ideas. Her intellect had more pliancy and impressionability than depth and thoughtfulness, more training than creativity, just as her entire nature contained more nervous vitality than spiritual strength.
She preferred managing people to dealing with affairs, and she was better at it.

Consolidation and modernization

Catherine was careful to conciliate the groups who had helped her to gain power. She scrapped Peter's unpopular proposals for the reform of the army, and created a Military Commission which devised a series of modernizing reforms which were implemented in the years 1764–65. The unpopular College of the Economy, established to administer ecclesiastical property, was abolished. Catherine rapidly gained in confidence, and by 1764 she announced the final secularization of church lands. She observed the forms of Orthodoxy, regarding the church as a moral arm of the state.

Her establishment of a Medical College in 1763 reflected Catherine's belief that the state should promote the health of the people. In 1768 she set a powerful example by having both herself and her son inoculated against smallpox by the English physician Thomas Dimsdale. Catherine was also concerned about the financial health of the empire. She inherited a serious inflationary situation, largely a consequence of the Seven Years War, which she tackled by banning the issue of copper coins and then by withdrawing them from circulation. Wars against Turkey, the escalating costs of local administration and the extravagance of Catherine's court put an end to this counter-inflationary policy and led to considerable increases in taxation. By liberalizing tariffs she promoted the development of overseas trade, the value of which more than quadrupled during her reign. Her Volga voyage of 1767 took her to parts of the empire which had not been visited by a reigning sovereign for many years, and brought home to her the social and economic diversity of her domains. She encouraged foreign immigrants to settle in Russia, offering free land and tax exemptions, and thus establishing an industrious community of Germans in the Volga region.

Allegorical portrait of Catherine II as Legislator by D.G. Levitsky, now in the Tretyakov Gallery, Moscow. Levitsky's use of flowing drapery tactfully concealed the empress' increasing girth. The Goddess of Justice is depicted in the top right-hand corner of the painting, holding a pair of scales. Dmitry Grigorievich Levitsky (1735–1822), the son of a priest who worked as an engraver at the Monastery of the Caves in Kiev, became the foremost painter of society portraits in Catherinian Russia.

The Legislative Commission and the *Nakaz*

The desire to strengthen her position may have been one of the reasons why Catherine called for the election of a Legislative Commission, with representatives of the nobility, towns, state peasants, non-Russian tribes and government departments. The serfs, who formed 90 per cent of the population, were not included. The Commission's stated purpose was to discuss a new code of laws. When the deputies gathered in Moscow in 1767 they were presented with a lengthy document written by Catherine herself, the *Bolshoi Nakaz* or *Great Instruction*. The *Nakaz*, which achieved the double distinction of being praised by Voltaire and banned by the French censors, drew heavily on Catherine's studies of the writings of Enlightenment thinkers such as Montesquieu, Beccaria and Bielefeld. The Cameralist ideas that had been influential in the German states in recent decades also influenced Catherine, who accepted the

CATHERINE II'S BOLSHOI NAKAZ

The *Bolshoi Nakaz* (Great Instruction) was laid before the members of the Legislative Commission summoned by Catherine II in 1767. The document offers some insight into the ideas and values of the empress, and into how she wished others to perceive those values and ideas.

6 *Russia is a European Power.*

9 *The sovereign is absolute; for no other authority except that which is concentrated in his person can act appropriately in a state whose expanse is so vast.*

10 *The expanse of the state requires that absolute power be vested in that person who rules over it...*

13 *What is the purpose of autocracy? Not to deprive people of their natural freedom, but to guide their actions so as to attain the maximum good...*

123 *The use of torture is repugnant to a healthy and natural mind. Humanity itself cries out against it and demands that it be totally abolished...*

365 *There are few ways that lead more directly to the attainment of honour than military service. To defend their fatherland and to conquer its enemies are the first right and the proper job of the nobles...*

367 *Yet still the proper dispensing of justice is no less required in time of peace than in war, and the state would be destroyed without it.*

494 *In such a great state, which extends its rule over so many different peoples, the mistake of forbidding or discriminating against various faiths would greatly endanger the tranquillity and security of its citizens...*

497 *One ought to be extremely cautious in the examination of cases concerning witchcraft and heresy. Accusations of these two crimes may excessively disturb the tranquillity, freedom, and welfare of the citizens and may be the source of innumerable torments unless the laws set proper bounds...*

view that the authority of the state should be used to regulate and improve morality, public health and commerce. The *Nakaz* condemned such arbitrary practices as torture, and defined the purpose of autocracy as guiding the actions of the people so as to attain the maximum good. Though the Legislative Commission debated many issues and presented statements of grievances to the empress, it did not produce a law code. The outbreak of the war with Turkey in 1768 brought an end to its sittings. It had served the purpose of conferring legitimacy on Catherine's rule.

Some historians have seen her failure to practise the Enlightenment doctrines that she preached as evidence of Catherine's hypocrisy. Others have suggested that she went through an enlightened phase in the early years of the reign, and then thought better of it, alarmed by the Pugachev rebellion (p. 135) and by the French Revolution. The *Nakaz*, though in part a statement of enlightened ideals, was not a liberal manifesto. It defined Russia as an absolute monarchy with fundamental laws. The codes, statutes and charters that Catherine issued in the period between 1768 and 1786 went some way towards defining those fundamental laws. Catherine enjoyed the flattering esteem of *philosophes* such as Voltaire and Diderot, with whom she corresponded, but her policies were dictated by a realistic assessment of the limitations of her power. Although she promoted an international essay competition on the future of the peasantry in 1765, Catherine did not abolish serfdom. She did not have the financial, military or bureaucratic resources to impose so sweeping a change on an unwilling nobility, on whom she relied to maintain order in rural Russia.

CATHERINE II AND VOLTAIRE

A contemporary portrait of Voltaire. François Marie Arouet (1694–1778), who assumed the name of Voltaire, was a French writer and philosopher. He condemned tyranny and superstition and advocated tolerance and freedom of thought. His correspondence with Catherine II was marked, on his side, by lavish flattery.

Voltaire to Catherine II

Ferney, 26 February 1769
...While you prepare to beat the Sultan, you are drawing up a code of laws. I am reading the preliminary Instruction, which your Imperial Majesty had the goodness to send me, and I have only put it down in order to finish my letter. Madam, Numa and Minos would have put their signature to your work, but would not perhaps have been capable of producing it. It is clear, concise, just, strict and humane. Rest assured that no-one in future will have greater renown than yourself; but in God's name, beat the Turks....

Oh, Madam, what a lesson your Majesty is giving to us petty Frenchmen, to our ridiculous Sorbonne and to the argumentative charlatans in our medical schools! You have been inoculated with less fuss than a nun taking an enema. The Crown Prince has followed your example. Court Orlov goes hunting in the snow after his inoculation against smallpox. Scipio would have done likewise, if that disease, which comes from Arabia, had existed in his time....

Madam, I am an old invalid of 75 years of age. Perhaps I talk nonsense, but at least I tell you what I think, which is quite rare when addressing persons like yourself. As I write, the 'Imperial Majesty' fades away before the person. My enthusiasm gets the better of my deep respect. I revere the lawmaker, the warrior, the philosopher.

Catherine II to Voltaire

St Petersburg, 15 [26 NS] April 1769
I have received, Sir, your splendid letter of 26 February. I shall do my very best to follow your advice. If Mustapha is not thrashed, it will certainly not be your fault or mine, or my army's; my soldiers are off to fight the Turks as if they were going to a wedding....

May you live to rejoice, Sir, when my brave warriors have beaten the Turks. You are aware, I think, that Azov, at the mouth of the Don, is already occupied by my troops. The last peace-treaty [the Treaty of Belgrade, 1739] stipulated that the place should be left unoccupied by both sides. You will have seen from the newspapers that we sent the Tatars packing in three different places, when they sought to pillage the Ukraine....

I am most vexed that your health is not responding to my wishes. If the success of my armies can help to improve it, I shall not fail to keep you informed of all our good fortunes. So far, God be thanked, I have had nothing but good news from all quarters: wherever the Turks or the Tatars show themselves, we send them away with a sound thrashing, and the Polish rebels most of all....

A medal struck to commemorate the Russian victory over the Turks at Chesme in 1770.

The Turkish War

Catherine understood the need to find allies against Russia's most dangerous neighbour, Turkey. Nikita Panin, her chief adviser on foreign policy until 1781, encouraged her to try to create a 'Northern System', an alliance which would include Prussia, Poland, the Scandinavian countries and Great Britain. The treaty of mutual assistance with Prussia in 1764 confirmed Peter III's alliance of 1762, and Frederick II helped to secure the election of Catherine's former lover Stanislaus Poniatowksi as King Stanislaus Augustus of Poland in the same year. Catherine's attempt to secure civil rights for the non-Catholic population of Poland provoked Catholic nobles into rebellion against his rule in 1768. Russian troops, sent to Poland to tackle the rebellion, clashed with Turkish forces on the frontier between Poland and Turkey and the Turks declared war on Russia in October 1768 (NS).

At first the war went well for Russia, whose forces defeated the Turkish fleet in the battle of Chesme (1770), and occupied Moldavia, Wallachia and the Crimea. Catherine then became the victim of her own

The Polish Plumb Cake. A satirical engraving concerning what proved to be the first Polish Partition. The cartoon was published in the *Westminster Magazine* in 1774.

The Cossack rebel and pretender to the throne Emelyan Pugachev in chains in a cage. A German woodcut.

success. The Prussians and the Austrians were reluctant to permit Russia territorial expansion unless they received compensation. In 1772 the first Partition of Poland was agreed, in which the three powers each took a slice of Polish territory, the Russians gaining the eastern part of Belorussia. Poland lost about one third of its land and half its inhabitants.

Truce talks with Turkey in 1772 were complicated by the danger of a war with Sweden, whose new king, Gustavus III, had ambitions to regain the territories that his country had lost to Russia. The threat of a northern war was averted, and in 1773–74 the Russians pressed their war with Turkey to a successful conclusion. The Treaty of Kutchuk Kainardji, signed in July 1774, brought the Russians significant territorial gains, the opportunity to develop a Black Sea fleet and rights of passage through the Straits and into the Mediterranean for merchant shipping. The Crimea was granted independence from Turkish rule. Though Catherine could claim that the war, into which she had blundered, had been brought to a successful conclusion, the costs were considerable. Tax increases, inflation and conscription had made her government unpopular.

Crises and responses

In 1773–74 Catherine faced the most dangerous internal challenge to her rule. A Don Cossack named Emelyan Pugachev, who claimed to be Peter III, initiated a revolt in September 1773. Pugachev's promise to liberate the serfs and to restore Cossack privileges attracted an estimated 200,000 supporters. The rebels slaughtered at least 1,500 noblemen and their families and more than 1,000 government officials. They were only dispersed after Catherine's troops had defeated them in a series of battles. Pugachev was betrayed by some of his supporters and was executed in Moscow in January 1775. The traditional liberties of all Cossacks, including those who had remained loyal, were curtailed. Satisfied that the revolt had not been stirred up by disaffected noblemen, Catherine granted a general amnesty to all participants in March 1775 and repealed a number of unpopular taxes. The reforms of local administration and the legal system which she then embarked on had been under consideration before the rebellion, which had emphasized the inadequacy of the existing structures.

The Statute for the Administration of the Provinces, promulgated in 1775, redrew provincial boundaries, creating 50 new provinces, each under the control of a governor appointed by and answerable to the empress. Provinces were subdivided into districts. Governors were empowered to establish boards of social welfare which would create schools, hospitals and other public institutions. Each province was given a system of law courts, including an equity court to which people arrested but not brought to trial could appeal. The nobility and townspeople were given the right periodically to hold assemblies and to elect officials. A Police Ordinance issued in 1782 laid down regulations for the policing of towns, charging the police not only with the task of maintaining order, but also with responsibility for public hygiene and morality.

CATHERINE II'S LOVERS

Stanislaus Augustus (formerly Count Poniatowski), king of Poland 1764–95. A state portrait by Bacciarelli.

Sergei Saltykov

Catherine's lover in the early 1750s. Saltykov, a courtier, may have been the father of her son Paul.

Stanislaus Poniatowski

Catherine's lover in the late 1750s, and the probable father of her daughter Anna Petrovna, who died in infancy. Poniatowski subsequently became king of Poland.

Grigory Orlov

A Guards officer, and an important figure in the coup which brought Catherine to power. They became lovers in 1761, and their relationship lasted for 11 years. Their son Alexei Bobrinskoy was granted lands by Catherine.

Alexander Vassilchikov

A young Guards lieutenant with whom Catherine had a brief affair in 1772–73. Her description of him as an 'excellent but very boring citizen' does not suggest great commitment on her side.

Grigory Potemkin

A cultured and able senior army officer, who remained an important member of Catherine's government until his death in 1791, even though they ceased to be lovers in 1776. There were rumours of a secret marriage between Potemkin and Catherine.

Peter Zavadovsky

A Ukrainian army officer and bureaucrat. An intelligent man, Zavadovsky assisted Catherine with the preparation of her reform of the local administration. Their affair ended in 1777, but Catherine continued to promote his career.

Simeon Zorich

A Serbian army officer with whom Catherine had a brief liaison in 1777–78. He was a compulsive gambler.

Ivan Rimsky-Korsakov

A young army officer who was dropped by Catherine in 1779 when she discovered that he was also having an affair with one of her ladies-in-waiting. He belonged to a branch of the same family as the 19th-century composer Nikolai Andreyevich Rimsky-Korsakov (1844–1908).

Alexander Lanskoy

A young Guards officer. Catherine's relationship with him began in 1780 and she was deeply upset when he died of diphtheria in 1784.

Alexander Yermolov

Catherine's relationship with Yermolov lasted for a few months in 1785–86

Alexander Mamonov

A handsome and cultured relation of Potemkin's. Catherine dismissed him in 1789 when she discovered that he was involved with several of her ladies-in-waiting.

Platon Zubov

Thirty years younger than Catherine, Zubov was her last favourite. He was the first of her lovers since Zavadovsky to play a significant political role, and the promotions that she heaped on him, which included the Governor-Generalship of New Russia and the Crimea, were beyond his abilities or deserts. In 1801 Zubov and his brothers played a prominent part in the conspiracy to overthrow Tsar Paul.

Gossip asserted that Catherine indulged in several other liaisons in the late 1770s, but there is no reliable evidence to support this view.

Alexei Grigorievich Bobrinskoy, Catherine II's son by Grigory Orlov. This portrait was painted in 1769 by Carl Ludwig Christinek.

Though the expansion of local administration enabled Catherine to streamline central government by abolishing a number of the Colleges set up by Peter the Great (p. 107), the cost of local administration increased sixfold by 1796, and the number of local officials more than doubled in the same period. The effectiveness of the reforms was limited. Corruption remained a serious problem. The new court system was handicapped by a lack of trained lawyers. At district level there were not enough literate and competent noblemen and townsmen to fill the new posts. The boards of welfare were hampered by a lack of funds. Catherine's attempt to transplant methods which had worked well in the German principalities to a vast empire with poor communications and a tiny nobility was unlikely to achieve dramatic results, but it did achieve significant improvements in the fields of justice, education and public health.

Private life

During the Pugachev rebellion Catherine embarked on the most important personal relationship of her life, her affair with Grigory Potemkin. Potemkin, a senior army officer, was a connoisseur of music as well as a courageous soldier. His good looks were somewhat marred by the loss of an eye. Catherine enjoyed his humour and his gift for mimicry, and her evident affection for him gave rise to rumours of a secret marriage. Though Potemkin was replaced in her bed in 1776 by a succession of young army officers, he remained highly influential until his death in 1791.

Catherine's reputation for sexual insatiability developed in her own lifetime, and has become firmly lodged in the public mind. Screen portrayals by Pola Negri and Marlene Dietrich, and a stage appearance by Mae West reinforced the myth. Mae West's comment on her own performance became part of the legend: 'Catherine was a great empress. She also had 300 lovers. I did the best I could in a couple of hours.' There is reliable evidence of only 12 lovers in Catherine's life, and some of these relationships were of long duration. In recent years feminist historians have argued that the myth of Catherine's insatiability arose from the anxieties of a male-dominated society confronted by a powerful and able woman ruler. Her letters suggest a warm-hearted person who craved affection, and her treatment of former lovers was usually generous.

Portrait of Prince Grigory Alexandrovich Potemkin (1739–91) by Volker, engraved posthumously in 1792. The artist has somewhat flattered his subject, who had lost an eye through the mistreatment of an infection by a quack doctor. Potemkin, who had been expelled from the University of Moscow for laziness and failure to attend classes, was so embarrassed by this disfigurement that he briefly contemplated taking holy orders. He chose instead a military career, distinguishing himself in the Turkish War. He was an important musical patron who attempted unsuccessfully to persuade Mozart to enter the Russian service.

The Smolny Institute, St Petersburg. This school for the daughters of the nobility was founded in 1764 by the Imperial Educational Society for Young Noble Ladies, of which Catherine II was patron. It was originally housed in the Smolny Convent. In 1806, ten years after the empress' death, the Italian Giacomo Quarenghi (1744–1817) began work on the new building, which was completed in 1808. In October–November 1917 the Military Revolutionary Committee of the Bolshevik Party organized their seizure of power from three rooms on the second floor of the building.

Social reforms

Catherine wished to encourage the emergence of 'estates', social groups with defined privileges and obligations who would be willing servants of the state. Her Charter to the Towns of 1785 placed urban local government in the hands of elected councils. The Charter to the Nobility, published in the same year, confirmed the nobles in their right to own property and serfs, and excluded those nobles who did not give service to the state from participation in local assemblies of the nobility and from election to local office. Noblemen were exempted from corporal punishment and personal taxation. The Charter also recognized that the land held by aristocrats was their legal property.

The empress wished to encourage education and founded the Smolny Institute, a boarding school for the daughters of the nobility, in St Petersburg. When she discovered that her reform of provincial administration was not resulting in a rapid spread of education she appointed a Commission on National Education in 1782 and established a teacher training college in 1783. The Statute on National Schools of 1786 laid down that there should be a high school in each provincial capital and a primary school in each district town, offering free education for boys and girls. By the end of the century over 300 schools had been founded, providing education for almost 20,000 pupils at a time. Educational practice fell short of the ideals that Catherine laid down. Corporal punishment was commonplace, though forbidden by the 1786 statute, and the vast majority of the population remained illiterate, since free education was not available to the children of serfs.

Although Catherine issued no statute on the subject of religious toleration, her government adopted a relatively enlightened policy towards the non-Orthodox and non-Christian subjects of the empire. The extra taxes payable by Old Believers were abolished in 1782 and the Jewish population was given legal equality in 1786, though from 1791 Jews could only enjoy these rights within the Pale of Settlement, an area designated by the government as the territory where they wished the great majority of the Jewish population to reside, and in 1794 they were forced to pay double taxes.

Wars and revolutions

The peace between Russia and Turkey achieved in 1774 was precarious. The Turks hoped to regain the Crimea, while Catherine wished to annex it. She also developed an interest in what became known as the Greek Project, the idea that Russia might conquer the European part of the Turkish empire and that her second grandson, appropriately christened Constantine, might rule a Christian kingdom based in Constantinople. No move against Turkey would be possible unless there was a favourable diplomatic situation in Europe. By the mid-1770s Panin's 'Northern System' was being challenged by Catherine's other advisers, including Potemkin. They argued that the Greek Project could only be achieved with Austrian support. The brief War of the Bavarian Succession (1778–79) between Austria and Prussia was ended by Russian and French mediation, a striking demonstration of Russia's enhanced status as a European power. Catherine cultivated the friendship of the Austrian emperor Joseph II, who visited her in 1780, and the two rulers reached a secret agreement in 1781 under which Joseph pledged military assistance to Russia if the Turks broke the Treaty of Kutchuk Kainardji.

Queen Catherine's Dream. A cartoon sometimes attributed to the English artist James Gillray (1757–1815). The devil tempts the empress by offering her Warsaw and Constantinople. The image reflects the anxiety about Russian ambitions that was to become a dominant theme of British foreign policy in the 19th century.

Catherine II and Joseph II, the Austrian emperor, on the occasion of the latter's visit to Russia in 1780. An engraving by Johann Hieronymus Loeschenkohl (fl. 1779–1807). Joseph rather resented Catherine addressing him as an equal in her letters, and referred to her as 'the Catherinized Princess of Zerbst'. During his visit he wrote: 'Apart from the amiability and charm of the empress and some of the foreigners it would really be a penance to take part in this journey.'

Catherine's response to the American War of Independence was at first one of neutrality. She turned down a request for support from King George III, hoping that Russia might play a mediating role in the conflict. In 1780 Russia took the lead in the creation of the League of Armed Neutrality, which asserted the rights of neutral shipping to enter belligerent ports. This stance gave an advantage to the Americans, though official recognition was not accorded to the United States by Russia until 1809.

The early 1780s offered a good opportunity for Russian expansion, since Britain and France were at war with each other. In 1783 Catherine ordered the annexation of the Crimea, an operation that was successfully carried out by Potemkin, who encouraged the economic development of the region. By 1785 a naval base had been established at Sevastopol. Catherine's tour of inspection of her new southern territories in 1787 gave rise to the expression 'Potemkin Villages', because Potemkin made sure that she saw only communities of apparently prosperous and happy peasants, but the saying should not be allowed to obscure his considerable achievements in the region.

The Second Turkish War, which began in the summer of 1787, was protracted and costly. Though Russia received Austrian assistance, the international climate was not otherwise favourable. Britain and Prussia were uncooperative, and in 1788 Gustavus III of Sweden declared war on Russia, hoping to regain lost territory. The Russo-Swedish War ended in a stalemate and was resolved by the Treaty of Verela in August 1790. The outbreak of the French Revolution in 1789 and the death of Joseph II, the Austrian emperor, in February 1790 further complicated the situation. Joseph's successor Leopold made a separate peace with Turkey later that year. Russian victories in 1791 made the Turks willing to discuss peace terms. In the Treaty of Jassy, signed in December 1791 (January 1792 NS), the Turks accepted the Russian annexation of the Crimea and conceded other Black Sea territories to Russia. Among Russia's gains was Odessa, which was soon developed into an important port.

In April 1792 France declared war on Austria. Russia did not join Austria and Prussia in the first anti-revolutionary coalition. Catherine was preoccupied with the problem of Poland, where revolution had

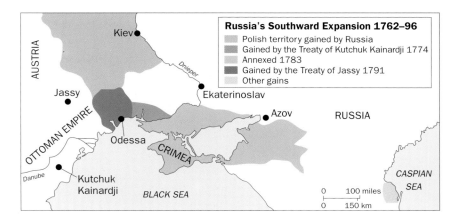

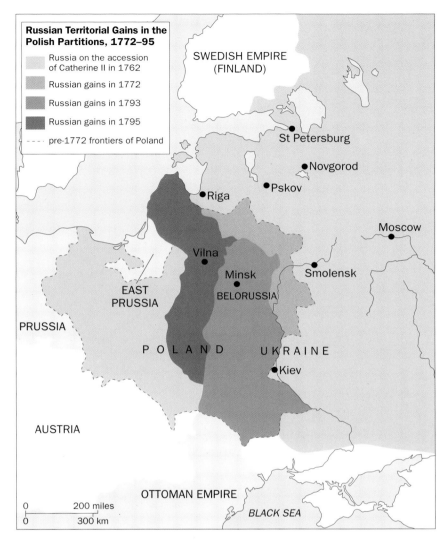

broken out in May 1791. She was unwilling to tolerate what she perceived as Jacobinism on her borders, but did not wish to offend Prussia and Austria by intervening without consulting them. She forewarned both powers of her intentions and in May 1792 sent Russian troops into Poland to crush the revolution. A second Partition was agreed between the three powers in January 1793. A second Polish revolt in the spring of 1794 provoked a further Russian invasion, in the course of which Russian forces massacred 20,000 Polish civilians in Praga, near Warsaw. A third and final Partition was agreed in 1795, and Poland ceased to exist.

Even after the overthrow of the French monarchy in 1792 and the execution of Louis XVI in 1793, Catherine remained reluctant to commit Russia to an anti-French coalition. By the time of her death in 1796 she had provided ships to assist the British war effort in the North Sea, and was planning to send Russian forces to the Holy Roman Empire to fight against the French. She had also sent a military expedition against Persia.

CATHERINE II AND CLASSICISM

Catherine II objected to the exuberance of Elizabethan taste as much as she disapproved of the frivolity of Elizabeth's lifestyle. A self-confessed sufferer from 'Anglomania', she disliked the rigid French formality of Elizabeth's gardens. 'At present I'm mad with love for English gardens,' she wrote to Voltaire in 1772, 'curved lines, gentle slopes, ponds in the form of lakes….' She had landscaped gardens laid out at Tsarskoe Selo in the English manner, and an English Palace was built at Peterhof in the Palladian style. She commissioned a dinner service from Josiah Wedgwood (1730–95), who also made an enamelled jasper portrait medallion of the empress in the early 1770s, based on a medal designed by Ivanov.

As a non-Russian who had gained power by means of a coup d'état in which her husband was murdered, it was important for Catherine publicly to establish herself as the successor of Russia's greatest rulers. She chose to do this in the classical style, commissioning, on the recommendation of Denis Diderot, the French sculptor Etienne Maurice Falconet

(1716–91) to produce an equestrian statue of Peter I. The emperor is depicted crowned with a victor's wreath, and dressed in a style that owes more to ancient Rome than to early 18th-century Russia. The design was influenced by the equestrian statue of Marcus Aurelius on the Capitoline Hill in Rome, but the rearing posture of the horse adds an urgency to the work that looks forward to early 19th-century Romanticism. The sculpture rests on a massive block of Finnish granite which took two years to transport from the quarry to St Petersburg, and which bears a dedicatory inscription in Latin: *PETRO PRIMO CATHARINA SECUNDA MDCCLXXXII* (To Peter the First from Catherine the Second 1782). Catherine was annoyed by Falconet's frequent complaints about the conditions in which he was obliged to work, and did not invite him back to Russia for the unveiling ceremony. The statue was the inspiration for another masterpiece, Alexander Pushkin's poem *The Bronze Horseman*.

It is sometimes said that Catherine II eschewed grandiose building projects, preferring a more intimate architectural style. The reality is more complex. Catherine kept her private

(Left) A Wedgwood cameo portrait of Catherine II dating from the late 18th century.

(Below) The Bronze Horseman. *Falconet's statue of Peter the Great.*

(Above) The Green Dining Room designed by Charles Cameron in the Catherine Palace at Tsarskoe Selo.

PETRO PRIMO
CATHARINA SECUNDA
MDCCLXXXII·

and public lives separate. The rooms which the Scots architect Charles Cameron (*c.* 1740–91) designed for her in Rastrelli's Catherine Palace at Tsarskoe Selo were relatively small in scale. Catherine described Cameron as 'Scottish by nationality, Jacobite by persuasion, [a] great designer nourished by antiquity.' There is no firm evidence that Cameron was a Jacobite, but he was unquestionably an expert on classical architecture, and the author of a book entitled *The Baths of the Romans*. The Green Dining Room and the Bedroom that he designed for Catherine at Tsarskoe Selo in the 1780s both show his love of classical ornament.

Catherine made substantial and important additions to the Winter Palace complex. The Small Hermitage was designed by Vallin de la Mothe in the 1760s as a private retreat for the empress. In the 1780s Giacomo Quarenghi (1744–1817) added the Hermitage Theatre. Another Italian architect, Antonio Rinaldi (*c.* 1710–94), was commissioned to build a palace for Catherine's lover Grigory Orlov. The Marble Palace, so-called because it was the first building in St Petersburg to be faced with the material, was completed in 1785.

The empress also patronized Russian architects. Ivan Yegorovich Starov (1743–1808) was commissioned to build a palace for her lover Grigory Potemkin. The Tauride Palace in St Petersburg was so named because Potemkin was granted the title Prince of the Tauride after his annexation of the Crimea. The Emperor Paul, as an act of petty revenge against his mother's memory, handed the palace over to the horseguards for use as barracks and stables. The building was restored and significantly altered in the 19th century. The Russian poet Gavriil Derzhavin (1743–1816) wrote of this building: 'Its exterior does not dazzle the eye with carving, gilt, or other sumptuous decorations. Its merit is in its ancient, refined style; it is simple, but majestic.'

(Right above) The painted ceiling of Catherine II's bedroom in the Tauride Palace, St Petersburg. The decorations were, like the palace itself, designed by Ivan Yegorovich Starov.

(Right) The exterior of the Tauride Palace, St Petersburg.

Natalya, the first wife of the Grand
Duke Paul. The ill-fated Wilhelmina of
Hesse-Darmstadt, who took the name
Natalya Alexeyevna when she converted
to Orthodoxy in order to marry Paul,
died in childbirth in 1776.

A contemporary drawing of Catherine II
with her grandchildren, the Grand Duke
Alexander (the future Alexander I) and
the Grand Duke Constantine. Falconet's
equestrian statue of Peter the Great
(p. 142) can be seen in the background.

Catherine as a cultural patron

Catherine sought to make her court the centre of Russia's cultural life.
Her literary output included satires, articles on Russian history, and
opera libretti. She encouraged the translation of foreign works into
Russian, and in 1783 founded the Russian Academy of Language, which
published the first Russian dictionary. She added a court theatre to the
Winter Palace, and subsidized public performances of plays. Censorship
operated in a liberal fashion until the beginning of the French Revolution. The empress patronized neoclassical architects such as the Scot
Charles Cameron and the Italian Giacomo Quarenghi, and made extensive purchases of European paintings.

The succession

In 1773 Catherine arranged a marriage between her son Paul and Wilhelmina of Hesse-Darmstadt, who was baptized into the Orthodox faith
under the name Natalya. Paul, who fell passionately in love with
Natalya, was blind to her frivolity and moral laxity. Shortly after the
wedding rumours reached Catherine from Italy of a pretender to the
throne who was claiming to be a daughter of Elizabeth. The mysterious
woman was kidnapped, brought to St Petersburg and interrogated. She
denied that she had ever claimed to be Elizabeth's daughter, and died in
the Peter and Paul Fortress, probably of consumption, in 1775. Her identity has never been established, but she has entered Russian legend as the
tragic 'Princess Tarakanova', who gave birth to a son in prison and
drowned when her cell was flooded.

Natalya died in childbirth in April 1776, as did her son. Paul was heart-
broken, but Catherine was determined that he should marry again

CATHERINE II'S DAILY ROUTINE

Catherine II walking with her dog in the gardens at Tsarskoe Selo. An engraving after a painting by Vladimir Lukich Borovikovsky (1757–1825) dating from 1796. The monument in the background was commissioned by Catherine in honour of Count Grigory Orlov.

I arise at six o'clock and until half past eight I read or write all alone in my study. Toward nine my secretaries arrive and I am with them until eleven. Then I dress and meanwhile chat with whomever is in my room. My toilet does not always last an hour, then I enter my reception room, I dine between one and two; after dinner I sew and have a book read to me until four; then those arrive who could not speak about business with me in the morning and I am with them until six, when I either go out for a walk, or to play, or to chat, or to a play. I sup between nine and ten, after supper I go to bed.

without delay. In a bid to overcome his reluctance she told him that Natalya had been conducting an adulterous affair with one of his closest friends. The empress' choice fell upon Princess Sophia Dorothea of Württemberg, whom Paul married in September 1776. Maria Feodorovna, as she was known in Russia, proved a much more satisfactory daughter-in-law, giving birth to a healthy boy in December 1777. Catherine took charge of the infant Alexander's upbringing, and Paul's second son Constantine, born in April 1779, was also educated under her supervision.

Reaction and death

Advancing age, ill health, and alarm at the revolutionary developments in France and Poland combined to make Catherine increasingly reactionary in her final years. Alexander Nikolaievich Radishchev's *Journey from St Petersburg to Moscow*, an indictment of social and political conditions in Russia, was banned. Radishchev, who is said to have fainted when he learned that his case was to be supervised by Sheshkovsky, the head of the Secret Expedition, was exiled to Siberia for ten years in 1790. Catherine tried to suppress Freemasonry, believing that masonic lodges were spreading revolutionary ideas. Even the works of Voltaire were proscribed, and in the last months of her life she imposed a strict censorship on foreign books and periodicals.

Catherine's health deteriorated in the 1790s. She put on weight, and her mobility was restricted by rheumatism and ulcers on her legs. It is possible that she considered disinheriting her son Paul in favour of her eldest grandson Alexander. She feared, justifiably, that Paul would undo her work, noting gloomily in 1787 that 'I cannot make my frame of mind hereditary.' On 5 November 1796 she suffered a stroke in her privy closet. She never regained consciousness and died on the evening of 6 November. When told that the empress was dying, Paul went to the Winter Palace and examined her papers. If there was a decree transferring the succession to Alexander, he must have destroyed it.

Slavophile historians, while acknowledging that she enlarged the empire and enhanced Russia's status as a great power, have written unfavourably of Catherine's German origins and Western ideas. For Soviet historians she was a ruler who identified with the interests of the nobility and did nothing for the peasant masses. Since the era of glasnost some Russian scholars have taken a more positive view of Catherine, and in 1996 the Russian Academy of Sciences organized a conference to mark the bicentenary of her death. Western historians have debated whether Catherine should be seen as an example of Enlightened Absolutism or Despotism. While it is difficult to believe in Enlightened Absolutism as a phenomenon, it is clear that Catherine was an innovator, both in her methods and her manner of government. Her reign can be seen as a dialectic between Enlightenment idealism and the political, economic and social realities of Russia. As she reportedly told Diderot: 'You work on paper, which will suffer anything. As for me, poor empress, I work on human skin, which is quite otherwise; irritable and ticklish.'

Павел   Paul
1796–1801

Александр I   Alexander I
1801–1825

Tsar Paul by Stepan Semyonovich Shchukin (1762–1828). This flattering portrait was painted at the time of his accession. The French painter Marie-Louise-Elisabeth Vigée-Lebrun, who met Paul, noted that he was '... exceedingly ugly. A flat nose, and a very large mouth furnished with very long teeth, made him look like a death's head.'

PAUL	
Full name	(Natalya
Paul Petrovich	Alexeyevna)
Romanov	Died 1776
Father	(2) 1776 Sophia
Officially Peter III,	Dorothea of
but possibly Sergei	Württemberg
Saltykov	(Maria Feodorovna)
Mother	Died 1828
Catherine II	*Children by (2)*
Born	**Alexander** (1777)
St Petersburg	Constantine (1779)
20 September 1754	Alexandra (1783)
Accession	Yelena (1784)
6 November 1796	Maria (1786)
Died	Catherine (1788)
St Petersburg	Olga (1792)
12 March 1801	Anna (1795)
Murdered	**Nicholas** (1796)
Wives	Mikhail (1798)
(1) 1773	
Wilhelmina of	
Hesse-Darmstadt	

PAUL

He appears lively and active, with a sensible, spirited countenance.

Benjamin Franklin

His features were ugly except the eyes, whose expression when he was not overcome with rage, was infinitely agreeable and gentle. When he was angry, his aspect was terrifying. Although his mien was ungraceful, he had a certain reserve of dignity, and especially of good manners, and a polite bearing towards women, which gave a real distinction to his person and proclaimed him a prince and a nobleman.

Princess Lieven, the wife of a prominent Russian diplomatist

Paul (1796–1801) was born in 1754. Officially he was acknowledged as the son of Grand Duke Peter (later Peter III) and his wife Catherine (later Catherine II), though Catherine subsequently hinted that the marriage was never consummated, and Paul was born during her affair with Saltykov. The Empress Elizabeth immediately removed Paul from the care of his parents. The murder of the man he believed to be his father in the coup which brought his mother to power made him hostile and

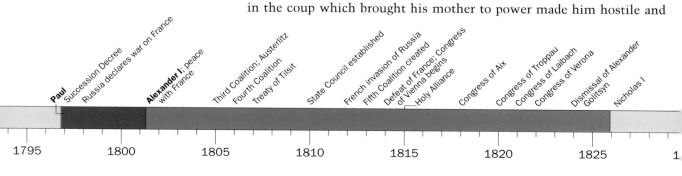

PAUL'S INSTRUCTIONS TO A WIFE

Paul's second wife, the Empress Maria Feodorovna, in an engraving by Rockstuhl after a portrait by G.B. Lampi (1751–1830).

At the time of his second marriage, in 1776, Paul drew up a detailed set of instructions for his bride. These show that he had some understanding of his own temperament, and a need to lead a carefully regulated existence.

It is appropriate for her above all to arm herself with patience and meekness in order to tolerate my ardour and volatile disposition and, equally, my impatience.... By subjecting ourselves to well-known rules, we protect ourselves from our own fantasies, which frequently become caprices, and ... we give an example to other people who are obliged to subject themselves to the same rules.... I said above that the exact fulfilment of the rules is one of the chief conditions which it is necessary to observe in life; I repeat this again, especially relative to the domestic regime. As long as we hold to the established rules, we spare ourselves much, including tedium, one of the chief enemies of man.... My own use of time is distributed such that, beginning at ten o'clock, when I am completely dressed, and until noon, I do not have a minute of free time.

suspicious towards Catherine. His education was supervised by Nikita Ivanovich Panin, who sought to rear him as an enlightened ruler. Paul's desire to carry Panin's precepts into practice was undermined by his temperament. He was obsessive, volatile and prone to violent, irrational rages.

Paul's first wife, Natalya, died in childbirth in 1776. He married his second wife, Sophia Dorothea of Württemberg, later that year. His feelings towards her may be judged from his description of her as 'not bad: large and well-shaped'. Maria Feodorovna, as she was known in Russia, gave him four sons and six daughters. The eldest sons, Alexander and Constantine, were educated under the supervision of Catherine II and did not enjoy close relations with their parents until they were teenagers. Paul lived at Gatchina and Pavlovsk, his country estates near St Petersburg, excluded from affairs of state by Catherine. He was critical of what he saw as the luxury and corruption of his mother's court, preferring

(*Right above*) A military parade at Gatchina. An engraving by G.S. Sergeyev dating from 1798. Paul was given Gatchina by his mother in 1784.

(*Right*) The Grand Palace at Pavlovsk, in an engraving of 1805 by G.L. Lory.

Engraving of Paul and his entourage wearing Prussian-style uniforms.

THE HISTORIAN KLIUCHEVSKY ON PAUL

In general, Paul's attempts to introduce legality into relations in which free will and accident were the sole operating agencies were so ill-conceived, and put forward so faultily, that there resulted less a weakening of the free will than so great an increase of fear and confusion in every heart, so complete a subjection of the whole community to depression and weariness, as never had been witnessed the eighteenth century through. We see the atmosphere best illustrated in the fact that whenever an officer was about to attend an Imperial Review (a ceremony from which one might depart either straight to Siberia or be promoted a step in rank) he would take with him to the review sufficient money to cover long-journey travelling expenses. And as for officers' wives, they stood so intimidated with the prevalent system of nocturnal arrests that, when retiring to rest, they would do so only if they had a hand of their husband clasped in one of theirs, that at least he might not be spirited away without their becoming aware of the fact.

simple pleasures such as drilling troops, playing chess and eating sausages. Gatchina became a cross between a model estate and an armed camp, with a private army, whose uniforms, drill and strict discipline reflected Paul's enthusiasm for things Prussian. He participated in the war with Sweden (1788–90) and was pleased to have been under fire, though the Swedes later apologized for shooting at him.

Paul's succession in 1796 was unchallenged. His insistence that the remains of Peter III be reburied alongside those of Catherine II in the Peter and Paul Cathedral was an ostentatious assertion of his own legitimacy. He sought to regularize the succession by issuing a decree in 1797 imposing the system of male primogeniture, and ruling that the successor must be Orthodox. Paul reversed many of Catherine's policies. The expedition which she had sent to fight the Persians was recalled. Dissidents imprisoned by her were released. The manners and customs of Gatchina were transferred to the capital, which became like an armed camp. The Secret Expedition's activities were expanded.

Reforms and censorship

The early years of the reign saw constructive reforms. A new military manual was issued, on the Prussian model. This, and the Prussian-style uniforms which Paul introduced, caused resentment. The living conditions of the private soldiers were improved. Paul also attempted to revive and centralize the system of government and to reduce its costs. He created Russia's first two ministries. A Ministry of Appanage was established in 1797 to administer the landholdings of the imperial family and a Ministry of Commerce was created in 1800. These institutions, larger and more efficient than the Colleges, established the pattern for the development of the imperial bureaucracy in the 19th century. His attitude to the peasants was paternalistic. In 1797 he urged landowners not to make serfs work on Sundays. He also recommended that serfs should only be required to work for three days a week on their owners' land. He forbade the breaking up of serf families. These measures were unpopular with the nobility, as was Paul's taxation of noblemen and his infliction of corporal punishment on them – both breaches of Catherine's Statute of the Nobility of 1785. Paul was instinctively anti-revolutionary. In 1800 he imposed a complete ban on the importation of books and music. The use of revolutionary vocabulary such as 'citizen' and 'society' was forbidden.

Foreign policy

The emperor's decision to join Austria, Britain and Naples in the Second anti-French Coalition was based on ideology, fantasy and hard-headed calculation. He wished to see the hereditary rulers of Italy restored to their thrones. The French occupation of Malta in 1798 profoundly affected him. Since boyhood he had been fascinated by the Knights of Malta. In 1798 he was elected Grand Master of the Order, and he dreamed of liberating the island. He saw France's incursions into the eastern

PAUL'S VIEWS ON GOVERNMENT

In 1788 Paul drew up a political testament in which he argued that Russia needed an autocratic system of government, while acknowledging that an autocracy is vulnerable to the frailties of the autocrat.

The object of every society is the happiness of each and all. Society cannot exist unless the will of everyone is directed to a common goal. This is what government is for, any kind of government. The best is that which most directly and advantageously reaches its goal.... The larger the land, the more difficult the means of fulfilling [the goal of happiness]; consequently the first care must be to facilitate them. The simplest means is to entrust power to a single person, but there are human incapacities inherent in it.

Count Peter Alexeyevich Pahlen (1745–1826), the chief architect of the plot to overthrow Paul. A contemporary engraved portrait. Pahlen was asked by his fellow-conspirators what would happen to the emperor in the coup d'état. He replied: 'One cannot make an omelette without breaking eggs.'

Mediterranean as a threat to Russia's growing Black Sea trade, and brought Russia into an improbable and short-lived alliance with Turkey in 1798. In the winter of 1798–99 a joint Turkish and Russian fleet commanded by Admiral Feodor Ushakov drove the French out of the Ionian Islands, which were occupied by the Russians.

The Russian land forces commanded by General Suvorov performed well in the Italian campaign of 1799, before conducting a brilliant retreat through the Swiss Alps. Paul withdrew from the coalition when he realized that the Austrians were bent on annexing territory in Italy rather than restoring the legitimate rulers. Napoleon's seizure of power in November 1799 caused Paul to consider negotiating with what he now saw as a counter-revolutionary French government. The negotiations were fruitless. Paul's terms – the restoration of pre-war governments in Italy, Germany and Malta – were unacceptable to Napoleon. Relations with Great Britain deteriorated because the British continued to support the Austrians, and refused to return Malta, which they occupied in 1800, to the Order. Paul imposed a trade embargo, revived the League of Armed Neutrality and planned an expedition to conquer India. Many Russian nobles, however, favoured a pro-British policy. Paul's irrational behaviour intensified their opposition. By 1799 disgruntled aristocrats and officers, resentful of severe discipline and the dangers of summary dismissal, had begun to plot his downfall.

The search for security

Paul's private life was complex. His passionate but probably platonic friendship with Catherine Ivanovna Nelidova placed a strain on his marriage for several years, but Nelidova and the empress eventually became firm friends and together exercised a moderating influence on his behaviour. In 1798 Paul became involved with Anna Lopukhina, and distanced himself from both the empress and Nelidova. He became obsessive about security, and commissioned a new, moated residence in St Petersburg, the Mikhailovsky Zamok. Paul insisted on moving himself and his family into the building in February 1801 before the plaster on the walls was dry.

The plot which resulted in Paul's murder was led by Count Peter Pahlen, the military governor of St Petersburg, who was able to secure the conspirators access to the Mikhailovsky Zamok. Their plan to overthrow Paul was approved by his heir, Alexander. The fact that they took an abdication document with them may suggest that they were not bent on murder. They made their way into the building on the night of 11–12 March 1801, and found the emperor hiding behind a screen in his bedroom. A scuffle ensued, during which Paul was brutally battered and then strangled with a sash.

Though the official announcement stated that he had died of apoplexy, Paul's murder soon became public knowledge. The view that he had been insane was convenient to his successors, and found its way into much historical writing in the 19th and 20th centuries. It is only recently that Paul's reign has come to be seen not as a lunatic aberration but

THE MIKHAILOVSKY ZAMOK

Paul diverted marble from the construction work on St Isaac's Cathedral in order to complete the Mikhailovsky Zamok (Michael Castle). The architects were Vincenzo Brenna (*c*. 1750–1804) and Vasily Ivanovich Bazhenov (1738–99), and the design was influenced by the emperor's fear of assassination. Paul wanted a fortified and secure residence in a central location in the capital, and the castle was equipped with a moat and drawbridges as well as secret staircases to enable the emperor to escape from danger. Work began in 1797 and was completed at the end of 1800. Five thousand workmen were

The principal façade of the Mikhailovsky Zamok. An engraving by Benjamin Paterssen (1750–1816). The drawbridges over the moat are clearly visible. Construction of the castle involved the demolition of the Summer Palace built by Rastrelli for the Empress Elizabeth.

employed on the project, which cost 18 million roubles. Such was the emperor's sense of urgency that huge iron plates were heated and applied to the walls to dry the mortar more quickly. Paul was assassinated in his bedroom only three weeks after moving in. In 1822 Alexander I handed the structure over to the School of Engineers, an institution of which Feodor Mikhailovich Dostoyevsky was probably the most distinguished alumnus.

as the period when tsarist autocracy assumed the shape that it was to retain during the 19th century. Paul's emphasis on military discipline, his creation of Russia's first ministries, his tightening of censorship, and his police-state paternalism were to be developed by his sons, Alexander I and Nicholas I.

The youthful Grand Dukes Alexander, Constantine and Nicholas depicted as cherubs in a painting by Vladimir Lukich Borovikovsky (1757–1825).

ALEXANDER I	
Full name	*Died*
Alexander Pavlovich Romanov	Taganrog 19 November 1825
Father	A fever
Paul Petrovich Romanov	*Wife*
Mother	1793 Princess Louise of Baden (Elizabeth Alexeyevna)
Sophia Dorothea of Württemberg (Maria Feodorovna)	Died 1826
Born	*Children*
St Petersburg 12 December 1777	Maria (1799) Elizabeth (1806)
Accession	
12 March 1801	

ALEXANDER I

Despite the regularity and delicacy of his features and the bright freshness of his complexion, his physical beauty was at first sight less impressive than the air of kind benevolence which won all hearts and instantly inspired confidence. His tall, noble and majestic figure, often stooping graciously like the pose of an ancient statue, was already threatening to become stout, but he was perfectly formed. His eyes, alert and expressive, were blue and he was a little short-sighted. His nose was straight and well shaped with a small agreeable mouth. The rounded contours of his face resembled those of his august mother, as also did his profile. His forehead was slightly bald, giving to his whole countenance an open and serene expression, and his hair – which was a golden blond in colour – was carefully groomed as on the heads of classical cameos or medallions so that it seemed made to receive a triple crown of laurel, myrtle or olive.

Countess Tiesenhausen, describing Alexander I in 1812

Alexander I in uniform. A portrait by Jacques-Louis David (1748–1825), the painter who exercised a dominant influence in France during the Napoleonic era. David was also a deputy during the revolution and voted for the execution of Louis XVI.

Born in 1777, Alexander I (1801–1825) was brought up by his grandmother Catherine II. His Swiss tutor La Harpe, a convinced republican, inculcated in his pupil a belief in the rule of law and a hatred of despotism. As an adolescent Alexander grew to resent his grandmother's tutelage, and to admire the military discipline of his father's household at Gatchina. The pressure to please both Catherine II and Paul, whose characters and attitudes were so different, contributed to the self-doubt from which he suffered. Shortly before his accession to the throne he told friends that he hoped to retire into private life abroad. His marriage, at the age of 15, to Princess Louise of Baden, known in Russia as Elizabeth Alexeyevna, was arranged by his grandmother. By 1803 he had taken a mistress, Maria Naryshkina.

During Paul's reign Alexander was given significant responsibilities, including the Presidency of the War College and the Military Governorship of St Petersburg. Alexander knew of the plot to overthrow his father but the murder of Paul filled him with guilt and remorse. The liberal measures that he instituted in the ensuing weeks may have been motivated by fear of his father's murderers. He announced his intention of returning to the style of government of his grandmother. Censorship was relaxed. The 1785 Charter of the Nobility was reaffirmed and a commission was appointed to draw up a new law code.

In June 1801 Alexander, confident of the loyalty of the army, felt able to dismiss Pahlen. The brief return to Catherinian policies was over. The Law Commission achieved nothing. The idea of a charter granting civil rights to the Russian people was rejected. The Permanent Council established at the beginning of the reign continued to function, but in the period 1801–03 the emperor relied on the advice of an Unofficial Committee of friends. Prince Adam Czartoryski, Count Victor Kochubei, Nikolai Novosiltsev and Count Paul Stroganov were men with a knowledge of Western ideas. Their influence over the emperor, who was given to regurgitating the half-digested liberal precepts of his tutor, alarmed conservatives, but the advice that the Unofficial Committee gave Alexander was cautious. They believed

THE HISTORIAN KARAMZIN ON ALEXANDER I

Autocracy has founded and resuscitated Russia. Any change in her political constitution has led in the past and must lead in the future to her perdition, for she consists of very many and very different parts, each of which has its own special civic needs; what save unlimited monarchy can produce in such a machine the required unity of action?

Alexander, inspired with love for the common good, and with the best intentions, took counsel, and, in accord with … the political system of foreign countries, established ministries. To begin with, let us call attention to the excessive haste with which this move was made. The ministries were created and set in motion before the ministers had been provided with an Instruction, that is, with a dependable, clear guide to help them carry out their important duties! Let us next inquire into their

utility. Ministerial bureaus have replaced colleges. Where work had been carried out by eminent officials such as a president and several assessors, men with long training and with a strong sense of responsibility for their whole office, we came to see insignificant officials, such as directors, filing clerks, desk heads, who, shielded by their minister, operated with utter impunity.

A village council in Russia.
An engraving from J.A. Atkinson's
*A Picturesque Representation of the
Manners of the Russians*, published in
1812. The function of such councils was
to determine the pattern of local
agriculture by deciding which family
would cultivate which areas of the
communally held land.

The battle of Austerlitz, 1805. An early
19th-century engraving. Austerlitz
(Slavkov in the Czech Republic) was
then in the Moravian region of the
Austrian empire.

that reform could only be achieved from above, and argued against the abolition of serfdom on the grounds that it would alienate the nobility and lead to a breakdown of order in the countryside. The Free Cultivators Law of 1803 permitted landlords to liberate serfs if they wished, but less than 0.5 per cent of serfs had been emancipated by 1825.

Early reforms

In September 1802 Alexander granted the Senate the power to reject laws which they regarded as unsuitable, though when the Senate exercised this right in the following year the emperor angrily imposed limits on it. Alexander believed that a ministerial system of government would enhance his power, and in 1802 he created eight new ministries. Ministers were to be appointed and dismissed by him, though the Senate had the right to receive annual reports from them and to question them. The Secret Expedition was abolished, and thousands of people imprisoned or exiled in the previous reign were released.

A decree of 1803 sought to create parochial schools in every village, offering free tuition to all, including serfs. In practice few serfs' children attended the schools. By 1825 there were over 1,400 state schools in Russia, and pupil numbers had reached 70,000. Secondary schools were set up in district towns and gymnasia in provincial capitals. New universities were opened at Kazan, Kharkov and St Petersburg, and all universities were granted a generous degree of self-government.

Foreign policy

In 1801 Alexander recalled the expeditionary force that his father had sent to attack India, restored diplomatic and trading relations with Britain and signed a peace treaty with France. The last move was unpopular with Russian conservatives. By the spring of March 1802 Europe was at peace, Napoleon having concluded the Treaty of Lunéville with Austria in February 1801 and the Treaty of Amiens with Britain in March 1802.

Alexander continued the expansionist policy of his predecessors, annexing Georgia in 1801. A war with Persia (1804–13) consolidated and extended Russia's gains in the Caucasus region, and the nominal control that Russia had since 1740 claimed over the Kazakh tribes was enforced in the course of the reign.

Peace in Europe did not last. Britain and France went to war in May 1803. Napoleon's continuing ambitions in the eastern Mediterranean alarmed Alexander. His attempt to arbitrate between the French and the British was rejected by Napoleon, whose coronation of himself as emperor in 1804 persuaded Alexander that peaceful coexistence with France was not possible. In 1805 he joined the British and the Austrians in the Third Coalition against France. The Russian campaign in Austria ended in disaster, partly because Alexander ignored the advice of his experienced commander, Mikhail Kutuzov. At Austerlitz, on 20 November (2 December NS) 1805, the Russians suffered at the hands of Napoleon their worst defeat since Narva (p. 99). Alexander narrowly avoided

The conference at Tilsit in 1807. This contemporary French engraving shows the meeting between Napoleon (on the left) and Alexander I (right) which took place on a raft moored in the middle of the River Niemen. The two leaders exchanged pleasantries, polite enquiries about their respective families, cravats and embroidered handkerchiefs.

Mikhail Mikhailovich Speransky (1772–1839). An early 19th-century engraved portrait. The son of a priest, Speransky married an Englishwoman, Elizabeth Stephens. She died a year later, and he never remarried.

capture, and spent the night after the battle in a peasant's hut, a tearful victim of remorse and stomach cramps. Austria made peace with France, the Holy Roman Empire was dissolved and Napoleon was able to restructure the German states. A Fourth Coalition was formed in 1806, involving Prussia, Russia, Great Britain and Sweden. Napoleon defeated the Prussians at Jena on 14 October 1806 (NS), and occupied Berlin. At the end of 1806 Turkey, influenced by France, provoked Russia into war by closing the Straits and deposing the rulers of Moldavia and Wallachia. Russia was ill-prepared for a war on two fronts. A decisive French victory at Friedland in June 1807 undermined Alexander's will to continue the war. On 25 June (7 July NS) he, Friedrich Wilhelm III of Prussia and Napoleon began peace talks at Tilsit.

Alexander agreed to hand over the Ionian Islands, and to withdraw his forces from Moldavia and Wallachia. He also committed Russia to membership of Napoleon's Continental System, which meant breaking lucrative trading links with Great Britain. Napoleon took control of Prussian Poland, creating a French satellite state, the Grand Duchy of Warsaw, and conceding only Bialystok to Russia. He also agreed to underwrite Alexander's plans to conquer Finland. The possibility of partitioning the European parts of the Ottoman empire between France and Russia was discussed. These concessions were not sufficient to convince educated opinion in Russia that Alexander had been successful at Tilsit. He himself seems to have regarded peace with France as a temporary expedient. The war against Sweden in 1808–09, in which Russia gained Finland, was unpopular with Russian conservatives, who felt that Alexander was acting on Napoleon's behalf.

The Speransky era

Alexander's principal adviser in the period 1807 to 1812 was his State Secretary, Mikhail Mikhailovich Speransky, who sought to modernize Russia's governmental institutions. In 1809 he introduced a system of examinations for promotion to the higher levels of the bureaucracy. He revived the work of the Law Commission, which produced a Civil Code in 1812. The Code, which was influenced by Napoleon's legal reforms, was unpopular with the nobility and was never implemented. Speransky also tackled Russia's finances, trebling government revenues in the period 1810–12 by increasing the soul tax and imposing a highly unpopular income tax, which the nobility saw as a breach of the 1785 Charter.

Speransky persuaded Alexander to establish an advisory State Council to prepare legislative proposals for the emperor's consideration. He also suggested the creation of a consultative State Duma elected by property owners. This proposal, which might have been the means of establishing a civic partnership between the autocracy and a section of the population, was rejected by Alexander, who feared that such an assembly would encroach upon his prerogative. In March 1812, aware that war with France was imminent, and that he needed to conciliate the conservatives, Alexander tearfully dismissed Speransky.

ALEXANDER I AND THE WAR OF 1812

Alexander, who took personal command of the Russian forces at the start of the war, had no intention of allowing Napoleon to penetrate deep into Russia. He favoured making a stand at Drissa, but soon realized that the fortifications there were inadequate and left the town on 4 July (16 July NS). Then, to the relief of his generals, he relinquished command of the army to General Barclay de Tolly and set out for Moscow, where he proved to be very effective in rallying support for the war effort.

The French Advance

The cautious Barclay de Tolly abandoned Vitebsk to the French, who occupied the town on 16 July (28 July NS). Barclay and General Bagration, whose personal relations were rancorous, managed to join forces at Smolensk, but they were outnumbered and Barclay decided to avoid a large-scale battle. The French entered Smolensk on 6 August (18 August NS). By then Alexander, who had returned to St Petersburg, was under considerable pressure to dismiss Barclay. On 8 August (20 August NS) he reluctantly appointed Kutuzov as commander-in-chief. Kutuzov chose to confront Napoleon's forces at Borodino, 70 miles west of Moscow. There, on 26 August (7 September NS) the Russians inflicted heavy casualties on the French at enormous cost to themselves.

The news of Borodino was greeted with enthusiasm in St Petersburg, but when it became apparent that Kutuzov had not gained a decisive victory and was retreating towards Moscow, public opinion turned against Alexander. On Sunday 1 September (13 September NS) Kutuzov made the decision to abandon Moscow in order to preserve the Russian army.

Napoleon in Moscow

The French entered Moscow on 2 September (14 September NS). That night fires broke out in the city, and in the course of the next few days much of Moscow

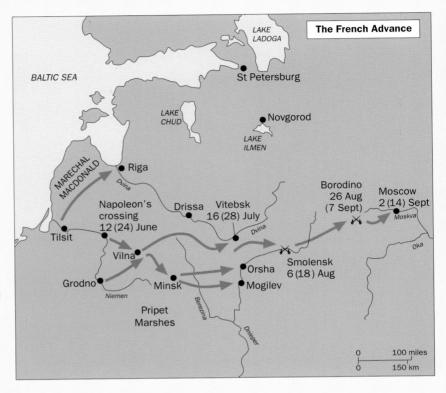

The fall and burning of Moscow (left) precipitated a religious crisis in Tsar Alexander I (above), who maintained an attitude of public defiance towards the French, despite his private misgivings.

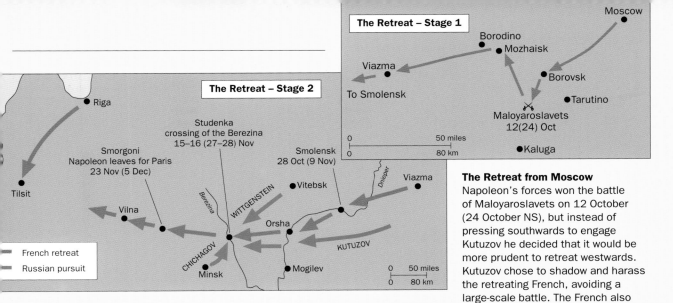

The Retreat – Stage 1

Moscow
Borodino
Mozhaisk
Viazma
Borovsk
To Smolensk
Tarutino
Maloyaroslavets
12(24) Oct
Kaluga

0   50 miles
0   80 km

The Retreat – Stage 2

Riga
Studenka
crossing of the Berezina
15–16 (27–28) Nov
Smorgoni
Napoleon leaves for Paris
23 Nov (5 Dec)
Smolensk
28 Oct (9 Nov)
Tilsit
Vitebsk
Viazma
Vilna
WITTGENSTEIN
Orsha
CHICHAGOV
KUTUZOV
Minsk
Mogilev

◼ French retreat
◼ Russian pursuit

0   50 miles
0   80 km

The Retreat from Moscow

Napoleon's forces won the battle of Maloyaroslavets on 12 October (24 October NS), but instead of pressing southwards to engage Kutuzov he decided that it would be more prudent to retreat westwards. Kutuzov chose to shadow and harass the retreating French, avoiding a large-scale battle. The French also had to contend with attacks from Russian partisans. An early and severe winter set in, slowing their progress, and the French found themselves menaced by Russian forces commanded by Wittgenstein and Chichagov. The destruction of the bridge over the River Berezina at Borisov threatened to cut off Napoleon's line of retreat. The French discovered a ford at Studenka, and the hasty construction of two trestle bridges in the shallow water enabled the remnants of the Grande Armée to escape from the trap on 15–16 November (27–28 November NS). At Smorgoni on 23 November (5 December NS) Napoleon took the decision to return to Paris. By then combat, harsh weather and starvation had further reduced the Grande Armée. An estimated 25,000 men crossed the River Niemen in December.

was destroyed. Though he later denied it, the burning of Moscow had been organized by its governor, Count Rostopchin. Alexander, dismayed at the news of the loss of Moscow and fearful of the impact it would have on opinion in St Petersburg, delayed the official announcement for 11 days.

Napoleon hoped that the capture of Moscow would force the Russians to come to terms, but Alexander rejected his attempts to negotiate. The nearness of winter, lack of food and the vulnerability of his supply lines limited Napoleon's freedom of manoeuvre. Of the 450,000 soldiers in his Central Army Group, only 100,000 had reached Moscow, the remainder having fallen victim to starvation, disease and battle. An attack on St Petersburg seemed too hazardous, and Napoleon decided to march south-westwards, hoping to defeat Kutuzov's forces at Tarutino before retreating to a less vulnerable position. Before they left Moscow on 7 October (19 October NS), the French attempted to destroy the Kremlin by detonating mines that they had laid under its buildings.

The French retreat from Moscow restored Alexander's popularity and confirmed his belief that he had a divine mission to rid Europe of Napoleonic rule. In the epilogue of his novel *War and Peace*, Lev Tolstoy analysed Alexander's contribution to the defeat of Napoleon thus: 'During the national conflict he is inactive because he is not needed. As soon as the necessity for a general European war becomes apparent, he is in his place at the given moment and, uniting the nations of Europe, leads them to the goal.'

(Below) Mikhail Bogdanovich Barclay de Tolly (1761–1818), appointed War Minister in 1810, was regarded with suspicion in St Petersburg because of his Scots ancestry.

(Above) Peter Ivanovich Bagration (1765–1812) was a descendant of the Georgian royal house. He was fatally wounded at the battle of Borodino.

(Right) Mikhail Ilarionovich Kutuzov (1745–1813) was a veteran of the Turkish Wars. His corpulence, and the loss of an eye in battle, did not curtail his amorous propensities.

The French Campaign, 1814. This celebrated painting by the French artist Jean-Louis-Ernest Meissonier (1815–91) depicts Napoleon and his troops in the final stages of the War of the Fifth Coalition. Meissonier's canvas, now in the Louvre, Paris, has been likened to 'a symphony by Berlioz played without drums and with tin for brass.'

The defeat of Napoleon

At Erfurt in October 1808 Napoleon accepted Russia's claim to Moldavia and Wallachia in return for Russian support in the event of a war between France and Austria. Alexander's contribution to Napoleon's victory over the Austrians in 1809 was negligible, as was Russia's territorial reward, the district of Tarnopol, north-east of the Carpathian mountains. By 1810 the costs to Russia of membership of the Continental System were all too apparent. The annual value of Russia's exports had fallen by 40 per cent, and the government was forced to inflate the currency. It was clear that France was not willing to give meaningful support in Russia's war against Turkey. On 31 December 1810 Alexander effectively abandoned his alliance with France by announcing that a higher tariff would be levied on overland imports to Russia than on goods coming in by sea. Neutral shipping had been delivering British goods to Russia for some time, and during 1811 British ships began to enter Russian ports.

Fearing a French attack, Alexander made peace with the Turks in May 1812. Russia agreed to evacuate Moldavia and Wallachia, but gained part of Bessarabia. Napoleon's invasion force crossed into Russian territory on 12 June (24 June NS) 1812. Outnumbered, the Russians avoided a large-scale battle until the enemy's forces, already depleted by hunger and disease, were less than 100 miles from Moscow. Mikhail Kutuzov, the Russian commander-in-chief, made a stand at Borodino, where the French lost 40,000 men in an inconclusive battle on 26 August (7 September NS). He then decided to abandon Moscow, a policy of which Alexander disapproved. Napoleon's army, reduced to 100,000 soldiers, entered the almost deserted city on 2 September (14 September NS). That night fires broke out and in the next few days 90 per cent of Moscow was destroyed. Baffled by the Russians' refusal to surrender and alarmed at the prospect of a Russian winter, Napoleon ordered a retreat from Moscow in October. Only a small remnant of his soldiers escaped from Russia. The rest had fallen victim to partisans, Kutuzov's forces and the severe weather.

During the 1812 War Alexander experienced a religious conversion, and became convinced that it was his duty to overthrow Napoleon and restore order in Europe. In 1813 he worked to construct a Fifth Coalition, negotiating agreements with Prussia and Austria. He took command of his armies, displaying personal heroism in the battle of Leipzig in October 1813. Overcoming Austrian and Prussian reluctance, Alexander insisted that the allies invade France. The Treaty of Chaumont (9 March 1814 NS) committed them to the total defeat of Napoleon, who abdicated on 11 April 1814 (NS), a few days after Alexander had led his victorious forces into Paris.

Peace-making

Alexander's behaviour in the years 1812–14 was a puzzling mixture of piety and profligacy. During a visit to England in 1814 he was impressed by the work of the Bible Society, and thereafter he annoyed the Orthodox hierarchy by supporting the Society's efforts to disseminate the scriptures in Russia. His sexual escapades in Vienna in 1814 abruptly gave way to domestic tranquillity, a transformation which the chief of the Austrian secret police cynically ascribed to the emperor's having contracted venereal disease. By 1815 Alexander had fallen under the influence of Baroness Julie de Krüdener, a religious enthusiast who encouraged his belief that God had chosen him to fulfil an historic purpose.

At the Congress of Vienna (1814–15), during which the powers attempted to shape the future of Europe, the British and the Austrians were unwilling to agree to Alexander's proposal to recreate Poland, and he had to settle for a truncated Kingdom of Poland under Romanov rule. Russian forces played no part in the final campaign against Napoleon who, heartened by the disputes between the allies, left his place of exile on Elba and made a bid for power which ended with his defeat at Waterloo on 18 June 1815 (NS).

Alexander wanted the Quadruple Alliance to be permanent, and supported the attempt to create a Congress System, with regular meetings between the allies to discuss the affairs of Europe. His suggestion that the alliance should be strengthened by a commitment to 'the immutable

The Congress of Vienna. A contemporary engraving. Seated behind the table are Alexander I of Russia (to the left) and Emperor Franz II of Austria. King Friedrich Wilhelm III of Prussia is standing between the Austrian emperor and the globe, and the Duke of Wellington is seated next to him.

principles of the Christian religion' was rejected by the British. Prussia and Austria, who shared the British unease at the size of Russia's armed forces, signed the Holy Alliance, though the Austrian Foreign Minister Metternich dismissed it as 'empty and sonorous'.

By the end of the Napoleonic Wars Russia had become the dominant military power in Europe. Tarnopol, an area acquired by Austria in 1772 as a result of the first Polish Partition, was granted to Russia by Napoleon in 1809. Under the Vienna Settlement of 1815 the Russians returned it to Austria. The Grand Duchy of Finland, hitherto ruled by the Swedes, was annexed by Russia in 1809 and retained until December 1917. Russia acquired Bessarabia from the Ottoman empire in 1812 under the terms of the Treaty of Bucharest. The southern part of Bessarabia was ceded back to the Turks in 1856 after the Crimean War and regained by Russia in 1878. Bessarabia was annexed by Romania in 1918. In 1815, at the Congress of Vienna, Russia was allotted most of the Napoleonic Grand Duchy of Warsaw. 'Congress Poland', as the kingdom became known, remained under Russian rule until 1917.

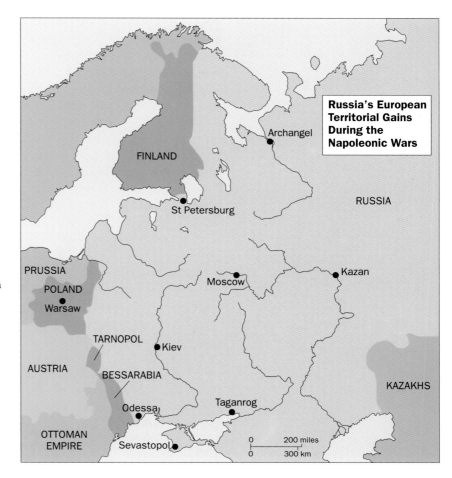

Russia's European Territorial Gains During the Napoleonic Wars

The retreat from constitutionalism

In November 1815 Alexander granted a constitution to Poland, guaranteeing important civil rights. When he addressed the opening session of the Polish Diet in 1818, he explained his intention of granting similar liberties in Russia when the time seemed ripe. In 1818 he instructed Novosiltsev to produce a draft constitution for Russia. Yet Alexander rejected his proposals, and also turned down Alexei Andreyevich Arakcheyev's scheme for a gradual emancipation of the serfs. Foreign revolts and a mutiny by members of the Semeonovsky regiment in 1820 convinced the emperor that evil revolutionary influences were at work and that repressive policies were required.

Arakcheyev, a general in the artillery who had served Alexander as War Minister from 1808 to 1810 and who exercised an increasing influence on domestic policy from 1815 onwards, was given charge of the new system of military colonies instituted by Alexander in 1815–16. The colonies were an attempt to end the system under which military service cut a recruit off from normal life for 25 years. They were populated by soldiers and their families, and by state peasants who farmed the land when the soldiers were on campaign. Although education and medical care were provided, the colonists resented the harsh, intrusive military discipline imposed by Arakcheyev, and there were several rebellions. The system was modified in the reign of Nicholas I and finally abandoned after the Crimean War.

By 1822 Alexander had come under the influence of the Archimandrite Photius, a reactionary Orthodox monk who lectured him on the perils of Protestantism, Freemasonry and Liberalism. Photius, who was an ally of Arakcheyev, helped to persuade Alexander to abandon his support for the Bible Society and in 1824 he secured the dismissal of Prince Alexander Golitsyn, a notable advocate of religious tolerance, from the post of Minister of Spiritual Affairs and Education. Yet

MILITARY COLONIES

Nicholas I's wife recollects, in a private memoir not intended for publication, the military colonies established in the reign of her brother-in-law Alexander I.

I felt more at ease with Prince Galitzin than with Arakcheyev who only spoke Russian, and imbued me with a certain instinctive dread.

At that time there was much talk of military colonies; they had been instituted about a year previously on the Emperor's initiative, but the execution of the scheme having been entrusted to Arakcheyev it was not being carried out gently but on the contrary by hard and cruel methods which left the poor peasants discontented. On our drive from St Petersburg we met here and there inhabitants of villages who, on their knees, begged that their lives might not be interfered with.

Etching from a contemporary portrait of Alexei Andreyevich Arakcheyev (1769–1834), an influential minister in the second half of the reign of Alexander I. Liberal contemporaries regarded him as an evil genius.

Alexander refused to suppress the secret societies which posed the greatest threat to political stability in Russia. 'I have encouraged and shared these illusions and errors myself,' he is reported to have said in 1821. 'It is not for me to punish them.' The Decembrists, as these groups later became known because some of their members participated in an uprising in December 1825, had by then concluded that the autocracy itself was an obstacle to progress.

The Congress System

At the Congress of Aix-la-Chapelle in 1818 Alexander's suggestion of an alliance to crush revolutions and to preserve the territorial settlement agreed at Vienna was unacceptable to the British, and alarming to Metternich, who felt that Alexander was too much under the liberal influence of Ioannis Kapodistrias, the Greek nobleman who was joint Foreign Minister of Russia with Nesselrode from September 1815 until June 1822. Alexander was persuaded to withdraw his proposals.

Metternich found Alexander's attitudes at the Congress of Troppau, which opened in October 1820, reassuringly conservative, though he was alarmed by Alexander's offer to send Russian troops to crush revolutions in Spain and the Kingdom of Naples. At the Congress of Laibach in 1821 the powers discussed the risings against Turkish rule in Greece, Moldavia and Wallachia. Alexander might have been expected to share Kapodistrias' enthusiasm for the Greek cause, but he was now convinced that armed rebellions were the work of the devil. At the Congress of Verona, which began in October 1822, Alexander agreed that the Turks should be left to settle matters in the Balkans.

The Congress System did not survive beyond the meeting at Verona. In the years that followed, Alexander pursued the idea that the Greeks should be given autonomy within the Ottoman empire. The other powers saw this as a bid to extend Russia's sphere of influence in the Balkans, and both the Turks and the Greeks rejected the proposal. By the autumn of 1825 Alexander may have been contemplating military action against the Turks.

The succession

The death of his younger daughter in 1808 left Alexander I childless. His brother Constantine had no issue and the hopes of the dynasty were therefore concentrated on the Grand Duke Nicholas, the third son of Tsar Paul. Alexander had come to regard Nicholas as a more suitable successor, partly because Constantine had contracted a morganatic marriage to a Polish countess. In 1822 Constantine, who was Viceroy of Poland, renounced his claim to the throne, and in the following year Alexander signed a secret proclamation designating Nicholas as his heir.

Drawing of the Grand Duke Constantine Pavlovich, brother of Alexander I and Nicholas I. Prince Czartoryski said of him: 'His heart is sound, but the rectitude of his judgment is a matter of chance.... Whether he loves or hates, it is always with violence.' The Marquis de Custine claimed that at a military review Constantine thrust his sword through the foot of a general in order to demonstrate the absolute discipline of Russian soldiers. Since the general remained both silent and motionless under this provocation, the experiment was deemed a success.

Elizabeth, wife of Alexander I, in a portrait by the French painter Marie-Louise-Elisabeth Vigée-Lebrun (1755–1842). Vigée-Lebrun recalled in her memoirs that '...the more sittings the Grand Duchess Elizabeth did for me, the kinder and more affectionate did she become.'

Death and the legend

Alexander suffered a serious attack of erysipelas, a streptococcal skin infection, in early 1824. The death of his illegitimate daughter Sophie, and the devastating floods in St Petersburg in November of that year, seemed to the emperor a punishment for his sins. During this period he grew closer to the Empress Elizabeth, but by 1825 her health was failing, and in September of that year Alexander took her to Taganrog on the Sea of Azov to winter in a warmer climate. The visit gave him the opportunity to inspect military units in the Crimea. While there he was taken ill with a fever, and he died at Taganrog on 19 November. His remains were taken to St Petersburg for burial early in 1826. Elizabeth did not long survive him. She died at Belev in April 1826. The fact that Alexander's body was not publicly displayed before burial helped to give rise to the popular myth that he was not dead, but had renounced the throne to become a wandering holy man.

Those who had dealings with Alexander I were charmed, puzzled and exasperated by him, and historians have pondered the discrepancy between the liberal sentiments of his youth and the repressive conservatism of his later years. Some have attributed this change to his religious conversion. Others have argued that his youthful idealism was a fashionable pose. Though many of Alexander's contemporaries believed him to be inconsistent or hypocritical, there is a common thread running through his reign. He was a consistent guardian of the imperial prerogative.

ALEXANDER I – DEATH AND THE LEGEND

There were many hermits and wandering holy men in 19th-century Russia, but one in particular became the subject of a persistent legend. Feodor Kuzmich first came to public notice in Siberia in 1836, and died in Tomsk in 1864. He was said to have a detailed knowledge of the imperial family and government affairs, and the rumour spread that he was none other than the Emperor Alexander I, who was said to have faked his own death in 1825 in order to devote himself to religion. By the time of Kuzmich's death it was widely believed that the Romanovs had taken a close interest in him, and there were people willing to claim that he resembled the emperor. Another version of the legend linked Kuzmich with the Princess Tarakanova, an 18th-century pretender to the throne. It was suggested that Princess Tarakanova was the offspring of the Empress Elizabeth and Count Razumovsky, that she was briefly married to Count Radziwill, and that Feodor Kuzmich was their son.

Whoever Feodor Kuzmich was, it is highly unlikely he was Alexander I. The emperor had been in poor health in the final years of his reign, and the idea that he could have lived to the age of 87 and endured the hardships experienced by Kuzmich is improbable. The rumours are contradicted by this account of a post mortem conducted on the emperor's body by an English doctor, Robert Lee, who was a Fellow of the Royal Society.

On the post-mortem examination of the body being made, the appearances observed were such as are most frequently met with in those dying from bilious remittent fever, with internal congestion. Two ounces of serous fluid were found in the ventricles of the brain, and all the veins and arteries were gorged with blood. There was an old adhesion between the dura and the pia mater at the back part, but of no great extent. The heart and lungs were sound, but too vascular. The liver was turgid with blood, and of a much darker colour than natural. The spleen was enlarged and softened in texture. The prevalence of fever in the Crimea during the autumn, the sudden change of the weather when the Emperor left the coast, the usual symptoms appearing in the course of a few days after quitting Perecop, as I had before observed in others, with the subsequent history of the disease, and the appearances after death, rendered it certain that the Emperor Alexander was cut off by the bilious remittent fever of the Crimea.

Nicholas I
1825–1855

Alexander II
1855–1881

Alexander III
1881–1894

Nicholas II
1894–1917

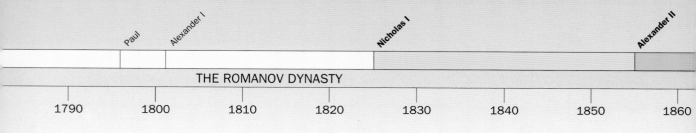

Paul

Alexander I

Nicholas I

Alexander II

THE ROMANOV DYNASTY

1790   1800   1810   1820   1830   1840   1850   1860

Nicholas I

Alexander II

Alexander III

Nicholas II

THE CHALLENGES OF MODERNIZATION

THE LAST FOUR ROMANOVS were all confronted by the same dilemmas. The strength of their empire could only be maintained by modernizing the economy and the administration, but modernization involved the emergence of an educated class likely to question the existing system and to aspire to a role in government. Governing a multinational empire in an era of increasing nationalism presented another set of challenges. The policy of Russification, which involved imposing the Russian language and culture on subject peoples and discriminating against their religious beliefs, alienated national groups such as the Poles and the Ukrainians.

The Decembrist Uprising of 1825 frightened Nicholas I into a reactive and reactionary conservatism which further alienated the educated classes. Alexander II emancipated the serfs and modernized Russia's institutions. This perestroika was insufficient to bridge the gulf that had opened between the autocracy and the intelligentsia and the Tsar Liberator fell victim to a terrorist bomb. His successor, Alexander III, set his face against constitutional reform but encouraged rapid industrial growth. Alexander's heir, Nicholas II, was temperamentally ill-equipped to deal with the consequences of that growth. He was forced to concede a limited constitution in 1905–06, thus feeding an appetite for change which he was unwilling to satisfy. The First World War proved fatal to a monarchy weakened by a reluctance to delegate power to able ministers and an unwillingness to rule in cooperation with civic-minded Russians.

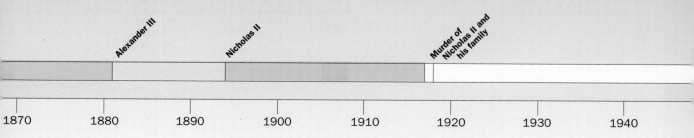
Alexander III · Nicholas II · Murder of Nicholas II and his family

1870   1880   1890   1900   1910   1920   1930   1940

Николай I Nicholas I
1825–1855

Александр II Alexander II
1855–1881

Nicholas I in uniform. A posthumous portrait dating from 1856, possibly by G.B. Rothmann. Contemporary observers were generally impressed by the emperor's physical appearance. The American historian John Motley described him as 'a regular-built Jupiter'.

NICHOLAS I	
Full name Nicholas Pavlovich Romanov *Father* Paul Petrovich Romanov *Mother* Sophia Dorothea of Württemberg (Maria Feodorovna) *Born* Gatchina 25 June 1796 *Accession* 14 December 1825 *Died* St Petersburg 18 February 1855 Pneumonia	*Wife* 1817 Charlotte, Princess of Prussia (Alexandra Feodorovna) Died 1860 *Children* **Alexander** (1818) Maria (1819) Olga (1822) Alexandra (1825) Constantine (1827) Nicholas (1831) Mikhail (1832)

NICHOLAS I

The dominant characteristic of his countenance is a worried severity – not a very agreeable expression, it must be said, despite the regularity of his features.... However, at rare intervals, lights of kindness temper the imperious or imperial look of the master; then an expression of affability suddenly brings back the native beauty of this classic head.

The Marquis de Custine

I do not think that Nicholas is a tyrant by nature, but only from conviction. He is persuaded that if he acted otherwise, public affairs could not succeed, and he is very well satisfied with the manner in which they have gone on during his reign. The habit of governing upon this principle has given him a taste for cruelty, for the habit of tyrannizing makes man a tyrant. The Russians say that it requires an iron hand to govern Russia, but that this hand should be gloved. Nicholas has the iron hand but he has forgotten the glove.

Ivan Golovine

The future Nicholas I was born in 1796. His education, supervised by General Count Lamsdorf, was spartan. He was made to sleep on a regula-

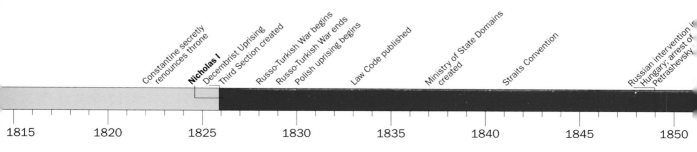

Constantine secretly renounces throne

Nicholas I
Decembrist Uprising
Third Section created

Russo-Turkish War begins
Russo-Turkish War ends
Polish uprising begins

Law Code published

Ministry of State Domains created

Straits Convention

Russian intervention in Hungary; arrest of Petrashevsky

1815   1820   1825   1830   1835   1840   1845   1850

THE LATE ROMANOVS

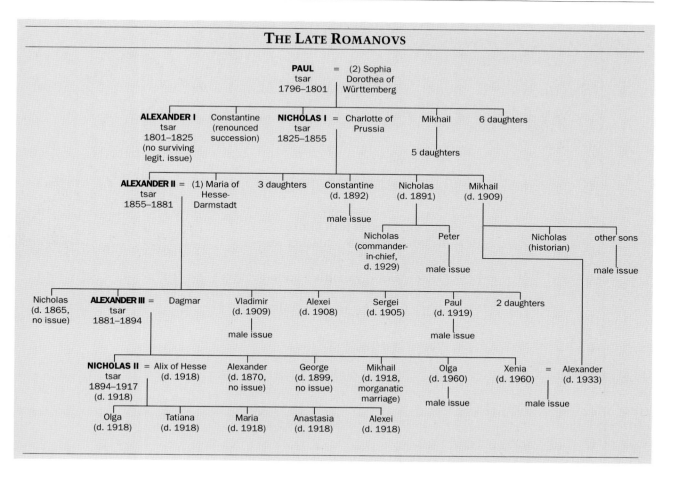

```
                          PAUL      =  (2) Sophia
                          tsar          Dorothea of
                          1796–1801     Württemberg

   ALEXANDER I    Constantine    NICHOLAS I  =  Charlotte of     Mikhail      6 daughters
   tsar           (renounced     tsar           Prussia
   1801–1825      succession)    1825–1855
   (no surviving                                              5 daughters
   legit. issue)

   ALEXANDER II = (1) Maria of   3 daughters   Constantine    Nicholas      Mikhail
   tsar            Hesse-                      (d. 1892)      (d. 1891)     (d. 1909)
   1855–1881       Darmstadt
                                               male issue
                                                      Nicholas        Peter        Nicholas      other sons
                                                      (commander-                  (historian)
                                                      in-chief,
                                                      d. 1929)          male issue              male issue

Nicholas   ALEXANDER III =  Dagmar   Vladimir    Alexei      Sergei      Paul       2 daughters
(d. 1865,  tsar                      (d. 1909)   (d. 1908)   (d. 1905)   (d. 1919)
no issue)  1881–1894
                                     male issue                          male issue

   NICHOLAS II = Alix of Hesse  Alexander    George      Mikhail       Olga        Xenia     =  Alexander
   tsar          (d. 1918)      (d. 1870,    (d. 1899,   (d. 1918,     (d. 1960)   (d. 1960)    (d. 1933)
   1894–1917                    no issue)    no issue)   morganatic
   (d. 1918)                                             marriage)     male issue             male issue

   Olga        Tatiana      Maria       Anastasia    Alexei
   (d. 1918)   (d. 1918)    (d. 1918)   (d. 1918)    (d. 1918)
```

tion military bed, a habit which he never gave up. Nicholas did not enjoy academic studies, but developed an ambition to serve as an officer and a simple faith in God, whom he regarded as a celestial Field Marshal requiring absolute devotion to duty. He joined the army in 1814, but, to his disgust, did not see action. During a visit to Berlin in 1815 he was deeply impressed both by Prussian militarism, and by Princess Charlotte, the daughter of King Friedrich Wilhelm III. They were married in 1817 and enjoyed a close and happy relationship. Alexandra Feodorovna, as Charlotte became known, gave birth to their first child, Alexander, in 1818.

Beneath Nicholas' stern demeanour lay a volatile temperament. On being told, in 1819, that his elder brother Constantine had no wish to rule, and that he himself might one day be emperor, he burst into tears.

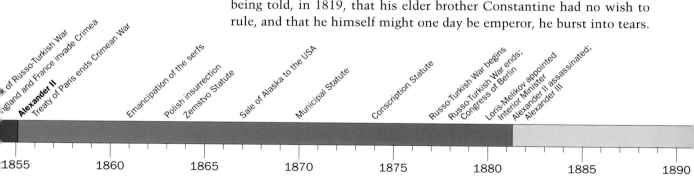

Start of Russo-Turkish War
England and France invade Crimea
Alexander II
Treaty of Paris ends Crimean War
Emancipation of the serfs
Polish insurrection
Zemstvo Statute
Sale of Alaska to the USA
Municipal Statute
Conscription Statute
Russo-Turkish War begins
Russo-Turkish War ends; Congress of Berlin
Loris-Melikov appointed Interior Minister
Alexander II assassinated; Alexander III

```
1855      1860      1865      1870      1875      1880      1885      1890
```

PALACE SQUARE

Alexander I and Nicholas I were important architectural patrons, who took an active interest in the projects which they initiated and sought to regulate the whole built environment. Alexander established a Committee for Construction and Hydraulic Works to supervise building in St Petersburg, both public and private, and its influence spread throughout the empire. The laws which required architects to conform to norms laid down by the government were abolished in the 1840s.

Alexander commissioned Karl Ivanovich Rossi (1775–1849), an architect of Italian ancestry, to create a square on the landward side of the Winter Palace. The site, though large, was awkward in shape, constrained by the Moika Canal and the Nevsky Prospect. Rossi converted the various residential buildings which occupied it into a warren of offices and courtyards to house the Ministries of Finance and Foreign Affairs and the General Staff. He then bound the whole together with a long, curving façade broken by a triumphal arch, and enlivened the roofline with a single dome. The monumental simplicity of the building, which was completed in 1829, offsets the rococo exuberance of the palace.

Nicholas I's reign saw the construction of new offices for the Senate and the Holy Synod and the New Hermitage.

In private Nicholas was willing to indulge in architectural whimsies, including a Gothick cottage at Tsarskoe Selo, but he required public buildings to embody his authority in stone and metal and, like his brother, favoured the classical style.

The Alexander Column in the centre of Palace Square, designed by Avgust Avgustovich Montferrand, the architect of St Isaac's Cathedral, was erected in 1829 as a monument to Alexander I, and to Russia's victory in the War of 1812. The column is a monolith of Karelian granite, and was designed to be taller than Trajan's Column in Rome or the column in the Place Vendôme in Paris.

In December 1837 the Winter Palace was seriously damaged by fire. Extensive rebuilding was required, and Nicholas insisted that this be done with all speed. The Marquis de Custine, a French visitor to Russia, recorded the human cost:

Finally, I saw the façade of the new Winter Palace, another prodigious product of the will of a man applied to aligning the strength of men against the laws of nature. The goal was attained, for in one year this palace rose up out of its ashes.... In order to finish the work in the period specified by the emperor, unprecedented efforts were required. The interior construction was continued under the bitterest cold of winter. Six thousand labourers were continually at work;

(Left) Palace Square and the Alexander Column. Rossi's General Staff building with its triumphal arch is visible in the background.

(Right) An ornamental staircase in the Pavilion Hall in the Little Hermitage. Designed by Andrei Stakenschneider (1802–65), the Pavilion Hall was completed in 1856. Its delicate decoration combines classical and Moorish elements.

(Below) The exterior of the New Hermitage (1852). This building was commissioned by Nicholas I to enable the public to visit the imperial art collections. Its architect was the German Leo von Klenze (1784–1864). The statues of Atlanteans supporting the lintels of the entrance were carved by Alexander Ivanovich Terebenev (1814–59).

(Bottom) The Winter Canal separates the New Hermitage and the Little Hermitage, on the left, from the Hermitage Theatre, which was built for Catherine II by Giacomo Quarenghi. The theatre is linked to the rest of the Hermitage complex by an enclosed bridge.

a considerable number died each day, but, as the victims were instantly replaced by other champions who filled their places, to perish in their turn in this inglorious gap, the losses were not apparent.... During freezes of 15 to 20 degrees below zero, 6,000 obscure martyrs ... were shut up in rooms heated to eighty-six degrees in order to dry the walls more quickly. Thus these wretches on entering and leaving this abode of death – now become, thanks to their sacrifice, the home of vanity, magnificence and pleasure – underwent a difference in temperature of 100 to 108 degrees. Work in the mines of the Urals is less injurious to life....

When Alexander I died, Nicholas hesitated before claiming the throne. He knew that he was unpopular with his fellow officers, who resented his pettifogging approach to discipline. Constantine refused to come to St Petersburg and make a public renunciation of his claim. Nicholas was finally driven to take power when an informer told him that a military uprising was imminent.

The Decembrists

The army officers and intellectuals involved in what became known as the Decembrist movement were members of secret societies founded after the Napoleonic Wars. Many of them had served abroad, an experience which encouraged them to question the political and social order in Russia. They believed that the ending of the autocracy and the abolition of serfdom were the keys to progress in Russia, and they were all in some sense nationalists, but there were serious disagreements about the kind of Russia that they wished to create. The Southern Society, whose leading figure was Colonel Pavel Pestel, wanted a centralized republic. The Northern Society, led by Nikita Muraviev, hoped for a federal constitutional monarchy. The uncertainty about the succession provided an opportunity which was seized by members of a weak and divided movement.

On 14 December 1825, hours after Nicholas had proclaimed himself emperor, troops led by dissident officers occupied Senate Square in St Petersburg, declaring their allegiance to Constantine and demanding a constitution. Nicholas, who led loyal soldiers to confront the rebels, was reluctant to shed blood but eventually ordered the artillery to open fire. The rising was crushed at the cost of 56 lives. The emperor returned to the Winter Palace, and spent the first night of his reign interrogating the leaders of the rebellion. Five of the Decembrists were executed, 31 were sentenced to life imprisonment with hard labour in Siberia, and 253 others received shorter sentences.

The Decembrist Uprising convinced Nicholas of the need for ceaseless vigilance and discipline. He made frequent, but superficial tours of inspection in the provinces, during which he dispensed instant punishments and rewards. He created institutions to enable him to rule directly, including the various Sections of His Majesty's Own Chancery. He ordered a detailed survey of the state of the empire, and a committee, formed on 6 December 1826, was charged with this task. Mikhail Speransky, recalled from exile, was one of its members. The committee endorsed Nicholas' conviction that change should be gradual, and that the autocracy was fundamentally sound.

Speransky's proposal of a new code of laws was rejected by the emperor on the grounds that it might arouse expectations of reform. Instead the Second Section of His Majesty's Own Chancery collected and published all the decrees that had been passed since 1649. Nicholas believed that this codification, which was completed in the 1830s, would help to ensure order.

The five executed Decembrist leaders. This engraving appeared in an emigré journal edited by the exiled Russian political theorist Alexander Herzen. When the five condemned men were taken out to be hanged, the ropes broke in three cases, so that the process had to be repeated. The condemned man Ryleyev's last words are reported to have been: 'Unhappy country, where they don't even know how to hang you.'

'Mrs Greece and her Rough Lovers'. An English caricature of 1828 concerning the crisis in the Balkans. The Turkish sultan has a copy of the Koran tucked in his sash, and the Russian emperor has a pamphlet entitled *Russian Politics of Self Interest*, a detail suggesting that the cartoonist took a cynical view of Russian motives in the Balkans.

Russian troops entering Adrianople. A French engraving of 1829. Adrianople (Edirne, in Turkey) was a strategically important town situated only 130 miles from the Turkish capital, Constantinople. The advance on Adrianople was led by General Diebich, known to his troops as Samovar Pasha on account of his bulbous shape.

Persia, Turkey and Greece

The emperor took active control of Russia's foreign policy, though Nesselrode, who continued to serve as foreign minister, exercised a restraining influence. Nicholas believed that war might lead to revolution, and preferred to work in cooperation with other powers, but he was willing to use force to extend Russia's influence. A war with Persia (1826–28) added the khanates of Erivan and Nakhichevan to the Russian empire, and secured the Russians the right to build a fleet on the Caspian Sea.

Nicholas regarded the Turkish sultan as the legitimate ruler of the Balkans, and was reluctant to encourage the Greeks in their bid for independence, preferring to cooperate with Britain and France in an attempt to secure autonomy for them under Turkish rule. He forced the Turks to sign the Akkerman Convention of 1826, allowing Russian merchant ships to use the Straits. When the sultan rejected the idea of Greek autonomy, a joint Russian, French and British naval force destroyed the Egyptian fleet, which had come to the aid of the Turks, in the battle of Navarino (October 1827). The following spring Russia went to war with Turkey.

The campaign provided Nicholas with his first experience of warfare, which proved more costly and horrific than he had imagined. Russian successes in the second year of fighting drove the Turks to seek peace. The Treaty of Adrianople (1829) secured Turkish recognition of Russia's territorial gains in Georgia and the Caucasus, and autonomy for Moldavia, Wallachia and Greece. At the London Conference of 1830 Russia, Britain and France agreed on the creation of an independent kingdom of Greece.

NICHOLAS I TO THE POLES

Nicholas told a delegation of Poles in Warsaw in 1835:

At my command a citadel is being erected here and I declare to you that in the event of the slightest disturbance I will order the destruction of your city. I shall demolish Warsaw and, of course, I will not rebuild it. Believe me, gentlemen, to belong to Russia and to be under her patronage is true happiness. If you will conduct yourselves properly, if you will fulfil all your obligations, then my fatherly solicitousness will extend to all and, in spite of everything that has happened, my government will always be concerned about your welfare.

The Polish Uprising of 1830–31. A contemporary engraving showing rebels attacking a prison in Leshno Street, Warsaw. The insurrection began with an assault on a brewery. The authorities happened to increase the price of beer on the very day that a group of army officers had planned to start a revolt, and public outrage turned their coup into a mass insurrection.

The Revolutions of 1830

The revolutions which broke out in France and the Low Countries in the summer of 1830 alarmed Nicholas. He was reluctant to recognize the new government of France. His announcement that Russian and Polish troops would assist the king of the Netherlands in crushing the Belgian nationalist uprising helped to provoke a rebellion in Poland, which ruled out Russian intervention in Western Europe.

The Polish uprising of November 1830 proved difficult to suppress. It was not until September 1831 that the Russian army recaptured Warsaw. Nicholas, who believed that Russia's control of Poland was essential to her future as a European power, treated the Poles with great severity. The Organic Statute of February 1832 abolished the Polish parliament and army and imposed a greater degree of direct Russian rule. Universities were closed down, and a process of Russification began, as a result of which high school students were forced to learn the Russian language. Similar policies were introduced in the Belorussian and Ukrainian provinces of the empire.

Internal policies

The economic growth in Russia during the reign owed little to government policies. Count Kankrin, finance minister from 1823 to 1844, believed that there was little that the state could do to promote economic growth. He opposed the construction of railways on the grounds that they would 'weaken the moral fibre of Russian society'. Nicholas, impressed by the speed with which the British government had been able to move troops from Manchester to Liverpool when there was trouble in Ireland, saw advantages in a railway system. Russia's first line, connecting Tsarskoe Selo with St Petersburg, was opened in 1837. Kankrin

A Russian popular print of 1857 showing the opening of a railway station. The first railway line in Russia, opened in 1837, linked St Petersburg and Tsarskoe Selo, with a short extension to Pavlovsk. The station there was designed by an English architect, who surrounded it with pleasure gardens named after those at Vauxhall in London, and also built a concert hall. Thus *Vokzal* entered the Russian language as the word for railway station. Cynics argued that the only purpose of the railway was 'to connect the capital with the cabaret', but the line became the first section of a rail route between St Petersburg and Moscow. The concert hall proved very popular, and Johann Strauss the younger was a conductor there over several seasons.

THE HISTORIAN KLIUCHEVSKY ON BUREAUCRACY IN THE REIGN OF NICHOLAS I

At the time of Nicholas' accession he was, to his dismay, informed that pending in the various tribunals under the Ministry of Justice there were no fewer than 2,800,000 cases, and that out of them as many as 127,000 persons were making a living at the Treasury's expense. And did the machine work the better, the more rapidly, for its achievement of complexity? Again a single instance, a return furnished by the Ministry of Justice in 1842, will suffice. From it we see that no fewer than 3,300,000 cases then were pending in the various legal institutions, and that for their exposition on paper no fewer than 33,000,000 folios had been used.

worked hard to strengthen the currency, though his efforts were to be undermined by the inflationary effects of the Crimean War. Exports of wheat increased, and a cotton industry developed, but Russia, hampered by serfdom and lack of capital, could not keep pace with the faster growing economies of the West.

Nicholas understood that serfdom was evil, but was unwilling to impose abolition on the nobility, and feared that it would lead to a breakdown of order. He encouraged General Count P.D. Kiselev, the head of the Fifth Section, to improve the lot of the 20 million state peasants, in the hope that the nobility might follow this example. In December 1837 (January 1838 NS) the Fifth Section was transformed into the Ministry of State Domains, with Kiselev as minister. Schools and model farms were built, and additional lands were allotted to the poorer communes. A minority of enlightened noblemen tried to improve the lot of their serfs, but the cautious legislation of the final years of the reign had little impact. A law of 1847 which allowed serfs to purchase land if their owner's estate was sold by auction was never put into practice, and few peasants were permitted to take advantage of the 1848 law enabling them to buy land with the consent of their owners.

Spending on education was increased, and new technical and vocational schools were opened. Count S.S. Uvarov, Minister of Education from 1833 to 1849, argued that the purpose of education was to produce pious, obedient and patriotic subjects. He was never quite able to overcome the emperor's distrust of the educated classes. Uvarov's doctrine of Official Nationality, based on the principles of 'Orthodoxy, Autocracy and Nationality', became the dominant ideology of the reign. These were shaky foundations on which to build. Strict government control had done nothing to strengthen the Orthodox church. An impoverished and poorly educated parish clergy had lost the respect of the educated classes. Nationality was a dangerous principle on which to base an empire with a multi-ethnic population. It was to lead future emperors further down the road of Russification, and to encourage the development of Panslavism.

GLINKA AND NICHOLAS I

In 1836 the composer Mikhail Ivanovich Glinka (1804–57) completed his opera *Ivan Susanin*. It tells the story of the heroic peasant who, during the Time of Troubles, saved Mikhail Romanov from the Poles at the cost of his own life. The theme of the opera, which is more widely known as *A Life for the Tsar*, naturally appealed to Nicholas I, though Glinka's memoirs do not confirm the story that Nicholas himself ordered that the title be changed. After its triumphant premiere in St Petersburg in November 1836, the work entered the repertoire, and performances of it marked many imperial occasions during the next 80 years. What Glinka's memoirs do make clear is that the emperor was a generous patron, but did not hesitate to tell creative artists how they could improve on their work.

Page from the illustrated programme for the gala performance of Glinka's A Life for the Tsar held on 7 May 1896 to mark the coronation of Nicholas II.

The success of the opera was complete … I was called to the imperial box on the side of the theatre. The Sovereign first thanked me for my opera, then observed that it was not good to have Susanin killed on stage. I explained to His Majesty that I had not been to the last rehearsal because of illness and could not know how things had been planned there but according to my programme the curtain should have been lowered as soon as the Poles attacked Susanin and his death recounted afterward by the orphan in the epilogue. After the Emperor had thanked me, the Empress did so, too, and then all the Grand Dukes and Grand Duchesses who were in the theatre. I soon received an imperial gift for my opera: a four-thousand-rouble ring made up of a topaz encircled by three rows of the finest diamonds. I gave it to my wife at once.

Mikhail Yurievich Lermontov (1814–41), a guards officer, poet and novelist. Like Pushkin, Lermontov was killed in a duel.

The Third Section of His Majesty's Own Chancery was created in 1826 as much to root out corruption and promote good behaviour as to hunt down subversives. Its first head, Count A.K. Benckendorff, described himself as 'the moral physician of the people'. All works distributed in Russia had to be examined by the censors to make sure that they did not offend against the principles of Official Nationality, and writers who questioned the status quo were harshly treated. Nevertheless the periodical press flourished, and Russian literature continued to develop in the hands of masters such as Pushkin, Lermontov and Gogol. Nor could censorship prevent the lively debate between the Slavophiles, who believed that Russia's was a uniquely valuable civilization, and that future reforms should be based on traditional values and institutions, and the Westernizers, who looked to Western Europe for ideas about how to change society. Nicholas was an important architectural patron, and enjoyed discussing plans with architects, and interfering with their designs.

PUSHKIN ON THE GERMAN BLOOD IN IMPERIAL VEINS

In his book *Russia under the Autocrat Nicholas I* Ivan Golovine recorded this anecdote about the writer Pushkin:

Pushkin delighted to represent the nationality of the reigning family in a very eccentric manner; he took a goblet and poured into it a glass of pure red wine in honour of Peter I, whose Russian origin could not be disputed, and added a glass of water for the father of Peter III … he poured out another glass of water in honour of Catherine II, a Princess of Anhalt … and poured a fourth glass of water for Maria Feodorovna, the mother of Nicholas I; then a fifth for the reigning Empress, by which time the liquor was so faintly tinged with red, that he raised a general laugh by asking the company to decide whether it was wine or water, and whether, by comparison, the present Tsars were Russians or Germans?

THE EMPEROR AND THE POET

For Russians Alexander Sergeyevich Pushkin (1799–1837) is not merely a great writer, but *the* great writer. He lived his entire life in the shadow of the imperial family. He was one of the first intake of boarders at the Imperial Lycée at Tsarskoe Selo, whose buildings adjoined the Catherine Palace. On graduation he entered the Ministry of Foreign Affairs as a civil servant. By 1820 his writings were causing concern to Alexander I, who gave him a posting in southern Russia to remove him from the capital. In 1824 Pushkin was confined to his family's estate in Pskov province on the suspicion that he was sympathetic to atheism. This exile meant that he had no opportunity to take part in the Decembrist Uprising, in which several of his friends were involved, but his absence from St Petersburg did not mean that he was out of danger, for his writings were found among the papers of all of the leading conspirators. In 1826 Pushkin wrote a supplicatory letter to Nicholas I, avowing that he had never belonged to any secret society, and asking for a relaxation of his exile on medical grounds. Nicholas summoned the poet to Moscow, and questioned him in the Kremlin. Asked whether he would have joined in the Decembrist Uprising had he had the opportunity to do so, Pushkin replied in the affirmative. He then promised 'to conduct himself in an honourable and decent manner', and was granted permission to reside in St Petersburg. In the matter of Pushkin's writing, Nicholas said: 'I myself will be your censor.'

The first work by Pushkin to be submitted to the emperor was his play *Boris Godunov*. Nicholas' response, conveyed to the poet through Count Benckendorff, the newly appointed head of the Third Section, was that the work should be rewritten as an historical novel after the manner of Sir Walter Scott. Pushkin tactfully pleaded that he lacked the ability to carry out such a revision. It was not until 1830 that the emperor consented to the publication of the play. Nicholas was no more pleased with the report on the future of Russian education which he required Pushkin to submit.

In February 1831 Pushkin married Natalya Nikolaievna Goncharova, a strikingly beautiful aristocrat who was a dozen years his junior. That summer the couple met the emperor and empress while walking in the gardens at Tsarskoe Selo. The imperial couple were both very taken with Natalya. Nicholas' offer to take the poet back into the civil service and to pay him a salary was accepted, and the emperor encouraged his historical researches, granting him access to the imperial archives. Pushkin continued to submit his work to Nicholas' personal censorship, and his loyalty was rewarded with court rank and the entrée to imperial social occasions. The price paid for this official recognition was a high one. The manuscript of his masterpiece

The Bronze Horseman came back from the palace studded with imperial question marks, and the work was not published in the poet's lifetime. One of the fruits of his historical researches, a monograph on Pugachev, had its title altered by Nicholas, who objected to *The History of Pugachev* on the grounds that a rebel could not possibly have a history, and insisted on *The History of Pugachev's Revolt*.

In November 1836 Pushkin received an anonymous letter proclaiming his election to the membership of the Most Serene Order of Cuckolds. Pushkin immediately challenged the Baron Georges-Charles d'Anthès, who was not only his wife's most persistent suitor but was shortly to marry her sister, to a duel. The emperor got to know of the challenge and personally persuaded Pushkin to abandon the idea of fighting d'Anthès. He also took the trouble to tell Pushkin's wife that, in view of her husband's reputation for jealousy, she should behave decorously, advice which was reinforced by a gift of 1,000 roubles, ostensibly to enable Natalya to buy a wedding gift for her sister. When Pushkin heard of this he thanked the emperor, and confessed that he had suspected Nicholas himself of paying court to his wife. There is no evidence that Natalya had by that time been the emperor's mistress, though the anonymous letter which Pushkin received contained a reference to D.L. Naryshkin, the wronged husband of Alexander I's mistress, and this may have fuelled the poet's jealous suspicions. Court and diplomatic gossip held that Natalya and Nicholas had a liaison some time after the poet's death.

On 27 January 1837 Pushkin broke his promise to the emperor and was fatally injured in a duel with d'Anthès. He died two days later. Nicholas is said to have written a note forgiving the poet, urging him to accept the consolations of the church, and promising to look after his wife and children. He did settle Pushkin's debts, and made financial provision for his family, but this private generosity was accompanied by vigorous attempts to ensure that the poet's funeral was a low-key affair. The emperor refused to sanction a national monument to Pushkin, and it was not until 1880 that a statue of the poet was unveiled in Moscow.

Pushkin as a student, in an engraving by E. Heilmann which clearly shows the poet's African ancestry. One of his maternal great-grandfathers was Abraham Petrovich Hannibal, a negro servant and protégé of Peter the Great.

The statue of Pushkin in Arts Square, St Petersburg, by M. Anikushkin.

THE UPBRINGING OF THE FUTURE ALEXANDER II

The Tsarevich Alexander. A contemporary engraving.

Maréchal Marmont, the distinguished French commander, visited Russia in 1826 on a diplomatic mission, and recorded these impressions of the upbringing of the Tsarevich Alexander, who was then eight years old.

The education which Nicholas has given his son is admirable. He is a charming prince, of rare beauty, whose good qualities have no doubt developed with time. I asked the Emperor to present me to him, and he replied: 'Do you want to turn his head? It would fill the little fellow with conceit if a General who has commanded armies were to pay him homage. I am much touched by your wish to see him, and this can be given effect to when you go to Tsarskoe Selo, where you will meet my children. You will be able to observe them and talk to them; but a ceremonial presentation is not desirable. I wish to make a man of my son, before making a Prince of him.

The Future of Turkey

In the 1830s Nicholas, fearing that the collapse of Turkey would lead to a disastrous war between the powers, supported the Turks against Mehmet Ali, the ruler of Egypt. In return, the Turks in 1833 signed the Treaty of Unkiar Skelessi, in which they promised to close the Straits to foreign warships if Russia was under attack. At a meeting at Münchengrätz in 1833 the rulers of Austria, Russia and Prussia agreed that Turkey should be preserved intact if possible, and that in the event of its collapse, they would cooperate to create a new order in the Balkans.

War was renewed between Turkey and Egypt in 1839. Russia worked with the other powers to ensure the survival of Turkey, and to force the French, who had supported Mehmet Ali, to accept a multilateral settlement of the crisis. The Straits Convention of 1841 included guarantees similar to those in the Treaty of Unkiar Skelessi. The crisis strengthened Nicholas' suspicions of the French and his belief that the Turkish empire was doomed. An official visit to Britain in 1844 left him convinced that he had secured an agreement with the British to cooperate in future crises in the Near East, but the British did not believe his assertions that Russia had no ambition to acquire Turkish territory.

Family affairs

The relationship between 'Nicks' and 'Mouffy', as the imperial couple affectionately called each other, became clouded in the 1840s. The doctors ruled that the empress' heart condition rendered the pleasures of the marriage bed unacceptably hazardous. Nicholas still loved his wife, but had for some years been attracted to one of her ladies-in-waiting, Varvara Nelidova. His affair with Nelidova began in 1845. Gossip attributed other infidelities to him, depicting a more colourful private life than he may have experienced. By the mid-1840s Nicholas appeared prematurely aged. He was suffering from pains in the legs and a liver complaint.

The 1848 Revolutions

Though Nicholas I became known as 'the Gendarme of Europe', his initial reaction to the revolutions which broke out in many European countries in 1848 was cautious. Fearing trouble at home, he did not wish to embark on military adventures abroad, but he was prepared to act when he believed that Russia's interests were threatened. In July 1848 he intervened to prevent the establishment of constitutional government in Moldavia and Wallachia, and when, in 1849, Polish inhabitants of the Austrian empire rose in support of the Hungarian revolutionaries he sent Russian troops to assist the Emperor Franz-Josef in crushing the rebellion. Nicholas also intervened to prevent Prussian aggression against Denmark and to restore the status quo in the German states by means of the Olmütz agreement of 1850.

Though Russia had not experienced serious unrest in 1848–49, the government tightened censorship and imposed stricter controls on universities. The number of students was reduced, and controversial

Feodor Mikhailovich Dostoyevsky
(1821–81). A portrait by Vasily Perov
(1833–82), completed in 1872.

'Clemency of the Russian Monster'.
An English cartoon of *c*.1832 concerning
Russian repression in Poland. It
illustrates the widely held view of
Nicholas I as 'the Gendarme of Europe'.

subjects such as constitutional law were eliminated from the curriculum. The Third Section and the police intensified their surveillance of society. The best-known victims of this repression were the intellectuals who met at the house of Mikhail Vasilievich Butashevich-Petrashevsky, to discuss social and political questions. Petrashevsky and his associates were arrested in 1849. Fifty-one of them were exiled, and 21, including the writer Dostoyevsky, were sentenced to death. The condemned men were placed in front of a firing squad, and only then was the commutation of their sentences to penal servitude announced.

The Crimean War

In the early 1850s a dispute arose about the control of the Christian holy places in Palestine. The French demanded that the Turkish sultan enforce the rights which his predecessors had granted to Roman Catholics. Those rights could only be restored at the expense of the Orthodox church, on whose behalf Nicholas intervened. He feared a

A Russian gun emplacement after its capture by British forces. One of the collection of photographs taken during the Crimean War by the English photographer Roger Fenton.

Lithograph of Nicholas I based on
a drawing from life made by Sir Edwin
Landseer (1802–73), the favourite painter
of Queen Victoria. Victoria wrote of
Nicholas I: 'He is stern and severe – with
fixed principles of duty which nothing
on earth will make him change; very
clever I do not think him, and his mind
is an uncivilized one; his education has
been neglected; politics and military
concerns are the only things he takes
great interest in.'

further expansion of French influence in the eastern Mediterranean,
and assumed that Austria and Britain would support him. He reasserted
Russia's claim to a general protectorate over the Christian population
of the Ottoman empire, but failed to browbeat the Turks into accepting
this. Russia broke off diplomatic relations with Turkey in May 1853,
and on 21 June (3 July NS) the Russian army marched into the Danubian
Principalities.

Britain and France, fearing that Russia intended to seize control of the
Straits, sent their fleets to Besika Bay in the hope of persuading the Russians
to negotiate. A peaceful resolution of the dispute might have been
achieved had not the Turks, encouraged by what they saw as British and
French support, refused to accept the compromise drafted by the powers
and demanded that the Russian army evacuate Moldavia and Wallachia.
The Russians refused to comply and in October 1853 the two countries
found themselves at war. The Turkish fleet was destroyed at the Battle of
Sinope in November. Britain and France entered the war on Turkey's side
in March 1854. Russia's diplomatic isolation was completed when
Austria demanded that she withdraw from the Principalities. Nicholas
was furious at what he saw as Austrian ingratitude, yet he complied with
the demand, aware that it was important to keep Austria out of the conflict.
The allies then decided to send an expeditionary force to the
Crimean peninsula in the hope of capturing the naval base at Sevastopol,
and ending Russian domination of the Black Sea. The Kingdom of Sardinia
declared war on Russia in January 1855.

The Crimean War demonstrated the relative backwardness of Russia.
The need to defend a vast empire and the lack of a developed railway
system prevented her generals from concentrating more than a fraction
of their manpower in the Crimea. In 1853 there was only one musket
for every two soldiers, and only 4 per cent of the infantry had rifles.
A technological gap had opened between Russia and the West, which
could only be closed by radical reforms, including the abolition of

THE TSARIST NATIONAL ANTHEM

Until 1833 the tune of the British
national anthem was used in court
ceremonies in Russia. A trip to Prussia
and Austria in that year brought home
to Nicholas I the fact that his empire
lacked an indigenous anthem. He
mentioned the matter to Benckendorff,
the head of the Third Section, who had
on his staff an officer of considerable
musical ability, Alexei Feodorovich
Lvov. Lvov (1798–1870) was the son
of the Director of the Imperial Court
Chapel, a post to which he succeeded

on the death of his father in 1836. He
quickly produced the music, and passed
it to the poet Vasily Zhukovsky, who was
one of the tutors of the Tsarevich
Alexander. Zhukovsky was, in Lvov's
words, 'by no means musical' and found
it difficult to write words suited to the
minor ending to the first cadence of the
tune. The result, performed in his
presence on 23 November 1833,
delighted Nicholas I, who told Lvov 'It is
really superb'. Lvov's rewards included a
transfer to the emperor's personal staff,
the gift of a gold snuff-box decorated
with diamonds, and the right to use the
first line of Zhukovsky's text – 'God

protect the Tsar' – as the motto on his
coat of arms. The tune was later used
by Tchaikovsky, first in the *Marche Slave*
(Op. 31, 1876) and then, more briefly,
in the *1812 Festival Overture* (Op. 49,
1880). Among Lvov's later compositions
were a violin concerto and several
operas, including a patriotic work
entitled *Boris the Headman or The
Russian Peasant and the French
Marauders* first performed in 1854. He
was an exceptionally talented violinist,
who impressed both Schumann and
Mendelssohn, whose violin concerto
he played in the Leipzig Gewandhaus
under the baton of the composer.

serfdom, a perestroika which the emperor had rejected as too risky. The war developed into a bloody stalemate in which half a million Russians died. Nicholas did not live to see its end. In February 1855 he caught a cold. His insistence on attending a military parade in freezing weather resulted in pneumonia, and he died on 18 February 1855.

Nicholas I was widely loathed by his contemporaries. The judgment of A.V. Nikitenko, the distinguished academic who also worked as a censor, that 'the main shortcoming of the reign of Nikolai Pavlovich consisted in the fact that it was all a mistake' has been echoed by many historians, who have depicted an era of unrelieved reaction and repression. Yet Nicholas understood that change was necessary, and his was an active government with some positive achievements to its credit. His belief that the pace and the nature of change must be dictated from above made him unwilling to consult Russia's educated class, and the rift between the autocracy and the intelligentsia widened during his reign.

ALEXANDER II	
Full name	(Maria
Alexander	Alexandrovna)
Nikolaievich	Died 1880
Romanov	(2) 1880 Catherine
also known as the	(Katia) Mikhailovna
Tsar Liberator	Dolgorukaya
Father	(Princess
Nicholas I	Yurievskaya)
Mother	Morganatic
Charlotte, Princess	marriage
of Prussia	Died 1922
(Alexandra	*Children by (1)*
Feodorovna)	Alexandra (1842)
Born	Nicholas (1843)
Moscow	**Alexander** (1845)
29 April 1818	Vladimir (1847)
Accession	Alexei (1850)
18 February 1855	Marie (1853)
Died	Sergei (1857)
St Petersburg	Paul (1860)
1 March 1881	*Children by (2)*
Assassinated	George (1872)
Wives	Olga (1873)
(1) 1841 Maria of	Boris (1876)
Hesse-Darmstadt	Catherine (1878)

Alexander II

ALEXANDER II

Alexander II certainly was not a rank-and-file man, but two different men lived in him, both strongly developed, struggling with each other; and this inner struggle became more and more violent as he advanced in age. He could be charming in his behaviour, and the next moment display sheer brutality. He was possessed of a calm, reasoned courage in the face of real danger, but lived in constant fear of dangers which existed in his brain only.

Prince Peter Kropotkin

When the Emperor talks with a man of spirit, he has the look of someone suffering from rheumatism caught in a draught.

Feodor Ivanovich Tiutchev, poet and Chairman of the Foreign Censorship Committee

Although Alexander II (1855–1881) is remembered as the 'Tsar Liberator', the emancipator of the serfs, he was no liberal. He believed that it was possible to maintain the autocracy while cautiously modernizing government and society. The 'Great Reforms' of the early years of the reign were largely the work of his ministers, though on occasion the emperor decisively shaped events by taking sides in disputes between them. Alexander was the victim of an austere, militaristic upbringing, and grew into a sensitive, asthmatic youth. His marriage in 1841 to Maria, the younger daughter of Grand Duke Ludwig II of Hesse-Darmstadt, was a love match, but his ardour soon cooled and a series of liaisons with aristocratic women ensued. Alexander received more preparation for the role of ruler than his father. As a member of the Council of State, the Finance Committee and other government bodies in the 1840s and early 1850s he supported Nicholas' repressive policies.

Ending the Crimean War

In December 1855 Austria threatened to join the war on the British, French and Sardinian side. Alexander, angered by what he saw as Austrian ingratitude and treachery, bowed to pressure from his advisers and agreed to discuss peace terms. The Treaty of Paris of March 1856 left Russia isolated. She was forced to cede Southern Bessarabia to Moldavia, and to give up both her Black Sea fleet and her claim to an exclusive protectorate over the Christian inhabitants of the Turkish empire. Reversing these setbacks became an important objective for the emperor and his newly appointed foreign minister, Alexander Gorchakov.

Reforms

The early years of the reign seemed to promise a general liberalization. Unpopular conservative ministers were dismissed, many political prisoners were freed, including 29 surviving Decembrists, and the censorship was relaxed. These measures may have been an attempt to encourage a body of public opinion in favour of the emancipation of the serfs. Though he told the Moscow gentry in 1856 that it would be 'better to begin eliminating serfdom from above than to wait for it to eliminate itself from below', Alexander's approach to this question was cautious.

The arguments for emancipation were compelling. It was difficult to farm profitably with servile labour. Unrest in the countryside demonstrated that serfdom was no longer an effective mechanism of social control. Levels of fitness and morale among peasant recruits to the army were low. Alexander's hopes of recruiting the support of the nobility for emancipation were largely disappointed, and he had to force the pace of reform. In late 1857 the Nazimov Rescript, a document committing the government to emancipation, was published. Alexander then permitted open discussion of the issue, and he intervened decisively in 1858 in

The Emancipation Proclamation being read out in public at Telav in Georgia. Alexander II knew that the settlement was unlikely to meet peasant expectations, and delayed its announcement until the first day of Lent in the hope of minimizing unrest.

favour of providing the emancipated serfs with land. The Emancipation Statute was finally promulgated on 19 February 1861.

It was a reform which in the short term satisfied nobody. The peasants resented having to pay for the land that was allotted to them. They remained bound to the *mir* or commune, with a social and legal status inferior to other Russians. The spring and summer of 1861 saw disturbances in all but one of the provinces to which the Emancipation Statute applied. Landowners felt that their interests had been ignored, though many of them were to benefit by selling land to their former serfs at a price higher than its market value. The state advanced the money for the transaction, and the peasants were obliged to repay the loan over a period of 49 years. These redemption payments were burdensome. The government lacked the administrative machinery strictly to enforce payment and massive arrears developed.

Though Alexander reacted to the unrest of 1861 by dismissing some of the ministers responsible for the Emancipation Statute, he understood that further reforms were necessary. Emancipation made central government responsible for millions of peasants who had previously been under the control of landlords. The Statute had created a new tier of local government, the *volost* (district), and in 1864 a system of elected regional councils, or *zemstva*, was established in Russia's European provinces. The Zemstvo Statute was not as liberal as it appeared. Alexander insisted on a system for electing the district and provincial assemblies and the zemstvo boards which ensured aristocratic dominance of those bodies. The taxational powers of the zemstva were limited, and their business was subject to interference from provincial governors, but they were able to accomplish useful work in the fields of primary education, road maintenance, public health and the relief of poverty. The existence of the zemstva created an appetite among the gentry for a say in national affairs, and they became a breeding ground for liberalism.

The judicial reforms of 1864 were largely the work of the Minister of Justice, Dmitry Zamiatnin. The creation of an independent judiciary, appointed for life, was intended to guarantee impartial justice for all Russians. These reforms pleased the liberal intelligentsia. Mikhail Reutern, Finance Minister from 1862 to 1878, introduced centralized budgeting and the auditing of departmental accounts. The traditional system of tax farming (whereby the tax collector was a businessman seeking to make a profit rather than a salaried official) was abolished, and a State Bank was created to provide loans to new businesses and industrial enterprises.

In late 1861 Alexander appointed a reforming Minister of Education, Alexander Golovnin. His 1864 Primary School Statute promoted the gradual development of public elementary education. The new primary schools were fee-paying, and offered only a basic curriculum. A Law on Secondary Schools was passed in 1864, giving the government the power to standardize the curriculum. The University Statute of 1863 lifted most of the restrictions imposed on the universities by Nicholas I in 1835.

ALEXANDER II POURS OUT HIS TROUBLES TO A FRIEND

Field Marshal Prince Bariatinsky, the Viceroy of the Caucasus, had been a close friend of Alexander's since boyhood.

St Petersburg, 8 January 1861
…Triumphant revolution in Italy threatens the whole of Europe. Towards spring time Austria will probably be attacked in the Venezia and will have at the same time to combat a new revolution in Hungary and Galicia. Spirits in Poland are also excited … and we must expect to see attempted uprisings there which, thanks to the energetic measures which we are taking will be, I hope, nipped in the bud. In addition to that it is more than probable that the rising in Hungary will be the signal for a general rising of all the Christian populations of Turkey, which will have as a result the fall of the Ottoman Empire in Europe. Now you know that this question touches us closely and that we cannot, whether we like it or not, remain spectators.
Add to this the excitement of spirits inside Russia produced by the question of Emancipation, which must be decided in a few weeks – and you will have a true idea of all the cares which oppress me! Confidence in the mercy of God is the only idea which sustains me and which gives me the courage to support all my daily worries. Have a little pity on me and don't add to them from your side. My wife thanks you for your letter and sends a thousand friendly greetings to you; as for me, I embrace you from the bottom of my heart. May God sustain us all! Alexander

Troubles

Demonstrations by Polish nationalists in 1860 and 1861 and a series of fires in St Petersburg in 1862, which were believed to be the work of insurrectionary arsonists, alarmed Alexander. The Poles were granted a degree of autonomy in 1862, but this concession failed to satisfy the nationalists, who demanded complete independence. The government's attempt to conscript the nationalists' leaders into the army provoked an insurrection in January 1863. The violence spread to parts of Lithuania, Belorussia and the Ukraine, and it took 15 months to suppress the insurgents. Polish autonomy was abolished. The study of Russian was made compulsory in Polish schools. Polish officials were sacked and replaced by Russians. The Catholic church was forbidden to communicate with the Vatican. The publication of books in Ukrainian was banned. This Russification caused much resentment.

In 1865 Alexander's son and heir Nicholas died of tubercular meningitis at the age of 21. Grief plunged the emperor into a severe depression. His family and ministers had to endure unpredictable outbursts of anger, and his wife withdrew into a life of piety and good works. Alexander's self-confidence was further

The bedroom of the Tsarevich Nicholas Alexandrovich. After the tsarevich's death in 1865, his parents preserved the room as a shrine to his memory, and commissioned this painting by E. Hau.

undermined in April 1866 when he was the object of an assassination attempt by a young nobleman, Dmitry Karakozov. The numerous public demonstrations of loyalty and gratitude for his escape could not console him. Some historians have seen the Polish insurrection and the Karakozov assassination attempt as turning points in the reign, marking the end of the 'Great Reforms' and the beginning of a period of 'Counter Reform'. Alexander certainly became more cautious, and appointed a number of conservative ministers such as Count Dmitry Tolstoy at Education and K.I. Pahlen at Justice. Laws in 1866 and 1867 limited the powers of the zemstva. Yet in other areas of government, reform continued.

Katia Dolgorukaya

In his late 40s Alexander fell in love with a teenage schoolgirl, Katia Dolgorukaya. Katia, an imperial ward since the death of her father, an impoverished aristocrat, was a boarder at the Smolny Institute in St Petersburg. They became lovers in 1866, shortly after Katia left the school. He installed her in a house on the English Embankment, close to the Winter Palace, and Katia bore him four children. The affair could not be kept secret, and the emperor's irascibility and inconsistency were attributed to her excessive physical and emotional demands. Gossip even blamed her for Alexander's chronic constipation, a condition which he sought to relieve by smoking a hookah while at stool. The strain of leading a double life, and the tensions in his relations with his heir, Alexander, who took his mother's side, affected the emperor's health.

(Below) The emperor's family. Alexander II, the Empress Maria Alexandrovna, and their eldest surviving son, the future Alexander III.

(Below right) The emperor's other family. A photograph of Alexander II, Katia Dolgorukaya and their two eldest children, George and Olga. The picture is from an album given to the emperor by his mistress to mark the twelfth anniversary of their liaison.

COURT BALLS IN THE REIGN OF ALEXANDER II

Alexander II and his wife in medieval costume for a court masquerade at Tsarskoe Selo.

A British diplomat, Lord Augustus Loftus, recorded his impressions of the Russian court in his memoirs.

The Court is very brilliant and admirably maintained. It has something of an Oriental grandeur. The Court balls, with the romantic appearance of the Circassian guard – the brilliant variety of uniforms – the Oriental costumes of the 'negroes' posted at the various doors – the picturesque appearance of the Cossacks – the magnificence of the ladies' toilettes (the perfection of a certain Mr Worth) and the splendour of their jewels (especially turquoises, diamonds and sapphires) – and the stately rooms of the Winter Palace, lit with thousands of wax candles, are

unsurpassed in beauty and splendour at any Court where I have resided. The guests are received by their Majesties with that grace and courtesy which at once gratifies and sets them at their ease; and there are no fêtes more enjoyable than those at the Winter Palace. There is one special fête called 'Le Bal des Palmiers', where the supper, in a salon transformed into a Winter Garden, is served at round tables encircling each palm tree. These palm trees are brought on each occasion from the conservatories at Tsarskoe Selo, and I was told that they require three years to recover from the exposure they undergo in one night's decoration.

Foreign policy

Until 1863 Gorchakov's and Alexander's thinking was dominated by the need for Russia to escape from isolation. Great Britain was implacably hostile and Prussia was regarded as too weak to be useful, a serious misjudgment of her potential. The French, who shared Russia's hostility towards Austria, seemed the most likely ally. Alexander's meeting with the Emperor Napoleon III at Stuttgart in 1857 led to an agreement early in 1859 that Russia would respond with benevolent neutrality when France made her bid to drive the Austrians out of Italy, and that France would assist Russia to revise the Treaty of Paris (1856).

Russia's southward expansion in western and central Asia was viewed with suspicion by the British, who believed that it threatened their control of India.

A cross commemorating the killing of demonstrators in Warsaw in February and April 1861. The inscription reads 'Memento. 25 27 February 8 April 1861'.

The alliance proved disappointing to both sides. The brief war between France and Austria in 1859 did not achieve everything that the French had hoped for, and they resented Russia's unwillingness to take a more active role against Austria. Alexander realized that by backing France he had helped to unleash revolution in Italy. The Polish insurrection of 1863 deepened his disillusionment, since Napoleon III joined the British and the Austrians in criticizing Russia's treatment of the Poles. Berlin was supportive of Russia, however, and this encouraged Alexander and Gorchakov to consider Prussia as a possible ally.

In the years 1863–70 the main focus of Russian foreign policy was on expansion in Asia. The Treaties of Aigun and Tientsin (1858) and Peking (1860) gained for Russia the left bank of the Amur River and the area between the Amur-Ussuri region and the Sea of Japan. Settlements were established at Khabarovsk (1858) and Vladivostok (1860). Alexander and Gorchakov understood that Russia's Pacific ambitions were viewed with suspicion by Britain and France, and saw the importance of securing American goodwill. Alaska, an area that was difficult for the Russians to exploit, was sold to the United States in 1867 for $7.2 million. In the

THE NOVGOROD MILLENNIUM MONUMENT

The Novgorod Millennium Monument, erected in 1862 to mark the millennium of the foundation of the Russian state.

In September 1862 Alexander II visited Novgorod for the millennium of the foundation of the Russian state. He approached the visit with some trepidation, since the gentry of the Novgorod region were in the main strongly opposed to the Emancipation. In the event the nobles assembled for the ceremonies proved to be docile. The emperor inaugurated a large and impressive memorial decorated with figures and bas-reliefs in bronze, created by a team of sculptors working to an overall design by Mikhail Mishekin and Ivan Shreder. The panels, which form a frieze around the base of the monument, depict grand princes, tsars and important military, religious and cultural figures.

An engraving depicting the arrival of the emperor and empress in the Novgorod Detinets (kremlin).

Treaty of St Petersburg (1875) Japan relinquished her claims to Sakhalin in return for sovereignty over the Kurile Islands. During Alexander's reign 37,000 square miles of Asian territory were added to the Russian empire.

Russia extended her dominance over Central Asia in the 1860s and 1870s, a policy which alarmed the British, who saw it as a threat to their control of India. The conquest of the Caucasus region was completed in a series of campaigns which began in 1857. In 1868 the Russians established a protectorate over Bokhara. Khiva was occupied in 1873. Kokand was annexed in 1876 and by the end of the reign Russia had gained control over the area of Turkmenia bordering on Persia and Afghanistan.

While Russia was preoccupied in Asia, the balance of power in Europe was changing. Prussia established her hegemony over the German states, which were unified in 1871. The Franco-Prussian War of 1870–71 provided Alexander and Gorchakov with the chance to repudiate those clauses of the Treaty of Paris which forbade the Russians from having a Black Sea fleet, an initiative endorsed by the powers in the London Convention of 1871. The new German empire represented a potential threat to Russian interests, but the Russian government preferred to rely on the Three Emperors' League with Germany and Austria-Hungary formed in 1873 rather than to seek an alliance with republican France.

Further reforms

The Municipal Statute of 1870 granted limited self-government to towns. The conservative Education Minister Count Dmitry Tolstoy insisted on a secondary school curriculum dominated by classical studies, in the mistaken belief that this would prevent the secondary schools from being a breeding ground for political dissidents, though he also increased government spending on education by 250 per cent. In 1871 women were permitted to enter the teaching profession and other areas of government employment.

Dmitry Miliutin, War Minister in 1861, introduced a new military statute and penal code in 1867 which regulated and moderated military discipline. His Conscription Statute of 1874 made the entire male population liable to the call-up, regardless of social status. Length of service was determined by level of education, with the maximum period of full-time service being six years. This reform made possible the development of a sizeable reserve, but the Russian army continued to lag behind its continental rivals in terms of equipment and organization.

Challenges to authority

Opposition to tsarism grew in the 1860s and 1870s. Some intellectuals placed their faith in revolution. By the late 1860s Sergei Nechaev, a young scripture teacher from the provinces, was preaching a nihilistic revolutionary creed. Nechaev's ruthless revolutionary authoritarianism, attacked by Dostoyevsky in his novel *The Devils*, was to have a significant influence on Lenin. Others believed that the answer to Russia's problems lay with the peasants. The attempts of these Populists politically to educate the peasantry by going to the countryside and preaching to them were unsuccessful. The Land and Liberty group, formed in 1876, began by living alongside the peasants in order to understand their mentality, and then sought to persuade urban workers to join the struggle for political reform. The government responded with mass arrests. Large-scale public trials provided the dissidents with a platform from which to spread their ideas.

In 1877 Trepov, the Governor-General of St Petersburg, ordered the flogging of a Populist detainee, although corporal punishment of political prisoners was illegal. This outrage pushed some Populists towards terrorist action. In 1878 a Populist named Vera Zasulich tried to kill Trepov. Though she did not deny her crime, Zasulich was found not guilty by a jury – a chilling repudiation of the standards of justice that Alexander II had attempted to establish. Sympathy for terrorism among the educated classes was a disturbing symptom of the final years of the reign. Land and Liberty split in 1879. One faction, known as the People's Will, dedicated itself to assassination as a means of provoking revolution. Alexander II was their principal target.

War with Turkey

During Alexander's reign the Panslavists, who believed that Russia should be the protector of all Slav peoples and should support those Slavs in the Balkans who aspired to be independent of Turkish rule, became increasingly influential. The Panslavists disapproved of the Three Emperors' League because it brought Russia into alliance with Austria-Hungary, whom they regarded as her principal rival for influence in the Balkans. Gorchakov would have preferred to pursue limited objectives by traditional methods but was forced to respond to the public demand for a more active foreign policy. The 'War in Sight' crisis of 1875 produced the first crack in the Three Emperors' League. Though Bismarck had no intention of going to war with France, he resented the heavy-handed way in which Gorchakov, in alliance with the British, protested against German policy. In the same year revolts broke out among the Serbian and Bosnian subjects of the Turkish empire. The Panslavists' demands for action in support of the rebels were strengthened when a Bulgarian rising was brutally put down by the Turks in 1876. Gorchakov's instinctive reaction to the crisis was to reach an accommodation with Austria-Hungary, but public clamour for intervention proved irresistible. Tchaikovsky's *Marche Slave*, which incorporated Serbian folk tunes and the Russian national anthem, expressed this mood. In April 1877 Russia went to war with Turkey, ostensibly in defence of the Bulgarians, but in reality in pursuit of prestige and territorial gain. The patriotic enthusiasm of the time is captured in some of the later chapters of Tolstoy's *Anna Karenina*.

On the Caucasian front the Russian armies did not achieve a decisive victory until November 1877, and in the Balkans stiff resistance by the Turks at Plevna held up the Russian advance until 28 November

Bulgarian refugees from Turkish atrocities returning to their homes with a Russian military escort. A contemporary engraving from the *Illustrated London News*. There was considerable popular sympathy for the Bulgarians in Britain and other Western European states, but Russian ambitions in the Balkans were viewed with suspicion.

The Congress of Berlin. A contemporary engraving. Gorchakov, the Russian Foreign Minister, is seated on the extreme left, and is touching the arm of Disraeli, the British Prime Minister, who is leaning on a cane. To the right of centre the German Chancellor Bismarck shakes hands with Peter Andreyevich Shuvalov, Russia's ambassador in London from 1874 to 1879.

(10 December NS). The Turks signed an armistice with Russia in January 1878. The Treaty of San Stefano of 19 February (3 March NS) 1878 allowed Turkey to retain a foothold in Europe and created a large Bulgarian state with an Aegean coastline. The Russians assumed that Bulgaria would be their satellite, but the powers were unwilling to accept such an extension of Russian influence. In July 1878 Russia bowed to international pressure at the Congress of Berlin and accepted a revision of the Treaty of San Stefano in which Bulgaria was considerably reduced in size. Although the Russians were allowed to keep their other territorial gains, in southern Bessarabia and in the Caucasus, it seemed to Pan-slavist opinion that the fruits of victory had been snatched away, and that the German Chancellor Bismarck, despite his claim to have been an 'honest broker', had sided with the Austrians.

The Dictatorship of the Heart

In April 1879 a doctor, Alexander Soloviev, fired five shots at the emperor from close range. An attempt was made to blow up the imperial train on 19 November 1879, and in February 1880 a terrorist bomb exploded in the banqueting hall of the Winter Palace. These events helped to

The wreckage of a train, blown up by terrorists in Moscow on 19 November 1879 in an unsuccessful bid to assassinate Alexander II. A contemporary engraving. Alexander was safely in the Kremlin at the time. He is reported to have asked: 'Am I a wild beast, that they should hound me to death?'

Count Mikhail Tarielovich Loris-Melikov (1825–88). The son of an Armenian merchant, Loris-Melikov fought with distinction against the Turks in the Crimean War, achieving the rank of Major General at the age of 30.

The assassination of Alexander II. A contemporary engraving. The terrorist Nikolai Rysakov threw a bomb under the coach in which the emperor was returning to the Winter Palace. Alexander, unhurt, got out of the coach to ensure that the wounded were being attended to and to question Rysakov. A second, fatal bomb, thrown by Ignaty Grinevitsky, exploded at his feet.

persuade Alexander that a new political approach was needed. In February 1880 he appointed General Count Mikhail Loris-Melikov as the head of a Supreme Administrative Commission with dictatorial powers. Loris-Melikov believed that short-term repression combined with constructive reforms would stabilize the political situation. By relaxing the censorship, removing some of the restrictions on the activities of the zemstva, and abolishing the unpopular salt tax, Loris-Melikov somewhat reduced the political tension. These policies became known as 'the Dictatorship of the Heart'. Unpopular conservative ministers, including Dmitry Tolstoy, were dismissed. The Third Section was abolished in August 1880 and its functions were handed over to the Minister of the Interior, a post which was given to Loris-Melikov.

The empress died in May 1880. A few weeks later Alexander married his mistress, in defiance of church law and the wishes of his family. Katia, now entitled Princess Yurievskaya, was not content with the status of morganatic wife. Loris-Melikov, a member of her social salon, suggested that further political liberalization might persuade public opinion to accept the proclamation of Katia as empress. He proposed the creation of a system of preparatory commissions, which would draft legislation on issues specified by the emperor. As well as officials chosen by the autocrat, the commissions would include elected representatives of the zemstva and the towns. On 28 January 1881 Alexander II accepted these suggestions, which fell far short of granting a constitution. The fact that no one had tried to assassinate him for a year may have convinced him that Loris-Melikov's blend of repression and reform was working. The proposals were due to be put to the Council of Ministers on 4 March 1881. On 1 March Alexander was being driven through the streets of St Petersburg when a terrorist threw a bomb at his carriage. Uninjured, Alexander got out to help the wounded and to question the perpetrator. A second assassin threw a bomb at his feet. The explosion smashed the lower part of the emperor's body. He was taken to the Winter Palace, where he died some hours later. A lock of Katia's hair was plaited into a crown and placed in the coffin. After the funeral Katia and her children went abroad. She died in Nice in 1922.

The French writer Anatole Leroy-Beaulieu commented shortly after Alexander's death that the emperor had made of Russia 'an incomplete and uncomfortable dwelling where friends and opponents of innovation felt almost equally ill at ease.' The reforms of his reign alienated conservative aristocrats but failed to secure the support of the liberal intelligentsia. An autocrat in name, Alexander had been forced to rely on his ministers and to exercise power by backing one bureaucratic faction and then another. His assassination strengthened the hand of the conservatives and removed reform from the political agenda.

Александр III   Alexander III
1881–1894

Николай II   Nicholas II
1894–1917

Alexander III. An engraving published in the *Illustrated London News* at the time of his death.

ALEXANDER III	
Full name Alexander Alexandrovich Romanov	*Died* Livadia 20 October 1894
Father Alexander II	*Wife* 1866 Marie Sophie Frederikke Dagmar of Denmark (Maria Feodorovna) Died 1928
Mother Maria of Hesse- Darmstadt (Maria Alexandrovna)	*Children* **Nicholas** (1868) Alexander (1869) George (1871)
Born St Petersburg 26 February 1845	Xenia (1875) Mikhail (1878) Olga (1882)
Accession 1 March 1881	

ALEXANDER III

The appearance of the tall, stately, vigorous man with the fine broad forehead betokens a mixture of strength and weakness, disdainful pride and invincible shyness, a mind constantly occupied with itself. This explains how he, who as a Prince was merely unsociable, has arrived at a degree of isolation within the last few years which surpasses anything ever shown by his predecessors.

H. von Samson-Himmelstierna, a German diplomat and writer

Alexander III was 6 ft 3 inches (1.9 m) tall. His robust physique and unsubtle mentality were reflected in his father's nickname for him – 'the bullock'. He enjoyed displaying his strength by bending pokers or rolling silver roubles into tubes between his fingers. Alexander experienced a limited education designed to fit him for a military career. On the death of his elder brother Nicholas in 1865 he became heir apparent, and in 1866 he married the Danish princess Dagmar, who had been betrothed to Nicholas. Tchaikovsky wrote his *Festival Overture on the Danish National Anthem* to mark the occasion. Maria Feodorovna, as Dagmar became known in Russia, was a diminutive, beautiful woman whose tact

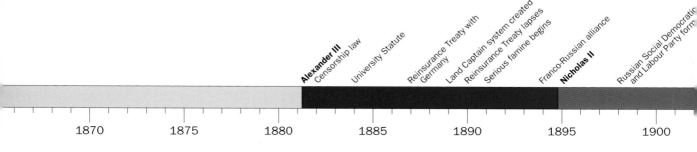

Alexander III · Censorship law

University Statute

Reinsurance Treaty with Germany

Land Captain system created

Reinsurance Treaty lapses

Serious famine begins

Franco-Russian alliance

Nicholas II

Russian Social Democratic and Labour Party form

1870   1875   1880   1885   1890   1895   1900

The Empress Maria Feodorovna (1847–1928), wife of Alexander III. A tinted photograph issued as a postcard.

Konstantin Petrovich Pobedonostsev (1827–1907). A line engraving from the *Leipziger Illustrierte Zeitung*, 1888.

and charm impressed the St Petersburg aristocracy and compensated for her husband's bluff taciturnity. Alexander gained significant experience of administrative and military affairs before his accession, attending meetings of the Council of Ministers, serving in the Russo-Turkish War and participating in the Supreme Administrative Commission under the chairmanship of Loris-Melikov.

The publication, on 29 April 1881, of an Imperial Manifesto asserting the new emperor's determination to defend the autocracy ended the hopes of those who believed that further reform was the only means of detaching the educated classes from the terrorists. The manifesto was the work of Konstantin Pobedonostsev, the Procurator of the Holy Synod, who had been one of Alexander's tutors. Loris-Melikov resigned. Alexander chose to rely on the advice of a small group of officials which included Pobedonostsev and Count Dmitry Tolstoy, who became Interior Minister in 1882. They encouraged the emperor's domineering approach to government, mistaking inflexibility for strength. Alexander believed that his father's reforms had weakened the monarchy, and was more in sympathy with the ideology of Official Nationality favoured by his grandfather Nicholas I (p. 171).

In August 1881 the Temporary Regulation on Measures for the Safety of the State was issued. The Regulation, which remained in force until 1917, conferred extensive powers of repression on central and provincial government, in particular on the Ministry of the Interior and therefore on the police. The censorship was tightened in 1882, and the University Statute of 1884 brought higher education back under the direct control of the state. Alexander encouraged the development of the Okhrana, a network of political police departments. These measures weakened the revolutionary opposition but did not destroy it.

In 1889 the office of Land Captain was created, a reform upon which the emperor insisted in the face of opposition from a majority of the State Council. The Land Captains, salaried officials appointed from the ranks of the propertied classes, were charged with supervising the lives of the peasants and acting as justices of the peace. The separation of the legal and executive powers established by Alexander II in 1864 was thus breached. A law of 1890 altered the character of the zemstva by increasing the representation of the gentry, restricting the peasant vote, and bringing zemstva boards under closer government control. A similar law of 1892 restricted the activities of the city dumas.

The emperor's strong prejudices against Poles and Jews found expression in an increased emphasis on Russification and the growth of official

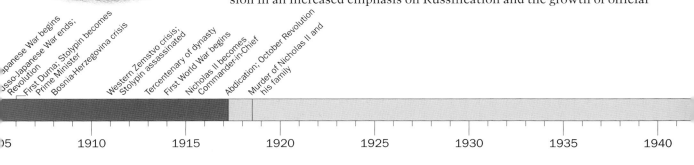

...panese War begins
...usso-Japanese War ends; Revolution
First Duma; Stolypin becomes Prime Minister
Bosnia-Herzegovina crisis
Western Zemstvo crisis; Stolypin assassinated
Tercentenary of dynasty
First World War begins
Nicholas II becomes Commander-in-Chief
Abdication; October Revolution
Murder of Nicholas II and his family

)5   1910   1915   1920   1925   1930   1935   1940

A PLEA FOR CLEMENCY REJECTED

Lev Tolstoy wrote to Alexander III in the early weeks of his reign, pleading with him to spare the lives of the terrorists who had murdered his father, Tsar Alexander II.

Sire, now you stand pure and innocent before yourself and before God, but you are at a crossroads. A few days more and, if the victory goes to those who think and say that Christian truths have no value except in words and that in life, blood must flow and death must reign, then you will lose forever your blessed state of purity and communion with God, and you will set forth along the dark road of 'reasons of State' that justify everything, even the violation of divine law. If you do not pardon, but execute the murderers, you will have done away with three or four individuals out of hundreds; but evil breeds evil, and thirty or forty more will spring up to replace those three or four.... The death penalty is useless against revolutionaries. Their numbers are not what counts, it is their ideas. To fight them, you must meet them on the ground of ideas. Their ideal is universal well-being, equality, liberty. To combat them some other ideal must be advanced, superior to theirs, larger than theirs.'

Tolstoy's letter was sent to Pobedonostsev, who refused to show it to the tsar, and wrote to Alexander in these terms:

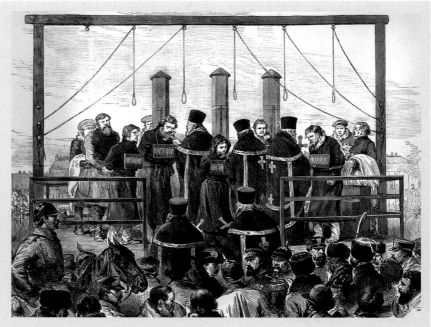

The execution of the assassins of Alexander II. A contemporary engraving from the Illustrated London News.

... in this moment, with the eyes of the entire Russian nation upon you, it is unthinkable that you should pardon the murderers of your father, the emperor of Russia – that you should forget the blood that has been shed, for which everyone (apart from a few weak-hearted and feeble-minded individuals) is crying vengeance, and people are already demanding to know why the sentence is so long in coming.... If one of these wretches should escape death, he will immediately begin to hatch new plots for undermining the government.

For the love of God, Sire, do not listen to misguided sycophants.

Alexander wrote across the letter 'Rest assured, no one will dare come to me with such a request, and I promise you that all six of them will hang.' One of the prisoners had her sentence commuted to life imprisonment because she was discovered to be pregnant. Sophia Perovskaya, the organizer of the conspiracy, and four men were publicly hanged on 3 April 1881.

anti-semitism. The first large-scale pogroms, outbreaks of popular violence against Jews tolerated or encouraged by the authorities, occurred in 1881. From 1887 a quota system limited the number of Jewish students admitted to universities. Religions and sects other than the Russian Orthodox church were forbidden to proselytize.

The Russo-Turkish War had deepened the government's indebtedness and undermined the value of the paper currency. Alexander's Finance Ministers sought to strengthen the currency, increase government revenue and modernize the economy. Bunge (1881–86) reduced the soul tax, which was finally abolished in 1887, and established a Peasant Land Bank in 1882. Reducing the burden of taxation on the peasants made it even more difficult to balance the budget, and Bunge never managed to

THE CHARACTER OF ALEXANDER III

This account of Alexander III's character was written by a contemporary German observer, H. von Samson-Himmelstierna.

The present Emperor's innate nature is impressionable, and ever prone to be at variance with itself; his contact with the world … has driven him to distrust and doubt both himself and others: in spite of his most strenuous endeavours to become a self-sufficient autocrat, he has never succeeded in the process. His characteristic reserve arises partly from an inborn and invincible shyness, partly from a want of self-confidence. The undeviating persistence in following out a given line of action represents a sense of duty which has been painfully acquired; it does not proceed from an inner necessity. The Emperor is almost impervious to the counsel and opinions of other people – not because he always has his own private opinion in which he puts implicit trust, but because he holds it as a duty to be and to appear incapable of being influenced, and because he fears the appearance of dependence still more than dependence itself.

do so. A decree of 1882 banned the employment of children below the age of 12, and limited the working hours of those under 15 years old. A factory inspectorate was established, yet working conditions remained primitive and hazardous. Strikes were made illegal. Bunge was dismissed because the emperor's conservative advisers regarded his policies as too progressive.

In promoting Vyshnegradsky, Finance Minister from 1887 to 1892, and his successor Sergei Witte, the emperor chose technocrats from outside the bureaucratic elite. Vyshnegradsky secured foreign loans, introduced an external tariff in 1891 to protect Russia's emerging industries, and embarked on a programme of railway building. By 1892 he had built up Russia's gold reserves and turned a trade deficit into a surplus. The government's revenues were boosted by increases in indirect taxation which bore most heavily on the poorest sections of society and the trade surplus was built largely on increased exports of grain, a risky policy in an empire whose agricultural productivity was low. That risk was emphasized by the terrible famine of 1891–92, with its attendant epidemics of cholera and typhus.

The government ordered the press not to use the word famine in its reports, and Vyshnegradsky argued against banning grain exports. The delay in imposing the ban meant that essential supplies of food continued to leave Russia for several weeks. By the autumn of 1891 it was clear that the government was incapable of dealing with the crisis, and Alexander III called for the formation of charitable organizations to provide food and medical assistance. The educated classes responded energetically to this command, and the zemstva played an important part in organizing relief. The famine thus brought about a flowering of civic activity and an upsurge of opposition to the government.

The famine of 1891–92. A contemporary engraving showing peasants pulling the thatch from the roofs of their houses in order to feed their horses. Without the horses, which were used for ploughing, there would be no harvest next year.

Alexander III of Russia and his great uncle Wilhelm I of Germany. An engraving published in *Der Berliner* in 1887.

Foreign policy

The emperor took a personal interest in foreign policy. The Balkan crisis of 1877–78 had destroyed the Three Emperors' League, leaving Russia diplomatically isolated. One of the first initiatives of the new reign was the signing of the Three Emperors' Alliance in June 1881. This secret treaty, of three years' duration, included a guarantee that if any of the three contracting powers – Russia, Austria-Hungary and Prussia – was at war with a fourth power the others would remain neutral. The alliance also committed the three powers to keeping the Straits closed to foreign warships, and to maintaining the status quo in the Balkans. N.K. Giers, a cautious bureaucrat who had been Gorchakov's deputy since 1875, was appointed Foreign Minister in 1882. He believed that good relations with Germany were vital to Russia's interests. Alexander accepted this approach for some years, despite his anti-German prejudices, since he wished to concentrate on internal affairs. The military budget was cut by a quarter in 1882, and the Three Emperors' Alliance was renewed in 1884.

A complex crisis in Bulgaria in the period 1885–87 demonstrated the weakness of Russia's international position. The realization that Germany was, under pressure, likely to back Austria against Russia made Alexander unwilling to renew the Three Emperors' Alliance in 1887. Anxious to avoid having to choose between Austria and Russia, the German Chancellor Bismarck negotiated a secret Reinsurance Treaty with the Russians in the same year, but when the Bulgars chose Ferdinand of Coburg, an Austrian protégé, to be their ruler, the tensions between Russia and Austria grew worse. A tariff war with Germany, and the publication by Bismarck of his 1879 Dual Alliance with Austria, deepened Russian suspicions of Germany. In 1890 Kaiser Wilhelm II refused to renew the Reinsurance Treaty, and Russia's isolation was complete.

A Russian railway station in the Far East. This engraving was published in 1896, five years after work had begun on the construction of the Trans-Siberian Railway.

Alexander turned to those advisers who favoured a closer relationship with the French, a policy which made economic sense, since France was a fruitful source of investment capital. Negotiations began in 1891 and a treaty was concluded in 1894. In return for a pledge to support France if she was attacked by Germany, Russia gained a French guarantee of support in the event that either Germany or Austria at Germany's encouragement attacked Russia.

Russian expansion in Central Asia reached its climax during the reign of Alexander III. As Russia's frontiers moved closer to Afghanistan in the early 1880s the British, who felt that their control of India was threatened, grew more alarmed. A confrontation, triggered by fighting between Russian and Afghan troops at Penjdeh in 1885, was resolved by diplomacy. A treaty with China in 1893 secured part of Chinese Turkestan for Russia. By then work had begun on the construction of the Trans-Siberian Railway, which Witte saw both as the key to the economic development of Siberia and as a means of projecting Russia's military power eastwards.

Personal life

The emperor preferred Gatchina to Tsarskoe Selo as a country residence, and spent little time in St Petersburg. He delighted in country pursuits, and getting drunk with his cronies, and was wont in his cups to lie on the floor and wave his arms and legs about. When his doctors forbade alcohol Alexander had a pair of wading boots made in which a flask could be concealed from the solicitous vigilance of the empress.

The marriage between Alexander and Maria was a happy one, and the emperor remained faithful to his 'Mimi'. Like her sister Alexandra, the consort of the future Edward VII of Great Britain, Maria was a domineering mother. Her three sons Nicholas, George and Mikhail grew into

Alexander III's study at Gatchina, his favourite residence. This watercolour drawing by E. Hau shows the family portraits with which the emperor surrounded himself.

PRACTICAL JOKES AT THE PALACE

Count Witte, who was appointed Finance Minister by Alexander III and who admired the emperor, left this account of life in the imperial family.

Alexander III ... was a stern father and while the children did not fear him, they were uneasy and constrained in his presence with the single exception of Mikhail, the favourite son, who was not only unrestrained, but even inclined to take liberties, as the following amusing anecdote, related to me by his valet, will indicate. Becoming impatient at the boy's impertinence and inattention during a stroll in the gardens early one summer morning, Alexander III snatched up a watering hose and gave Mikhail a good dousing. Without further ado they went in to breakfast, the youth changing his drenched clothing. After that the Emperor retired to work in his study and as usual indulged in his habit of occasionally leaning out of the window, but was met with an altogether unusual deluge from the upper window, where Misha had stationed himself with a pailful of water in anticipation of the Imperial appearance fenestral. There is very little doubt that none but Mikhail would have dared to think of such a stratagem, and there is no doubt whatsoever that nobody else could have executed it with impunity.

Alexander III surrounded by his family. Clockwise from the left: Mikhail, the Empress Maria Feodorovna, the Tsarevich Nicholas (later Nicholas II), Xenia, George and Olga.

WITTE ON ALEXANDER III

Sergei Witte, who regarded Alexander III as a strong and competent ruler, left this pen portrait of the emperor in his memoirs.

Alexander III was undeniably a man of limited education. I cannot agree, however, with those who would class him as unintelligent. Though lacking perhaps in mental keenness, he was undoubtedly gifted with the broad sympathetic understanding which in a ruler is often far more important than rational brilliancy. Neither in the Imperial family nor among the nobility was there anyone who better appreciated the value of a rouble than Emperor Alexander III. He made an ideal treasurer for the Russian people, and his economical temperament was of incalculable assistance in the solution of Russia's financial problems.

diffident, immature young men. Mikhail was his father's indulged favourite, but Nicholas was an object of exasperation to Alexander, who referred to him as 'girlie' and doubted whether he had the willpower required of an autocrat.

Last days

In 1888, during a railway journey, Alexander grew irritated at the slow speed of his train and ordered that it should go faster. His ministers ignored warnings that one of the two locomotives was antiquated, and that any acceleration would be dangerous. The elderly locomotive and

The train crash at Borki on 17 October 1888. A line-drawing by an eyewitness. The incident resulted in the resignations of the Minister of Communications and the Chief Inspector of Railways, who had suffered a broken arm in the crash.

several carriages were derailed. Alexander is said to have saved his wife and children by supporting the collapsed roof of the imperial saloon on his shoulders until help arrived. The accident at Borki probably contributed to the physical decline of the emperor. Over the next few years he suffered from back pain, headaches and kidney problems. By the time that Bright's disease was diagnosed it was too late to save his life. He died at Livadia in the Crimea on 20 October 1894, surrounded by his family.

Though many historians have seen Alexander III's reign, with its 'counter-reforms', as the period when tsarism finally and fatally alienated Russia's educated classes, contemporaries believed that he had strengthened the monarchy. In 1894 the opposition was weak and divided, the finances of the state had been restored, and Russia was experiencing rapid industrialization. The crises that his heir was to face were crises of modernization, symbolically prefigured in the railway accident at Borki. It remained to be seen whether the antiquated administrative structures of Russia were capable of coping with the political, social and economic changes consequent upon its rulers' insistence on accelerated economic growth.

NICHOLAS II

NICHOLAS II	
Full name	*Died*
Nicholas Alexandrovich Romanov	17 July 1918 (NS) Shot by a Bolshevik firing squad
Father Alexander II	*Wife* 1894 Princess Alix of Hesse (Alexandra Feodorovna)
Mother Marie Sophie Frederikke Dagmar of Denmark (Maria Feodorovna)	Died 1918, shot by a Bolshevik firing squad
Born St Petersburg 6 May 1868	*Children* Olga (1895) Tatiana (1897)
Accession 20 October 1894	Maria (1899) Anastasia (1901)
Abdication 2 March 1917	Alexei (1904) All murdered 1918

Nicholas II

Nicholas II was without doubt an honest person and a good family man, but he was by nature extremely weak-willed. He had never prepared himself to reign, nor did he like it when this burden fell upon him. He, as well as his wife, hated court etiquette and did not conform to it. After conscientiously hearing out the usual reports of his ministers, that so bored him, he would run out of the conferences into the open air to chop wood, his favourite pastime.

Pavel Miliukov, historian and leading Russian liberal

Nicholas II (1894–1917) was a shy, slightly built man who found public life uncongenial. He was not lacking in intelligence, but service in fashionable regiments and a sentimental education in the arms of the ballerina Mathilde Ksheshinskaya had done little to prepare him for responsibilities which would have taxed the powers of the ablest statesman, and a grand tour of Europe and the Far East in 1890–91 failed to broaden his mind. An attempt on his life by a deranged Japanese policeman left him with a strong dislike of the inhabitants of that country, whom he scornfully termed 'monkeys'. As tsarevich he had dutifully chaired the Special Committee on Famine Relief and the Siberian Railway Committee, as well as attending meetings of the Committee of Ministers, but he preferred country life and simple outdoor pleasures to state papers and public affairs.

Among Nicholas' mentors was Pobedonostsev, the Chief Procurator of the Holy Synod. Pobedonostsev's recollection of a bored tsarevich picking his nose during one of their tutorials suggests that historians may have exaggerated his influence on the future ruler, yet Nicholas

HISTORICAL PAINTING AND THE SLAVIC REVIVAL

The modern view of Russia's tsarist past is coloured by the work of Russian 19th-century painters who were fascinated by the Muscovite period. Vasily Ivanovich Surikov (1848–1916) produced works which were much admired by the authorities, perhaps because their political content was partly concealed beneath virtuoso technique and historical pageantry. His *The Morning of the Execution of the Streltsy* was completed in 1881, the year in which Alexander III refused to commute the death sentences on the assassins who had killed his father. Peter the Great watches, his face set in an expression of implacable anger, as the condemned *streltsy* are brought in carts to the place of execution outside the walls of the Moscow Kremlin.

Nikolai Nikolaievich Ge (1831–94) produced a number of historical canvases, of which the most famous is *Peter the Great Interrogating the Tsarevich Alexei* (1871), another work which conveys both Peter's cruelty and his strength of purpose.

Other artists who turned to historical painting in the 1880s included Ilya Efimovich Repin (1844–1930). His *Tsar Ivan with the Body of His Son*, completed in 1885, shows Ivan the Terrible clutching the son whom he has just fatally injured. The canvas can be seen as an indirect attack on autocracy, but Repin appears to have been more interested in the melodramatic psychology of the situation.

Viktor Mikhailovich Vasnetsov (1848–1927) also preferred subjects from a remoter past. Inspired by a genuine enthusiasm for Muscovite art and architecture, Vasnetsov was less interested in reading political messages into the past than in achieving richness and authenticity of detail.

(Above) The Morning of the Execution of the Streltsy *by Vasily Ivanovich Surikov.*

(Left) Peter the Great Interrogating the Tsarevich Alexei *by Nikolai Nikolaievich Ge.*

The Church of the Saviour on the Spilled Blood, St Petersburg, designed by Alfred Parland.

The Historical Museum, Moscow, designed by Vladimir Osipovich Shervud.

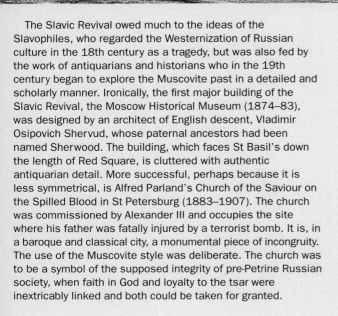

Nicholas II's masquerade costume, made by Kaffi, the Imperial Theatrical Costumier, for a costume ball in February 1903. The caftan was a copy of the parade dress worn by Tsar Alexei Mikhailovich.

The Slavic Revival owed much to the ideas of the Slavophiles, who regarded the Westernization of Russian culture in the 18th century as a tragedy, but was also fed by the work of antiquarians and historians who in the 19th century began to explore the Muscovite past in a detailed and scholarly manner. Ironically, the first major building of the Slavic Revival, the Moscow Historical Museum (1874–83), was designed by an architect of English descent, Vladimir Osipovich Shervud, whose paternal ancestors had been named Sherwood. The building, which faces St Basil's down the length of Red Square, is cluttered with authentic antiquarian detail. More successful, perhaps because it is less symmetrical, is Alfred Parland's Church of the Saviour on the Spilled Blood in St Petersburg (1883–1907). The church was commissioned by Alexander III and occupies the site where his father was fatally injured by a terrorist bomb. It is, in a baroque and classical city, a monumental piece of incongruity. The use of the Muscovite style was deliberate. The church was to be a symbol of the supposed integrity of pre-Petrine Russian society, when faith in God and loyalty to the tsar were inextricably linked and both could be taken for granted.

Nicholas II was fascinated by the Muscovite period. He preferred the traditional title of 'tsar' to that of 'emperor', and named his son after his favourite 17th-century predecessor. He shared his father's suspicion of cosmopolitan, Westernized St Petersburg, which both men saw as a nest of interfering bureaucrats and treasonous intellectuals, and much preferred Moscow. He enjoyed wearing elaborate 17th-century costumes at fancy dress balls. His tendency to retreat into a romanticized version of the past did not help him to deal with the complexities of a present which he found unpalatable.

QUEEN VICTORIA ON THE MARITAL PROSPECTS OF ALIX OF HESSE

Queen Victoria's prescient misgivings about the proposed marriage between her granddaughter Alix of Hesse and the Tsarevich Nicholas were expressed in this letter to Victoria, Princess Louis of Battenberg, dated 21 October 1894.

All my fears about her future marriage now show themselves so strongly and my blood runs cold when I think of her so young most likely placed on that very unsafe throne, her dear life and above all her husband's constantly threatened and unable to see her but rarely. It is a great additional anxiety in my declining years! Oh, how I wish it was not to be that I should lose my sweet Alicky.

The wedding of Nicholas II and Princess Alix of Hesse. A contemporary engraving from the Illustrated London News.

came to share his belief in autocracy both as a divinely ordained system and as the only workable form of government for the vast Russian empire.

In November 1894, a few weeks after his accession to the throne, Nicholas married Alix of Hesse, a German princess who, as the favourite granddaughter of Queen Victoria, had received a thoroughly English upbringing. Alexandra Feodorovna, as Alix became known in Russia,

The coronation procession of Tsar Nicholas II in the Moscow Kremlin, 14 May 1896. The tsar is walking beneath an ornamental canopy which is carried by the senior generals of the imperial retinue, who are wearing caps made of lambskin.

The funeral, on 18 May 1896, of the victims of Khodynka. The size of the mass grave indicates the scale of the disaster, in which more than 1,000 people were killed. The imperial couple's presence at a ball given by the French ambassador on the evening of the tragedy was widely viewed as evidence of their callousness, though Nicholas and Alexandra had only agreed to attend because their advisers were anxious not to upset the French.

Sergei Yulievich Witte (1848–1915). This picture of the Russian statesman was given away with a French brand of chocolate. President Theodore Roosevelt, who met him in 1905, commented that '... he struck me as a very selfish man, totally without ideals.' Witte was known to have written his memoirs. When he died Nicholas II ordered that his papers be put under seal, but the statesman had placed the typescript of the book in his wife's safe deposit box, and it was published after the downfall of the dynasty.

espoused Orthodoxy with all the zeal of a convert. Nicholas' and Alexandra's coronation in Moscow in May 1896 was attended by tragedy. A public celebration at Khodynka, a suburb of Moscow, got out of hand during the distribution of souvenirs, and more than 1,000 people were crushed to death.

Alexandra's reserved manner alienated her from St Petersburg society, which she regarded as frivolous and immoral. She found a formidable rival in the popular Dowager Empress Maria Feodorovna, who continued for some years to exercise a dominant influence over the emperor. Nicholas and Alexandra preferred the bourgeois comforts of the Alexander Palace at Tsarskoe Selo to the magnificence of the Winter Palace. Their first daughter, Olga, was born in 1895. Tatiana (1897), Maria (1899) and Anastasia (1901) further enlarged the family, but her failure to produce a male heir preyed on Alexandra's mind, and made her the more ready to resort to quack doctors and faith healers.

Government and governed

The emperor conscientiously spent hours dealing with trivial matters and even stamped his own letters. He preferred to deal with ministers individually, believing that this would preserve his power, yet he was unable to provide the clear sense of direction that was needed. Nicholas viewed able and energetic ministers such as Sergei Witte with suspicion, fearing that they might encroach on the royal prerogative. His ministers found the emperor courteous, evasive and liable to change his mind.

Witte, who was Minister of Finance from 1892 to 1903, believed that rapid industrial growth could only be achieved by state intervention. He sustained and strengthened Vyshnegradsky's protectionist policy and his efforts to create a strong currency and to attract foreign investment. He also encouraged the construction of the Trans-Siberian Railway. Output of coal and pig iron trebled in the 1890s, and by the end of that decade Russia had a railway network of 31,940 miles. The influx of peasants into

NICHOLAS II MAKES CLEAR HIS DETERMINATION TO DEFEND THE AUTOCRACY

Nicholas II soon made it clear that he intended to rule in accordance with his father's principles. This speech, which he addressed to representatives of the zemstvos in January 1895, had probably been written by Pobedonostsev.

I know that recently, in zemstvo assemblies, there have been heard voices carried away by senseless dreams about the participation of zemstvo representatives in governmental affairs. Let everyone know that, devoting all my strength to the good of my people, I will preserve the principles of autocracy as firmly and undeviatingly as did my unforgettable late father.

These words moved the historian Kliuchevsky privately to predict that Nicholas II would be the last tsar. The Coronation Manifesto of 1896 reinforced the message that the pace of change and the agenda of reform would be determined by the autocracy.

The cover of Nicholas II's Coronation Manifesto.

the booming industrial cities – the population of St Petersburg more than doubled in the period 1890–1914 – was not accompanied by improvements in housing and infrastructure, and when recession hit the Russian economy in the early years of the new century mass unemployment was added to the miseries experienced by urban workers. By then the revolutionary opposition had begun to assume a more coherent form. In 1898 Russia's various Marxist organizations came together to form the Russian Social Democratic Labour Party, and in 1901 various groups who believed in the possibility of peasant revolution coalesced as the Socialist Revolutionary Party. The Russian Social Democratic Labour Party split into two factions, the Bolsheviks and the Mensheviks, in 1903. The Bolsheviks, under the dynamic, ruthless and centralizing leadership of Vladimir Ilyich Lenin, were to be the ultimate beneficiaries of the collapse of tsarism.

The spread of education and the development of the zemstvo system were creating a new class of literate, civic-minded public servants. In 1895 Nicholas dismissed the zemstvo movement's hopes of playing a greater role in government as 'senseless dreams'. By 1904 the zemstvo

NICHOLAS II REACTS TO THE DEATH OF A GENIUS

An extract from a letter which Nicholas II wrote to his mother in November 1910.

As you must have heard, Tolstoy is dead. This event is being much discussed and written about a great deal – a great deal too much, in my opinion. Fortunately, he was buried quickly, so that not many people were in time for the funeral at Yasnaya Polyana and everything went off in an orderly and calm manner. Everyone expected demonstrations and disturbances – when nothing happened they were rather surprised.

Portrait of the writer Lev Nikolaievich Tolstoy (1828–1910) by Ivan Nikolaievich Kramskoy (1837–87). The painting was completed in 1873.

leaders and the Union of Liberation, a liberal political movement founded in that year, were calling for the creation of an elected duma (parliament) with legislative powers.

Foreign policy

The emperor's approach to foreign policy, in which he took a strong interest, was influenced by prejudice and by family loyalties. He believed that by correspondence and personal meetings with Kaiser Wilhelm II he could maintain stable relations with Germany, using the Franco-Russian alliance as a lever. Cousin Willy had good reason to encourage Cousin Nicky's ambitions to expand Russian influence in the Far East, and those ambitions were not necessarily misguided. Nicholas' mistakes were to overestimate the naval and military capabilities of Russia, and to underestimate the Japanese.

Russian penetration of Manchuria and the Liaotung Peninsula in the 1890s, and Russian ambitions with regard to Korea created hostility between Russia and Japan. Nicholas believed that a strong foreign policy would restore the popularity of the monarchy. His refusal to withdraw troops from Manchuria and his rejection of Japanese proposals for the

(*Above*) The Alexander Palace Egg of 1908, made by the firm of Fabergé and presented by Nicholas II to his wife as an Easter gift. Peter Carl Fabergé (1846–1920) was appointed goldsmith and jeweller to the imperial court early in the reign of Alexander III, and in 1884 he was commissioned by the emperor to make a jewelled Easter egg as a gift for the Empress Maria Feodorovna. Alexander III commissioned further eggs, and the tradition was maintained by Nicholas II. The Alexander Palace Egg is made of nephrite and decorated with gold, silver and precious stones. It bears the initials of the empress and miniature portraits of her five children. Each of the Fabergé imperial eggs contained a surprise; in this instance a tinted gold and enamel model of the Alexander Palace at Tsarskoe Selo, the favourite residence of Nicholas and Alexandra. The egg is preserved in the State Museums of the Moscow Kremlin.

(*Right*) In the 1890s Russia secured extensive influence in Manchuria from the Chinese and work began on the Chinese Eastern Railway, completed in 1903. Having used diplomatic pressure to force Japan to withdraw from the Liaotung Peninsula and northern Korea, Russia then leased Liaotung from China in 1898 and was granted the right to develop a naval base at Port Arthur. After the Russo-Japanese War, Russia was forced to give up Liaotung and her influence in Manchuria, and Japan gained the southern half of Sakhalin Island.

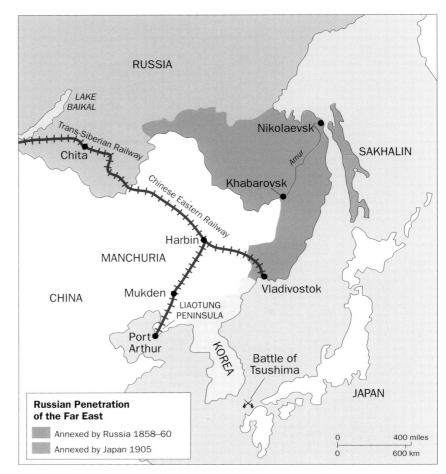

Russian Penetration of the Far East

- Annexed by Russia 1858–60
- Annexed by Japan 1905

A Japanese woodblock print of the battle of Tsushima. The battle took place on 27 May 1905 (NS). It is often asserted that it only lasted 45 minutes. In fact firing commenced shortly after 2 pm, and it was not until 7.30 that evening that the crippled Russian flagship *Suvorov* finally sank with all hands.

creation of Russian and Japanese spheres of influence in Manchuria and Korea made war inevitable. A Japanese surprise attack on Port Arthur on 26–27 January (8–9 February NS) 1904 inflicted serious damage on Russia's Pacific Fleet, and the Russians found themselves engaged in a war for which they were ill-prepared. In 1905 they experienced a series of humiliating defeats, culminating in the battle of Tsushima in May. Russia's Baltic Fleet had been ordered to sail for the Pacific in October 1904. In the first phase of this ill-fated cruise the Russian ships encountered a number of British fishing vessels on the Dogger Bank, and opened fire on them in the belief that they were Japanese torpedo boats. When, seven months later, the Baltic Fleet reached the Straits of Tsushima which separate Korea from Japan, it was virtually annihilated by the Japanese in a brief but devastating naval engagement. Admiral Rozhdestvensky, the Russian commander at Tsushima, survived the battle and was subsequently acquitted by a court martial. The Russian government had no alternative but to negotiate. Under the Treaty of Portsmouth, signed on 23 August (5 September NS) 1905, Russia was forced to withdraw her remaining troops from Manchuria, to cede Port Arthur, the Liaotung Peninsula and the southern half of Sakhalin to the Japanese and to give them a free hand in Korea.

The 1905 Revolution

By the time the war ended, Russia was experiencing a revolutionary crisis. Nicholas' refusal to allow the zemstvo movement a national assembly had alienated liberals, and his pursuit of Russification drove

NICHOLAS II'S ANTI-SEMITISM

A contemporary French satirical cartoon documenting police brutality against Jews.

A number of extremist right-wing groups emerged during the turbulence of 1905. The largest, the Union of the Russian People, was supported by the tsar and funded by the government. The Union's paramilitary groups, the Black Hundreds, beat up and murdered liberals, left-wingers and Jews. There were pogroms all over Russia following the publication of the October Manifesto. In Odessa, 800 Jewish people were murdered. The authorities subsidized the printing of anti-semitic leaflets and even distributed vodka to arouse the mob. Sergei Witte recalled Nicholas's own anti-semitism in his memoirs.

The Emperor was surrounded by avowed Jew-haters, such as Trepov, Plehve, Ignatiev, and the leaders of the Black Hundreds. As for his personal attitude towards the Jews I recall that whenever I drew his attention to the fact that the anti-Jewish riots could not be tolerated, he either was silent or remarked: 'But it is they themselves, i.e. the Jews (His Majesty always used the opprobrious zhidy [yids], instead of yevrei [hebrews]) that are to blame.' The anti-Jewish current flowed not from below upward, but in the opposite direction.

the nationalities of the western part of the empire into revolutionary militancy. The government's repressive policies were strong enough to outrage educated opinion but not strong enough to extinguish opposition. The main causes of unrest were, however, economic: mass unemployment and poor living and working conditions in urban Russia, and poverty and land-hunger in the countryside, intensified by bad harvests.

In an attempt to contain working-class unrest, Sergei Zubatov, the head of the Moscow Okhrana, had established government-controlled trades unions. In St Petersburg the 'police union' was run by a priest, Father Gapon, who developed a genuine sympathy for the workers. On Sunday 9 January 1905 he led a peaceful march on the Winter Palace, to petition the emperor to alleviate the misery of the workers. Police and troops opened fire, killing and injuring hundreds of unarmed demonstrators. Though Nicholas was not in St Petersburg at the time, and not directly responsible for what happened, 'Bloody Sunday' seriously damaged the image of the emperor as the 'Little Father' of the Russian people. In the early months of 1905 strikes, terrorism and peasant violence escalated. Military force was needed to restore order, and incidents of mutiny, including the rising by the crew of the battleship *Potemkin*, alarmed the authorities. In May a Union of Unions was established under the chairmanship of the distinguished liberal historian Pavel Miliukov. This brought together representatives of professional organizations to demand the establishment of a parliament. When, on 6 August 1905, the emperor announced his intention of creating a purely consultative duma, the Union of Unions rejected this proposal as inadequate.

In October a general strike developed, paralysing the railways and industry. Even the corps de ballet at the Mariinsky Theatre came out in solidarity. In St Petersburg a soviet, an elected workers' and soldiers' council, was established to supervise the strike. Witte attempted to bring home to Nicholas the dangers of the situation, telling him that he must either introduce constitutional reforms or institute a military dictatorship. Nicholas instinctively favoured the latter course but was dissuaded from it by his kinsman, the Grand Duke Nikolai. When offered the job of military dictator, the grand duke took out his revolver and threatened to shoot himself unless the tsar accepted Witte's proposals for constitutional reform. Witte agreed to serve on condition that he was allowed effectively to function as prime minister, choosing other ministers and determining policy. On his advice Nicholas issued the October Manifesto (on 17 October) in which he conceded the creation of an elected legislative duma, and guaranteed certain fundamental civil rights to the Russian people. The promise of a parliament drove a wedge between the middle-class moderates, who were alarmed at the level of disorder, and the industrial workers. The regime felt confident enough to use troops to crush the workers' movements in St Petersburg and Moscow and to curb peasant unrest.

THE 1905 REVOLUTION

3 January	A strike begins at the Putilov Armaments factory in St Petersburg
9 January	'Bloody Sunday'
4 February	Assassination of the Grand Duke Sergei
18 February	Publication of the Bulygin Rescript
Late February	Beginning of agrarian disturbances
18 April	Outbreak of industrial unrest in Poland
8–9 May	Establishment of the Union of Unions
14–24 June	Mutiny on the *Potemkin* and riots in Odessa
6–8 July	Congress of zemstva and town councils in Moscow
6 August	Manifesto announcing the creation of a consultative Duma
27 August	Autonomy granted to universities, which become centres of free speech and political opposition
8 October	Railway strike begins. It soon develops into a general strike
12–18 October	Founding Congress of the Constitutional Democrat (Kadet) Party
17 October	Publication of the October Manifesto
18–21 October	Pogrom in Odessa. Anti-semitic violence spreads to other regions
19 October	Council of Ministers appointed with Witte as Chairman
3 December	Arrest of leaders of the St Petersburg Soviet
8–18 December	Insurrection in Moscow
11 December	Electoral Law for the election of the Duma published

(all dates Old Style)

Bloody Sunday

Father Gapon, who organized the demonstration on 9 January 1905, had been encouraged in his activity among the workers by Sergei Zubatov, the chief of the Moscow Okhrana, who believed that the government should control and supervise the workers' movement. Gapon and his followers were patriotic and religious, and believed that if only the tsar understood the plight of the workers he would help them. The demonstrators were unarmed, and had deliberately placed women and children at the front of the processions in the mistaken belief that the troops would not shoot at them. More than 100 men, women and children were killed, and the political attitudes of many St Petersburg workers were transformed by what happened. Gapon himself escaped, but was murdered in mysterious circumstances in 1906.

The *Potemkin* Mutiny

Sergei Eisenstein's film *Battleship Potemkin* has ensured that the events in Odessa form an important part of the popular view of the 1905 Revolution. The incident began when sailors on the *Potemkin* refused to eat maggot-infested meat. Their leader, Vakulenchuk, was shot on the orders of the captain. The crew mutinied, killed some of the officers and sailed the ship to Odessa, where a large-scale strike was in progress. Vakulenchuk's body, laid out at the bottom of the marble steps which lead from the harbour to the city centre, became a temporary shrine. Troops were sent to disperse the crowd that had gathered round the bier. They opened fire, and 2,000 people were killed, either by bullets or because they drowned in the sea attempting to escape. The *Potemkin* put out from Odessa, and the mutineers sought refuge in Romania. The mutiny was an isolated incident. No other ships' crews joined in. The great majority of army units remained loyal to the regime, and though their over-zealous reactions on 'Bloody Sunday' and in Odessa brought the tsar's government into disrepute, the armed forces were to play a vital part in crushing the revolution.

A postcard image of the events on Bloody Sunday in St Petersburg. The caption reads 'At the Winter Palace. 9 January 1905'. 'Lord, how painful and sad', Nicholas wrote in his diary.

Nicholas II and the October Manifesto

Nicholas II explained his decision to sign the October Manifesto in this letter to his mother.

Peterhof, 19 October 1905
My dearest Mama,
I do not know how to begin this letter.

We have been through such grave and unprecedented events that I feel as if the last time I wrote to you was a year ago.... There were only two ways open: to find an energetic soldier and crush the rebellion by sheer force. There would be time to breathe then but, as likely as not, one would have to use force again in a few months; and that would mean rivers of blood, and in the end we should be where we started. I mean to say, government authority would be vindicated but there would be no positive result and no possibility of progress achieved. The other way out would be to give the people their civil rights, freedom of speech and press, also to have all laws confirmed by a State Duma – that, of course, would be a constitution. Witte defends this very energetically. He says that, while it is not without risk, it's the only way out at the present moment. Almost everybody I had an opportunity of consulting is of the same opinion. Witte put it quite clearly to me that he would accept the Presidency of the Council of Ministers only on the condition that his programme was agreed to, and his actions not interfered with. He and Alexei Obolensky drew up the Manifesto. We discussed it for two days, and in the end, invoking God's help, I signed. My dear Mama, you can't imagine what I went through before that moment.... From all over Russia they cried for it, they begged for it, and around me many – very many – held the same views. I had nobody to rely on except honest Trepov. There was no other way out than to cross oneself and give what everyone was asking for.

A street barricade in St Petersburg, 1905.

The St Petersburg Soviet

The St Petersburg Soviet (Council) of Workers' Deputies arose out of the general strike in October 1905. It first met on 13 October, and was soon publishing a newspaper, *Izvestia* (*News*). The young Leon Trotsky quickly emerged as the dominant figure in the Soviet, and the editor of *Izvestia*. Trotsky played an important part in calling off the general strike, realizing that it had no chance of success and that its continuance would provide the government with a pretext for further bloodshed. He was a realist, who understood that the Soviet could achieve little in the present situation, other than giving the workers organizational experience. On 3 December 1905 police and troops arrested Trotsky and other leaders, and suppressed the Soviet. Trotsky was imprisoned in the Peter and Paul Fortress, where discipline was surprisingly relaxed and he was able to enjoy playing leapfrog in the courtyard with some of his fellow prisoners.

The Moscow Insurrection

Marxists in Moscow reacted to the news of the arrest of the leaders of the St Petersburg Soviet by planning an insurrection. Workers' militias were formed, and they managed to seize control of most of the railway stations and of many of the inner suburbs. Soviets emerged in various districts to direct events, but the insurrectionists were not sufficiently organized to mount a concerted attack on the city centre and the Kremlin. The government moved in artillery and reinforcements from St Petersburg, and the insurrection was suppressed in the course of several days of heavy fighting. More than 1,000 were killed, many of them innocent civilians.

A demonstration by workers in Moscow in October 1905. Among the slogans on their banners are 'Workers of all lands, unite!' and 'Down with Autocracy!'.

(Above) Nicholas II dressed as a private in the Russian army, his son Alexei on his shoulder. This popular photograph was taken in 1909 when, in order to test the new army uniform and kit, Nicholas marched 25 miles in nine hours.

(Above right) Rasputin with a group of admirers. The third woman (standing) from the left is Anna Vyrubova, close friend of the Empress Alexandra. Anna developed an intense belief in Rasputin's mystical powers, and encouraged the empress to trust the *starets*.

(Below) Members of the Duma leaving the Tauride Palace in St Petersburg. This 1910 watercolour was sold as a postcard.

Personal crises

On 30 July 1904 Alexandra gave birth to a son, Alexei. It soon became apparent that the baby was a haemophiliac. This hereditary disorder was then untreatable, and few sufferers survived into middle life. Nicholas and Alexandra kept the precise nature of the tsarevich's condition a secret, though they could not conceal the child's ill health. Alexei's bleeding attacks, any one of which might prove fatal, were a great trial for his parents.

In October 1905 Nicholas and Alexandra were introduced to Grigory Efimovich Rasputin, a *starets* (elder or holy man) of Siberian origin who had acquired a reputation in St Petersburg society for prophecy and healing. To Nicholas and Alexandra he seemed an embodiment of the traditional Russian peasant virtues of devotion to God and loyalty to the tsar. His apparent ability to heal her son's bleeding attacks soon made Alexandra deeply dependent on him. The extent of his political influence has been exaggerated by historians, but his influence over the imperial couple became widely known and served to discredit them.

Political reaction

The Fundamental Laws of 23 April 1906 conceded the shadow of constitutional democracy, but not the substance. The emperor retained the right to declare war and to make peace, and the power to dissolve the Duma. Ministers would be appointed by him and responsible to him alone. They would not be obliged to resign if the Duma passed a motion of censure against the government. The creation of the State Council, an upper chamber with a power of veto, the majority of whose members were to be appointed by the emperor, reduced the legislative power of the Duma. Most importantly, the crown reserved to itself the sole right to alter the Fundamental Laws.

Nicholas was no more willing to see his prerogatives limited by a prime minister than by a parliament. In April 1906 Witte was dismissed

NICHOLAS II DESCRIBES THE MURDER OF STOLYPIN

Nicholas II wrote this letter to his mother in September 1911, shortly after the events it recounts.

I felt rather tired, but everything went off so well and so smoothly that I was kept going by my own good spirits, when suddenly, on the 1st, at the theatre, this dastardly attempt was made on Stolypin's life. Olga and Tatiana were with me at the time. During the second interval we had just left the box as it was so hot, when we heard two sounds as if something had been dropped. I thought an opera glass might have fallen on somebody's head, and ran back into the box to look.

To the right I saw a group of officers and other people. They seemed to be dragging someone along: women were shrieking, and directly in front of me in the stalls Stolypin was standing. He slowly turned his face towards us and, with his left hand, made the sign of the cross in the air.

Only then did I notice that he was very pale and that his right hand and uniform were blood-stained. He slowly sank into his chair and began to unbutton his tunic. Fredericks and Professor Rein helped him. Olga and Tatiana came back into the box and saw what had happened. While Stolypin was being helped out of the theatre there was a great noise in the corridor near our box; people were trying to lynch the assassin. I am sorry to say that the police rescued him from the crowd and took him to an isolated room for his first examination. He had been badly man-handled however, and two of his teeth had been knocked out. Then the theatre filled up again, the national anthem was sung, and I left with the girls at eleven. You can imagine with what emotions!

Peter Arkadyevich Stolypin (1862–1911). He anticipated a violent end: a will written a few years before his death stipulated that he should be buried wherever he was assassinated.

and replaced by the elderly Ivan Goremykin, who could be relied on to resist the demands of the First Duma, in which reformist parties such as the Constitutional Democrats and the Octobrists were strongly represented. The emperor's assumption that the majority of Russia's peasants were loyal to the throne and would vote for monarchist candidates had proved unfounded. The First Duma was dissolved in July 1906, after sitting for only two months. The Second Duma proved no more biddable, and when it was dissolved in June 1907, a new Electoral Law was promulgated which, by reducing the weighting given to the votes of peasants and workers and increasing that given to the votes of landowners, produced a conservative-dominated Third Duma which was allowed to run for its full term, from 1907 to 1912. The Fourth Duma, elected in that year, was broadly similar in its composition.

Stolypin's reforms

In July 1906 Goremykin was replaced as Prime Minister by the Interior Minister, Peter Arkadyevich Stolypin, whose vigorous suppression of disorder led to the hangman's noose becoming known as 'Stolypin's necktie'. Stolypin believed that economic and social progress was essential to the saving of the Russian monarchy. Whereas Witte had concentrated on building up industry, Stolypin tried to tackle the more fundamental problem of the food supply. He believed that the traditional communal system of farming and paying taxes was an obstacle to agricultural modernization, and sought to create a class of prosperous, enterprising and productive peasants. The redemption payments by means of which the liberated serfs were supposed to pay for their land had already been abolished, and legislation in 1906 and 1907 allowed peasants to opt out of the communal system and consolidate their strips of land into single holdings. The assumption was that the emerging class of prosperous farmers would be loyal because they would have a stake in the existing order.

Stolypin himself believed that this 'wager on the sober and the strong' would need 20 years of peace to work. By 1914 only 98,000 of Russia's 12 million peasant households had taken the opportunity to withdraw from the commune system, and some historians argue that the emergence of this body of prosperous peasants destabilized rural society by generating class antagonism. Stolypin had to contend not only with the innate conservatism of the Russian peasantry, but with the fact that the emperor and the landowning nobility did not share his Westernizing vision. Nicholas vetoed Stolypin's plan to abolish the limitations on the civil rights of the empire's Jewish population and attempted to block his proposal to set up elected zemstva in Russia's western provinces. By 1911 Stolypin was an isolated figure. The assassin whose shots fatally injured him during a gala performance at the Kiev Opera House in September of that year had connections with the secret police. After his death the powers of the Prime Minister were reduced, and government was once again characterized by inter-departmental rivalries and by a lack of direction.

On the eve of war

In 1913 the emperor presided over the celebrations marking the 300th anniversary of the Romanov dynasty. The enthusiasm of the crowds confirmed Nicholas in his belief that the regime was still popular with the mass of the Russian people. The reality was more complex. There were no major agrarian disturbances at the time, but there was large-scale industrial unrest in the years 1912–14. The revolutionary parties who might have exploited the situation were weak and divided, and many of their leaders were in exile. Although the strikes in the early months of 1914 had a political character, and the Bolsheviks were gaining support among the workers, the empire was not on the brink of revolution. Yet fundamental problems remained unsolved. The peasants still hoped for radical land reform. Middle-class liberals were deeply disillusioned by the emperor's handling of the Duma. Nicholas himself was pinning his hopes on the Union of the Russian People, a right-wing, anti-semitic movement founded in 1905 which sought to encourage popular support for the monarchy.

Russia and the Balkans

The war with Japan had demonstrated the limitations of Russia's power. Stolypin's policy was to seek peace abroad in order to have the opportunity to carry out reforms at home. Agreements with Britain signed in 1907 resolved the tensions between the two powers over Persia and Afghanistan, but contributed to the growing belief in Berlin that Germany was encircled by hostile powers. Since no further expansion was possible in Central Asia, and Russian ambitions in the Far East had been thwarted it was natural that Russian statesmen should concentrate on the Straits and the Balkans. There too Russia was thwarted, gaining no compensating benefit from the Austrian annexation of Bosnia and Herzegovina in 1908, a humiliation which infuriated educated opinion in Russia.

In the years 1912–14 industrial unrest at home made the idea of a more active foreign policy tempting. The Balkan Wars of 1912 and 1913 caused an upsurge of Panslavist enthusiasm in Russia. By the time of the assassination of the Austrian Archduke Franz-Ferdinand and his wife at Sarajevo in June 1914, Nicholas was very receptive to the arguments of those ministers who believed that the Russian people would lose confidence in the autocracy if Russia did not take a stand in the Balkans, and prepared to ignore those, including Rasputin, who prophesied that war would destroy the dynasty. Russian mobilization in support of Serbia

The People's House (*Narodny Dom*) in St Petersburg decorated with imperial emblems in readiness for a visit by Tsar Nicholas II during the tercentenary year of 1913.

The assassination of the Archduke Franz-Ferdinand and his wife Sophie at Sarajevo on 28 June 1914.

Nicholas II and his cousin once removed the Grand Duke Nikolai Nikolaievich, commander-in-chief of the Russian army. Although the grand duke shared Alexandra's mystical enthusiasms, the empress came to view him with suspicion, believing that he was upstaging her husband as a focus of patriotic enthusiasm. In the summer of 1915 Nicholas, ignoring the advice of his ministers, dismissed him and appointed himself commander-in-chief. The grand duke escaped into exile and died, childless, in 1929.

helped to turn a Balkan crisis into a European conflict, and on 19 July (1 August NS) Germany declared war on Russia.

The First World War

The decision to go to war was a gamble on the government's ability to reassert Russia's international prestige. In the short term, the gamble paid off. Panslavists, patriots and liberals could all find reasons for regarding the war as a crusade. A wave of anti-German feeling swept Russia, and the capital city was given the Russian name of Petrograd. A quick victory would undoubtedly have strengthened the regime, but early successes against the Austrians were balanced by defeats in East Prussia at the hands of the Germans, and the prolongation of the war into 1915 revealed serious weaknesses in the Russian army. Shortages of equipment, problems of transport and supply and a lack of trained manpower hampered the war effort.

By the spring of 1915 the press and the opposition were loudly condemning the incompetence of the government. Nicholas responded by sacking some of his most unpopular ministers and also the Grand Duke Nikolai Nikolaievich, the commander-in-chief. The emperor's decision to take supreme command himself exposed him to direct blame for subsequent military defeats. It had the positive effect of bringing the military and civilian branches of the government closer together, but it removed the emperor from Petrograd from August 1915 onwards. As at the time of the famine of 1891–92, the educated classes felt that, given the chance, they could manage things better than the bureaucrats. The zemstva and the towns formed organizations to provide medical care and canteens for the troops.

Many of Nicholas' ministers urged him to come to an agreement with the Progressive Bloc, a loose and unreliable alignment of liberal and moderate nationalist parties in the Duma which was calling for the creation of 'a government of public confidence'. The emperor rejected this suggestion and, in September 1915, prorogued the Duma. Its members involved themselves in war relief work, strengthening their links with the zemstva and municipal organizations, and developing political links with the officer corps which were to prove important in 1917.

At first events seemed to justify the emperor's refusal to share power. The military situation improved, and in the summer of 1916 Russian forces commanded by the energetic, intelligent and adaptable General Alexei Brusilov achieved an impressive, though not decisive victory. On the home front, however, an effectively leaderless government was confronted by a worsening economic situation. With the emperor absent at headquarters for long periods of time, the empress' influence on his thinking grew even stronger. Alexandra and her daughters had spent long hours nursing patients in military hospitals and the rumours that 'the German woman', as she became known, was conspiring to achieve a compromise peace settlement were unfounded. Yet the influence that she exercised on ministerial appointments became public knowledge, as

LETTER OF THE TSARITSA TO THE TSAR, DECEMBER 1916

Tsarskoe Selo Dec 13th 1916
My own dearest Angel,
Tenderest thanks for your dear card…. It's all getting calmer & better, only one wants to feel Your hand – how long, years, people have told me the same – 'Russia loves to feel the whip' – its their nature – tender love & then the iron hand to punish and guide. – How I wish I could pour my will into your veins. The Virgin is above you, for you, with you, remember the miracle – our Friend's* vision.

Soon our troops will have more force in Roumania. – Warm & thick snow. – Forgive this letter, but I could not sleep this night, worrying over you – don't hide things from me – I am strong – but listen to me, wh. means our Friend & trust us through all – & beware of Trepov – you can't love or venerate him. I suffer over you as over a tender, softhearted child – wh. needs guiding, but listens to bad advisers whilst a man of God tells him what to do. Sweetest Angel, come home soon…. I love you too deeply & cry over your faults & rejoice over every right step. God bless & protect, guard & guide you.
Kisses without end. Y. truest, Wify.

*Rasputin, who was to be murdered a few days later

did her increasing reliance on the advice of Rasputin, whose views she relayed to the emperor. Rasputin's scandalous private life helped to bring the imperial family into disrepute. The group of aristocrats and right-wing politicians who murdered the *starets* in December 1916 believed that they could save the monarchy by removing him. By then Russia was in crisis. Hyperinflation was eroding middle-class savings, and problems of transport and marketing had led to food shortages in Russian cities whose populations had been swelled by the rapid growth of industry to meet the demands of the war.

The February Revolution

The collapse of the monarchy was sudden. On 23–24 February (8–9 March NS) 1917 food riots broke out in Petrograd. On 25 February Nicholas, who was at army headquarters in Mogilev, decided that military force should be used to restore order. Next day some units obeyed their officers' orders to fire on the crowd, but others mutinied. The emperor once again rejected calls for a government of public confidence, and dismissed the Duma. On 27 February the mutinies spread. The government had lost control of the capital, and Nicholas ordered that troops from the front be sent to Petrograd to restore order. He set out for Tsarskoe Selo by train. Arriving at Malaya Vishera on 1 March, he was informed that

The imperial family. The Tsarevich Alexei is seated in front of the Empress Alexandra. The Grand Duchess Anastasia is seated next to the emperor, and the Grand Duchesses Maria, Tatiana and Olga are behind their parents.

Petrograd, February 1917. Students and soldiers take aim at policemen who were using the attic windows of buildings in the city centre as firing positions. Though this photograph appears to have been posed, such exchanges of fire did take place during the February Revolution.

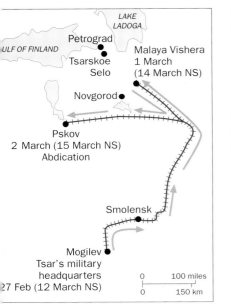

LAKE LADOGA

GULF OF FINLAND

Petrograd

Tsarskoe Selo

Malaya Vishera
1 March
(14 March NS)

Novgorod

Pskov
2 March (15 March NS)
Abdication

Smolensk

Mogilev
Tsar's military
headquarters
27 Feb (12 March NS)

0   100 miles

0   150 km

the line to the capital was blocked by revolutionaries, and ordered that his train should be diverted to Pskov.

On 27 February a Provisional Committee of the Duma and a Workers' and Soldiers' Soviet had been set up in Petrograd. On the night of 1–2 March the Duma Committee and the Soviet agreed to form a Provisional Government. Nicholas' chances of retaining power now depended on the willingness of his senior generals to use troops to crush the revolution. The generals, who had come to trust the Duma politicians as a result of working with them on war-relief committees, accepted the judgment of Mikhail Rodzyanko, the President of the Duma, that only the emperor's abdication could prevent a complete breakdown of order in Petrograd. General Alexeyev, the army Chief of Staff, and other senior officers communicated this judgment to the emperor at Pskov by telegram on 2 March. Nicholas abdicated on behalf of himself and his son, leaving the throne to his brother Mikhail. Public hostility soon persuaded Mikhail to renounce the throne, and on 3 March (16 March NS) 1917 tsarist government came to an end.

Some historians believe that the Russian monarchy was already doomed by 1914, and that Nicholas II's refusal to cooperate with the Duma was his most serious mistake. Others point out that Russia made significant progress, economically, socially and even politically, in the years 1906–14 and that but for the catastrophe of the First World War a genuine constitutional monarchy might have evolved. It is difficult to believe, however, that a constitutional monarchy on the Western European model would have worked in an empire as vast and as economically and socially underdeveloped as Russia. Some sort of partnership between the monarchy and the educated classes might have been possible but for the mutual antagonism that had developed between them during the 19th century. The unwillingness of successive emperors to trust the civic instincts of the educated classes, and the willingness of sections of the intelligentsia to embrace nihilism and revolutionary violence doomed the Russian monarchy.

EPILOGUE

The imperial family in captivity. This photograph shows them sitting on the roof of a greenhouse at the Governor's House in Tobolsk, where they arrived in August 1917, and where they remained until the spring of 1918.

Wall painting in the Russian Orthodox church in Emperor's Gate, London, depicting Nicholas and Alexandra and their family. The members of the imperial family were canonized by the Russian Orthodox Church Abroad in 1981. Here they are shown in the company of other martyrs.

After his abdication, Nicholas and his family spent five months at Tsarskoe Selo as prisoners of the Provisional Government. The demeanour of the emperor and empress was dignified and uncomplaining. To Russia's new rulers the captives were an embarrassment, and they tried to persuade the British government to grant asylum to the Romanovs. King George V, the tsar's first cousin, accepted his advisers' view that welcoming Nicholas and Alexandra would discredit the British monarchy in the eyes of the labour movement, and the request was refused. In the summer of 1917 the family was moved, for their own safety, to Tobolsk in Western Siberia. On the night of 25–26 October (7–8 November) the Bolsheviks seized control of Petrograd and established a government.

The accession to power of a clique of ruthless revolutionaries who needed to fight and win a civil war in order fully to establish their control over Russia placed the imperial family in great danger. In the spring of 1918 the Romanovs were moved to Ekaterinburg, the principal Bolshevik stronghold in the Urals region. In the course of their last journey Nicholas and Alexandra passed through Rasputin's home village of Pokrovskoe, fulfilling the *starets'* prophecy that: 'Willing or unwilling, they will come to Tobolsk and they will see my village before they die.' In Ekaterinburg they were imprisoned in the house of an engineer named Ipatiev. There was an accidental but fearful symmetry in the choice of the family's final residence, since the first of the Romanovs, Mikhail, had emerged from the Ipatiev Monastery to accept the throne in 1613.

In the early hours of the morning of 17 July 1918 (NS) a Bolshevik firing squad led by Yakov Yurovsky, acting on orders from the highest level of the Soviet government in Moscow, executed the whole family, their doctor and three servants in a small basement room of the Ipatiev house. The bodies were taken out into the forest, and thrown down a mine shaft. The official press releases announced the execution of Nicholas but claimed that his family had been moved to a more secure location, a lie which gave rise to much uncertainty about their fate. The killing was justified by the assertion that White (anti-Bolshevik) forces were approaching Ekaterinburg with the intention of rescuing the former tsar and his family. Ekaterinburg did fall to the Whites later that month, but the fact that the Bolsheviks murdered 17 other members of the Romanov family in the course of the Civil War suggests a deeper motive. Years later Trotsky, by then an exile, wrote: 'Actually, the decision was not only expedient but necessary. The severity of this summary justice showed the world that we would continue to fight on mercilessly, stopping at nothing. The execution of the tsar's family was needed not only in order to frighten, horrify and dishearten the enemy, but also in order to shake up our own ranks to show that there was no turning back, that ahead lay either complete victory or complete ruin.'

Since 1918 a number of people have claimed to be one of the members of the imperial family, and to have survived the massacre in the Ipatiev house, thus contributing to the rich tradition of royal pretenders in Russian history. Developments in the study of DNA have made it possible to discount these claims, even in the case of Anna Anderson, who insisted that she was the Grand Duchess Anastasia. The same techniques have been used to identify the remains of Nicholas and Alexandra, three of their children, their doctor and their servants, which were first discovered in 1979 a dozen miles north-west of Ekaterinburg by a local historian, Alexander Avdonin. The remains were buried in the Peter and Paul Cathedral in St Petersburg on 17 July 1998, 80 years to the day after

Ekaterinburg, July 1998. A guard of honour watches over the skeletons identified by scientists as the remains of the Romanovs and their servants.

TSARS ON FILM

Nicholas II had an ambivalent attitude to film. On the one hand he employed a succession of court cinematographers to record the life of the imperial family. On the other hand he wrote the following indictment of the medium in the margin of a police report in 1913:

I consider that cinematography is an empty matter, which no one needs. It is even something harmful. Only an abnormal person could place this farcical business on the level of an art. This is silliness and we should not attribute any significance to such trifles.

The early Communist leaders developed a clear understanding of the power of film to shape people's ideas and emotions. In the 1930s and 1940s a few feature films were made which focused on the lives and achievements of past rulers.

Vladimir Petrov's two-part *Peter the First* (1937–39) explored politically safe themes. Stalin was a known admirer of Russia's first emperor.

Sergei Eisenstein believed that he was playing safe in choosing to make a film about Alexander Nevsky. Stalin supported the project, and approved of the film's anti-German content. *Alexander Nevsky* was completed in 1938 and widely praised. Then, in August 1939, it was abruptly withdrawn from circulation because the USSR had signed a non-aggression pact with Nazi Germany, and not shown again until the German invasion of 1941. Vsevolod Pudovkin was more fortunate in his timing. His *Minin and Pozharsky*, a film about the leaders of the Second National Army during the Time of Troubles, was strongly anti-Polish, and came out in 1939, the year in which the USSR invaded eastern Poland.

It was Stalin who decided that Eisenstein should direct a film about Ivan IV. *Ivan the Terrible* was made in two parts. The first, which was released in 1944, won a Stalin prize.

(Opposite above) Nikolai Simonov in the title role of Vladimir Petrov's Peter the First. *Petrov also directed* 1812, *a patriotic film about Napoleon's invasion of Russia which was released in 1944.*

(Opposite left) Nikolai Cherkasov as Ivan in a scene from Part One of Eisenstein's Ivan the Terrible.

(Left) Pola Negri as Catherine the Great in the 1924 silent film Forbidden Paradise *directed by Ernst Lubitsch.*

Alexei Petrenko as Rasputin, in a scene from Elem Klimov's Agoniya. *Petrenko played the part of Peter I in Alexander Mitta's 1976 musical* The Tale of Tsar Peter Arranging Arap's Wedding.

The second, completed in 1946, did not please the authorities. Eisenstein and Nikolai Cherkasov, the actor who played the part of Ivan, were summoned to the Kremlin in February 1947 for a late-night meeting with Stalin at which the dictator explained why he disliked the film. Eisenstein had portrayed the tsar as subject to doubt and remorse. 'Ivan the Terrible executed someone and then he felt sorry and prayed for a long time', Stalin complained. 'God hindered him in this matter. Tsar Ivan should have been even more resolute.' The film was suppressed and not shown in public until 1958, ten years after Eisenstein's death and five years after the death of Stalin.

Soviet cinema largely ignored the lives and achievements of Russia's women rulers, though Catherine the Great featured in Feodor Ozep's *Princess Tarakanova* (1938), and it was left to Western film makers to fill the gap. Pola Negri played the part of Catherine in a silent film, Ernst Lubitsch's *Forbidden Paradise* (1924), and Elisabeth Bergner, Marlene Dietrich and Tallulah Bankhead all tackled the role. The Hollywood view of Catherine II was summed up by Mae West, who produced a screenplay about the empress: '... a pre-incarnation of myself: a Slavic-German Diamond Lil, just as low in vivid sexuality, but on a higher plane of authority.' The film was never made, and the Broadway version, *Catherine was Great*, was damned by the critics. 'Mae West slips on the steppes' summed up their view.

Few films about the tsarist past were made in Russia in the period between Stalin's death and the era of glasnost. The most distinguished was Elem Klimov's *Agoniya*, a film about Nicholas II and Rasputin which was completed in 1975 but which met with official disapproval and was not released until ten years later. The last tsar is portrayed as a decent though weak-willed man, and the exploration of Rasputin's character is subtle and thorough, suggesting shrewdness of judgment and human sympathy as well as debauchery.

Russian women holding icons and portraits of the Empress Alexandra and Tsar Nicholas II. There was significant support in Russia in 1998 for the suggestion that the murdered Romanovs should be canonized.

The tomb of the Grand Duke Kirill Vladimirovich in the Peter and Paul Cathedral in St Petersburg. The inscription documents his birth at Tsarskoe Selo in 1876, his death in Paris in 1938, his burial in Coburg in the same year and his reburial in St Petersburg in 1995.

the murders took place. The ceremony was surrounded by controversy. Patriarch Alexei II did not officiate, because the Russian Orthodox church had not accepted the authenticity of the remains, but marked the anniversary by holding a service in the Dormition Cathedral of the Holy Trinity and St Sergius Monastery, near Moscow. It is likely that, during the next few years, the Russian Orthodox church will canonize Nicholas, Alexandra and their children as martyrs, as the Russian Orthodox Church Abroad did in 1981.

The funeral was a potential source of embarrassment to President Boris Yeltsin, who in 1977, as a local Communist Party official, carried out Leonid Brezhnev's order that the Ipatiev house should be demolished to prevent it from becoming a monarchist shrine. At the last minute Yeltsin announced his intention of attending the ceremony. In a brief address he described the murders at Ekaterinburg as 'one of the most shameful pages of our history'.

The 1998 anniversary served to emphasize the divisions within the Romanov family. The most active claimant to the Russian throne, the Grand Duchess Maria Vladimirovna, chose to attend the liturgy at the Holy Trinity and St Sergius Monastery with her son, the Grand Duke George, born in 1981. Other senior members of the family were present at the funeral service in St Petersburg. Maria is the grand-daughter of Grand Duke Kirill, a first cousin of Tsar Nicholas II. Her claim is not universally accepted. According to the complex 1797 Law of Succession the crown should pass to a male if there is an eligible male of the blood royal. The criteria for eligibility included the stipulation that the heir should marry with the permission of the reigning tsar. In 1905 the Grand Duke Kirill married Victoria Melita of Hesse, the divorced wife of the Empress Alexandra's brother, without the permission of Nicholas II. No living Romanov fully meets the exacting criteria of the 1797 Law, though there are male Romanovs who could, if they wished, make a strong case for their claims to the throne, particularly Prince Nicholas Romanov, born in 1922. He is a direct descendant of Tsar Nicholas I in the male line, since his great grandfather was the tsar's third son Nicholas. Unless the Russian people desire a restoration of the monarchy, the debate will remain academic.

For the Communists who ruled Russia from 1917 to 1991, the legacy of the tsarist past was hard to handle. The approach to the writing of history in Russia was transformed, and academics were required to follow the party line. Gifted men and women nevertheless continued to carry out valuable research under difficult conditions. The more chronologically remote their field of enquiry was, the greater their freedom of investigation.

At first there was a tendency to write off tsarist rule as entirely negative, but this soon gave way to a number of other approaches. The policies and achievements of some of Russia's imperial rulers were interpreted as part of the process of historical progress that Karl Marx had analysed. Thus Ivan the Terrible's Oprichnina came to be seen

Decorative mosaic from the Moscow Metro, a showpiece of the Soviet era. Peter I is depicted leading his troops at the battle of Poltava.

as an attempt to reduce the power of the boyar aristocracy, and the technological and economic progress encouraged by Peter the Great could be admired. Indeed Peter was dubbed 'the first Bolshevik'. It became possible to see positive aspects even in the reign of so recent a figure as Alexander II. Secondly, the Communists' insistence on incorporating into the USSR as much of the former tsarist empire as possible meant that criticism of tsarist imperialism was not encouraged. Thirdly the need to rally the population to meet the German onslaught in 1941 led Stalin to encourage a patriotic view of Russia's past. Alexander Nevsky was an obvious hero. Parallels came to be drawn between Napoleon and Hitler, and the war of 1812 came to be seen as a liberation struggle fought against a bourgeois colonial aggressor. Since Stalin was an autocrat who encouraged a cult of his own personality and responded brutally to criticism, there were good reasons for Russian historians to emphasize the achievement of past autocrats and to play down or justify their brutality. These approaches continued long after Stalin's death in 1953.

In the 1980s, under glasnost, it became acceptable for Soviet historians to look at the careers of rulers, such as the Empress Elizabeth, who had been dismissed in the Stalinist era as luxury-loving parasites, and to study court politics. Since the collapse of Communism there has been strong interest in Russia in the reign of Nicholas II. Postcards and photographs of the imperial family are widely available. A special exhibition of costumes, jewellery, paintings and memorabilia from that era was mounted at the Hermitage in St Petersburg in 1994. The nascent capitalism of the New Russia has seized on the imperial past as a heritage to be exploited. Matryoshka dolls painted with crude likenesses of Russia's emperors and empresses are hawked in the streets, and by 1996 a new brand of cigarettes had appeared named after Peter I.

The revival of imperial statuary in the 1990s. Journalists visiting the studio of the Russian sculptor Vyacheslav Klykov to inspect his new statue of Nicholas II.

This brand of cigarettes is named after Peter the Great. The slogan reads: 'PETER I Always first!'

SELECT BIBLIOGRAPHY

Sources in translation and original English sources

Alexandra Feodorovna, Empress *A Czarina's Story* tr. and ed. U. Pope-Hennessy (London and Brussels: Nicholson and Watson, 1948)

Alexei Mikhailovich, Tsar *Introduction to the Falconry Regulation of 1656* in *Slavonic Review* Vol. III, no. 7, 1924, pp. 63–64 (London: School of Slavonic and East European Studies, University of London)

Barbaro, J. and Contarini, A. *Travels to Tana and Persia* tr. W. Thomas and S.A. Roy (London: Hakluyt Society, 1874)

Berry, L.E. and Crummey, R.O., eds *Rude and Barbarous Kingdom* (Madison: University of Wisconsin Press, 1968)

Bing, E.J. ed. *Letters of Nicholas II and his Mother* (London: Ivor Nicholson and Watson Ltd, 1937)

Bussow, Conrad *The Disturbed State of the Russian Realm* tr. G.E. Orchard (Montreal: McGill-Queen's University Press, 1994)

Catherine II, Empress *Memoirs* tr. M. Budberg (London: Hamish Hamilton, 1955)

Collins, S. *The Present State of Russia* (J. Winter for D. Newman: London, 1671)

Cross, S.H. and Sherbowitz-Wetzor, O.P. *The Russian Primary Chronicle* (Cambridge, Mass.: Medieval Academy of America, 1953)

Custine, Marquis de *Journey for Our Time* tr. P.P. Kohler (London: Arthur Barker, 1953)

Fennell, J.L.I. ed. and tr. *The Correspondence between Prince A.M. Kurbsky and Tsar Ivan IV of Russia 1564–1579* (Cambridge: Cambridge University Press, 1955)

Gibbes, C.S. *Tutor to the Tsarevich* compiled J.C. Trewin (London: Macmillan, 1975)

Glinka, M.I. *Memoirs* tr. R.B. Mudge (Norman: University of Oklahoma Press, 1963)

Golovine, A. *Russia under the Autocrat Nicholas I* (London: Henry Colburn, 1846)

Herberstein, Sigismund von *Description of Moscow and Muscovy* ed. Bertold Picard, tr. J.B.C. Grundy (London: J.M. Dent, 1969)

Herberstein, Sigismund von *Rerum Moscoviticarum Commentarii* tr. R.H. Major (London: Hakluyt Society, 1851)

Jackman, S.W. ed. and tr. *Romanov Relations: the Private Correspondence of Tsars Alexander I, Nicholas I and the Grand Dukes Constantine and Michael with their Sister Queen Anna Pavlovna* (London: Macmillan, 1969)

Jenkinson, A. et al. *Early Voyages and Travels in Russia and Persia* ed. E.D. Morgan and C.H. Coote (London: Hakluyt Society, 1886)

Kleinmichel, Countess *Memoirs* tr. V. Le Grand (New York and London: Brentano's, 1923)

Kropotkin, M. *Memoirs of a Revolutionist* ed. C. Ward (New York: Horizon Press, 1968)

Kurbsky, Prince A.M. *History of Ivan I* ed. and tr. J.L.I. Fennell (Cambridge: Cambridge University Press, 1965)

Lentin, A. ed. and tr. *Voltaire and Catherine the Great Selected Correspondence* (Cambridge: Oriental Research Partners, 1974)

Margeret, J. *Estat de l'Empire de Russie et Grande Duché de Moscovie* tr. and ed. C.S.L. Dunning (Pittsburgh: Pittsburgh University Press, 1983)

Miliukov, Paul *Political Memoirs 1905–1917* ed. A.P. Mendel, tr. C. Goldberg (Ann Arbor: University of Michigan Press, 1967)

The Nikonian Chronicle, Vol. 5, ed. S.A. Zenkovsky, tr. S.A. and B.J. Zenkovsky (Princeton and New Jersey: Darwin Press Inc., 1989)

Olearius, A. *The Travels of Olearius in Seventeenth-Century Russia* tr. and ed. S.H. Baron (Stanford, California: Stanford University Press, 1967)

Pares, B. ed. and tr. *Letters of the Tsaritsa to the Tsar* (London: Duckworth and Co., 1923)

Possevino, A. *Moscovia* ed. H.F. Graham (Pittsburgh: University Center for International Studies Publications Section, 1977)

Saint-Simon, Duc de *Memoirs* tr. St John Bayle (London: Samuel Bagster and Sons Ltd, 1902)

Samson-Himmelstierna, H. von *Russia under Alexander III and in the Preceding Period* tr. J. Morrison (London: Fisher Unwin, 1893)

Staden, H. von *The Land and Government of Muscovy* tr. T. Esper (Stanford: Stanford University Press, 1967)

Trotsky, L.D. *Diary in Exile* tr. E. Zarudnaya (London: Faber and Faber, 1959)

Vernadsky, G. ed. *A Source Book for Russian History from Early Times to 1917* Vols 1–3 (New Haven: Yale University Press, 1972)

Victoria, R.I. *Queen Victoria in her Letters and Journals* ed. C. Hibbert (London: John Murray, 1984)

Vigor, Mrs *Letters From a Lady who Resided some Years in Russia to her Friend in England* (London: J. Dodsley, 1775)

Witte, Count S.Y. *Memoirs* tr. A. Yarmolinsky (London: William Heinemann, 1921)

Modern references and works by Russian historians translated into English

Alexander, J.T. *Catherine the Great: Life and Legend* (Oxford: Oxford University Press, 1989)

Almedingen, E.M. *The Emperor Alexander I* (London: Bodley Head, 1964)

Anderson, M.S. *Peter the Great* (London: Thames and Hudson, 1978)

Andreyev, V. *His Majesty Lord Novgorod the Great* (Novgorod: Zemlya Novgorodskaya, 1995)

Anisimov, E.V. *Empress Elizabeth: Her Reign and Her Russia* tr. J.T. Alexander (Gulf Breeze: Academic International Press, 1995)

Berton, K. *Moscow: An Architectural History* (London: Studio Vista, 1977)

Bobrick, B. *Ivan the Terrible* (Edinburgh: Canongate, 1990)

Brayley-Hodgetts, E.A. *The Court of Russia in the Nineteenth Century* (London: Methuen, 1908)

Britten Austin, P. *1812 The March on Moscow* (London: Greenhill Books, 1993)

Byrnes, R.F. *V.O. Kliuchevskii, Historian of Russia* (Bloomington: Indiana University Press, 1996)

Carr, F. *Ivan the Terrible* (Newton Abbot and London: David and Charles, 1981)

Carrère d'Encausse, H. *The Russian Syndrome* tr. C. Higgitt (New York: Holmes and Meier, 1992)

Channon, J. and Hudson, R. *The Penguin Historical Atlas of Russia* (Harmondsworth: Penguin Books, 1995)

Chew, A.F. *An Atlas of Russian History* (New Haven: Yale University Press, 1970)

Choldin, M.T. *A Fence Around the Empire* (Durham, N. Carolina: Duke University Press, 1985)

Conte, F. ed. *Great Dates in Russian and Soviet History* (New York: Facts on File, 1994)

Crummey, R.O. *The Formation of Muscovy* (London: Longman, 1987)

Curtiss, M. *A Forgotten Empress: Anna Ivanovna and Her Era* (New York: Frederick Ungar, 1975)

Deutscher, I. *The Prophet Armed: Trotsky 1879–1921* (Oxford: Oxford University Press, 1954)

Dukes, P. *The Making of Russian Absolutism* 2nd ed. (London: Longman, 1992)

Dukes, P. *Catherine the Great and the Russian Nobility* (Cambridge: Cambridge University Press, 1967)

Edmonds, R. *Pushkin: the Man and His Age* (London: Macmillan, 1994)

Fennell, J.L.I. *The Crisis of Medieval Russia* (London: Longman, 1983)

Fennell, J.L.I. *Ivan the Great of Moscow* (London: Macmillan, 1961)

Figes, O. *A People's Tragedy* (London: Jonathan Cape, 1996)

Fuhrmann, J.T. *Tsar Alexis, His Reign and His Russia* (Gulf Breeze: Academic International Press, 1981)

Goodwin, J. *Eisenstein's Cinema and History* (Urbana: Illinois University Press, 1993)

Grabbe, P. and Grabbe, B. eds *The Private World of the Last Tsar* (Boston and Toronto: Little, Brown and Co., 1984)

Grunwald, C. de *Tsar Nicholas I* tr. B. Patmore (London: MacGibbon and Kee, 1954)

Habsburg-Lothringen, G. von and Solodkoff, A. von *Fabergé: Court Jeweler to the Tsars* (New York: Rizzoli, 1979)

Halperin, C.J. *Russia and the Golden Horde* (Bloomington: Indiana University Press, 1985)

Hamilton, G.H. *The Art and Architecture of Russia* 3rd ed. (New Haven: Yale University Press, 1983)

Hanbury-Williams, J. *The Emperor Nicholas II as I Knew Him* (London: Arthur L. Humphreys, 1922)

Hartley, J.M. *Alexander I* (London: Longman, 1994)

Holden, A. *Tchaikovsky* (London: Bantam Press, 1995)

Hosking, G. *Russia People and Empire* (London: HarperCollins, 1997)

Hughes, L. *Sophia Regent of Russia 1657–1704* (New Haven: Yale University Press, 1990)

Hyde, H.M. *Princess Lieven* (London: George G. Harrap, 1938)

Karamzin, N.M. *Memoir on Ancient and Modern Russia* tr. R. Pipes (Cambridge, Mass.: Harvard University Press, 1959)

Keenan, E.L. *The Kurbskii–Groznyi Apocrypha* (Cambridge, Mass.: Harvard University Press, 1971)

Keep, J.L.H. *Soldiers of the Tsar: Army and Society in Russia 1462–1874* (Oxford: Clarendon Press, 1985)

Keep, J.L.H. *The Regime of Filaret* in the *Slavonic and East European Review*, Vol. 38, 1960

Kenez, P. *Cinema and Soviet Society 1917–1953* (Cambridge: Cambridge University Press, 1992)

Kliuchevsky, V.O. *A Course in Russian History* tr. N. Duddington (Chicago: Quadrangle Books, 1970)

Koslov, J. *Ivan the Terrible* (London: W.H. Allen, 1961)

Lawton, A. *The Red Screen: Politics, Society, Art in Soviet Cinema* (London: Routledge, 1992)

LeDonne, J.P. *Ruling Russia. Administration in the Age of Absolutism 1762–1796* (Princeton, New Jersey: Princeton University Press, 1984)

Leonard, C.S. *Reform and Regicide: The Reign of Peter III of Russia* (Bloomington: Indiana University Press, 1993)

Lieven, D. *Nicholas II* (London: Pimlico, 1993)

Lincoln, W.B. *Nicholas I Emperor and Autocrat of All the Russias* (London: Allen Lane, 1978)

Longworth, O. *Alexis Tsar of All the Russias* (London: Secker and Warburg, 1984)

Madariaga, I. de *Russia in the Age of Catherine the Great* (London: Weidenfeld and Nicholson, 1981)

Madariaga, I. de *Catherine the Great: A Short History* (New Haven: Yale University Press, 1990)

Massie, R.K. *Peter the Great* (London: Victor Gollancz, 1981)

Massie, R.K. *The Romanovs: The Final Chapter* (London: Jonathan Cape, 1995)

Massie, S. *Pavlovsk, the Life of a Russian Palace* (London: Hodder and Stoughton, 1990)

McConnell, A. *Tsar Alexander I, Paternalistic Reformer* (Arlington Heights: A.H.M. Publishing Corporation, 1970)

McGrew, R.E. *Paul I of Russia* (Oxford: Clarendon Press, 1992)

Miller, D.B. *The Coronation of Ivan IV of Moscow* in *Jahrbücher für Geschichte Osteuropas* 15, 1967, pp. 559–74

Miller, D.B. *The Velikie Minei Chetii* in *Forschungen der Osteuropaischen Geschichte* 26, 1979, pp. 263–382

Moss, W.G. *A History of Russia. Vol. 1 to 1917* (New York: McGraw-Hill, 1997)

Mosse, W.E. *Perestroika under the Tsars* (London and New York: I.B. Tauris and Co. Ltd, 1992)

O'Brien, C.B. *Muscovy and the Ukraine* (Berkeley: University of California Press, 1963)

O'Brien, C.B. *Russia under Two Tsars – the Regency of Sophia* (Berkeley: University of California Press, 1952)

Olivier, D. *The Burning of Moscow* (London: Allen and Unwin, 1966)

Palmer, A. *Alexander I: Tsar of War and Peace* (London: Weidenfeld and Nicholson, 1974)

Pereira, N.G.O. *Tsar Liberator: Alexander II of Russia 1818–1881* (Newtonville: Oriental Research Partners, 1983)

Pipes, R. *Russia under the Old Regime* (Harmondsworth: Penguin Books, 1990)

Platonov, S.F. *The Time of Troubles* tr. J.T. Alexander (Lawrence, Kansas: University Press of Kansas, 1970)

Presniakov, A.E. *The Formation of the Great Russian State* (Chicago: Quadrangle Press, 1970)

Presniakov, A.E. *The Tsardom of Muscovy* (Gulf Breeze, Florida: Academic International Press, 1978)

Raeff, M. *Understanding Imperial Russia: State and Society in the Old Regime* tr. A. Goldhammer (New York: Columbia University Press, 1984)

Ragsdale, H. *Tsar Paul and the Question of Madness* (New York: Greenwood Press, 1988)

Riasanovsky, N.V. *A History of Russia* 5th ed. (Oxford: Oxford University Press, 1993)

Riasanovsky, N.V. *The Image of Peter the Great in Russian History and Thought* (New York: Oxford University Press, 1985)

Rogger, Hans *Russia in the Age of Modernisation and Revolution* (London: Longman, 1990)

Saunders, D. *Russia in the Age of Reaction and Reform* (London: Longman, 1992)

Schakovskoy, Z. *Precursors of Peter the Great* tr. J. Maxwell Brownjohn (London: Jonathan Cape, 1964)

Shatz, M.S. *Western Influence in Russia after Peter the Great* in *Canadian American Slavonic Studies* Vol. 24, no. 4, 1990 (Bakersfield: California State University)

Soloviev, S.M. *History of Russia, Vol. 25 Rebellion and Reform* ed. and tr. L.A.J. Hughes (Gulf Breeze: Academic International Press, 1989)

Solzhenitsyn, A. *The Russian Question* tr. Yermolai Solzhenitsyn (London: Harvill Press, 1995)

Stone, N. *The Eastern Front 1914–1917* (London: Hodder and Stoughton, 1975)

Talbot Rice, T. *Elizabeth Empress of Russia* (London: Weidenfeld and Nicolson, 1970)

Taylor, R. and C. eds *The Film Factory: Russian and Soviet Cinema in Documents 1896–1939* (London and New York: Routledge, 1988)

Tisdall, E.E.P. *The Dowager Empress* (London: Stanley Paul, 1957)

Troyat, H. *Tolstoy* tr. N. Amphoux (Harmondsworth: Penguin Books, 1970)

Troyat, H. *Peter the Great* tr. J. Pinkham (London: Hamish Hamilton, 1988)

Vernadsky, G. *Russia at the Dawn of the Modern Age* (New Haven: Yale University Press, 1959)

Vernadsky, G. *The Tsardom of Moscow* (New Haven: Yale University Press, 1969)

Ware, T. *The Orthodox Church* (Harmondsworth: Penguin Books, 1963)

Wieczynski, J.L. ed. *The Modern Encyclopaedia of Russian and Soviet History* (Gulf Breeze: Academic International Press, 1976)

Willan, T.S. *The Early History of the Russia Company* (Manchester: Manchester University Press, 1956)

Wipper, R. *Ivan the Terrible* tr. J. Fineberg (Moscow: Foreign Languages Publishing House, 1947)

Yaney, G.L. *The Systematization of Russian Government* (Urbana: University of Illinois Press, 1973)

Young, R. *Timothy Hackworth and the Locomotive* (Shildon: Stockton and Darlington Railway Jubilee Committee, 1923)

Illustration and Text Credits

Sources of illustrations
a=above, c=centre, b=bottom, l=left, r=right

The following abbreviations are used to identify sources and locate illustrations. BAL = The Bridgeman Art Library, London; BM = Copyright The British Museum; DW = David Warnes; Hermitage = The State Hermitage Museum, St Petersburg; JMS = John Massey Stewart Picture Library; KAM = Kremlin Armoury Museum, Moscow; Novosti = Novosti (London). Rovinsky = Rovinsky, *The Sources of Russian Iconography*, 1884–91. All maps drawn by Philip Winton.

2 JMS. **5** a–b National Museum, Copenhagen; de Vicquefort, *Voyages du Sieur Adam Olearius*, 1718; Hermitage; *L'Illustration*, October 1903. **6** Musée du Versailles, Photo © RMN. **7** a JMS; b Novosti. **8** F.Solutsev, *Antiquities of the Russian Empire*, 1849. **9** a Aleksandr Alekseevich Kochevnik; b Braun and Hogenberg,*Civitas Orbis Terrarum*, 1570. **10** State Historical Museum, Moscow. **12** r Novosti; b Mosfilm. **15** l–r Novosti; National Museum, Copenhagen; JMS; Novosti. **16** Novosti. **20** a Hans Weigel, *Trachtenbuch* , 1566; b Novosti. **21** Narodowe Museum, Cracow. **22** a By kind permission of the British Library; b DW. **23** al KAM; ar JMS; b DW. **26** a Narodowe Museum, Warsaw; b Adam Olearius, *Vermeherte newe Moskawitsche und Persanische Reise*, 1656. **27** JMS. **29** DW. **30** National Museum, Copenhagen. **31** a Novosti; b KAM. **33** Novosti. **35** Novosti. **36** a Tretiakov Gallery, Moscow; b KAM. **37** DW. **39** a Walker Art Gallery, Liverpool, courtesy Board of Trustees of the National Museums and Galleries on Merseyside; c JMS; b Science Museum/Science & Society Picture Library. **42** Novosti. **43** a Novosti; b Germanisches Nationalmuseum, Nuremberg. **45–49** l&r Novosti. **51–52** Rovinsky. **53** JMS. **54** a JMS; b Tretiakov Gallery, Moscow. **56** a Bibliothèque Slave, Paris; b State Russian Museum, Moscow. **57–58** Novosti. **61** l–r JMS; JMS; JMS; The Royal Collection © Her Majesty Queen Elizabeth II. **63** Novosti. **64** a&b Novosti. **64** a State Historical Museum, Moscow; b de Vicquefort, *Voyages du Sieur Adam Olearius*, 1718. **67** Palazzo Pitti, Florence. **68–69** JMS. **70** JMS. **71** Novosti. **73** N.A. Noudenov, *Moskvy, Snimkis Vidov Mestnostei*, 1886. **74** F.Solutsev, *Antiquities of the Russian Empire*, 1849. **75** DW. **79** Novosti. **80** a Rovinsky; b Jan Struys, *Reyseni*, 1671. **81** Palazzo Pitti, Florence. **82** a DW; b BAL. **83** a Novosti; cr JMS; cl &b KAM. **84** Novosti. **86** l KAM; r JMS. **87** a&bl Novosti; br KAM. **89** a Novosti; b Hermitage. **88** Hermitage/BAL. **91** a Hermitage; b State Historical Museum, Moscow. **92** Novosti. **93** a Hermitage; b BM. **94** JMS. **95** a Royal Holloway & Bedford New College, Surrey/BAL; b The Royal Collection © Her Majesty Queen Elizabeth II. **96** Johann Georg Korb, *Diarium Itineris in Moscoviam*, 1699. **97** a DW. **98** a JMS; b Armémuseum, Stockholm. **100–01** Hermitage. **102** a Hermitage/BAL; c BM; b JMS. **103** b DW. **104** a Hermitage; b Novosti. **105** Musée du Versailles. **106** Hermitage. **109** Hermitage. **111** l–r JMS; Novosti; Novosti; JMS. **112–13** Hermitage. **114** a Novosti; b JMS. **115** Novosti. **117** KAM. **120** Novosti. **121** a The V&A Picture Library; b Tretiakov Gallery, Moscow/BAL. **122** a JMS; c&b DW. **124** a Novosti; c&b DW. **125** a JMS; b Novosti. **126** Novosti. **128** Novosti. **129** Nationalmuseum, Stockholm. **131–32** Novosti. **134** a Musée Carnavelet, Paris; b Hermitage. **135** a *Westminster Magazine*, 1774; b Rovinsky. **136** l Nationalmuseum, Stockholm; b Hermitage/BAL. **137** Novosti. **138** JMS. **139** a Rovinsky; b Vienna Historisches Museum. **142** a The V&A Picture Library; c BAL; b JMS. **143** a BAL; b JMS. **144** a&b JMS. **152** a J.A. Atkinson, *A Picturesque Representation of the Manners and Customs of the Russians*, 1812; b JMS. **153** a © Bibliothèque Nationale de France, Paris; b JMS. **146** Hermitage/BAL. **147** Pavlovsk Palace, St Petersburg. **148** JMS. **150** a The Victoria and Albert Museum, London/BAL. **151** JMS. **155** a–b JMS; Hermitage; JMS; Hermitage; Hermitage/BAL. **156** Musée du Louvre, Paris. **157** Österreichisches Nationalbibliothek, Vienna. **159** State Historical Museum, Moscow. **160** JMS. **161** Musée du Montpellier. **163** l–r Novosti; JMS; Novosti; JMS. **164** Private Collection. **166** JMS. **167** a–b DW **169** a BM; b Bibliothèque Nationale de France, Paris. **170** Novosti. **171** BM. **172–73** JMS. **175** a BM; b V&A Picture Library. **176** BM. **177** JMS. **178** Hulton Getty. **179** *Illustrated London News*, September 1856. **181** l&r JMS. **183** a Historical Museum, Warsaw; b *Illustrated London News*, September 1862. **186** a BM; b *Illustrated London News*, November 1879. **187** a Hulton Getty; b Novosti. **188** JMS. **189** a JMS; b *Leipziger Illustrierte Zeitung*, 1888. **190** BM. **191** *Illustrated London News*, October 1891. **192** a *Der Berliner*, 1887; b E. Ukhtomsky *Travels in the East of Nicholas II, Emperor of Russia*, 1896. **193** Private Collection/BAL. **194** a Private Collection; b *Illustrated London News*, 1888. **195** *New York Herald*, May 1896. **196** a&b Novosti. **197** a Tim Crosskeys; c KAM. **198** a *Illustrated London News*, November 1894; b JMS. **199** a Novosti; b JMS. **200** a JMS; b Tretiakov Gallery, Moscow. **201** Novosti. **202** BM. **203** JMS. **204** a&bl *L'Illustration*, November 1905; br Novosti. **206** a&b JMS. **207** JMS. **209** b JMS. **210** Novosti. **211** JMS. **212** a JMS; b Russian Church, Emperor's Gate, London, Photo: JMS. **213** Associated Press. **214–15** Mosfilm. **216** a Popperfoto/Reuters; b DW. **217** a DW; bl Novosti; br DW.

Sources of quotations

Alexander, John T. *Catherine the Great: Life and Legend* (Oxford Univ. Press: Oxford, 1989) pp. 5–6 [Carloman de Rulhière, p. 130]; p. 114 [Catherine II, p. 145]

Alexandra Feodorovna, Empress *A Czarina's Story* tr. and ed. Una Pope-Hennessy (Nicholson and Watson: London and Brussels, 1948) p. 35 [p. 159]

Alexei Mikhailovich, Tsar *Introduction to the Falconry Regulation of 1656* in *Slavonic Review* Vol. III, no. 7, June 1924, tr. uncredited (School of Slavonic and East European Studies, Univ. of London) pp. 63–64 [p. 78, with two modifications to avoid the use of the word 'gay']

Anisimov, E.V. *The Reforms of Peter the Great: Progress through Coercion in Russia* tr. John T. Alexander (Armonk: New York, and M.E. Sharpe: London, 1993) p. 296 [p. 98]

Anisimov, E.V. *Empress Elizabeth: Her Reign and Her Russia* tr. J.T. Alexander Gulf (Academic International Press: Gulf Breeze, Florida, 1995) pp. 70–71 [p. 123]; pp. 185–86 [Fonvizin, p. 125]; p. 249 [p. 127]

Barbaro, J. and Contarini, A. *Travels to Tana and Persia* tr. W. Thomas and S.A. Roy (The Hakluyt Society: London, 1874) pp. 163–64 [p. 16]

Berry, L.E. and Crummey, R.O. eds *Rude and Barbarous Kingdoms* (Univ. of Wisconsin Press: Madison, 1968) p. 362 [Chancellor, p. 30]; p. 238 [Fletcher, p. 46]; p. 238 [Fletcher, p. 47]; p. 362 [Horsey, p. 48]

Bobrick, B. *Ivan the Terrible* (Canongate: Edinburgh, 1990) p. 329 [Queen Elizabeth I, p. 39]

Brayley-Hodgetts, E.A. *The Court of Russia in the Nineteenth Century* (Methuen: London, 1908) Vol. I, pp. 137–38 [Robert Lee, p. 161]; Vol. II, p. 70 [Augustus Loftus, p. 182]

Bussow, Conrad *The Disturbed State of the Russian Realm* tr. and ed. G. Edward Orchard (McGill-Queen's Univ. Press: Montreal, 1994) p. 78 [p. 51]; pp. 61–62 [p. 52]

Custine, Marquis de *Journey for Our Time (The Journals of the Marquis de Custine)* ed. and tr. P. Penn Kohler [Arthur Barker: London, 1953] p. 72 [p. 164]; pp. 52–53 [pp. 166–67]

Fennell, J.L.I. ed. and tr. *The Correspondence between Prince A.M. Kurbsky and Tsar Ivan IV of Russia 1564–1579* (Cambridge Univ. Press: Cambridge, 1955) pp. 3, 37, 73, 75, 181, 191–93, 247 [p. 41]

Glinka, Mikhail Ivanovich *Memoirs* tr. Richard B. Mudge (Univ. of Oklahoma Press: Norman, Oklahoma, 1963) p. 108 [p. 172]

Golovine, Ivan *Russia under the Autocrat Nicholas I* (Henry Colburn: London, 1846) pp. 305–06 [p. 164]; pp. 246–47 [p. 172]

Herberstein, Sigismund von *Rerum Moscoviticarum Commentarii* tr. R.H. Major, 'Notes upon Russia' Vol. 1 (The Hakluyt Society: London, 1851) p. 24 [p. 16]; p. 50 [p. 28]

Herberstein, Sigismund von *Description of Moscow and Muscovy* ed. Bertold Picard, tr. J.B.C. Grundy (J.M. Dent: London, 1969) p. 44 [p. 25]

Hughes, Lindsey *Sophia Regent of Russia 1657–1704* (Yale Univ. Press: New Haven, 1990) p. 28 [Collins, p. 69]; pp. 93–94, tr. Hughes [Hövel, p. 86]; p. 268, tr. Hughes [Catherine the Great, p. 86]; pp. 227–28, tr. Hughes [Sophia to Golitsyn, p. 88]

Hyde, H. Montgomery *Princess Lieven* (George G. Harrap: London, 1938) p. 28 [p. 146]

Karamzin, N.M. *Memoir on Ancient and Modern Russia* tr. Richard Pipes (Harvard Univ. Press: Cambridge, Mass., 1959) p. 113 [p. 50]; pp. 127–28 [p. 116]; p. 129 [p. 120]; pp. 130–33 [p. 137]; pp. 139 and 149 [p. 151]

Kenez, P. *Cinema and Soviet Society 1917–1953* (Cambridge Univ. Press: Cambridge, 1992) p. 16 [Nicholas II, p. 214]

Kliuchevsky, V.O. *A Course in Russian History: The Seventeenth Century* tr. Natalie Duddington (Quadrangle Books: Chicago, 1970) pp. 5–6 [p. 66]; p. 350 [Alexei to Ordin-Nashchokin, p. 71]; [p. 76]

Kluchevsky (sic), V.O. *A History of Russia* Vol. 2, tr. C.J. Hogarth (J.M. Dent: London, 1912) p. 93 [p. 33]; Vol. 5, tr. C.J. Hogarth (J.M. Dent: London, 1931) pp. 126–27 [p. 148]; p. 180 [p. 171]

Kropotkin, Prince Peter *Memoirs of a Revolutionist* tr. C. Ward (Horizon Press: New York, 1968) p. 242 [p. 177]; p. 151 [p. 179]

Leonard, Carol S. *Reform and Regicide: The Reign of Peter III of Russia* (Indiana Univ. Press: Bloomington, 1993) p. 8 [R. Keith, p. 128]; p. 139 [Louis XV, p. 128]

Letters of Nicholas II and his Mother ed. Edward J. Bing (Ivor Nicholson and Watson Ltd: London, 1937) pp. 260–61 [p. 200]; pp. 264–68 [p. 207]; pp. 185–88 [p. 205]

Letters of the Tsaritsa to the Tsar 1914–1916 ed. Sir Bernard Pares (Duckworth and Co: London, 1923) pp. 453–54 [p. 210]

Lieven, D. *Nicholas II Emperor of all the Russias* (Pimlico: London, 1994) p. 71 [Nicholas II, p. 200]

Lincoln, W. Bruce *Nicholas I Emperor and Autocrat of All the Russias* (Allen Lane: London, 1978) p. 227 [Nicholas I, p. 170]

Longworth, O. *Alexis Tsar of all the Russias* (Secker and Warburg: London, 1984) p. 86 [Alexei to Odoevsky, p. 69]; p. 133 [Alexei's shopping list, p. 77]

Margeret, J. *Estat de l'Empire de Russie et Grande Duché de Moscovie* tr. and ed. C.S.L. Dunning (Univ. of Pittsburgh Press: Pittsburgh, 1983) p. 59 [p. 49]; p. 75 [p. 51]

Massa, Isaac *Short History of the Muscovite Wars* tr. and ed. G. Edward Orchard (Univ. of Toronto Press: Toronto, Buffalo and London, 1982) p. 183 [p. 62]

The Memoirs of Catherine the Great tr. from the French by Moura Budberg (Hamish Hamilton: London, 1955) p. 372 [p. 119]

The Memoirs of Count Witte tr. A. Yarmolinsky (Heinemann: London and New York, 1921) pp. 40–41 [p. 194]; pp. 38–39 [p. 194]; p. 190 [p. 203]

Miliukov, Pavel *Political Memoirs 1905–1917* ed. A.P. Mendel, tr. C. Goldberg (Univ. of Michigan Press: Ann Arbor, 1967) p. 117 [p. 195]

The Nikonian Chronicle Vol. 5, ed. S.A Zenkovsky, tr. S.A. and B.J. Zenkovsky (Darwin Press Inc.: Princeton and New Jersey, 1989) pp. 155–56 [p. 24]

Olearius, Adam *The Travels of Olearius in Seventeenth-Century Russia*, tr. and ed. Samuel H. Baron (Stanford Univ. Press: Stanford, Cal., 1967) p. 62 [p. 62]; p. 100 [p. 65]

Palmer, A. *Alexander I: Tsar of War and Peace* (Weidenfeld and Nicholson: London, 1974) p. 218, citing Choiseul-Gouffier *Historical Memories* (London, 1904) p. 82 [Countess Tiesenhausen, p. 150]

The Politics of Autocracy: the Letters of Alexander II to Prince A.I. Bariatinskii 1857–1864 ed. Alfred J. Rieber (Mouton and Co.: Paris and the Hague, 1966) p. 143, tr. Warnes [p. 180]

The Pskov Chronicle tr. G. Vernadsky, cited in G. Vernadsky *Russia at the Dawn of the Modern Age* (Yale Univ. Press: New Haven, 1959) p. 135 [p. 29]

Queen Victoria in her Letters and Journals: a Selection by Christopher Hibbert (John Murray: London, 1984) p. 329 [p. 198]

Ragsdale, Hugh *Tsar Paul and the Question of Madness* (Greenwood Press: New York and London, 1988) p. 19 [Franklin, p. 146]; pp. 51–52, 53 and 54 [Paul, p. 147]; p. 56 [Paul, p. 149]

Riasanovsky, N.V. *A History of Russia* 5th ed. (Oxford Univ. Press: Oxford, 1993) pp. 234–35 [Stalin, p. 91]

Saint Pierre, Michel de *Le Drame des Romanov* (Editions Robert Laffont: Paris, 1989) p. 59, tr. Warnes [Van Zeller, p. 84]

Saint-Simon, Duc de *Memoirs* Vol. 3, tr. St John Bayle (Samuel Bagster and Sons Ltd: London, 1902) p. 364 [p. 90]; p. 365 [p. 106]

Samson-Himmelstierna, H. von *Russia under Alexander III and in the Preceding Period* tr. J. Morrison (Fisher Unwin: London, 1893) [p. 188]; pp. 13–14 [p. 191]

Schakovskoy, Zinaida *Precursors of Peter the Great* (Jonathan Cape: London, 1964) p. 63 [Berlioz, p. 29]

Soloviev, Sergei M. *History of Russia* Vol. 25, ed. and tr. L.A.J. Hughes (Academic International Press: Gulf Breeze, Florida, 1989) pp. 84–86 [Feodor III, p. 85]

Solzhenitsyn, A. *The Russian Question* tr. Yermolai Solzhenitsyn (Harvill Press: London, 1995) pp. 9–10 [p. 91]

Trotsky, L.D. *Diary in Exile* tr. E. Zarudnaya (Faber: London, 1959) pp. 80–81 [p. 213]

Troyat, H. *Tolstoy* tr. Nancy Amphoux (Penguin: Harmondsworth, 1970) pp. 559–62 [p. 190]

Troyat, H. *Peter the Great* tr. J. Pinkham (Hamish Hamilton: London, 1988) p. 193 [Margravine of Bayreuth, p. 112]

Vallotton, H. *Pierre le Grand* (Librairie Arthème Fayard: Paris, 1958) p. 286, tr. Warnes [Canon de la Naye, p. 106]; pp. 299–300, tr. Warnes [Peter I to the Tsarevich Alexei, p. 107]

Vernadsky, George ed. *A Source Book for Russian History from Early Times to 1917.* Vol. 1 (Yale Univ. Press: New Haven, 1972) p. 188 [Timofeyev, p. 53]; pp. 205–06 [Pozharsky, p. 58]; pp. 404–05 [Nakaz, p. 133]

Vigor, Mrs *Letters from a Lady who Resided Some Years in Russia to her Friend in England* (J. Dodsley: London, 1775) pp. 73 and 106 [pp. 114, 115 and 119]

Voltaire and Catherine the Great Selected Correspondence ed. and tr. A. Lentin (Oriental Research Partners: Cambridge, 1974) pp. 56–58 [p. 134]

Western Influence in Russia after Peter the Great tr. M.S. Shatz *Canadian American Slavic Studies* Vol. 24, no. 4 (California State Univ.: Bakersfield, 1990) p. 453 [Kliuchevsky, p. 131]

Wipper, R. *Ivan Grozny* tr. J. Fineberg (Foreign Languages Publishing House: Moscow, 1947) pp. 93 and 105 [p. 45]

Żółkiewski, Hetman Stanislaus *Expedition to Moscow* tr. Jedrzej Giertych (Polonia Publications: London, 1959) p. 47 [p. 53]

Author's note

My thanks go to Professor Andrew Pettegree for his encouragement, to Professor Norman Stone, whose teaching stimulated my interest in Russian history, and to Edmund Cavendish and Jonathan Bromley for their critical and perceptive comments on sections of the manuscript. None of them bears any responsibility for the content of the book. Thanks are also due to Gillian Holt, unflappable co-leader on many eventful school visits to Russia, and to Vladimir Pavlovich Krasnov, Konstantin Vladimirovich Krasnov and the late Andrew Milne for providing some important insights. I am indebted to Ruslan Muratovich Mergenov for his expertise in Old Church Slavonic. The staff of the Cambridge University Library rendered invaluable assistance, and Dr John Blatchly and Alexander Alexeyevich Kochevnik both contributed illustrations. I am also very grateful to the Society of Our Lady of the Isles, under whose hospitable roof parts of the book were written.

INDEX

Page numbers in *italic* refer to the illustrations

Åbo, Treaty of (1743) 121
Adashev, Alexei 33, 38, 40
Adrianople 169, *169*
Ahmed, khan of the Great Horde 19–20
Ahmed III, Sultan 105
d'Alembert, Jean le Rond *130*
Alexander I, Tsar 6, 11, 111, 150–61; *6, 111, 150, 151, 154*; architectural projects 166; Catherine II and 145, 147; Congress System 157, 160; *158*; death 161; foreign policy 152–53; military colonies 159; and Paul's murder 149; and Pushkin 173; Quadruple Alliance 157–58; reforms 152; retreat from constitutionalism 159–60; Speransky era 153; succession 160; War of 1812 154–55, 156–57
Alexander II, Tsar 177–87, 217; *163, 177*; assassination 187, 190, 197; *187*; assassination attempts 181, 186–87; *186*; childhood 165, 174; court balls 182; *182*; Crimean War 178; 'Dictatorship of the Heart' 187; emancipation of serfs 163; foreign policy 182–84; and Katia Dolgorukaya 181, 187; *181*; Populist opposition 184–85; reforms 178–79, 181, 184, 189; troubles 180–81; war with Turkey 185–86
Alexander III, Tsar 181, 188–95; *163, 181, 183, 188, 192, 193, 194*; character 191; death 195; foreign policy 192–93; industrial growth 163; personal life 193–94; railway accident 194–95
Alexander the Jagiellonian, king of Lithuania 20, 21; *21*
Alexander Nevsky, Grand Prince 8, 9, 12, 53, 215, 217; *12*
Alexandra Feodorovna, Tsaritsa (wife of Nicholas I) 165, 174
Alexandra Feodorovna, Tsaritsa (wife of Nicholas II) 198–99, 206, 209–10, 212, 213, 216; *210, 212, 216*
Alexandrovskaya Sloboda 41, 42; *43*
Alexei, Tsarevich (son of Alexei Mikhailovich) 79, 80
Alexei, Tsarevich (son of Nicholas II) 206; *206, 210*
Alexei Mikhailovich, Tsar 23, 61, 68, 69–81, 83; *4, 61, 69, 70*
Alexei Petrovich, Tsarevich 93, 106–07; *107*
Ali-Khan 20
alphabet, Cyrillic 27
Alphery, Mikifer 50
Anastasia Nikolaievna, Grand Duchess 199, 213; *210*
Anastasia, Tsaritsa (wife of Ivan IV) 32, 40, 44, 59
Andrei the Elder (brother of Ivan III) 17
Andrusovo, Treaty of (1667) 73
Anisimov, Evgeny 98, 127
Anna, Empress 93, 111, 113, 115–17, 118, 120; *113, 115, 117*
Anna Leopoldovna, Regent 117, 118, 119, 126
anti-semitism 190, 203
Anton-Ulrich, Duke of Brunswick-Wolfenbüttel 117, 119
appanage 9
Apraxin, Field Marshal 127
Arakcheyev, Alexei Andreyevich 159; *159*
Archangel 38

army, reforms 34, 99–100, 184
Asia 183–84, 193
Assembly of the Land 33, 43, 49, 59, 64, 65, 68, 70
Augustus II, king of Poland 95, 96, 100, 105, 116
Augustus III, king of Poland 117
Austerlitz, Battle of (1805) 152–53, *152*
Austria 67, 121, 148, 152, 157, 176, 182–83, 185
Avvakum, Archpriest 74, 85
Azov 68, 93, 117; *93*

'Baby Brigand' (son of False Dmitry II) 58, 64
Bagration, General Peter Ivanovich 154; *155*
Bakhchisarai, Treaty of (1681) 85
Balkans 169, 185–86, 192, 208–09; *169*
Barclay de Tolly, General Mikhail Bogdanovich 154; *155*
Bariatinsky, Field Marshal Prince 180
Basil the Blessed, St 36
Batu Khan 8, 22
Bayreuth, Margravine of 112
Belgorod Line 68
Belorussia 9
Belsky family 31
Benckendorff, Count A.K. 172, 176
Berlin, Congress of (1878) 186; *186*
Bestuzhev-Riumin, Alexei Petrovich 120, 121, 126, 127; *126*
Biron, Ernst Johann 115–16, 117, 118
Bismarck, Prince Otto von 185, 186, 192; *186*
Black Hundreds 203
Black Sea 135, 140, 149, 176, 178, 184
Blaeu, Jan 23
Bobrinskoy, Alexei Grigorievich *136*
Bolotnikov, Ivan 54, 59
Bolsheviks 200, 208, 212–13
Bolshoi Nakaz 132–33
Bono, Marco 23
Boris (brother of Ivan III) 17
Boris Godunov, Tsar 15, 23, 39, 42, 46–47, 48–50, 52, 56; *15, 39, 49*
Borodino, Battle of (1812) 154, 157
Boyar Duma 25, 64, 65, 105
Boyar Romanov, house of the, Moscow *54*
boyars 25, 26, 107; *26*; *mestnichestvo* system 34, 45, 85; Oprichnina 42; Peter I trims beards 97; *97*; power of 15; and Vasily Shuisky 53–54
Brand, Karsten 91
Britain 121, 176, 178
Bulgaria 185–86, 192; *185*
Bunge, N.K. 190–91
Burnet, Gilbert, bishop of Salisbury 94
Bussow, Conrad 51, 52
Byzantium 9, 27, 31

calendar 13, 97–98
Cameron, Charles 143, 144; *142*
Casimir IV, king of Lithuania 17, 19, 20
Catherine I, Empress 106, 111, 112–13; *100, 101, 112*; marriage to Peter I 100–01, 109; Tsarskoe Selo 124
Catherine II, Empress (Catherine the Great) 6, 109, 111, 117, 130–45, 172; *7, 111, 128, 129, 131, 132, 139, 144, 145*; and Alexander I 151; *Bolshoi Nakaz* 132–33; and Classicism 142–43; cultural patronage 144; death 145; demolishes Kolomenskoe 83; on Empress Elizabeth 119; films about 215; *215*; Greek Project 139; and Ivan VI 119; lovers 136, 137; marriage to Peter III 129; murder of Peter III 128, 130; Pugachev rebellion 135; reforms 131, 137, 138–39, 148; succession 144–45, 146–47; and Voltaire 134; wars and revolutions 134–35, 139–43
Catherine Palace, Tsarskoe Selo *124, 142–43*

Catherine Pavlovna, Grand Duchess 11
Catholic church 180
Chancellor, Richard 30, 39
Charles X, king of Sweden 71
Charles XII, king of Sweden 98–99, 100, 104, 105, 108; *98*
Chesme, battle of (1770) 134
Chosen Council 33
Church of the Saviour on the Spilled Blood, St Petersburg 197; *197*
Classicism, Catherine II and 142–43
Collins, Samuel 69, 77, 79
Communists 216–17
Congress System 157, 160; *158*
Constantine XI, Emperor 21
Constantine Monomachus, Emperor 32, 37
Constantine Pavlovich, Grand Duke 160, 165, 168; *150, 160*
Constantinople 10, 27, 28, 48
Contarini, Ambrogio 16
Copper Rebellion (1656) 77–78
Cossacks 47, 48; *47*; capture Azov 68; Mazepa 104; Pugachev rebellion 135; rebellion against Vasily Shuisky 54; Stepan Razin's rebellion 80–81; support for Mikhail 63; Thirteen Years War 71, 72; uprising against Poles 57–58; Zarutsky rebellion 64
Crimea 9, 19–20, 89, 135, 139, 140
Crimean War 171, 175–77, 178
Custine, Marquis de 164, 166–67
Cyril, St 27

Daniel (son of Alexander Nevsky) 9
Daniel, Metropolitan 28, 29
David, Jacques-Louis *151*
Decembrists 160, 178; Uprising (1825) 163, 173, 168; *168*
Deulino, Treaty of (1618) 64, 65, 67
Devlet-Girey, khan of the Crimea 43
Diderot, Denis 133, 145
Dimsdale, Thomas 131
Dmitry (son of Ivan III) 24–25
Dmitry of Uglich, Prince 48, 50, 52, 53, 56; *56*
Dmitry Donskoi 9
Dolgorukaya, Katia 181, 187; *181*
Dolgoruky, Prince Mikhail 87
Dolgoruky family 112, 114, 115
Don Cossacks 47, 68, 80–81
Dormition Cathedral, Moscow 22; *22, 23*
Dostoyevsky, Feodor Mikhailovich 175, 184; *175*
Duma 206–07, 208, 209, 210, 211; *206*

Eisenstein, Sergei 12, 204, 215; *12, 215*
Ekaterinburg 13, 212–13, 216
Elizabeth, Empress 111, 117, 118–27, 144, 146, 217; *111, 113, 118, 121*; as Catherine I's heir 113, 115; coup 116, 119, 120; court intrigues 126; court life 121–22; cult of Alexander Nevsky 12; death 127; domestic policies 123–26; palaces 124–25; *124–25*; Seven Years War 127; succession question 120, 127, 129; War of the Austrian Succession 121
Elizabeth I, queen of England 39, 42, 47, 48, 50; *39*
Elizabeth Alexeyevna (wife of Alexander I) 151, 161; *161*
Emancipation Statute (1861) 179; *178*
England 6, 39, 94–95
Enlightenment 132–33, 145
Evelyn, John 94

Fabergé, Peter Carl *201*
Faceted Palace, Moscow 23; *23*
Falconet, Etienne Maurice 142; *142, 144*
False Dmitry I 49, 50, 51–53, 54, 56; *51, 52*

False Dmitry II 49, 54–55, 56, 57, 58, 63, 64; *57*
False Peter 54
famines 191; *191*
February Revolution (1917) 210–11
Fennell, John 12
Feodor I, Tsar 15, 23, 46–48, 54, 56, 64; *15, 46, 48*
Feodor II, Tsar 51
Feodor III, Tsar 79, 84–86; *61, 84*
Filaret, Patriarch 50, 52–53, 55, 57, 59, 63–64, 65–66, 67, 68; *65*
Filipp, Metropolitan 24, 42
films 12, 137, 214–15
Filofei 28
Finland 153, 158
Finland, Gulf of 20–21, 43, 47, 64, 100
Fioravanti, Aristotele 22; *23*
First World War 163, 209–10, 211
Fletcher, Giles 46, 47
Florensky, Pavel Alexandrovich 7
Fonvizin, Denis 125
France: alliance with Alexander II 182–83; Franco–Prussian War 184; Napoleonic Wars 152–53, 154–55, 156–57; Peter I visits 105–06; Revolution 133, 140, 141, 144; Seven Years War 127; treaty with Alexander III 193; War of Austrian Succession 121
Franklin, Benjamin 146
Franz-Ferdinand, Archduke 208; *209*
Franz-Josef, Emperor 174
Frederick the Great, king of Prussia 121, 129, 134; *121*
French Revolution 133, 140, 141, 144
Friedrich Wilhelm I, king of Prussia 106
Friedrich Wilhelm III, king of Prussia 153
Funikov, Nikita 43

Galloway, Christopher 23
Gapon, Father 203, 204
Gatchina 147, 148, 151, 193; *147, 193*
Ge, Nikolai Nikolaievich 196; *196*
Gerasimov, M. *45*
Germany 192–93, 201, 208, 209
Giers, N.K. 192
Glinka, Mikhail Ivanovich 172
Glinskaya, Yelena 29, 30, 31
Glinsky, Mikhail 31
Glinsky, Yury 31, 32
Glinsky family 31, 32
Godunov family 47 *see also* Boris Godunov; Feodor II
Gogol, Nikolai Vasilievich 172
Golden Horde 8, 9, 47
Golitsyn, Prince Alexander 159
Golitsyn, Prince Dmitry 114, 115
Golitsyn, Prince Mikhail Alexeyevich 117
Golitsyn, Vasily 85, 88, 89; *89*
Golitsyn family 115
Golovine, Ivan 164, 172
Golovnin, Alexander 179
Gorchakov, Alexander 178, 182, 183, 184, 185; *186*
Gordon, Patrick 92–93
Goremykin, Ivan 207
grand princes 8–10
Great Embassy (1697–98) 93–96
Great Horde 19–20
Great Northern War 98–100, 104, 105, 108
Great Schism 61, 73–76
Gregorian Calendar 13, 97–98
Gregory XIII, Pope 13
Griaznoi, Vasily 42
Gustavus III, king of Sweden 135, 140
Gustavus Adolphus, king of Sweden 64, 67

Habsburg empire 67, 121 *see also* Austria

Hangö, battle of Cape (1714) 105
Hastings, Lady Mary 39
Hebdon, John 77
Herberstein, Sigismund von 16, 25, 28; *28*
Hermitage, St Petersburg 143, 217; *167*
Hermogen, Patriarch 48, 57, 58, 59, 64
historical painting 196
Holy Roman Empire 26, 141, 153
Holy Trinity and St Sergius Monastery, Sergiev Posad (Zagorsk) 27; *27, 31*
Horsey, Sir Jerome 39, 48

Ibrahim, khan of Kazan 20
Ice Palace 6, 117
icons *27*
Interregnum 14, 46, 56–59
Istomin, Charion 108
Ivan III, Grand Prince (Ivan the Great) 16–25, 26–28; *15, 16, 20, 24*
Ivan IV, Tsar (Ivan the Terrible) 6, 15, 22, 29, 30–45, 59; *5, 15, 30, 31–33, 45*; abdication 44; coronation 31–32; *32*; correspondence with Kurbsky 41; death 45; Eisenstein's film 215; *215*; empire 34–35; and England 39; Kazan cathedral 36; Livonian War 38–40, 43; marriages 32, 44–45; Oprichnina 41–43, 216–17; reforms 33–34, 38; succession 44, 46–47
Ivan V, Tsar 86, 87, 89, 91, 92, 115, 117; *88*
Ivan VI, Tsar 117, 118–19, 120, 126, 130; *119*
Ivan the Great Belltower, Moscow 23; *23*
Ivan the Younger (son of Ivan III) 21, 24
Ivangorod 21

James I, king of England 50, 64
Jan Olbracht, king of Poland 21
Jan Sobieski, king of Poland 81, 96; *81*
Japan 184, 201–02, 208; *202*
Jesuits 53
Jews 139, 189–90, 203, 207
Joachim, Patriarch 76, 86
Job, Patriarch 47–48, 49, 51
Johannes, king of Denmark 21
Joseph, abbot of Volokolamsk 25
Joseph II, Emperor 139, 140; *139*
Judaizers 24, 25
Julian Calendar 13, 97

Kankrin, Count 170–71
Karakozov, Dmitry 181
Karamzin, Nikolai Mikhailovich 11, 50, 116, 120, 137, 151
Kardis, Treaty of (1661) 72
Karl Friedrich, Duke of Holstein-Gottorp 113
Kazan 9, 20, 26, 34–35, 36–37; *35*
Keith, Robert 128
Khmelnitsky, Bogdan 71, 72; *70*
Khodynka 199; *199*
Khovansky, Prince Ivan 87, 88
Kiev 8, 10, 27, 70, 73, 75, 89
Kirill Vladimirovich, Grand Duke 216; *216*
Kiselev, General Count P.D. 171
Klimov, Elem 215; *215*
Kliuchevsky, Vasily Osipovich 11–13, 33, 66, 76, 115, 120, 131, 148, 171
Kneller, Sir Godfrey 95; *95*
Knights of Malta 148, 149
Kobyla, Andrei Ivanovich 32
Kolomenskoe 77, 83; *83*; Church of the Ascension *29*
Korb, Johan Georg 96
Kotoshikhin, Grigory 26
Kozlovsky, Prince 7
Krekshin, Petr 87
Kremlin *see* Moscow Kremlin
Kropotkin, Prince Peter 177, 179

Ksheshinskaya, Mathilde 195
Kulikovo Field, Battle of (1380) 9
Kurbsky, Prince Andrei 40, 41, 42, 45
Kutchuk Kainardjii, Treaty of (1774) 135, 139
Kutuzov, Mikhail 152, 154, 155, 157; *155*
Kuzmich, Feodor 161

Lake Chud, Battle of (1242) 12
Land and Liberty group 185
land ownership, *pomestie* 18, 33
Lanskoy, Alexander 136
Leblond, Jean-Baptist 102
Lefort, François 92–93, 94; *92*
Legislative Commission 132–33
Lenin, Vladimir Ilyich 184, 200
Leopold I, Emperor 95
Leopold II, Emperor 140
Lermontov, Mikhail Yurievich 172; *172*
Leroy-Beaulieu, Anatole 187
Leslie, Alexander 67
Lestocq, Armand 121, 126
Leszczyński, Stanislaus 116–17
Lieven, Princess 146
Lithuania 10, 19, 20–21, 26
Livonia 20–21
Livonian Order 19, 21, 40
Livonian War 38–40, 41, 43
Loftus, Lord Augustus 182
Lomonosov, Mikhail Vasilievich 122; *122*
Lopukhina, Anna 149
Lopukhina, Evdokia (wife of Peter I) 93, 97, 106, 113, 114
Lopukhina, Countess Natalya 126
Loris-Melikov, Count Mikhail 187, 189; *187*
Louis XV, king of France 105–06, 117, 128; *105*
Lubitsch, Ernst 215; *214–15*
Lvov, Alexei Feodorovich 176

Magnus, prince of Denmark 43
Makary, Metropolitan 31, 32, 34, 40
Malta 148, 149
Maly, Petrok 23
Mamonov, Alexander 136
Manchuria 201
Margaret, Captain Jacques 49, 51
Maria of Tver 17, 21
Maria Alexandrovna, Empress (wife of Alexander II) 177, 187; *179, 181*
Maria Feodorovna, Empress (second wife of Paul) 145, 147, 149, 172; *147*
Maria Feodorovna, Empress (wife of Alexander III) 188–89, 193, 199; *189, 194*
Maria Nikolaievna, Grand Duchess 199; *210*
Maria Theresa, Empress 126
Maria Vladimirovna, Grand Duchess 216
Marmont, Maréchal 174
Marx, Karl 216
Marxism 200
Massa, Isaac 62
Matveyev, Artamon Sergeyevich 70, 85, 87; *87*
Mazepa 104
Mehmet Ali 174
Mengli-Girey, khan of the Crimea 19, 26
Mensheviks 200
Menshikov, Prince Alexander Danilovich 93, 100, 102, 109, 112, 113, 114; *92*
Merrick, John 64
mestnichestvo (precedence) system 34, 45, 85
Methodius, St 21
Metternich, Prince Clemens 158, 160
Mikhail, Ivan 83
Mikhail Romanov, Tsar 15, 58, 59, 62–68, 212; *5, 54, 61, 62, 63, 64, 65*
Mikhailov, Ivan 83
Mikhailovsky Zamok, St Petersburg 149; *150*
Miliukov, Pavel 195, 203
Miliutin, Dmitry 184

Miloslavsky, Prince Ilya 69, 70, 77
Miloslavsky family 79, 84, 86, 87
Minin, Kuzma 58–59, 215; *58*
Mniszek, Marina 50, 53, 54–55, 58, 64; *51, 52*
Mohammed-Emin 20
monasteries 27; *27*
Morozov, Boris Ivanovich 69, 70
Moscow, *9, 10*; appanage era 9; fires 32, 36, 43, 70, 154–55, 157; German Quarter 74, 92; *73*; 1905 Revolution 205; *205*; rise of 9–10; War of 1812 154–55, 157; *154*
Moscow Historical Museum 197; *197*
Moscow Kremlin 6, 21, 22–23, 59, 82, 155; *9, 15, 22–23*
Münnich, Count Burkhard von 118, 120
Muscovy 10, 43, 50, 55
Muscovy Company 39, 47

Nakaz, see Bolshoi Nakaz
Napoleon I, Emperor 111, 149, 152–53, 155, 156–57, 217; *153, 156*
Napoleon III, Emperor 182, 183
Narva, siege of (1700) 99, 100
Naryshkina, Natalya 79, 87, 91, 92; *87*
Naryshkin faction 80, 85, 86, 87
Natalya Alexeyevna (first wife of Paul) 144–45; *144*
national anthem 176
navy, Anna and 116
navy, Peter I and 93, 100
Nechaev, Sergei 184
Nelidova, Catherine Ivanovna 149
Nelidova, Varvara 174
Nerchinsk, Treaty of (1689) 88
Netherlands 94
Nicholas I, Tsar 150, 160, 164–77, 189; *150, 163, 164, 176*; architectural projects 166, 172; *167*; Crimean War 175–77; *175*; Decembrist Uprising 163, 168; 1830 revolutions 169; 1848 revolutions 174–75; foreign policy 169; and Glinka 172; internal policies 170–72; marriage 165, 174; and Pushkin 173
Nicholas II, Tsar 193–94, 217, 195–211; *5, 163, 194, 195, 206, 209, 212, 216, 217*; abdication 212; Alexei's haemophilia 206; coronation 199, 200; *198*; execution 212–16; February Revolution 210–11; and films 214, 215; First World War 163, 209–10; foreign policy 201–02; government 199–201; marriage 198–99; 1905 Revolution 202–05; and Stolypin's reforms 207–08
Nicholas Alexandrovich, Tsarevich 180, 188; *180*
Nikolai Nikolaievich, Grand Duke 203, 209; *209*
Nikon, Patriarch 71, 74–76, 80, 85; *74*
Nikonian Chronicle 24
Non-Possessors 25
Novgorod 8, 9, 10, 17–18, 58, 64; *9, 19*; Millennium Monument 183; *183*
Novi, Alevisio 22
Nystad, Treaty of (1721) 108

Obolensky, Prince Ivan 31
October Manifesto 203, 204, 205
Odessa 203, 204
Odoevsky, Prince Nikita 69, 70
Okhrana 189, 203, 204
Old Believers 75, 76, 85, 88, 108, 139; *97*
Olearius, Adam 62, 65; *65*
Olga Nikolaievna, Grand Duchess 199; *210*
Oliva, Treaty of (1660) 72
Oprichnina 41–43, 44, 45, 47, 216–17
Ordin-Nashchokin, Afanasy Lavrentievich 70, 71–72, 79; *71*
Orlov, Alexei 130
Orlov, Grigory 129, 130, 136, 143, 145

Orsha, Battle of (1514) 26; *26*
Orthodox church 27; Catherine II's reforms 131; and death of Nicholas II 216; Elizabeth and 120; Great Schism 61, 73–76; Peter I's reforms 108; 'Possessors' and 'Non-Possessors' struggle 25; under Vasily III 28
Osterman, Andrei 114, 115, 116, 118, 120
Ottoman empire 9, 175–76, 178 *see also* Turkish wars

Pachomius, bishop of Astrakhan 65
Pahlen, K.I. 181
Pahlen, Count Peter Alexeyevich 149, 151; *149*
painting, historical 196
Palace Square, St Petersburg 166; *166–67*
Panin, Nikita Ivanovich 147
Panslavists 171, 185, 186, 208, 209
Paris, Treaty of (1856) 182, 184
Parland, Alfred 197; *197*
Patriarch's Palace, Moscow 75
Patrikeyev, Prince 25
Paul, Tsar 124, 129, 143, 144–45, 146–50, 151; *111, 129, 146, 148*
Pavlovsk 147, 171; *147*
People's Will 185
Pereiaslavl, Treaty of (1654) 71
Peresvetov, Ivan 33
Peter I, Tsar (Peter the Great) 61, 70, 82, 90–109, 116, 120, 172; *5, 61, 79, 86, 88, 90, 91, 92, 94, 103, 105, 106, 217*; aims 93; builds St Petersburg 6, 101–03; calendar 13; cult of Alexander Nevsky 12; death 109, 112; *109*; early life 77, 79, 91–93; European tours 93–96, 105–06; films about 215; first boat 92, 122; Great Northern War 98–100, 104, 105, 108; *104*; in historical paintings 196; joint reign with Ivan V 86–87; marriages 89, 100–101; *101*; reforms 97–98, 99–100, 104–05, 107–08, 109, 217; Sophia's regency 89; statue of 142; *142*; streltsy revolts 87, 96–97, 196; taxation 104; title 108, 109; trims boyars' beards 97; *97*; and Tsarevich Alexei 106–07; Tsarskoe Selo 124
Peter II, Tsar 109, 112, 114, 115; *114*
Peter III, Tsar 120, 122, 126, 127, 128–30, 134, 135, 146, 148; *129, 130*
Peter and Paul Cathedral, St Petersburg 148, 213, 216; *102–03*
Peter and Paul Fortress, St Petersburg 102–03, 122
Peter Petrovich (son of Peter I) 109
Petrashevsky, M.V. 175
Petrov, Simon 83
Petrov, Vladimir 215; *215*
Photius, Archimandrite 159
Pissemsky, Feodor Andreyevich 39
Pobedonostsev, Konstantin 189, 190, 195–98, 200; *189*
pogroms 190, 203; *203*
Poland: Livonian War 43; nationalist insurrection 180, 183; *183*; Partitions 135, 140–41; *135*; Polish Uprising (1830–31) 170; *170*; Treaty of Eternal Peace with Russia (1686) 89; *89*; Union of Lublin 43; War of the Polish Succession 116; wars with Russia 64, 67–68, 70–73
Polianovka, Peace of (1634) 68
Polotsky, Simeon 77
Poltava, Battle of (1709) 104; *104, 217*
pomestie land tenure 18
Poniatowski, Stanislaus 129, 134, 136; *136*
Populists 184–85
Possessors 25, 28
Potemkin mutiny (1905) 203, 204
Potemkin, Grigory 136, 137, 139, 140, 143; *137*
Pozharsky, Prince Dmitry 58–59, 215; *58*

Preobrazhensky Guard 92, 104, 112, 119, 120; *104*
Preobrazhensky Prikaz 104, 107
Primary Chronicle 27
Prus 21
Prussia 96, 129–30, 182–83, 184
Prut, Battle of (1711) 105
Pskov 26, 28, 64, 71, 210
Pskov Chronicle 29
Pudovkin, Vsevolod 215
Pugachev, Emelyan 135, 173; *135*
Pugachev rebellion 133, 135
Pushkin, Alexander Sergeyevich 142, 172, 173; *173*

Quarenghi, Giacomo 143, 144; *167*

Radishchev, Alexander Nikolaevich 145
railways 170, 194–95, 199; *171, 192, 194*
Rasputin, Grigory Efimovich 206, 208, 210, 212, 215; *206, 215*
Rastrelli, Bartolommeo Francesco 124–25, 143; *122*
Razin, Stepan 80–81; *80, 81*
Razumovsky, Alexei 116, 120
Red Square, Moscow 35, 53, 197; *63*
Repin, Ilya Efimovich 7, 196
Reutern, Mikhail 179
Revolution (1905) 202–05
Revolution (1917) 210–13
Riazan 26
Rimsky-Korsakov, Ivan 136
Romanov, Prince Nicholas 216
Romanov family 32, 50, 54, 55, 61, 63–64, 82, 161, 208, 216
Rossi, Karl Ivanovich 166; *167*
Rozhdestvensky, Admiral 202
Rtishchev, Feodor Mikhailovich 77
Rublev, Andrei 27; *27*
Ruffo, Marco 23
Rulhière, Claude Carloman de 130
Rurik 8, 26, 28, 66
Rurikid princes 8, 15, 64
Russian Social Democratic Labour Party 200
Russification 163, 170, 171, 180, 189, 202–03
Russo-Japanese War (1904–05) 201–02; *202*

Safa-Girey, khan of Kazan 34
St Basil the Blessed, Cathedral of (Cathedral of the Intercession), Moscow 35, 36; *37, 63, 65*
St Petersburg 116, 200; Alexander I's and Nicholas I's projects 166–67; *167*; February Revolution 210–11; *211*; 1905 Revolution 203, 204–05; *204, 205*; Peter I builds 6, 101–03; *102–03*
Saint-Simon, Duc de 90, 106
Salt Rebellion (1648) 70
Saltykov, Sergei 129, 136, 146
Saltykova, Praskovia (wife of Ivan V) 89
Samson-Himmelstierna, H. von 188, 191
Secret Department 78–79
Secret Expedition 130, 145, 148, 152
Semeonovsky Guard 92, 159
serfs 111, 123–26; Catherine II and 132, 133; Decembrists and 168; emancipation 163, 178–79; *178*; under Alexander I 152, 159; under Nicholas I 171; under Paul 148
Sergius of Radonezh, St 27
Seven Years War 127, 131
Shafirov, Peter 93, 109
Shah-Ali, khan of Kazan 34
Shakhovskoi, Prince Grigory 54
Shapka Monomakh 31–32, 37; *31, 87*
Shein, Mikhail Borisovich 67, 68
Sheremetieva, Yelena 44–45
Shervud, Vladimir Osipovich 197; *197*

Sheshkovsky, Stepan Ivanovich 130
Shuisky, Prince Andrei 31
Shuisky, Vasily 48, 52, 53–57, 59; *53, 55*
Shuisky family 31
Shuvalov, Ivan 120, 122, 126; *120*
Shuvalov, Peter 123
Shuvalov family 116, 120
Siberia 47, 85, 114, 116, 193; *114*
Sigismund III, king of Poland 55, 57, 67; *55*
Simeon Bekbulatovich, Grand Prince 44
Skopin-Shuisky, Prince Mikhail 54, 55; *54*
Skuratov-Belsky, Grigory Liukanovich 42
Slavic Revival 197
Slavophiles 91, 145, 172, 197
Slavs 8
Smolensk 26, 58, 64, 67, 71, 73, 154
Smolny Convent, St Petersburg *122*
Smolny Institute 138; *138*
Socialist Revolutionary Party 200
Solari, Pietro Antonio 22–23
Solomonia Saburova 28–29
Soloviev, Alexander 186
Solzhenitsyn, Alexander 91
Sophia, Regent 6, 61, 82, 86, 87–89, 91, 92, 96–97; *7, 86, 88*
Sophia Palaeologue 21, 24–25; *24*
Sorsky, Nil 25
Spasskaya (Redeemer) Tower, Moscow 23; *23, 63, 65*
Speransky, Mikhail 6, 153, 168, 153; *153*
Stalin, Joseph 12, 45, 91, 215, 217
Starov, Ivan Yegorovich 143; *143*
Stefan Báthory, king of Poland 43, 47; *43*
Stoglav Council 34
Stolbovo, Treaty of (1617) 64
Stolypin, Peter Arkadyevich 207–08; *207*
streltsy revolts 87–88, 96–97, 196; *87, 96*
Stroganov family 47, 66
Sudebnik 19, 33
Summer Palaces, St Petersburg 124, 150; *103*
Supreme Privy Council 113, 115, 116
Surikov, Vasily Ivanovich 196; *196*
Suvorov, General 149
Sweden: Great Northern War 98–100, 104, 105, 108; invades Poland 71–72; Thirty Years War 67; war with Ivan III 20–21; wars with Russia 57, 64, 140, 148, 153
Sylvester, Archpriest 33, 40

Tamerlane 9
Tarakanova, Princess 144, 161, 215
Tatars 8–9, 12, 17, 19–20, 22, 31, 43, 47, 68; *20*
Tatiana Nikolaievna, Grand Duchess 199; *210*
Tauride Palace, St Petersburg 143; *143, 206*
Tchaikovsky, Peter Ilyich 13, 176, 185, 188
Terem Palace, Moscow 82, 98; *82–83*
Teutonic knights 12; *12*
Third Section 172, 175, 176, 187
Thirteen Years War 70–73
Thirty Years War 67
Three Emperors' League 184, 185, 192
Tiesenhausen, Countess 150
Tilsit, Treaty of (1807) 153; *153*
Time of Troubles 46–59, 63, 66, 172, 215
Timofeyev, Ivan 53
Tiutchev, Feodor Ivanovich 177
Tolstoy, Count Dmitry 181, 184, 187, 189
Tolstoy, Lev 155, 185, 190, 200; *200*
Trezzini, Domenico 102; *103*
Trotsky, Leon 45, 208, 213
Tsarskoe Selo 124–25, 142, 143, 145, 166, 170, 171, 173, 193, 199, 212; *124, 142*
Tsushima, Battle of (1905) 202; *202*
Turkish wars 81, 85, 89, 93, 96, 105, 117, 133, 134–35, 140, 153, 156, 169, 185–86, 189, 190; *134*

Twelve Apostles, Church of the, Moscow *75*

Ugra, River 20
Ugra, Stand on the (1480) 20
Ukraine 9, 71, 72, 81
Ulozhenie 70, 74
Union of Liberation 201
Union of the Russian People 203, 208
Unkiar Skelessi, Treaty of (1833) 174
Uvarov, Count S.S. 171

Van Zeller 84
Vasily II, grand prince of Moscow 10, 17
Vasily III, Tsar 22, 24, 25–29; *28*
Vasily Shuisky, *see* Shuisky, Vasily
Vasnetsov, Viktor Mikhailovich 196
Vassilchikov, Alexander 136
Vatican 21
Vedrosha River, Battle of (1500) 21; *20*
Verela, Treaty of (1790) 140
Viazma 20
Victoria, queen of England 176, 198
Vienna, Congress of (1814–15) 157, 160; *158*
Vigée-Lebrun, Marie-Louise-Elisabeth 146, *161*
Vigor, Mrs 114, 115, 119
Vikings 8
Vinius, Andrei 67
Viskovaty, Ivan 33, 38, 43
Vladimir I, grand prince of Kiev 8, 27; *8*
Vladimir Monomakh, grand prince of Kiev 32, 37
Vladimir-Suzdal 8
Voltaire 132–33, 134, 142, 145; *134*
Vorontsov, Mikhail 127
Vorontsov family 31, 116, 120
Vyrubova, Anna *206*
Vyshnegradsky, I.A. 191, 199

Waldemar Christian, prince of Denmark 68
War of the Austrian Succession 121
War of the Bavarian Succession 139
War of 1812 156–57, 166, 217
War of the Polish Succession 116
'War in Sight' crisis (1875) 185
West, Mae 137, 215
Westernizers 91, 172
Wilhelm I, Kaiser *192*
Wilhelm II, Kaiser 192, 201
William III, king of England 95
Winter Palace, St Petersburg 125, 143, 144, 166–67, 168, 182, 186, 187, 199, 203; *125, 204*
Witte, Count Sergei 191, 193, 194, 199, 203, 206–07; *199*
Wipper, R. 45
Wladyslaw IV, king of Poland 55, 57, 63, 64, 67; *67*

Yelena Stepanova 24–25
Yeltsin, Boris 13, 216
Yermak, Hetman 47
Yermolov, Alexander 136
Yury, Grand Prince 9
Yury Dolgoruky 22

Zamiatnin, Dmitry 179
Zaporozhian Cossacks 47, 71, 80
Zarutsky, Hetman Ivan 64
Zavadovsky, Peter 136
Zealots of Piety 73
Zemsky Sobor *see* Assembly of the Land
zemstvo system 179, 200–201, 209
Żółkiewski, Hetman Stanislaus 53
Zorich, Simeon 136
Zotov, Nikita 91
Zubatov, Sergei 203, 204
Zubov, Platon 136